The seven veils of privacy

Manchester University Press

The seven veils of privacy

How our debates about privacy conceal its nature

Kieron O'Hara

MANCHESTER UNIVERSITY PRESS

Published by Manchester University Press
Oxford Road, Manchester M13 9PL

www.manchesteruniversitypress.co.uk

British Library Cataloguing-in-Publication Data
A catalogue record for this book is available from the British
Library

ISBN 978 1 5261 6302 8 hardback
ISBN 978 1 5261 6303 5 paperback

First published 2023

Typeset by Newgen Publishing UK

To the memory of Yorick Wilks (1939–2023)
Brilliant scientist, distinguished computational
linguist, wonderful man

Contents

Preface   *page* ix

Introduction: the goal of this book   1

Part I: A concept in disarray?   5

Disarray 1: defining privacy – two approaches   7
Disarray 2: using 'privacy' – a reference list   22
Disarray 3: agreement and disagreement   40

Part II: Explaining the disarray   45

Explanation 1: is privacy an essentially contested concept?   47
Explanation 2: is 'privacy' a family resemblance term?   60
Explanation 3: privacy definitions are overburdened   66

Part III: A framework for privacy discourses   77

Level 1: conceptions   85
Level 2: architecture and affordances   103
Level 3: phenomenology   112
Level 4: preferences   124
Level 5: norms   142
Level 6: regulation   157
Level 7: rights, morality and politics   170

Part IV: Commentary on the framework   207

Commentary 1: the interplay of the levels   209
Commentary 2: privacy across space and time   217
Commentary 3: is there a level 0?   228

Contents

Part V: Topics in privacy studies   239

Level 1 topic: group privacy   241
Level 2 topic: security algorithms do not define privacy   250
Level 3 topic: design for apparency   257
Level 4 topic: consent does not define privacy   261
Level 5 topic: the private sphere does not define privacy   267
Level 6 topic: data protection does not define privacy   273
Level 7 topic: community values versus privacy   283

Conclusion: privacy in the time of COVID   299

References   310
Index   361

Preface

In my mild, suburban way, I am what is known as a 'privacy advocate' (Bennett 2008). I believe: that my business is my business; that we can do without advice and nudges from well-intentioned busybodies; that we should reserve the right to resist pressure to make ourselves open and legible to the state and powerful companies; that we should be able to entertain scurrilous opinions without risking a visit from the thought police; and that Mark Zuckerberg is a ghastly fellow. However, this is not a work of privacy advocacy.

It is about privacy, admittedly, prompted by a feeling that in the raging privacy wars not everyone is on the same battlefield. That there are wars to be had I am convinced, but I am not sure that we can't sustain more rational and polite debate. I will not try to untangle the knots into which we have got ourselves, because, to borrow one scholar's phrase, 'the tangle itself is the subject' (Spacks 2003, 15). To that end, I want to map the battlefield(s), to uncover some of the arguments' assumptions and path dependencies, and possibly help people avoid talking past each other. I don't pretend to be able to resolve the arguments, and I won't try; I will give my opinions, while highlighting alternative views. Rather, I set out a framework that I hope will spruce up our conceptual hygiene.

I have tried to be as multi-disciplinary as I can, because privacy demands a range of data and research techniques, and I have kept the discussion general, so as to exclude nobody. Although I am critical of many great works, I remain in awe of the brilliant literature the topic has spawned since Samuel Warren and Louis Brandeis' seminal paper of 1890, and a remark of Danny Weitzner's that we needed to 'go back to Westin' was the germ of this project. In particular,

I have enjoyed revisiting Alan Westin's *Privacy and Freedom* (which independently of its main topic is a marvellous primer on the practice of American politics in the mid-century), Irwin Altman's *The Environment and Social Behavior*, Ferdinand Schoeman's *Privacy and Social Freedom*, Beate Rössler's *The Value of Privacy*, Daniel Solove's *Understanding Privacy* and Helen Nissenbaum's *Privacy in Context*. Hannah Arendt's *The Human Condition* has much to say, and is as thought-provoking as anything by her, although its perspective is different from the rest of the literature. The major significant papers are collected in Schoeman's essential *Philosophical Dimensions of Privacy*, including Ruth Gavison's 'Privacy and the limits of law', which is probably closest to my own position. Of the clutch of recent works, who knows what will stand the test of time? Woodrow Hartzog's *Privacy's Blueprint* has impressed me as much as any.

It will be noticed that some of those publications date from decades ago – the dust of ages hasn't obscured their profundity. It does mean, however, that some authors' assumptions about social roles and use of pronouns are of their time. When I quote such works, I do so exactly, and won't put virtue-signalling '*sic*'s following masculine, feminine or gender-binary neuter pronouns, all of which are evident in the variety of material quoted. My own use of pronouns is intended, of course, to signal nothing and offend no one, and follows the publisher's guidelines, although like all restrictive guidelines they produce awkwardness and interfere with authors' self-expression. Such guidelines are also frequently updated, so offence may still be caused in future. On the subject of quotes, when I quote from literary works, TV programmes or films, the aim is illustration; such documents, if there are written sources at all, tend to go through several editions, so I haven't bothered to include full citations.

My thanks to many audiences who have sat through talks giving renditions of the framework, and helped me refine it with difficult questions and constructive remarks. My greatest intellectual debt is to Mark Elliot, my colleague in the United Kingdom Anonymisation Network UKAN, whose willingness to get deeper into detail than is strictly seemly has forced me to clarify, defend and adapt my ideas. I have had wonderful and inspiring conversations over the years with many others, including Nigel Shadbolt, Wendy Hall, Reuben Binns, Max Van Kleek, Mireille Hildebrandt, Charles Raab, Marion Oswald, Elaine Mackey, Lizzie Coles-Kemp, Sophie Stalla-Bourdillon, Michael Veale, Alison Knight, Claudia Pagliari, Les Carr, Steve Wood, Iain Bourne, John Taysom, Guy Cohen, Lilian Edwards, Andrew Charlesworth, Ian Brown, Ross Anderson, many members of UKAN, and, not least, Caspar Bowden. Caspar's death at the dreadfully early age of fifty-three deprived us of a doughty campaigner for privacy. Particular thanks are due to Martin Kraemer who gave me detailed comments on the whole *opus* and to two anonymous reviewers for MUP for their constructive criticisms. If you think this book is crummy, this is not of course the responsibility of any of these people, but think how bad it *could* have been without their inspiration.

Introduction: the goal of this book

'Privacy' and related ideas have been somewhat controversial in political, legal and academic circles for some time. For some, the concept is ultimately incoherent, however directly it speaks to a deeply felt human instinct. For others, its centrality and open-endedness have led to its being hi-jacked to support all sorts of causes and policies from abortion to employment to anti-vaccination. More think it a weapon for the selfish individual against the community, threatening security or the freedom of the press. Still others lament its passing or fight to preserve it. Over these debates lie the twin shadows of a growing technocratic state with an endless thirst for information about its citizens and private companies with the extraordinary knack of converting behaviour into representations, extracting value from our most trivial decisions and preferences.

'Privacy has an image problem' (Cohen 2013, 1904). The debates about it are stymied by divergent views on its definition, purpose and value, and 'support for all these possible [views], in almost any combination, can be found in the literature' (Gavison 1980, 348). Legal experts find it near-useless. Following an exhaustive survey, Daniel Solove concluded that privacy is 'a concept in disarray' because 'nobody can articulate what it means' (2008, 1; cf. Prosser 1960, 117; Westin 1967, 5). Raymond Wacks argued that it was 'too vague and unwieldy a concept to perform useful analytical work' (2010, xi). Philosophers are even more scathing. For Julie Inness it's 'chaos', investigating it 'resembles exploring an unknown swamp' (1992, 3), 'the majority of [privacy] conflicts are intimately related to the disorder of the implied privacy theories underlying the conflicting positions' (1992, 4), and privacy law is like unto 'a haystack in a hurricane' (1992, 11). Helen Nissenbaum saw 'a fractured, ambiguous, perhaps even incoherent concept' resulting in a 'conceptual morass' (2010, 2).

Solove's interrogation produced the stoic realisation 'that privacy is a plurality of different things and that the quest for a singular essence of privacy leads to a dead end. There is no overarching conception of privacy – it must be mapped like terrain, by painstakingly studying the landscape' (2008, ix). I have much sympathy with the pluralistic, bottom-up methodological implications of this claim, a denial both of what philosopher Ferdinand Schoeman called the *coherence thesis*, that there is something in common with (most) privacy claims (1984b, 5), and of Inness' hope that despite their 'strife-ridden nature', there is 'a core of shared privacy intuitions' (1992, 25n.11).

Despite commentators' despair, for the majority of people private life goes on, different from ten years ago but still recognisable. Some commentators accuse us of apathy, indifferent to the remote-seeming risks we run. Digital technologies delight their users with new experiences and conveniences. In more dictatorial places, people either learn ways of communicating that minimise their exposure, or simply retreat, happy or resigned, into the shrinking private sphere where government does not enforce its writ. So many different things going on, so many sociotechnical changes; the very complexity challenges the prospects of action (Baruh and Popescu 2017).

In a sense, this book is an attempt to press the reset button. The debates move so quickly and ramify into so many areas of life that nothing seems settled, yet at its root, privacy seems a simple matter. Most of us navigate private and public life without going to court, complaining to our representatives, ceasing to use privacy-invasive services or even worrying overmuch. Behavioural psychologists have discovered that even those who claim to be concerned about their privacy don't bother much about it when push comes to shove.

In this book, I want to demystify it. I wish to argue that our disagreements about the role and value of privacy obscure a large amount of agreement on the topic. The term itself is relatively consistently applied, despite the many and varied debates about when and where it should be defended, the wide cultural variation across time and space, and the uses to which it is put (Gavison

1980, 347). I will not go so far as to defend the coherence thesis, although I think accounts of privacy's *incoherence* are exaggerated. Solove's term 'disarray' is a strong one, since quite a few concepts are accompanied by heterogeneity and debate without being disarrayed. Demystification will not, I hasten to add, solve all the problems associated with privacy or even suggest solutions. What I hope to do is to make dialogue more productive by disentangling various coexisting agendas.

In short, privacy is a highly complex social phenomenon, and I want to provide a framework to enable us to negotiate that complexity.

To be more specific, there are a number of common differences of legal, academic and technological opinion, and I think at least some of these can be defused without too much collateral damage. As we trundle through the debates in this book, we will come across some particularly important oppositions. *First*, privacy as control over one's relationships *versus* privacy as a state of withdrawal. *Second*, privacy as active and empowering for the individual *versus* privacy as passive, being let alone. *Third*, privacy as only or primarily relevant to individuals *versus* privacy as also applying to (some) groups. *Fourth*, privacy as primarily relating to information flow *versus* privacy as more widely implicated in a range of social relationships. *Fifth*, privacy as a normative good *versus* privacy as a variably valued, context-dependent state with unpredictable costs and benefits. *Sixth*, privacy as constructed out of better-formed concepts (reductionism) *versus* privacy as a first-order phenomenon. *Seventh*, privacy as a human right *versus* privacy as an often strong preference. *Eighth*, privacy as a utilitarian notion whose value relates to the goods it provides *versus* privacy as something people want, at least sometimes, intrinsically and for its own sake. *Ninth*, privacy as incoherent *versus* privacy as clear and meaningful. *Tenth*, privacy as a technical construct of expert discourse *versus* privacy as a term in common use among competent native speakers of English requiring no expertise to understand. I won't go through these disputes methodically, and there are doubtless several more that I gloss over. However, by the end of the book, it should be clear that in each case, I am a supporter of the second option, which is not to say that the opposing positions don't have some plausibility.

The two disputes that are my main focus are the *ninth* and *tenth*. I aim to establish that privacy is pretty clear, and pretty intuitive. The other eight are also discussed, but in less detail and not always decisively.

As has been noted by a range of commentators, usage of the term 'privacy' is highly variable, at least in academic and legal discourse, and many would concur with Inness that 'such disagreements cannot be explained away by appealing to extraneous considerations. Although certain debates on privacy may be resolvable without directly addressing questions about the concept, the majority of these conflicts are intimately related to the disorder of the implied privacy theories underlying the conflicting positions' (1992, 4). In the first part of the book, I examine the nature of this disorder critically. In the second part, I attempt to show that many of the disputes stem from *attitudes toward* privacy, rather than a dispute about *what it is*. Or, put another way, the implied privacy theories may be disordered, but *contra* Inness the disorder is extraneous – redundant overlays intended to swing debates in particular directions, typically concerning non-conceptual issues such as privacy's value, social expectations or the law.

Parts III and IV will jointly develop a framework for avoiding these problems. This consists of a layered view of different types of privacy discourse, in which separate questions and controversies arise that sometimes connect with each other but that have different relations to the overarching idea of privacy. In Part III, each of these layers or levels will be described and surveyed. Part of my contention is that at least some of the debates are a direct result of illicit crossover between the levels, so that, for instance, one party is talking about social norms while another is discussing the law (it seems obvious that such people are at cross purposes, although it is rarely noted – a refreshing exception being Wacks 2010, 43–44). Part III artificially separates these layers for clarity's sake; Part IV emphasises how they interact and interleave. The concluding Part V looks at particular instances of debates illustrating the different levels.

Part I

A concept in disarray?

Our first task will be to investigate privacy discourse and especially to interrogate the statement that there is widespread conceptual confusion. This theme will be placed in counterpoint with a nagging sense that 'privacy' is a term that non-specialists are happy with and are able to use without it provoking disagreement or dispute on its own account.

This will be covered in three chapters. In the first, the academic position is reviewed. The 'golden age' of privacy literature of the period 1890–1975 will be evoked by three classic papers at ease with the idea of privacy, and then contrasted with our own 'silver age' from the mid-1960s on where the notion itself is seen as problematic and a cause of uncertainty. The second chapter shifts to the 'ordinary' use of the term, some of the general properties of privacy in relatively ordinary circumstances. At this stage, my focus is on the application of the English language term in Western democracies, but I will aim to transcend this parochial context later. The upshot of the second chapter is that while the word has a sprawling range of application, it is hardly out of control. Maybe the concept is rescuable after all? The third chapter compares two views of the disagreements, preparatory to an examination in Part II of influential explanations of why privacy's meaning is so hard to pin down.

Disarray 1: defining privacy – two approaches

The reason of a thing is not to be enquired after, till you are sure the thing itself be so. We commonly are at *what's the reason of it?* before we are sure of the thing.

John Selden (1584–1654), *Table Talk*, cxxi

In this chapter, I will consider the relation between being sure of privacy and asking what's the reason of it. I will argue that the suspicion that we are not sure of the thing is relatively recent, by contrasting the literature pre- and post-1975. Pre-1975, privacy scholars were, more or less, sure that their readers would fully understand what they were writing about. Hence they did not feel the need to define privacy in order to speculate on its reason. More recent writers tend to be more inhibited.

The old style: three classic papers

How did the earlier writers get away without defining privacy? I will review the arguments of three classic papers, two from law and one from philosophy, showing how their authors framed it as an understood input to their reasoning.

Samuel Warren and Louis Brandeis, 'The right to privacy' (1890)

The first great paper on privacy, still worth reading, is Warren and Brandeis (1890). The story of its genesis and creation is told, not necessarily reliably, in Prosser (1960, 104–105), but suffice it to say that the society wedding of the daughter of one of the authors was spoiled by the intrusion of a photographer of the 'yellow press', which prompted a programme of legal research to determine whether there was an implicit right to privacy in US law sufficient to repel such unwelcome invasion. The authors thought they found it, famously conceived as a 'right to be let alone' (the phrase is an Americanism, the British English version being a 'right to be *left* alone'), arguing that the implementation in law of statutory and constitutional protections against government interference were matched by common law protections against invasions by other citizens in a 'fitly tempered' composite.

They were not directly concerned with *defining* privacy – their interest was in finding *rights* to privacy *within* American law, as part of the 'full protection of person and of property' (1890, 75) that was the purpose of common law. They traced the evolution of the right to life from a basic set of rights to security and protection from physical harms, to a broader right to what they called an 'inviolate personality' (1890, 82), which included, on their account, 'the right to be let alone' (1890, 75), protected by diverse areas of law including slander, contract, breach of confidence, trade secrets and private property (1890, 78–86). 'It is our purpose,' they wrote, 'to consider whether the existing law affords a principle which could properly be invoked to protect the privacy of the individual; and if it does, what the nature and extent of such protection is' (1890, 77).

How could they possibly write about privacy without saying what it is? They talked of 'the private life, habits, acts, and relations of an individual' (1890, 88), without setting out what those might be in any more detail, or how they could be distinguished from public life. In other words, they blithely assumed that the reader of their paper would be well aware of what privacy is, and how it is observed and breached in everyday (bourgeois American) life. Given that collusion with the reader, they would explain how and to what extent privacy was protected in American law. They did not define it, and clearly felt no pressing need to do so.

They wrote of the 'right to be let alone'. Does that function as a *de facto* definition, as a number of authors have assumed? No: it is not a *characterisation* of privacy but rather the form that privacy protection takes *when made into law* (on their account). The 'unwarranted invasion of individual privacy ... is reprehended' (1890, 87); in other words, there are protections in law against privacy breaches *when they are not warranted or legitimate*. Hence, the resources available in law that were specifically uncovered or postulated by Warren and Brandeis cannot exhaust the meaning of privacy because some breaches are warranted, and hence not covered.

They gave examples, largely to do with unwanted publicity, but made no attempt to determine exactly what individual privacy was, nor to determine the exact point at which a breach would be warranted, beyond offering general guidelines such as that retiring individuals should have greater protection than those in public life. They also accepted that legal protection would 'in practice' only stretch to the 'more flagrant breaches' (1890, 88), implying that some privacy breaches were *not* protected legally, because too minor. Furthermore, one would not, even if protected, be granted redress against 'invasion of privacy by oral publication' (1890, 89). However privacy is defined, that definition cannot coincide with its definition in law, because some privacy is protected against breach and some not. Note that this is not simply a contingency of enforcement (as with class C drugs, which are defined in law but only irregularly policed). Law itself makes a key distinction within privacy cases, taking an interest in some and not others, and so cannot describe them exhaustively.

Warren and Brandeis also accepted that some information might be published in protected circumstances, thereby breaching privacy under cover of the law. For example, 'the right to privacy is not invaded by any publication made in a court of justice ... or in any body quasi public', publication, that is, 'of any matter ... in its nature private' (1890, 88). In other words, a legal process itself might breach privacy – a warranted breach, but a breach nonetheless. They explicitly noted that the *right* to privacy is not breached by such a process, but privacy itself is.

It cannot follow from this that the principle they detected ('the right to be let alone') helps define privacy. Simply because the right to X = the right to Y, it cannot be concluded that X = Y. Compare: the right to life = the right not to be killed by unauthorised entities, but life ≠ not having been killed by unauthorised entities, because otherwise Sir Isaac Newton would still be alive, as he was not killed by an unauthorised entity, not even the apple. Hence, even if the right to privacy is the right to be let alone, it does not follow that privacy is by definition being let alone. Furthermore, if the right to X = the right to Y, it certainly does not follow that X = the right to Y, so privacy is absolutely *not* the right to be let alone, and Warren and Brandeis did not make such a claim. Indeed, it is arguable that they asserted not an identity, but that the right to privacy was a special case of the right to be let alone (Gavison 1980, 388n.48).

William Prosser, 'Privacy' (1960)

'Shall the courts thus close the front entrance to constituted authority, and open wide the back door to idle or prurient curiosity?' (Warren and Brandeis 1890, 90). In our second classic paper, William Prosser, an expert on tort law, took up the task of examining how well the back door was secured, setting out precisely the torts that he detected as present in law to protect the privacy of individuals against their curious fellows. He found his predecessors' optimism exaggerated, because the torts he discovered hardly furnished a 'broader principle' (1960, 105) of integrated coverage of a right to be let alone but were instead a smallish set of discrete and discontinuous protections (1960, 107).

He was concerned that the use of the p-word by Warren and Brandeis had nudged the courts into amalgamating and widening these torts over time (1960, 124). Initially, many privacy cases failed, including a lady whose image had been used without her permission in an advertisement (1960, 105), but by the 1930s, many states recognised privacy rights to some extent (1960, 106). While Warren and Brandeis had focused on publication, Prosser also found protections from intrusion into legitimately private situations, whether in person or using devices such as microphones (1960, 108). This first tort he saw as a 'mental' interest filling the gaps between trespass, nuisance, infliction of mental distress and constitutional protections against government interference (1960, 109). He left the reader to understand the general idea, restricting himself to giving examples of legitimate intrusions (such as police fingerprinting). A second tort was the public disclosure of private facts (a separate ground for action from breach of confidence – 1960, 110), upon which Warren and Brandeis had concentrated. Again, Prosser mobilised the reader's pre-legal understanding to show how this tort provides only partial coverage of 'private' (undefined) facts. A third tort was false light, public disclosure of misleading representations or falsehoods, and a fourth was the unauthorised appropriation of someone's identity. All of these were defined against an understood background of pre-existing mores (1960, 114).

Prosser also considered that privacy law was in 'disarray', but that 'almost all of the confusion is due to a failure to separate and distinguish these four forms of invasion, and to realise that they call for different things' (1960, 117). The right to privacy was a mirage comprising 'four distinct kinds of invasion of four different interests of the plaintiff, which are tied together by the common name, but otherwise have almost nothing in common except that each represents an interference with the right of the plaintiff ... "to be let alone" ' (1960, 107).

As an example of the resulting confusion, a published photograph of a married couple embracing in public had been found both in breach and not in breach of their privacy rights at different times, but Prosser explained the two cases as being based on different types of invasion. The publication of the photograph *per se* did not breach their privacy *rights*, because they embraced in a *public* place, so could not reasonably have expected to go unnoticed. There *was* a privacy breach, being 'singled out from the public scene' (1960, 111), but the issue for the courts was whether their *rights* had been invaded. 'The law of privacy is not intended for the protection of any shrinking soul who is abnormally sensitive about such publicity' (1960, 112). However, when their photograph was republished to illustrate an article about reprehensible types of love, the husband as plaintiff won his case because they were placed in a false light, the third of the four torts (1960, 117). Privacy was breached by the photograph, but the breach was only *actionable* in the context of the false light tort, not public disclosure. The law therefore was not intended to enforce privacy, and following Warren and Brandeis' example, Prosser made no attempt to define it.

Consent would nullify a tort, but only if properly informed (1960, 107–108). Privacy is breached whether or not consent is granted; however, valid consent is a sufficient *defence* for the intruder against legal action (also 1960, 123).

Similarly, public figures have diminished rights to privacy, by virtue of being of legitimate public interest (1960, 118–121), but the loss of their rights does not affect their privacy. Rather, the breach is identical for public and private figures, but their legal protection is different. Public figures' 'personalities and their affairs already have become public, and can no longer be regarded as their own private business' (1960, 119), even though 'there must certainly be limits as to their own private lives into which the publisher cannot go' (1960, 120). Note that Prosser explicitly described a boundary *within* their private lives; his claim was not that the law *defines* the boundary between their sacrosanct private lives and publishable public lives, but rather that they *have* private lives (which he trusted the reader to recognise), parts of which are sacrosanct in law and parts not, the boundary drawn with 'rough proportion' (1960, 121–122).

Prosser deplored the way in which, in the wake of Warren and Brandeis' influential analysis, the same term had been applied to disparate and 'loosely related' torts, creating pressures to increase their range, integrate them and encroach on other fields – thereby weakening the position of defendants. His argument boiled down to the claim that there ideally would be a strong *disconnect* between the law as it related to privacy, and our understanding of privacy itself (1960, 124), and he attempted to achieve this by identifying and disaggregating the four torts. All of this without any actual definition of privacy; once more, the reader was expected to understand.

Judith Jarvis Thomson, 'The right to privacy' (1975)

Those papers were on the specific topic of the law, and their authors eschewed both conceptual and empirical analysis of privacy, never leaving the law library. A similar pattern can also be seen in a philosophical classic. Judith Jarvis Thomson began her account with the opening line that 'the most striking thing about the right to privacy is that nobody seems to have any clear idea of what it is' (1975, 272), but the most striking thing about that sentence is that its object is not privacy, but rather the *right* to it. Her analysis wrestled with this right, arguing that, in so far as it *can* be detected, it could just as easily be represented as a special case of other rights. Wielding Occam's razor, she concluded that there was no need to postulate it.

She dismissed the right to be let alone with the example of a man whose house is put under pervasive surveillance. If he has rights to privacy, these have surely been breached, but he has been let alone, so that can't be the basis for reaching this conclusion. Equally, hitting him over the head is hardly letting him alone, and yet this doesn't seem like a *privacy* violation (also Gavison 1980, 357; Allen 1988). She worried plaintively, 'Where is this to end? Is *every* violation of a right the violation of the right to privacy?'

She examined a series of examples of supposed breaches of the right to privacy, and cashed them out in other terms, rights of dignity and respect for the person (1975, 273), property rights (1975, 275–277), and rights not to be caused distress (1975, 282–284) or annoyance (1975, 285–286). This led her to postulate a 'right to privacy cluster', and to raise the question whether or not any of the rights in this cluster weren't also in other clusters, thereby rendering it otiose (1975, 284), and derivative (1975, 286). At no time in the paper did she explain what she meant by privacy, assuming that the reader would recognise the interest at play in her examples without prompting. Whether there was a *right* to privacy was determined by a thorough interrogation of intuitions with respect to how privacy violations implicated other rights. She never said that there is no such thing as privacy, only that our rights to it can be more parsimoniously described.

Hence these three classic papers adopted similar strategies. Warren and Brandeis and Prosser looked for protections in the common law, while Thomson's more normative paper considered what ethical protections there *ought* to be. All assumed that the reader would recognise privacy in their examples. Their conclusions were quite different – Warren and Brandeis that a right to be let alone exists in American common law, Prosser that their proposal is better disaggregated into discrete torts, and Thomson that many kinds of ethical principle jointly cover the areas where a subject can legitimately demand privacy protection.

They implicitly endorsed a tripartite division between privacy breaches about which a subject does not care, breaches about which a subject may care but has no rights of redress, and breaches which are/ought to be protected. These are not mutually exclusive – in particular, subjects may waive their rights. What none of them did was *set out what a privacy breach consists in.* It would seem to follow from that lacuna that understanding privacy is prior to understanding its regulation, and so interrogating law or ethics will not be particularly informative about privacy, if what one wants is a conceptual analysis. They also shared an ostensive view of privacy – one knows it when one sees it, the descriptions of their examples were sufficient. The law, on the other hand, needs grounds and criteria; Prosser in particular supplied these *for his torts.* Thomson's case was that when one sets out legitimate ethical objections to a breach of privacy, one will be able to do so using terms that are independent of the concept itself.

The modern view

Our classic authors, between 1890 and 1975, wrote as if the concept of privacy can look after itself, and they had faith in it as a meaningful term. We see similar confidence in early rights declarations, such as the UN's Universal Declaration of Human Rights of 1948, which states 'No one shall be subjected to arbitrary interference with his privacy, family, home or correspondence, nor to attacks upon his honour and reputation. Everyone has the right to the protection of the law against such interference or attacks' in Article 12. The European Convention on Human Rights, adopted in 1953, similarly states in Article 8 that 'Everyone has the right to respect for his private and family life, his home and his correspondence'. What privacy *is*, what everyone has the right to respect for, is not stated, although juxtaposed with family, home and correspondence, and presumably was expected to emerge from case law.

Such faith in meaning is less in evidence in more recent analyses. Solove wrote, not that no one knows what the *right* of privacy is but rather that the *concept* itself is in disarray and no one can articulate what *it* is (2008, 1), squashing Thomson's consoling thought that privacy rights are covered by other clusters, and ruling out the search within the law for privacy-related material (2008, 37). Hence, for Solove, 'to begin to solve some of the problems of privacy, we must develop an approach to conceptualizing privacy to guide policymaking and legal interpretation' (2008, 2). He agreed with his predecessors that conceptual problems are prior to law, but whereas Warren and Brandeis and Prosser were comfortable that law rested on a shared conceptual understanding, Solove denied that foundation, requiring that conceptual analysis be done. Law can't provide decent remedies because of failure 'to adequately conceptualize the problems that privacy law is asked to redress' (2008, 2).

Inness, like Solove, demanded a conceptual account alongside the normative, and rejected the pre-1975 approach. She took issue with Thomson's claim that we should abandon 'our quixotic quest for privacy's conceptual and normative core' (1992, 32), resuming the quest herself. As we have seen, Thomson's claim concerned normative matters, and she neglected the conceptual (Inness 1992, 29), but Inness rejected this option, apparently expecting the normative to deliver the conceptual: 'Even if Thomson is justified in avoiding defining privacy, her argument that the *right* to privacy lacks coherence fails to entail that privacy itself cannot be defined; we can clearly define privacy in terms of the disparate rights it covers' (Inness 1992, 39n.3, her emphasis). I will argue that it shouldn't be defined by rights at all, and *a fortiori* not by enumerating them, and more generally it remains to be explained why a core is needed that simultaneously delivers accurate conceptual and normative accounts.

Jargon, gammon and spinach

I don't know, offhand, what the collective noun for definitions is. A lingo of definitions? A jargon of definitions? Whatever it is, thanks to the prevalence of the modern view, we certainly have one. As revealed painstakingly by surveys (Solove 2008; Jarvis 2011), lots of people have tried to define privacy, and jointly produced a dog's breakfast of differing and incompatible views, often plausible in some contexts and hopelessly off the mark in others.

Nissenbaum observed three strategies that commentators have adopted: (i) try to map common usage of the term; (ii) narrow the concept down to something more coherent, taking Occam's razor to common usage; and (iii) define a specific, narrow, idea relevant to a particular area of interest and ignore the wider field (2010, 2–3; Rössler 2005, 6–7). For Nissenbaum (i) is problematic, because respecting heterogeneity 'while delineating a concept to support policy, moral judgement, and technical design seems a hopeless ambition'. Others agree; Wacks produced a more robust version of Thomson's argument, that because privacy is all things to all people, it is too nebulous a foundation upon which to build legal rights (2010, xi).

On the other hand (ii) and (iii) are both aimed at practical theory (2010, 113), but this is often bought at the cost of comprehensiveness. The usual method of implementing them is 'to locate the essential elements common to the aspects of life we deem "private" and then formulate a conception based on these elements' (Solove 2008, 12), which depends on there being common elements to be discovered. Most existing definitions make one of two types of error: either they generalise too far from paradigm cases and include extraneous features, or they focus on narrow details, thereby missing out on intuitive aspects. Indeed, some theories combine both solecisms (Solove 2008, 13).

Solove's survey of definitions produced the following clusters:

- The right to be let alone (Solove 2008, 15–18; Warren and Brandeis 1890), a type of seclusion or non-interference, so that one is in control of one's life, not the subject of the attention of others.
- Limited access to the self (Solove 2008, 18–21; Van Den Haag 1971; Gavison 1980; Allen 1988), also a type of withdrawal, isolation or anonymity, relative to others.
- Secrecy (Solove 2008, 21–24; Posner 1978, 1983), avoidance of public disclosure of previously concealed information.
- Control (Solove 2008, 24–29; Westin 1967; Altman 1975; Wasserstrom 1978), the ability to determine who, if anyone, should be given access to information about oneself.
- Personhood (Solove 2008, 29–34; Bloustein 1964; Benn 1971; Reiman 1976), the preservation of foundational aspects of the self from outside influence.

- Intimacy (Solove 2008, 34–37; Fried 1968; Inness 1992), the limitation of access to those areas that draw their meaning from emotional life.

This is a wide range, with some overlap but no consensus. Many are based on specific issues, which may be artefacts of our particular times and circumstances, and don't seem to cover the whole space. Definitions may be biased towards those situations where privacy is the centre of attention, in the law courts or the media, in all likelihood where it is under attack, and therefore focusing on the causes of the irritation – missing many of the quotidian, unremarked and uncontroversial aspects of privacy.

Taxonomies and typologies

Perhaps one way around this disarray is to try to bring it all under a single umbrella, in a taxonomy or typology (Koops et al. 2017, 494–495). Roger Clarke and Finn et al. both developed taxonomies based on what is kept private – the person, behaviour, data, communication and so on (Clarke 1988; Finn et al. 2013; Wright and Raab 2014), but these were ultimately not too satisfactory. In the first place, Clarke's taxonomy was developed in order to be open to new technological developments, but he found he still had to augment it as technology moved on (Koops et al. 2017, 497–500); in today's innovative world, future-proofing is hard. Furthermore, both taxonomies were biased toward data protection, and privacy rights. They may help underpin areas of privacy law, but don't provide an account of privacy itself.

Koops et al. (2017) produced an interesting and principled typology for clarifying academic debate, intended to be a coherent, elegant structure that respected cultural diversity and non-legal contexts. Their approach was a methodical trawl through constitutional protections in a range of countries with disparate legal systems (Koops et al. 2017, 506–509). Several clusters were discerned, focusing on the object of protection (2017, 541), ranging from a general private sphere, particular things (such as computers), relationships (such as family life or communications), aspects of the individual and personal data (2017, 510–539).

Table 1: Typology of privacy types

	Personal zone, solitude	Intimate zone	Semi-private zone, secrecy	Public zone, inconspicuousness
Freedom from, being let alone	Bodily privacy	Spatial privacy	Communi-cational privacy	Proprietary privacy (private property)
		Informational privacy		
Freedom to, self-development	Intellectual privacy	Decisional privacy	Associational privacy	Behavioural privacy

Source: Koops et al. 2017

These were tidied by putting them in a matrix, with four 'zones' of privacy, in the spirit of Westin's *Privacy and Freedom* (1967), and two benefits. The zones were the private zone/solitude, the intimate zone, the semi-private zone/secrecy and the public zone/inconspicuousness (Koops et al. 2017, 545–554). The different benefits alluded to whether privacy empowered individuals, or enabled them to be let alone (Koops et al. 2017, 556–563). This produced $4 \times 2 = 8$ types, with information privacy as 'an overlay relating to each underlying type' (2017, 566), giving the matrix of Table 1.

As a guide to legal attitudes to the types of privacy worthy of pro-tection, it is valuable and well-crafted. Could it tell us about privacy in non-legal contexts? It is not clear; their criticism of Finn et al., that 'it can be confusing to discern if each privacy type mentioned is actually linked to a privacy right or to a privacy threat, or an aspect of privacy that needs attention or regulation' (Koops et al. 2017, 503), seems to apply just as well to their own work.

There are other taxonomies based on academic but non-legal principles. I have already mentioned Westin's four types of privacy (1967), which was intended to provide a firmer basis for policy. Pedersen's six types of privacy (1997) were developed empiric-ally from a survey and so are focused around the preferences of ordinary people; I will discuss these in the next chapter. Solove him-self, having despaired of defining privacy, developed a taxonomy of harmful privacy *breaches* (2008), which I will discuss in more detail in Part V, Level 6.

But taxonomies to define privacy won't fix the problem that Solove set, because, on the basis of the results of his survey, privacy is too protean a beast. 'Any attempt to locate a common denominator for all the manifold things that fall under the rubric of "privacy" faces an onerous choice. A common denominator broad enough to encompass nearly everything involving privacy risks being overinclusive or too vague. A narrower common denominator risks being too restrictive' (Solove 2008, 37). Apologies for lapsing into logical formalisms briefly, but if a definition of privacy looks like $P \equiv_{df} X$ for some necessary and sufficient condition X, then a typology even of nine types of privacy such as that of Koops et al. still looks like a disjunctive definition: $P \equiv_{df} X_1 \vee \ldots \vee X_n \vee \ldots \vee X_9$. There is no real difference in principle between a definition in terms of a condition and a nine-strong typology of privacy functioning as a more complex disjunction. If the former is impossible, on the arguments of Solove, then the latter is not going to work as a definition of privacy either. If privacy is a concept in disarray, then a neat matrix isn't going to get to grips with it.

Taxonomies, by linking a group of theories may improve on broad definitions by targeting a wider variation of uses, but will still suffer from the same problem. The relative neatness of the theory will still fall foul of the messiness of the use of the term. Furthermore, the taxonomy itself will have to contain descriptions of its component parts – it is all very well having a matrix, but 'bodily privacy' and the other terms in it still need to be defined, and those definitions are also going to have problems with the coarseness of their grain.

Why now?

It is clear that there is no shortage of people giving their definitions of privacy, whether one-liners or more structured taxonomies. There is no consensus; the single definitions contradict each other, and the taxonomic approach only manages conflicting views under one structure. I will revisit many of the specific definitions in

Part III. For now, let us note that the modern view of privacy demanded definitions, and got them, in quantity, and we are not obviously a lot better off. The number of definitions probably reflects the range of ways in which privacy is perceived to be in trouble.

Why did this need to define emerge? It is not easy to give a comprehensive explanation of why a particular approach appears to be adequate at one time and not subsequently. Why did the discourse shift during the 1960s and the 1970s from 'people sometimes care about privacy, so when and how should it be protected?' to 'what is privacy, so we can protect it?'

One obvious reason is that once someone has defined privacy, that definition is there to be reasoned about and critiqued. One method of critique is to posit a competing definition that achieves what the first failed to do. That definition is open to further critique, and *voilà*, before we know it a jargon of definitions has blossomed.

Beyond that, perhaps privacy was less of an issue when our three classic papers were written. Fewer cases came to court; for example, there were nearly twice as many privacy cases before the European Court of Human Rights (1,625) in 2009 (admittedly a bumper year) as in the first forty years of its existence (1959–98, 837 – van der Sloot 2017a, 36–37), while damages awarded have been rising steadily (van der Sloot 2017b). By this measure, it looks increasingly salient, in Western democracies at least, as a social value and a perceived problem needing conceptual analysis.

Social change will no doubt have contributed. Changing boundaries between the public and private spheres and evolving relations between the sexes probably played their part (Rössler 2005, 4). Individualism may also mean that our communal support networks have declined.

Another possible reason for the urge to define is the increasingly prominent issue of cultural diversity. Our classic authors assumed a cohort of readers not dissimilar to themselves (three of them based in Boston, with Prosser the Dean of Law at Berkeley), with the shared understanding characteristic of the American *haute bourgeoisie*. If we assume the wider range of experience of a more diverse readership, then such a consensus may be unrealistic. Privacy will be seen and valued differently by a person brought up by a nanny in a large house on a secluded, walled estate and a person from a large family in a small apartment with constant exposure to the behaviour and scrutiny of extended family, neighbours and an aggressive police force (Chao et al. 2018), before we even consider the position of vulnerable persons or groups who may be faced, perhaps daily, with insecurity, abuse or repression.

However, the most obvious change since the mid-1960s is the ubiquity of digital technology, which eliminated all the old obstructions and obscurities of paper files, replacing them first with searchable databases, then with aggregated profiles of individuals and groups, and ultimately with a real time flood of rich and linkable data about an extraordinary range of activities. One fascinating aspect of Westin's pioneering *Privacy and Freedom* (1967) is its in-depth study of the transformative surveillance technology of the 1960s, that at times reads like a script of *The Man From UNCLE*. Westin focused on bugging, lie detectors, personality testing and subliminal suggestion, as well as information processing by computer (1967, 189–364). The evolution of these powerful technologies resulted in privacy becoming simultaneously more important, more threatened, and less valued (or at least more frequently traded off).

In which case it is no coincidence that Westin, who pioneered the technological focus of privacy studies, felt obliged to provide a definition (Solove n.d.). Since digital technologies directly manipulate data, this has put the spotlight on informational privacy and data protection, and so the field appears more coherent than it did in Prosser's day. However, informational privacy is only one type of privacy, and an account that deals only with it (e.g. Westin 1967; Fried 1968) is clearly inadequate *qua* theory of *privacy*, though possibly valuable in the reduced domain.

While technological threats to informational privacy dominate and unbalance the field, there are more privacy issues than those. Once definitions appeared in that area, they would inevitably appear in others, perhaps only tangentially related. Solove's literature review connected privacy to a number of related but separate notions – human rights, benefits to individuals (and concomitant costs to society), consent, control of information flow, intimacy and sex, freedom, empowerment, identity (and the risk of identity theft) and so on. Each required definitions relevant to the legal issues involved, and the diversity of these perhaps contributed to definitional disarray.

Disarray 2: using 'privacy' – a reference list

If commonly cited definitions of privacy are routinely inconsistent with each other, and if no consensus can form around a definition, maybe we really don't know what we are talking about. Yet most people seem comfortable with the word, or at least as comfortable as they are with other abstractions like 'problem', 'strangeness', 'helpfulness' or 'wishy-washiness'. The authors of the three classic papers thought that we did know about privacy and expected their readers to bring their own understanding. This would no doubt vary, but what might it look like?

Privacy features centrally in our lives in myriad ways, and we have a rich vocabulary with which to describe it. I would further claim that we don't have very much difficulty in identifying it when we have it or when we don't. Most people are well aware of what it is like to snoop, be snooped upon and be free of snoopers, and this folk understanding is rarely referenced in the privacy literature, an omission I hope to correct. I will not go so far as political scientist John Gilliom, who promised his readers 'no excursions to visit aging legal texts or the writings of dead philosophers, few official policy experts or authorities, or almost no attorneys, judges or privacy advocates' [ahem!]. My aim is to reconnect these authorities with basic insights on privacy, which will require many such archaeological expeditions. But his foregrounding 'people who are seldom seen and rarely heard, but who may well know more about the nature and implications of surveillance than all of the foregoing experts put together' (2001, xii) is surely on the right track.

In this chapter I will attempt to synthesise an ordinary language account of privacy, relating to the use of the term by English speakers of the twenty-first century. I am aware that this is a parochial exercise, but that does not concern me right now (the issue of cultural variance will be addressed later, in Parts III and IV). The aim is to provide a heuristic anchor, a broad catalogue of unreflective uses that – however we treat the legal-academic discourse – must surely be the starting point for our privacy debates. These heterogeneous uses will not constitute a *definition* of privacy, but between them they will erect a standard against which we can measure definitions written by more august persons.

Schoeman argued that privacy has 'for something' and 'with someone' elements, decomposing a privacy attribution into subjects, matters, people, roles and contexts (1992, 106–107), and I hope to respect this complexity. One may be private in one sense (e.g. spatially), and not in another (e.g. informationally). One may be private relative to person A and not relative to B. We do of course also talk of privacy in absolute terms, and that would mean that one was private with respect to everybody (or, sometimes, everybody that matters).

When a subject does not have privacy of a particular type relative to an other, then I will write of a *breach* of privacy by that other. I mean 'breach' to be a neutral term – it does not mean that the other necessarily intended to breach the subject's privacy or that it was an unwelcome act. A single action may breach privacy in more than one way; for instance, surveillance, a kind of attention, may lead to new information about the subject. A breach of privacy may be accidental, or coincidental, or deliberately aimed for by the subject. A breach may also be potential, not actual, so that, for instance, information about the subject has been stolen but not yet published (I will discuss this in more detail in Part III, Level 2).

This is slightly non-standard. 'Breach' is often, but not always, used as a negative term, but we need a term that also expresses complicit, consensual and unexceptionable losses of privacy, and this is how I will use it in this book (if you think of a better term, please just substitute it in). Other more clearly negative terms often used include 'violation' and 'invasion' of privacy, both of which imply wrongdoing or at least some show of force, coercion or subterfuge with respect to an unwilling subject (Gavison 1980, 347). I will avoid these terms, except where discussing another's text, so as not to imply moral judgement.

Privacy, then, is relative and contextual, and because of that, privacy and breaches of privacy may coexist. This is not inconsistency. One might, for example, keep some information private from one's work colleagues, and not from one's partner (or *vice versa*). Because of this, privacy may facilitate a loss of privacy without paradox. For instance, if there were two antagonistic social groups A and B, one might want to keep a strong level of privacy with respect to A, in order to integrate with, and cede privacy within, B (Schoeman 1992, 156). Medieval monasteries had this property, where the monks were private from the world but had very little privacy of any kind from their fellows (Saltzman 2019, 65–123); Petrarch in the fourteenth century noted that unaffiliated religious hermits had far more privacy than monks who surrendered theirs with their monastic vows (Webb 2007, 151).

Privacy is often seen as a good for the subject, all things being equal, and a breach, therefore, a harm. However, different people may react differently to breaches; one person may not care whether their medical history was broadcast, whereas another might. One person may object strongly to being stared at, whereas another might not. Some might actually prefer their privacy breached, and so my working assumption is that the costs and benefits of privacy and privacy breaches cannot be assigned without knowing more about the context, the people involved (subjects and potential intruders), their preferences and interests, the purposes for which privacy is required/rejected and so on.

Associated with a breach is a *remedy*. When privacy has been breached, what might restore it or the *status quo ante*? For instance, surveillance may be remedied simply by withdrawing the attention or scrutiny. Interference may require some sort of compensation for opportunities missed – for instance, if someone was prevented from selling a family heirloom and missed the chance to make a killing, they may deserve to be compensated financially. Some types of privacy breach may not be remedied easily; a leak of information may result in its being permanently in the public domain.

In this chapter, I will sketch a list of major types of privacy. It is not intended to be exhaustive or definitive, or to relate to law or human rights. I call the product the *reference list*, a rough but fairly comprehensive classification of everyday uses of the term 'privacy', which will orient us in our discussions through the book as we examine scholarly arguments about the concept itself. What the relationship is between the reference list and any final refined definition of 'privacy' I leave open for now – but the reference list is unambitiously descriptive, not normative. Whatever privacy turns out to be, it should cover a decent proportion of the list.

The reference list

The reference list comprises the following eight types of privacy, each of which will be explained in more detail in this section. I characterise them briefly in terms of the relation between a subject, whose privacy it is and an other. The labels for each type are obviously ten dollar words that do not feature in quotidian speech, but I hope these are recognisable everyday uses of the word 'privacy'.

- *Informational privacy*, where information about the subject is kept from or not known by the other. *Example breach*: my criminal conviction is published in a local Facebook group.
- *Decisional privacy*, where the agency of the subject is not influenced or coerced by the other, or where the other is not empowered to make decisions for the subject. *Example breach*: my interfering parents-in-law choose a hideous carpet for our living room.
- *Ownership*, or *private property*, where objects, land or other items are in the possession, and under the control, of the subject, and the other is unable to use or appropriate them without permission. *Example breach*: someone has used my mug again for their coffee.
- *Psychological privacy*, where the subject's moods, thoughts and motives are not communicated or revealed to the other. *Example breach*: when my colleague invites himself over for dinner, I can't stop a look of horror spreading over my face.
- *Ideological privacy*, where the political and/or religious belief system and/or associations of the subject are not remarked or used as the basis of discrimination by the other. *Example breach*: I am reprimanded for wearing a religious symbol in the workplace.
- *Spatial privacy*, where the other is denied physical access to the subject or to the subject's space, or is unable to contaminate the space (e.g. by littering). *Example breach*: a fellow passenger on the train sits far closer to me than is necessary.

- *Attentional privacy*, where the subject is not the object of interest, scrutiny or interrogation from the other. *Example breach*: Someone intercepts my telephone calls.
- *Extrinsic privacy*, where the subject's lifeworld is protected from intrusions from (the actions of) others. *Example breach*: I am compelled to listen to my neighbours' rows through the thin wall between our apartments.

I claim that the reference list broadly covers privacy as understood by a competent English speaker without a theoretical axe to grind. If you need to know with what methodology it was developed, it was this: *I made it up*. Now I have done so, others can refer to it, be rude about it and say what's wrong with it, and don't have to make their own up, so I consider this a great service for humankind. If you think you can do better, you probably can, but this is adequate for its purpose.

I don't claim that the reference list is either complete or definitively structured. Although it is undoubtedly messy, it is at least tractable, relatively full and plausibly structured, and so is of heuristic value. I don't think it is contradictory or inconsistent, although in any particular context one of these types of privacy may be thwarted by another. Koops et al. criticised one taxonomy because 'it feels more like a list than a typology, lacking a unifying underlying logic or structure' (2017, 503), and to that charge I plead guilty too.

I will now outline the eight elements of the reference list in a little more detail. In some of the types, I will suggest a few subtypes. As this is not an ontology in the strict sense, draw no semantic conclusions from that. For instance, if I say type A has subtypes B and C, that does not mean that all As are either Bs or Cs, that Bs and Cs are mutually exclusive, that all Bs are As and all Cs are As or anything of such precision. It is as if I had said that some men are chartered surveyors and others are motorbike couriers; the two don't exhaust the class of men, one could be both a surveyor and a courier in one's spare time, and one could be either a surveyor or a courier without being a man. I mention subtypes to draw attention to examples of privacy that might be treated separately, both to note how I classify them, and to help flesh out the wider class.

Informational privacy

Informational privacy is the most discussed and debated type of privacy nowadays. It means simply that some item of information about the subject is not known or revealed to the other. With an informational privacy breach, some people might know the information and others not, or the information may be widely or universally known. Information might be observed directly, volunteered or inferred. The questions of what counts as information about someone, whether we can quantify it, and if so how, are tricky ones which I won't go into (Gavison 1980, 351–353).

One type of information deemed particularly important is *personal data* or *personally identifying information* (PII), which can be linked to an identifiable individual, or be the basis of action concerning them (Murphy 1996). This is the foundation of data protection, discussed in Part V, Level 6. The problem with a leak of personal data is that it tells someone about a known and traceable person, and so may be used against them.

One potential subtype of informational privacy is *confidentiality*, where information is revealed to someone, often occupying a fiduciary role like financial advisor or doctor, in confidence, so that the other only uses that information in their role (typically for the subject's benefit) and does not pass it on to others outside the role. The possibilities of using breach of confidence as a means to regulate privacy have been debated for some time (Gilles 1995; Phillipson 2003; Witzleb 2007). Another possible subtype is *secrecy*, where the information is allowed to circulate around an in-group, and active steps are taken to prevent the information reaching the out-group.

These subtypes have provoked debate; while some have defined privacy as secrecy or the concealment of information (Posner 1978, 1981, 1983; Bauman 2010, 11), others baulk at the inclusion of confidentiality or secrecy as subtypes of information privacy (Inness 1992, 60–61; Rössler 2005, 5). Richard Wasserstrom raised the example of the record of an arrest. While that is a piece of information about someone, the arrestee cannot reasonably demand that it is kept secret, as it is also a public matter. However, if someone discovered that inferences were being drawn from it that, for example, stopped them getting a security clearance or a job, then they might reasonably complain that the information out of context is potentially misleading, since many people are arrested without being guilty or charged with an offence (1978, 326–327). Whether this is a breach of privacy is a moot point; I would say it is, though others demur (e.g. Post 2001).

The information that the subject gives in confidence may not concern them at all (it may be about a business). Similarly, many secrets have no personal focus (for instance, trade secrets, state secrets or military secrets). Only confidential or secret information *about a subject* can be a matter of privacy (for the hidden complexities of this idea, Gavison 1980, 352–353). A doctor who publicises a patient's poor health, a friend who tweets the details of the private wedding of a celebrity – both seem intuitively to breach privacy, given the fiduciary nature of the roles in play (Rachels 1975; Nissenbaum 2010, 141–143). But some argue that these are breaches of privacy *simpliciter*, and that the facts that a confidence has been broken or a secret revealed don't add anything important. On this view, confidences and secrets are simply different and distinct from privacy (in one formulation, confidentiality *serves*, but is not a type of, privacy – Lowrance 2012, 33). If information is given about a subject in confidence by a third party which is then revealed, we might be drawn to say that there was a breach of the *subject's* privacy and a separate and conceptually distinct breach of the *third party's* confidence. I don't want to resolve such questions here; few doubt that informational privacy is an important type, even if we might debate exactly what it contains, and for the purposes of the reference list we can treat its types to some extent as black boxes.

Decisional privacy

A decisional privacy breach is where an intended action of the subject is prevented by the other, or the subject is coerced into one course of action or an artificially narrow choice. Influence does not have to involve force: it could include ridicule or hostility, and even praise may be an undue kind of influence (Rössler 2005, 85).

Decisional privacy became prominent with its use to protect the private sex lives of Americans by the Supreme Court in the 1960s and 1970s. The original decision that confirmed the constitutional right to abortion, *Roe v Wade*, was couched in terms of the decisional privacy of women to abort their foetuses. Some have argued that decisional privacy is really a type of freedom, not privacy (Thomson 1975; Gavison 1980, 356–358; Wacks 2010, x), while Beate Rössler effectively opened the category so wide that it is closer to what I call below attentional privacy (2005, 79–110).

A subtype of decisional privacy is *economic privacy*, where the exchanges that the subject wishes to make are not prevented or influenced by the other. An economic privacy breach might be when the subject's attempt to purchase something is prevented or coerced, even by a tax or tariff. Another subtype is *contract*, where individuals voluntarily take on commitments to restrain their future actions and agree to binding judicial arbitration.

Private property

This is of course a long-standing legal concept, but property relations and systems exist in most if not all societies independently of and prior to their legal regulation, and I include it here in this highly general non-legal sense (cf. Waldron 1985). Ownership may be a legal right, but it can also be an affective relational state. For instance, a child may have small items of property – marbles, toy cars, sea shells found on the beach – which could never be legislated over. A dispute between two children over who owns a sea shell would never come to court, however rich and proud their parents. Nevertheless, although I don't want to restrict this type of privacy to a legal concept, feelings of ownership are often intertwined with quasi-legal ideas about what ownership entails, so that even children with sea shells express legalistic ideas of objectivity of ownership and ownership rights (Friedman et al. 2018). I suspect but cannot prove that property law, which is ancient and fundamental, grew organically out of social and psychological ideas of ownership and incorporated many of the conventions that surrounded them, feeding back into them over the centuries in a loop of mutual influence, but let's not go into that hypothesis here.

Very little of the philosophical literature mentions property (except speculation about property rights over personal data – P. Schwartz 2004), and so I do not discuss it in detail in this book. However, privacy is important for liberalism, and there has traditionally been a link between property and liberalism, as exemplified by Locke's philosophy or in Hayek's argument that:

> the system of private property is the most important guarantee of freedom, not only for those who own property, but scarcely less for those who do not. It is only because the control of the means of production is divided among many people acting independently that nobody has complete power over us, that we as individuals can decide what to do with ourselves. (2001, 108)

Hannah Arendt pushed back against this Hayekian thesis (1998, 67n.72) during her discussion of property, in which she also made the point that possession of private property has often, perhaps paradoxically, been seen as the *entrée* into *public* life, in Western antiquity which was her own focus but also in the first modern democracies where property qualifications were needed for suffrage. Her starting point was the Greek city states, which saw property principally as land, a fixed geographical part of the city, and traced the expansion of the notion to include wealth, owned objects, income and ultimately capital (1998, 58–69). However, the suggestion by the sociologist Georg Simmel, that the development of the money economy facilitated social inclusion of groups marginalised by class or social position (2004, 221), may be a means of reconciling these two viewpoints. As property became fungible via money and exchange, the barriers to previously excluded groups to full participation in public life became lower (since the exchange-value of property as expressed in money became more important than its specific type, while money itself is a valuable type of property), so that the freedom claimed by Hayek was spread more widely.

Psychological privacy

If a subject has psychological privacy, the other does not know what motives, attitudes, perceptions, etc. underlie their actions. It relates to what Alan Westin called *reserve* (1967, 35), the second of his four types of privacy. In Cartesian philosophy, the mind is a necessarily private realm (Williams 1978, 84–86), but consideration of the more social nature of mind and language, such as Wittgenstein's private language argument, shows this to be an illusion (Wittgenstein 1953, §§243–271). Psychological privacy can be, and often is, breached. Facial expressions are precisely that: expressive. A 'poker face' is needed in cards, while the ability to manage one's own expressions and read others' is essential for successful interaction (Schneider et al. 2013).

Psychological privacy has often been treated ambivalently, a necessary interior space that may conceal unpleasant or unworthy thoughts (Spacks 2003, 55–86). In the Bible, Jesus fulminated against the scribes and Pharisees, 'like unto whited sepulchres, which indeed appear beautiful outward, but are within full of dead men's bones, and of all uncleanness' (Matthew 23:27). The Catholic sacrament of penance or confession was intended to prevent the evil that can be nurtured behind psychological privacy, and the religious life tried to expose thoughts as well as deeds to scrutiny. In the fourth century, St John the Dwarf said that the Devil 'rejoices over nothing so much as over those who do not manifest their thoughts' (Webb 2007, 22–23).

Complex social life can lead to powerful norms of etiquette, requiring internalisation of 'proper' conduct, which, while it is 'a device for self-concealment' (Spacks 2003, 12), may also create space for an impulsive personality that could betray the individual (Schoeman 1992, 118). We seem here to be in the space of Nietzsche's *Genealogy of Morals*, Freud's *Civilization and its Discontents* and Stirner's *The Ego and its Own*, as outsized characters emerge and may need to be concealed or suppressed by conventions of civility (Post 1989; Shils 1997; Thomas 2018).

In our post-Freudian age, people have become concerned about the involuntary disclosure of emotions and thoughts (Wasserstrom 1978, 322). Slips of the tongue and other tell-tale unconscious disclosures are one constant threat (Sennett 2002, 24–25). Another is scientific investigation, beginning with pseudosciences such as phrenology or Lombroso's theory of criminal physiological traits, ultimately bequeathing the polygraph and the personality test (Westin 1967, 233–309). A third is the interpretation of signals from data created from our online activity and social networks (Pentland 2008; Kosinski et al. 2013).

Ideological privacy

Ideological privacy is on the surface similar to psychological privacy, but it does not involve ignorance on the part of the other. The belief system of a person may be widely known, but whether they are Marxist, conservative, feminist, racist, green or whatever is not held against them. An ideological privacy breach is where the subject is somehow punished or ostracised for their religious or political affiliation. Ideological privacy is closer to decisional privacy, as a determinant of freedom of action (indeed, the reader may prefer to reclassify it as a subtype of decisional privacy). Ideological privacy is rarely discussed in the literature, except when it is under threat, for example where ideals of religious and sexual privacy clash (Markey 1995; Ibarra 2020) or where data is used to infer ideological preferences (Volkova et al. 2014; Ansari et al. 2020; Kosinski 2021).

Spatial privacy

This is close to Westin's third type of privacy, *solitude* (1967, 33–34). We might make a distinction between *personal space*, which is mobile and accompanies the individual, and *territory*, a fixed piece of geography claimed and occupied, maybe temporarily, by an individual (like their house, garden, office, favourite bar stool or poolside sun lounger reserved with a beach towel) or by a group. A spatial privacy breach may be where the other enters the subject's space without permission, but breaches need not always be actual intrusion; other types of breach include contaminating or defiling territory or objects, for example by depositing litter. Groups' territorial issues range from organisations hiring space for events, to the subtle formation and maintenance of gangland territory, and at least sometimes these will be referred to using privacy vocabulary, such as 'this is a private meeting' (cf. Gover and Bradley 2004; Bradley and Gover 2010).

It can simply refer to 'personal space', the distance around the human body within which the subject feels comfortable (which itself will vary depending on whether the other is an intimate, an acquaintance, a stranger, an authority figure and so on). It also varies across cultures (Hall 1966; Altman 1975, 52–102; Sorokowska et al. 2017).

I would include actual physical contact or interference with the body as a subtype, as it would seem to be impossible without intrusion into personal space. Because of the severity of the worst cases here, many would prefer to place bodily interference in a type on its own (and of course in the most serious cases the breach of privacy is hardly the worst aspect – McClain 1995). However, my focus is not specifically on assaults, but all types of invasion of space as a class, including ones that are highly welcome, such as cuddling loved ones, and others that are meaningless and accidental, such as people cramming together in a crowded lift, or bumping into a stranger on the street.

Spatial privacy may sometimes require private property, or at least rights over a space such as a house, garden or flat. As Arendt noted, in the Greek city states, the only property that mattered was territory (1998, 66). Conversely, private property as a whole has sometimes been conceived as a subtype of territoriality. 'Not only is a person's home a castle, but so is his or her automobile, pen, typewriter, clothing, watch, and book' (Altman 1975, 108).

Attentional privacy

This, including much of what Warren and Brandeis brought under the catch-all term 'being let alone', means one is not the object of attention (surprisingly rarely mentioned by commentators, Gavison 1980, 353–354 being an exception). Note that being *let* alone does not entail *being* alone (*contra* e.g. McStay 2014, 40); one might just as often say 'leave *us* alone' as 'leave *me* alone'.

Attentional privacy has important subtypes, which have many links and crossovers. One is that one's behaviour is not the subject of *scrutiny*, and particularly not being noted or recorded, ready for recall and examination in the future. Another is that one's *appearance* is not open to scrutiny. Many cultures emphasise specific aspects, such as body parts (including the face, open mouth, hair and the not coincidentally named private parts) or even underwear, that should not be revealed or subject to attention. A third is that one is not *questioned*, held to account or interrogated. A fourth subtype is one's speech being free from *eavesdropping*, and by extension, communications being free from interception. A fifth is being free from *publicity*, such as the publication of images for the attention of 'a public'. A sixth is not being the subject of discussion, speculation or *gossip* (whether true or false) by others.

Although all of these apply (to an extent) to groups as well as individuals, a seventh subtype, concerning groups and associations in particular, is a lack of *interference* in their membership, constitution, rules, meetings or activities, or analogously for someone serving in a corporate role, no oversight. The corresponding breach, *transparency*, is becoming more important for both organisations and the occupants of roles within them (Fung et al. 2007). It may be argued that occupants of roles need privacy temporarily in which to deliberate, negotiate or develop policy freely, especially in contested areas.

> In most instances, the privacy required is a temporary one, and the interests of a democratic society in knowing what its elected and appointed officials are doing can be properly served by pulling back the curtain of privacy after the bargains have been struck and implemented. At that stage, democratic statesmen are held responsible for their acts. (Westin 1967, 413)

A totally transparent environment would make everyone more guarded, and communication correspondingly less frank and effective (Posner 1978, 339; Mulgan 2007). The modern idea of transparency would surprise our ancestors; an indicative simile in Purcell's opera of 1692, *The Fairy-Queen*, runs 'Love, like counsels of the wise, / Must be hid from vulgar eyes.'

An attentional privacy breach might be perpetrated by *direct perception*, or alternatively via a recording, photograph or video capturing the event enabling *asynchronous scrutiny* later. Some breaches of attentional privacy enable direct connection to be made between a person and whatever was observed, which clearly ups the stakes (such breaches in particular threaten Westin's fourth type of privacy, *anonymity* – 1967, 34–35). In such a case, there is scrutiny of an identifiable individual. Compare the private detective deliberately following a specific person, and a pedestrian passing the same person during an aimless stroll, unaware of their identity.

Extrinsic privacy

In any particular context, some people impinge on our awareness and others don't (Marková 1987; Wimpory et al. 2000; Holt and Yuill 2014; Oceja et al. 2014; Knowles and Dean 2018; Rabelo and Mahalingam 2019). We are aware of, alert for, engaged with, people we know, especially intimates and our children, even if we are doing something else and not talking to them. If they say something, we take note and respond. Intimacy is at least partially characterised by affective awareness – even if not paying attention right now, we are unconsciously alert to the other's every movement and word, ready to engage with them at any stage.

We are also alert to people in certain roles even if we are not specifically taking direct notice of them. For instance, in the dentist's waiting room, we keep half an eye out for the receptionist who we expect to call us for our appointment, but we treat the other patients as insensible mannequins. If they speak, even address us directly, we are apt not to notice until they cough theatrically or tap us on the shoulder. They are present in our space but not in our phenomenological lifeworld. At least sometimes we use the language of privacy to express this, which sociologist Erving Goffman (1971) described as *obtrusion*, and I call extrinsic privacy.

We tend to notice extrinsic privacy when it is breached disagreeably. Examples include being subjected to loud mobile phone calls or the exhibitionist antics of amorous lovers. Their failure to protect their own privacy breaches the extrinsic privacy of others, as, for example, when Rebecca West complained about being 'awakened in a hotel bedroom by the insufficiently private life of my neighbours' (West 2020, 21). It also includes unwanted communications like unsolicited telesales and obscene phone calls.

Human rights lawyer Ruth Gavison suggested that this is not a type of privacy, and that we only use this language by a false analogy with other types of intrusion (1980, 358). This is possible, but the point of the reference list is to capture our everyday use of the language of privacy, a project with which Gavison was generally sympathetic (1980, 347).

Earlier I suggested solitude was related to spatial privacy. There is also a kind of solitude, or aloneness-in-a-crowd, when there are lots of people about who happen not to intrude into (or are excluded from) our lifeworld. This is distinct from anonymity, although it often accompanies it; anonymity is being among people while not the subject of attention or scrutiny (a type of attentional privacy), while extrinsic privacy is not having the crowd impinge upon our consciousness. In his *Meditations*, Roman emperor Marcus Aurelius chastised those who sought physical solitude, 'since at any moment you choose you can retire within yourself. Nowhere can a man find a quieter or more untroubled retreat than in his own soul,' a thought echoed by medieval monastic theologians such as Bernard of Clairvaux (Webb 2007, 64–65). One need not be anonymous to have this kind of solitude: awed socialite Chips Channon noted in his 1923 diary that 'Royalties in public always behave as if they were enjoying great privacy' (Channon 2021, 69), and he might have been describing the situation centuries earlier, when royals such as James IV and Mary of Burgundy were depicted at prayer in private oratories set in public churches, oblivious to crowds of onlookers (Nash 2008, 271–275).

Commentary

The types in the reference list are not intended to be mutually exclusive. Someone observing another in the shower learns information about them, scrutinises them and may also be invading their space. Someone subject to eavesdropping may be having their informational or psychological privacy breached, as well as attentional privacy. They may also combine: for example, Mark Elliot suggested to me a ninth type of privacy that he called *deliberative* or *intrinsic* privacy and sketched as 'having the freedom and space to take time to consider, reflect and process information'. I've no strong objection to including this, but my instinct is to parse it as a variable combination of psychological, ideological, spatial, attentional and extrinsic privacy.

Privacy applies to a particular subject, which may be an individual, or a group. There is already controversy in this first statement; many scholars think that groups have no privacy interests. However, this is almost impossible to credit in ordinary language terms, given that privacy is valued particularly highly in many situations involving more than one individual, including the family, the household, political or religious meetings, parties and sexual relationships. My instinct – I have no empirical measure or proof of this statement, it is purely an opinion – is that in everyday discourse, the idea of privacy is invoked most often in relation to small, tight-knit groups such as these. The privacy of an individual *stricto sensu* is a relatively rare concern in everyday experience, as is the privacy of a wider or more formal group, such as a private meeting. I will return to this topic in more detail in Part V, Level 1.

If an account misses or fails to cover something from the reference list, then I will take this as *prima facie* evidence that it is not a *complete* account of privacy. The claim that privacy is in 'disarray' or 'chaos' will then amount to there being no satisfactory account of privacy that covers most of and not much beyond the reference list. What 'satisfactory' means is unspecified, and will ultimately depend on the purposes of those developing the account. A stronger claim, hinted at, for example, by Annabelle Lever, is that any decent reference list will include 'a cluster of somewhat contradictory ideas' (2012, 7), and that therefore it is impossible that an account of privacy could be both satisfactory and cover the list. The list would then have to be pruned until inconsistency was removed. I don't see inconsistency in the reference list, although it is certainly heterogeneous.

Because I propose the list for heuristic value, and because I don't claim it is complete or watertight, it is quite possible to come up with a different list, with additional factors or fewer, arranged similarly or differently. Different methods may produce entirely different groups; for instance, Pedersen (1997) suggested a list of six: solitude, isolation, anonymity, reserve, intimacy with friends and intimacy with family, and noted how 'little correspondence' (1997, 155) there was between that empirical account and Westin's normative one. The empirical methodology behind Pedersen's list will recommend it in many readers' eyes, while I claim that the reference list, established by observation and introspection, more or less covers the linguistic space.

Anita Allen's defence of privacy paternalism included an orientation exercise based on 'everyday meanings of privacy', although she cut the cake a little differently. Her focus was deliberately narrowed to spatial and informational privacy, but she also mentioned other types as being out of scope (2011, 4). Two of these, decisional and psychological (she called it 'intellectual') privacy, also appear in the reference list. To these she added two more. 'Associational' privacy is freedom of association, which I and others agree is important (Schoeman 1992). Her account assumed that privacy was a matter only for individuals, and so she needed an extra type to cover the privacy interests of groups, whereas the reference list specifically applies both to individuals and groups. It is likely that associational privacy can be dispensed with in the reference list, because we can reason about the privacy of the group. One's ability to join groups may be subsumed under decisional or ideological privacy, and there will be attentional privacy issues too. Allen's final type, 'proprietary' privacy, is freedom from misrepresentation that damages reputation. However, not only does this stray from an everyday meaning of privacy, it also is more to do with rights (it is what is breached by Prosser's false light tort) than actual privacy. Where there is a genuine privacy interest here, I would locate it under attentional privacy, where I included gossip. Hence, although Allen's set of 'everyday meanings' has a different structure from the reference list, it covers much, if not all, of the same ground.

Fine – I am prepared to be persuaded. The reference list aspires to be nothing more than a rough and ready standard. If a privacy theory misses something from the reference list, then we might reasonably ask for an explanation. As an example, consider Inness' account in which intimacy is the key first-order phenomenon that motivates privacy, so that only those types of privacy implicated in intimacy are genuine. On her account these are informational, attentional and decisional privacy (Inness 1992, 56–73). She might have added extrinsic privacy – hard to be intimate when listening to one half of someone's phone call. But even with this addition she did not cover the reference list, so I will take that as *prima facie* evidence that her account of privacy is incomplete (cf. Rössler 2005, 70).

However, Inness might legitimately respond with her own rationale, and consciously reject or downgrade other items on the reference list. Intimacy has a track record in the literature; it was one of the four types of privacy Westin described, defined as the position of a small group or pair who carry on their business together uninterfered with by others (1967, 34). Pedersen distinguished between intimacy with family and with friends as first-order classes (1997), but that seems to marginalise a third type of intimacy between lovers (which again could be split between the physical intimacy of all sexual relations, and the deep psychological intimacy which applies only to people in love).

However, in those accounts intimacy was only part of the story. Personally, I would class it not as a type of privacy but as behaviour facilitated by those types of privacy Inness defined. Romantic partners may also require psychological and decisional privacy, while some less loving associations might also benefit from economic privacy. Rössler distributed intimacy across her three main types of privacy: informational, decisional/attentional, spatial (2005, 6). I don't think intimacy, important though it is for obvious reasons, raises sufficiently distinct issues to demand special treatment, but others have held the opposite view. All up for debate, nothing decided yet, and it will be discussed in detail in Part III, Level 7.

One item that might but doesn't appear in the reference list is the *private sphere*, complementary to the *public sphere*, or in other words the general, open-ended areas of *social* life where it is illegitimate and legitimate, respectively, for those in authority, and in particular the state, to interfere or interact; i.e. where one is *in private* and *in public* respectively (Aristotle 1995; Arendt 1998; Sennett 2002). It could be added, but I see it as derivative from at least some, possibly even all, of the reference list, governed by norms about what is appropriate and inappropriate. I will discuss the two spheres in detail in Part V, Level 5.

Finally, privacy is seen differently through time and across cultures, as will be evident throughout this book (see Part IV in particular). Within living memory, ideas and ideals of privacy about matters such as sex, dress, news and gossip have evolved. Whether the face, head, hair, legs or arms can be open to scrutiny depends on where you are; in some countries, one can go about minimally dressed on the beach but is expected to cover up in church. These variations are real enough but don't affect the reference list. If a culture was completely unconcerned by, say, informational privacy, that does not mean that we couldn't discuss it in the context of that culture, even if only to remark that it is not salient in it.

Disarray 3: agreement and disagreement

The reference list sketches a common-sense understanding of privacy. It is a long enumeration of heterogeneous components but not completely unwieldy; they have one or two things in common, structurally. It is challenging but not chaos. So why the disarray of Disarray 1, why the imagery of swamps and hurricane-blown haystacks? There still seems to be a gap between ordinary usage, messy but tractable, and the disarrayed academic literature. Why?

There are two views of the divergence. A narrow view, which I will defend in the rest of this book, is that it is a local disagreement about the (primarily legal) resources available (primarily to Americans) to protect privacy. Prosser, for instance, was concerned for defendants' rights and thought an open-ended privacy tort would overwhelm even reasonable defences, while Solove argued that, partly thanks to Prosser's influence (Richards and Solove 2010), the common law had proved incapable of regulating digital modernity equitably. On this narrow view there is no need to postulate that the two had differing ideas of privacy (although they might) but only that they had differing views about the legal context of the time of writing.

An alternative characterisation of the divergence, to which Solove seemed to veer, and that I wish to challenge, is that incompatible views of privacy resulted in different ideas of how the law should treat it, and conceptual confusion led to poor regulation. If we define it in an over-constrained way, an attenuated privacy law results. But the law needs to protect it over a range of complaints, breaches and torts, and because of its plural and omnipresent nature we must have 'some notion of what privacy is' in order to balance it 'against countervailing interests', such as freedom of speech (Solove 2008, 12). On this second view, whether one's view of privacy law is constrained or expansionist correlates with one's view of privacy's value; Prosser and Thomson couldn't have thought much of it, because they played down its protections, while Warren, Brandeis and Solove accepted it as an important democratic value and tried to maximise its protection. Solove went further than Warren and Brandeis, arguing that we must understand the elusive concept in order to give form and structure to its legal protection. He set out an expansive and pluralistic understanding of privacy and a pragmatic view of its value (2008, 87–88), which he then used to develop a taxonomy of privacy problems, to 'aid the development of the body of law that addresses privacy' (2008, 10).

But, as I will argue in the rest of this book, it is circular to see this as a disagreement about privacy itself. If we need to understand privacy *qua* concept before we can make authoritative legal pronouncements about it, is it right that most of the literature surveyed by Solove was legal literature? Will it help fix the definition of privacy as an input to law to exhibit the US Restatement of Torts or a judgement of the European Court of Human Rights as the main evidence that, for instance, 'sexual activity has long been considered private' (Solove 2008, 54), or a US Supreme Court judgement to show that privacy is not violated if information about illegal activities is revealed (2008, 68)? If the attempt to make the law robust and conceptually clear requires large quantities of input from legal scholars and jurists, can it be sufficiently objective and distanced from its own (supposedly inadequate) past?

Not that Solove ignored philosophy, ethics, political science, psychology, sociology and anthropology; far from it. But even there, he took the same view of the relation of privacy to those disciplines as he did with law – the definition of privacy is not prior to debates about it, but rather needs to be resolved within them.

For instance, he represented Thomson as arguing 'that privacy is reducible to other conceptions and rights' (Solove 2008, 37). But she explicitly discussed only *rights* to privacy. Rights and the things they are rights *to* are clearly distinct. Most obviously, one can have rights and be denied them; specifically, one can have a right to privacy guaranteed by every court in the land, and still have no privacy, which is why we have courts to enforce legal rights. It is consistent to argue that (i) privacy is identical to neither a right nor a collection of rights, (ii) there is such an irreducible thing as privacy, (iii) we have rights to it, while still agreeing, with Thomson, that (iv) privacy rights are more coherently or parsimoniously defended as rights to other things.

If, on the other hand, the distinction between philosophical accounts of what privacy *is*, and legal/moral accounts of its normative *value*, collapses, then confusion about its value surely entails confusion about the concept itself, as if the value was immanent in the concept. But until that distinction has been *shown* to collapse, nothing in Thomson's position, whether or not one endorses it, entails that privacy is reducible to anything else. The aim of the rest of this book is to prop up the distinction.

Solove's book included this splendid rhetorical flourish, as arresting as the opening line of Thomson's classic:

> Thus privacy is a fundamental right, essential for freedom, democracy, psychological well-being, individuality, and creativity. It is proclaimed inviolable but decried as detrimental, antisocial, and even pathological. Some claim that privacy is nearing extinction; others argue that the threat to privacy is illusory. It seems as though everybody is talking about 'privacy,' but it is not clear exactly what they are talking about. (Solove 2008, 5)

This could have real policy implications. Openness advocate Jeff Jarvis made a similar point to bolster his view that privacy is a busted flush, an outdated value, and that if we worried less about it, we could do more advantageous things, such as share data for individual benefit and the common good.

> Do you feel any closer to a definition of privacy? I don't. I see a confused web of worries, changing norms, varying cultural mores, complicated relationships, conflicting motives, vague feelings of danger with sporadic specific evidence of harm, and unclear laws and regulations made all the more complex by context. (Jarvis 2011, 101–102)

It is hard to disagree with this. But the specific point he made is interesting: if the concept melts away into individual concerns, norms, motives, harms and laws, then it has no definition, and it is nothing but a Wizard of Oz behind the curtain. But we can flip this round – people talking about their concerns, norms, motives or whatever, cannot thereby define privacy, *and yet the conversation flourishes.*

The disagreements and debates that are held up as evidence of disarray tend to concern value, not definition. Privacy breaches naturally concern us, especially those we are not used to, that we dislike, that are impertinent, that may be risky for us down the line. If, for example, information about me is valuable to others who have gained it legitimately, this may be uncomfortable for me. So there is a reason for me to try to restrict the information, and a reason for the others to let it flow. Now we have a debate, but it is not a debate about the *nature* of privacy. It is clearly a privacy breach, because I am no longer private in the relevant sense; the argument is about the breach's legitimacy.

In other words, Solove's claim that we don't know what we are talking about is overblown. We are talking about privacy, and our understanding, as the authors of the three classic papers would agree, most likely coincides, and is probably expressed by something like the reference list.

We can generate a Solove-style paragraph about other concepts, for instance taxation.

> Thus taxation is a fundamental duty, a means to keep the state going, promote citizenship and inclusion, redistribute wealth and decrease inequality, promote certain types of behaviour and disincentivise others, or maintain the social contract. It is decried as state-sponsored theft, oppression and a disincentive to thrift, innovation and self-reliance. Some claim that we should tax wealth, others income, property, carbon dioxide, consumption, cigarettes, imports, luxuries, land, financial transactions or inheritances. Some want taxes to be progressive, others at a flat rate, and still others want negative income taxes. *It seems as though everybody is talking about 'taxation,' but it is not clear exactly what they are talking about.*

The first four sentences of this paragraph are all expressions of genuine disputes, but the italicised conclusion is odd – surely these disagreements about taxation do not imply *we don't know what it is*. It's a compulsory financial charge or levy in kind legitimately imposed by the state or authoritative body on those within its jurisdiction, such that evasion is subject to punishment, isn't it? Analogously, we shouldn't take the mere fact of heterogeneity of opinion *concerning* privacy as an indication that the concept *itself* is in disarray, any more than the above paragraph implies the same about the concept of taxation.

In this book, I want to defend the idea that privacy is subject to more agreement than many scholars accept. The 'concept in disarray' actually turns out to generate remarkably little dissent *about its application*, although we clearly think differently about whether it is good, desirable or important. We may not care whether or not we have privacy, or alternatively may prefer not to have it, but in the vast majority of circumstances we know it when we see it.

Hence the question is not quite whether we disagree or agree about the term 'privacy' (since there is clear disagreement!) but rather whether the fractious legal-academic discourse signals any problem with the concept. In Part II I will argue that it does not, and to do that I will look at a number of diagnoses of the academic disagreements.

Part II

Explaining the disarray

While commentators have been trying to neaten up the idea of privacy to make it intellectually usable in policymaking and legislation, my interest is in exploring its *complexity*. The reference list is but an initial step of this enquiry, not the end point. To move us toward that end, in Part II I will look at some specific explanations of the apparent disarray of the concept. These will help pinpoint the meaning of 'disarray', showing exactly what those concerned about the nature of privacy understand by the unusability of the term.

The first two are influential explanations taken from the literature: first that of Deirdre Mulligan and colleagues, that privacy is an *essentially contested concept* (as defined by W. B. Gallie), and then that of Solove himself, that 'privacy' is a *family resemblance term* (as defined by Ludwig Wittgenstein). These explanations were intended to assuage concerns about incoherence by defending the value of pluralism in moral discourse.

I will argue that while neither explanation achieves what it intends, the reasons they fail are still instructive about the nature of disarray. This will lead to a third explanation, which will pave the way to a framework to attempt to resolve the problems, which will be the subject of Part III.

Explanation 1: is privacy an essentially contested concept?

The first explanation of the disarray that we will review is that of Deirdre Mulligan and colleagues (2016), in which they argued that disputes about privacy are to be expected, indeed welcomed, because it is an *essentially contested concept* (ECC). ECCs were defined by philosopher W. B. Gallie as normative ideas in which dispute is neither accidental, nor a sign of conceptual confusion. They are concepts so value-laden that no amount of argument or evidence can ever lead to agreement on their correct application; examples include social justice, democracy and duty (Gallie 1956a).

These concepts evoke disagreement not only at the margins but also about paradigm cases, inviting adversarial debate. Both sides broadly agree that they are arguing about the same thing, jointly acknowledge some paradigm examples, and understand, if imperfectly, their opponent's position. Nevertheless, their disagreement is fundamental. Even so, the dispute is itself productive, helping inform and generate political institutions and practice that optimise social agreement with respect to the concept. The very process of robust debate helps keep interest in and understanding of the concept alive, rendering it relevant for audiences, and integrating it into the argy-bargy of quotidian politics.

Hence recognition of privacy as an ECC could be an important step forward, as we could try to create institutions that took the need for contestation into account. It would deflect the critique of those like Jarvis (2011) who wish to sideline it and counter Solove's claim of conceptual disarray (2008), by providing a road map toward greater analytical rigour.

In his seminal paper (1956a), Gallie set out seven criteria for recognising ECCs, and Mulligan et al.'s procedure was to work through them methodically, showing how each is exemplified by privacy. In this chapter, I will argue that the fit is not perfect, conceding the cases for five of the criteria, which we need not consider, while working through the other two in detail. The two criteria I challenge are that privacy, if an ECC, is *appraisive*, that it signifies a valued or disvalued achievement (Collier et al. 2006, 216), and *open*, that it 'admits of considerable modification in the light of changing circumstances' (Gallie 1956a, 172). The purpose of these arguments is neither to quibble, nor to establish definitively that privacy is not an ECC. Rather, the aim is to show that privacy behaves differently from other ECCs in illuminating respects.

Is privacy appraisive?

The first of Gallie's conditions is that an ECC is appraisive. Mulligan et al. were happy that privacy is such a concept:

> The best, most true conception of privacy is both hotly contested and normatively desirable. While the results of its use are not always positive, and those who can demand it do not always choose to avail themselves of it, it is always valued, and those who can successfully claim privacy have power over those who cannot. (2016, 5)

They also added that ECCs can be descriptive as well as normative, so that the concept of privacy can 'both ... describe states that satisfy the conditions for a particular conception of privacy, and ... posit its normative value' (2016, 6).

This may seem somewhat circular. Many types of privacy are not particularly desirable (e.g. some types of solitude), and everyone has to balance privacy against the joys of being visible to one's network. We construct our lives by a careful negotiation of privacy with publicity (Altman 1975), picking and choosing our moments. Some are thrust upon us, such as a near-universal demand that we go to the toilet in privacy, while in other circumstances it is proscribed, so that, for example, any money I earn must be reported to the taxman. Tech firms that use data heavily argue that our privacy is less valuable to us than the innovative services they provide through its analysis, as evinced by the large take-up of those services. Many dispute that the value of privacy is generally positive; there are anti-patriarchal arguments against the practice of veiling women, for example (Moors 2009; Brems 2014), and some feminists have argued that privacy is little more than a racket to maintain a safe space in which gendered abuse may occur (MacKinnon 1987, 100). Different cultures have taken more pejorative views of it; it has often been commented that the Ancient Greek word for a private person, *idiotes*, is where we get our modern-day 'idiot' (Arendt 1998, 38), and the Latin root of 'private', *privare*, signified deprivation (an outgrowth of the same root) rather than gain. Privacy doesn't always have this privative character (as Arendt pointed out, private property rather suggests the opposite – 1998, 61), and Sparkes (1988) made a strong case that *idiotes* had a far wider and not necessarily negative range of meaning and connotation than we nowadays assume, but neither was it unalloyedly positive.

This is atypical for an ECC – we do not, for instance, try to balance episodes of the ECC justice with alternative episodes of injustice. If we found out, say, that some people were being treated justly and others unjustly in some respect, we would all agree (i) that that is wrong, and (ii) that the only right solution would be to treat everyone justly (though we may disagree about how to do that).

Privacy behaves differently. If we found that some people had privacy and others not without good reason, for instance in a Scandinavian country in which most people had their tax returns published, some well-connected people managed to avoid publication, we would also agree that this is wrong. However, in this privacy-related case there are two equally good remedies: we could either stop publishing tax returns at all (privacy for all), or we could make sure that even the well-connected had their returns published (privacy for no one). We would not reason analogously in the case of justice, that a possible response to the unequal distribution of justice would be to treat everyone unjustly.

To repeat, we may disagree about *how* to treat everyone justly, but it would always be everyone's unequivocal aim, because 'justice' is appraisive. For example, suppose we were in a society in which one would be hanged for stealing an apple; we may argue that this is a disproportionate punishment for the crime, and that no one should be hanged for it. But that is not an argument that 'no one should receive justice'. Rather, in this case, the argument would be that the punishment is more severe than the perpetrator deserves, and therefore is *unjust*. All perpetrators deserve punishment, but if the choice is between them going free and being executed, they will not receive justice either way, and the second choice is the greater injustice. No one in this argument is suggesting that theft go unpunished, only that the punishment does not fit the crime. This is precisely the sort of dispute to be expected if justice is an ECC – it's what it means to be contested. There is no such dispute over the circumstances of the tax return case, the decision of whether to publish or not is purely pragmatic, and the fact that we are presented with a choice of how to proceed is a first hint that privacy does not have the appraisive force of a paradigmatic ECC such as justice.

As Gallie put it, 'to use an essentially contested concept means to use it against other uses and to recognize that one's own use of it has to be maintained against these other uses' (1956a, 172); we agree about our attitudes to the concept, but disagree about whether it applies in particular cases. We all agree, for instance, that we should do our duty (although we may sometimes fail to do so), but disagreement about duty tends to be over what it actually is in a context – agreement on its *value*, disagreement on its *application*. A British republican who refuses to stand for the national anthem *God Save the King* denies that it is a British person's duty to do so (disagreement on application). It is not that the republican agrees with the monarchist that standing is a duty, albeit one the republican prefers, on balance, to neglect; this would constitute *agreement* on application in the context.

Collier et al. put forward an illustrative list of nine ECCs: democracy, justice, rule of law, citizenship, abortion, war, genocide, rape and hate crime (2006, 212). Agreement on value and disagreement on application is the normative valence characteristic of debate about all (but one – see below) of these. To take one in more detail, genocide, there is a great deal of dispute about the deaths of over a million Armenians in 1915 and the actions of the Ottoman government. The dispute boils down to the application of the term 'genocide' to the events, against the background of agreement that the term only applies to heinous and unconscionable crimes against humanity. It is not the case that there is general agreement about the application of the term and disagreement about whether particular genocides were positive or negative. 'Well, that was one of the better genocides.' Everyone agrees that genocide is always monstrous, but the defenders of the Ottomans dispute whether the deaths constitute genocide at all. Agreement over value, disagreement over application. Similarly, when US Secretary of State Mike Pompeo declared the mistreatment of the Uighurs of Xinjiang Province by the Chinese government a genocide, the ensuing debate was not about the evil of genocide but whether China was engaged in it at all (Finlay 2022; Enos 2020).

All but one of Collier et al.'s example ECCs exhibit this pattern of agreement-on-value-disagreement-on-application. The one incongruous concept in their list, abortion, is markedly unlike the others (and therefore I would argue misplaced). Where abortion is concerned, disagreement is over *value*, while there is usually little dispute about whether a set of events is or is not an abortion. There have been cases in Latin America where women have been jailed for illegal abortions that appear to have been miscarriages, but these stem from accusations that the miscarriage was deliberately induced, i.e. about a fact in the case, rather than the application of the term (indeed, 'miscarriage' is arguably a better candidate as an ECC than 'abortion' – Reiheld 2015). Where the facts are agreed, there is no argument over whether a case is an abortion; indeed, clinics advertise abortion services. Disputes concern abortion's *evaluation* – is it a type of murder? Is it a woman's right? Is a foetus a person? Are threats to the mother's health paramount? The long and interminable debate in America is not about what terminations count as abortions but rather which abortions should be legal (if any). *Agreement* on application, *disagreement* on value. Abortion is very much an outlier, mistakenly added to Collier et al.'s list, because it is not appraisive.

How does privacy shape up as an appraisive term? Solove's 'nobody knows what they are talking about' paragraph is surely testimony to disagreement about value, while silent on application (2008, 5). Westin ran a series of surveys for three decades on public attitudes to privacy, and generated robust, if not always comparable, findings (Kumaraguru and Cranor 2005, 19), supporting his view that people naturally divided into three groups.

> Fundamentalists are generally distrustful of organizations that ask for their personal information, worried about the accuracy of computerized information and additional uses made of it, and are in favor of new laws and regulatory actions to spell out privacy rights and provide enforceable remedies. ... [Pragmatists] weigh

the benefits to them of various consumer opportunities and services, protections of public safety or enforcement of personal morality against the degree of intrusiveness of personal information
sought and the increase in government power involved. ... The
Unconcerned are generally trustful of organizations collecting their
personal information, comfortable with existing organizational
procedures and uses[,] are ready to forego privacy claims to secure
consumer-service benefits or public-order values[,] and not in favor
of the enactment of new privacy laws or regulations. (Kumaraguru
and Cranor 2005, 5)

An interesting grouping, indicating disagreement – but disagreement less over what privacy *is*, than its *value*. The fundamentalists
take it as a positive good, the pragmatists see advantages in it, and
the unconcerned are, er, unconcerned. Over the years, Westin's
surveys never elicited any obvious debate about what privacy was,
and his critics didn't argue that because it is a contested concept,
his survey methodology was flawed. Like the authors of the three
classic papers of Part I, Westin expected his respondents to bring
their own understanding to the party – *despite* the fact that in his
book he had felt obliged to define it.

In 1999 the CEO of Sun Microsystems, Scott McNealy, in
a notorious intervention, prepared us for digital modernity by
telling us 'You have zero privacy: get over it!' (Rauhofer 2008).
He did not try to argue that we still have privacy, on a different,
contested definition of it. He *accepted* the understanding of
privacy used by advocates and instead disputed that it was of
value or significance in a digital world. Agreement on application, disagreement on value, the *opposite* pattern from ECCs
(compare: if one upbraided Bashar al-Assad or Nicolás Maduro
about the wretched conditions in their benighted nations, it
is impossible to imagine either of them saying 'You have zero
justice: get over it'). It is, however, the same pattern as abortion.
McNealy's shocked interviewer commented specifically that 'he's
right on the facts, wrong on the attitude'. Jarvis argued that while
new technologies 'make possible entirely new ways to gather and
share information [and] bad things could happen', they also 'present new opportunities, which we could miss if we are too busy
building our bunkers. Presses print gossip but also art' (2011, 68).
Agreement on application, disagreement on value. A third

example is Inness' criticism of Robert Bork's attacks on privacy; her disagreement centred around its *value*, which he downplayed and thought should not be protected by law, not his *use* of the term (Inness 1992, vii).

We can approach the difference from another direction. I can ask for privacy, and I will need to give my reasons, which may be good ('I'd like some privacy, as I want to change my trousers') or bad ('I'd like some privacy, as I want to plan a terrorist attack'). But I need no reason to ask for justice, because it is appraisive. I need reasons for privacy because it is probably isn't appraisive; the normative force of my request depends not on what I am requesting (privacy) but rather on the force of the reason I want it. Of course, we may question what counts as justice – we would expect to, as it's an ECC – but the request for it has an absolute force that privacy cannot match.

As privacy is an outlier with respect to the criterion, with very different properties to other ECCs, it would seem reasonable to question whether privacy is appraisive. While we might agree with Mulligan et al. that 'the ability to traverse descriptive and normative explains part of the complexity and dynamism of contests over privacy' (2016, 6), we should also note that in those contests we agree for the most part about the descriptive aspects (application) and disagree about the normative (value), whereas it is characteristic of paradigm ECCs that there is agreement about their normativity but disagreement about descriptions of concrete situations, the exact reverse. Political scientist William E. Connolly argued that applying an ECC to a context is both to describe it and to ascribe a value to it (1983, 22), but when we argue that a context is private, we only describe it and leave its value open to debate.

The upshot is that privacy is not appraisive. This may or may not be fatal for its status as an ECC; while Collier et al. maintained that Gallie's criteria are not sufficient conditions (2006, 215), Baldwin argued that security cannot be an ECC with a parallel argument to mine in this section (1997, 10–12). However, my concern is less whether privacy is an ECC than on the nature of our agreement and disagreements about it. With that in mind, let us consider a second criterion.

Is privacy open?

Gallie's criterion of openness is that an ECC changes through debate. This clearly applies to privacy, as can often be seen following technological development (Mulligan et al. 2016, 7–8). To illustrate openness, Mulligan et al. considered two models of privacy, the nineteenth-century model of being let alone (Warren and Brandeis 1890) and the twentieth-century model of data protection. With the advent of new technology, each time the concept of privacy shifted to 'protect what people valued. … Practitioners in the later context could have jettisoned the concept. Rather than discard it, they sought to transform it, and to do so by arguing over its meaning' (Mulligan et al. 2016, 8).

However, the nature of its modification differs from the usual evolution of ECCs through time, and it will again be informative to compare privacy and contrast. I will consider two ways in which privacy diverges from paradigm ECCs, which give the account some interesting wrinkles.

Transformation versus accretion

The first wrinkle is that the concept of privacy isn't *transformed*. What we see is *addition* or *accretion*, not transformation. In the new context of digital information processing, a new aspect or conception of privacy appeared that was not evident or readily predictable before the technology was in place, which got added to the already bulging file of phenomena under the rubric of privacy. The previous incarnation, being let alone, *continued* to be a *bona fide* type of privacy unchanged and unchallenged. Similarly, even older conceptions of privacy remained unchanged and unaffected by the technologically enabled conceptions of privacy against which Warren and Brandeis railed, such as portable cameras. New technologies, practices, or norms implicate privacy in ways that don't affect older aspects. There is no *transformation* from the older cases, merely addition to them.

How does that compare with an ECC? Gallie wrote that 'Any essentially contested concept is persistently vague, since a proper use of it by P_1 in a situation S_1 affords no sure guide to anyone else as to P_1's next, and perhaps equally proper, use of it in some future situation S_2' (1956a, 172n.1). Suppose S_2 is not a new type of situation, it's just in the future, but well within our understanding and experience. No new technology or practices are in place, its description familiar to those acquainted with S_1. Then there is no reason, I contend, to suggest that P_1's use of the concept privacy will change from their original use; their previous use is a sure guide (I think Mulligan et al. would concur with this in the absence of technological change such as they highlighted). If something was classified as a breach of data privacy in 1990, it would probably be so classified in 2010. If not, P_1 would have some explaining to do.

On the other hand, if S_2 is a *new* type of situation, then there *is* an indeterminacy in P_1's use, of the type to which Gallie drew attention, but this may not add *vagueness*, as it may be fairly clear what would be said, at least in some circumstances. Cheap, simple face and voice recognition technology is only just being deployed in the public arena; we can think about what it would mean, and very few people have suggested that it is not going to be a powerful threat to privacy (Gates 2011). We may certainly disagree over whether the threat will be offset by correspondingly large gains in areas like security or well-being, but that our privacy will be diminished by the technology does not appear to be contested by anyone.

The cognitive linguistics of categorisation makes a distinction between 'the adaptation of concepts to new circumstances, [and] the application of a particular concept to new domains at a given point in time' (Collier et al. 2006, 235; Taylor 2003). In the former case, adapting the concept brings with it the possibility that its application to past circumstances changes. We see this retrospective effect in the adaptation of paradigmatic ECCs, but we don't tend to see it in the case of privacy.

In his discussion of democracy as an ECC, Gallie pointed out that 'democratic targets will be raised or lowered as circumstances alter, and democratic achievements are always judged in the light of such alterations' (1956a, 186). In democratic Athens of the fifth century BC, slaves and women could not participate in the public space. In the nineteenth century, property qualifications for the vote were routine and women's suffrage the exception. Such polities would not be called democracies by today's standards, although a modern commentator writing a book about democracy usually discusses these societies in early chapters to illustrate how norms have evolved (e.g. Stasavage 2020, 3–97). 'Empirically democracy has a different meaning in the two eras' (Collier et al. 2006, 224). New democratic practices have not left the characterisation of the past unchanged. From our perspective of universal suffrage, freedom of contract, freedom of association and freedom of speech, a slaveowning society like Athens is not a democracy, though it might have a few democratic characteristics. From Plato's perspective, Athens was a democracy pure and simple. The concept has been open to change over the millennia.

This contrasts with the historical development of privacy. There is no difficulty in redescribing Aristotle's public/private distinction in the *Politics*, and the perennial tensions between the needs of the private household and the wider community, using modern vocabulary (Roy 1999). Peeping Tom disturbed the privacy of Lady Godiva in the eleventh century by witnessing her nakedness, and judgements of his voyeurism have not changed in the intervening millennium. He breached her privacy then, and he breached her privacy from our own perspective too. In the twenty-first century, his spiritual descendants have new technologies to fall back upon, and our understanding of privacy and its breaches has extended to encompass them, but not in such a way as to alter past judgements. Revenge porn and upskirting are breaches of privacy that Peeping Tom could only have dreamt of, but the classification of his eponymous voyeurism as a breach of privacy remains solid.

In the cases Mulligan et al. described, crises were triggered by the appearance of a new technology (box cameras in the 1890s; digital data processing in the 1980s). The use of such technologies immediately presented themselves as novel privacy conundrums; people of the time appeared to classify these quite unproblematically alongside other types of privacy breach with which they were already familiar.

If we are to say that the people of the 1890s and 1980s transformed their concepts of privacy, an explanation is surely required as to why this should happen, i.e. what was it about the

box camera and data processing that prompted the transform-
ations? But these technologies seem not to have been perceived as
challenging old ideas. It would appear that the application of the
old concept to the new context was fairly evident to most; presumably it wasn't simply coincidence that the concept changed as
the technologies began to be used. The application of the old concept to the new technological context did not require, and did not
prompt, a *transformation* of the concept affecting its application
in the old contexts, but its *extension* to the new circumstances
where people spotted a resemblance.

Our *perceptions* of what types of privacy *we have a right to* have
altered. It is obvious that the *law* of privacy has changed over time,
as all law must. And social *norms* related to privacy have varied
across time and space. None of this entails that the notions of when
we do and do not have privacy have shifted very much at all. They
have been added to, as technology has improved and behaviour
changed, but they have not been transformed.

The legal context

The second wrinkle in Mulligan et al.'s account of openness is
that their examples and responses all presupposed a specific legal
context, mainly from the US, but also including the Organisation
for Economic Co-operation and Development's (OECD) data
protection guidelines (OECD 2013) and EU regulation. None of
these responses was conceptual or involved conceptual change;
they were all attempts to cajole the state into protecting breaches
of privacy that were *antecedently* perceived both as breaches and
as harms. Such legal responses are therefore not shifts in the concept of privacy, although they may signal additions to the concept in some new technologically mediated contexts.

The usual narrative of an ECC, on the other hand, is that it
changes, not as a result of new contexts emerging, so much as continuous argument and disputation causing the two sides to alter
their positions to accommodate points made by their opponents.
The phenomena to which Mulligan et al. drew attention were
created by new cases being brought to law as a result of the facili-
tation of privacy breaches by novel technologies that might not

have been covered by older *laws*, but whose conceptual *interpretation* as privacy breaches was pretty straightforward.

Their bias toward legal issues is also evidenced by their discussion of Supreme Court decisions, including *United States v Jones*, in which the police installed a GPS tracker on a suspect's car, and *Kyllo v United States* about police use of thermal imaging equipment to 'see' patterns of heat inside a house. In each case, the question was not really whether these were breaches of privacy, because they obviously were; it is hard to see privacy as being so 'open' as to leave any dispute in either case. The question being answered was the quite separate, technical and parochial one of whether they were unreasonable searches under the Fourth Amendment of the US Constitution which is nothing to do with privacy and everything to do with the law of a single nation. In the case of *Kyllo*, one justice argued (with the minority) that a search with thermal imaging was reasonable on the ground that the police were inferring from data, not searching. Whether an inference is a search is an interesting semantic question no doubt, but it has very little to do with whether someone's privacy has been breached, and the justice didn't pretend that it had. Kyllo's privacy *had* been breached unequivocally by these inferences, whether or not they were technically searches in US law. In the end, the majority found that the Fourth Amendment protected a person's right 'to be free from unreasonable governmental intrusion' in their home (Mulligan et al. 2016, 7).

Note also that the Amendment only protects against *government* searches, but the breach of privacy exists irrespective of whether the intrusion is carried out by a government official or a private agent (or indeed whether the intrusion is reasonable or otherwise). For instance, if a government official took it upon their own initiative to search a house, the only question relevant to the Fourth Amendment would be whether this was part of a warranted government search in which the official was playing their legitimate role, or whether on the contrary it was simply some unofficial vendetta. The question as to whether the observation *was a breach of privacy* cannot surely hang on whether the snooper was following orders or acting on their own initiative.

Conclusion: more agreement than contestation

All in all, privacy is an unlikely ECC. It is not contested as ECCs are typically contested. However, this exercise has been valuable. It has shown us first that the patterns of debate about privacy differ from those about other ECCs – most particularly, we tend to agree in our uses of the term, and disagree about the value we place on it – completely the opposite way round to usual examples of ECCs, such as justice, democracy or genocide. The concept is less like the genuinely appraisive concepts that Gallie examined and more like a concept whose boundaries we generally agree on but upon the *value* of which we may still fundamentally disagree (such as abortion, tax or the weather). In passing, it is interesting, in this context, that the non-appraisive concept abortion behaves rather like privacy in the debates we have about it, because – as we shall see later – legal defences of abortion rights in the US rest heavily on rights to privacy.

Second, it has shown that the concept has not been transformed by social and technical change over the years but rather has merely accumulated more facets or what I will refer to later as conceptions. Third, we have seen that legal changes follow the evolution of those conceptions, and so the law is at best a lagging indicator of conceptual change. These three points together mean that using ECC theory to explain privacy's 'disarray' is not going to work – it tells a story of conceptual *agreement*, not disagreement, and of *stability* of meaning, not transformation. The phenomena we would expect to see were privacy an ECC simply aren't in evidence.

Gallie was concerned to provide sufficient precision for conceptual debate about complex and disputed ideas in politics and moral philosophy. His scheme was intended to replace what he saw as a weaker theory, the family resemblance theory of Ludwig Wittgenstein (1953), and he saw ECC as a clear improvement (Gallie 1956b). Yet ECC theory is too demanding to apply to privacy, and so Mulligan et al.'s strategy failed to explain the conceptual disarray. Solove himself advocated family resemblance as an explanatory resource (2008), and it too is informative about the disarray, although not as Solove intended. This will be the topic of the next chapter.

Explanation 2: is 'privacy' a family resemblance term?

The pluralism that Solove discerned in the use of the term 'privacy' led him to Wittgenstein's family resemblance theory of meaning, in which 'privacy is not defined by looking for a common denominator in all things we view under the rubric of privacy. ... Privacy is not one thing, but a cluster of many distinct yet related things' (Solove 2008, 40; Wittgenstein 1953); 'the meaning of a word comes from the way a word is used in language, not from any inherent connection between the word and what it signifies' (Solove 2008, 42).

When we look at instances of the uses of some terms – Wittgenstein wrote of games in the first instance (1953, §§65–71) – 'you will not see something that is common to all, but similarities, relationships, and a whole series of them at that ... a complicated network of similarities overlapping and criss-crossing: sometimes overall similarities, sometimes similarities of detail' (1953, §66). The uses exhibit a *family resemblance*. Solove suggested that 'privacy' is such a term – there is nothing common to all instances of privacy, but they form a kind of chain of similarity and analogue. Hence (i) we should not expect to find a common denominator or means of generalising across cases of privacy, any more than we should expect to find a common property of games, and (ii) the failure to find necessary and/or sufficient conditions does not mean that the term 'privacy' is incoherently used (Hart 1983). Solove welcomed the use of privacy as an umbrella term, bringing together interconnected but distinct phenomena (2008, 45). Bringing a family resemblance theory of meaning to bear would enable us to rid ourselves of visions of 'rigid conceptual boundaries and common denominators' (2008, 44).

Each new application of the term stands in need of explanation, but without recourse to abstract concepts or universals (2008, 43–44).

Family resemblance injects nuance into the question 'is this the same (type of thing) as that?' This depends crucially on the context, and intended contrasts. Is being spied on while dressing the same thing as being prevented from purchasing contraception? In one sense, no: the actions and their effects are utterly disparate. In another sense, yes: they are both breaches of privacy. There is family resemblance both between the *types* of privacy on the reference list and between the *instances* of privacy within each type; hence we can integrate or disaggregate the reference list relative to different contrastive classes.

Solove convinces that 'privacy' is a family resemblance term. The question for us is whether this will do the explanatory work that he wishes it to do. Does family resemblance explain the disarray and disagreement in the definitions of the term?

Let's revisit the original theory. Wittgenstein's target was a view of language and definition which he himself had espoused in previous works, alongside Gottlob Frege and Bertrand Russell in the early twentieth century, that concepts can be defined so that (i) they can be analysed or decomposed into a combination of more primitive concepts, which (ii) can be used to determine whether something is an instance of the concept or not (Russell 1956; Wittgenstein 1961; Frege 1980). So, for example, if we define privacy as control of access to ourselves, then we (i) understand privacy in terms of these other concepts 'self', 'control' and 'access', and (ii) are able to deduce certain facts about any instance of privacy (viz. that someone with privacy is in control of some kind of access to himself). Conceptual analysis outputs necessary and sufficient conditions of its application in more primitive terms. On this Fregean view, a concept is incoherent if it is neither primitive nor has such a decomposition, although it is perfectly possible for someone to use a coherent concept coherently without knowing what the definition is or being able to do the decomposition (these are everyday language skills). The definition becomes evident only upon careful logical analysis, which enables us to apprehend what it is that all instances have in common. Such a universalist view might be held about all language or could be narrowed down to apply only to concepts in certain carefully choreographed contexts, such as science or the law.

After writing his early masterpiece the *Tractatus Logico-Philosophicus* in this technical-positivist vein, Wittgenstein retired from philosophy in 1919 to become a (spectacularly bad) primary school teacher, having persuaded himself that he had solved all philosophical problems with conceptual analysis and logic. The positivists, including his younger self, thought that the practical value of language had to rest on a logical substructure that would explain it. If there was no such substructure, then how, they had asked, could there be agreement and regularity? However, during his extended sabbatical, he came to doubt that this view would work – in particular that logic and mathematics were stable enough to act as the foundations for all thought – and developed a second, completely different view, based on the insight that language is a tool for doing things, that it has an indefinite range of functions, and that his earlier essentialism was therefore misplaced, an artificially neat imposition upon messy reality.

The later Wittgenstein was therefore addressing a somewhat different problem to Solove's. He certainly argued that terms whose use is characterised by family resemblance cannot be defined by necessary and sufficient conditions, but he did not suggest that they cannot be explained; indeed 'my concept of a game [is] completely expressed in the explanations I could give' (1953, §75). Solove wanted to use family resemblance theory to explain the disarray in and disagreement about the concept of privacy, but Wittgenstein argued that family resemblance explained the *lack* of disarray in a term's use.

Solove's point was that if there was a conceptual substructure of necessary and sufficient conditions, then the concept of privacy would not be in disarray; that it *was* in disarray showed that there was no such substructure. His position was still in thrall to the Fregeans and positivists – no necessary and sufficient conditions entailed no coherence.

The later Wittgenstein, however, flipped this around. As there *can* be no such substructure and yet language is *not* in disarray, the substructure was simply a philosophical fiction or myth. Hence he avoided using the word 'concept' as the referent of a term, arguing instead that its meaning is contained in its use. The idea of a 'concept' gave the (false) impression that the term 'privacy' really did refer to something, *viz.*, the concept of privacy. On the Fregean account, the concept could then be decomposed into conditions that we could use to check whether the term was being used correctly. The family resemblance theory blew that whole idea out of the water.

Typically, where use of a term is characterised by family resemblance, we explain via pointing, showing examples or paradigms. Different people point to different exemplars, and there will be tricky borderline cases where there will be differences of opinion or a vague application. Furthermore, we often agree about what is vague or tricky (for instance, most people recognise that blood sports, or gladiatorial games, or certain types of bullying, are problematic uses of the term 'game', although we grasp easily why the term is used in such a context, as for example in *The Hunger Games* books and films). We even agree about analogies and metaphors (e.g. the 'Great Game'). It is clear from the relatively commonplace examples that Wittgenstein used that he did not think that these borderline phenomena are problematic – we all recognise a game when we see one, and we are almost always in agreement about the usage of the term 'game', and we almost always agree on what is a borderline case, even if we don't agree about which side of the border they fall. Wittgenstein argued that that this *only* seems odd if we assume that 'game' must be definable in terms of necessary and sufficient conditions, so that all games must have something in common. What on Earth could the Great Game have in common with hopscotch?

Solove was keen to resolve indeterminacy in the use of the term 'privacy', but the notion of family resemblance doesn't provide the necessary resources. Wittgenstein's project was simply to show that a conceptual definition is not necessary to ground agreement in the use of a term. Solove's was the opposite, for he was trying to explain why we do *not* agree on the use of the term 'privacy'. The family resemblance argument, if we accept it, shows that we don't *need* a definition to agree in the use of a term. It does not, however, suggest that a term about whose use we do *not* agree is coherent; neither does it provide any explanation of how it could be coherent.

This is a key difference. Wittgenstein's point about games was that we *agree* on how we use the term, not only in clear cases, but also in analogies and grey areas, and because meaning, for Wittgenstein, is essentially connected with the use of terms, we therefore agree on the meaning of 'game' despite the lack of necessary and sufficient conditions. Yet Solove's problem with privacy stems from his claim that we *don't* have that kind of agreement. If we *do*, then the problem cannot be as Solove frames it. If we do not in fact agree on our usage of the term privacy, then family resemblance has nothing to explain, and worse, there *can* be no family resemblance between the different uses of the term (since there is no resemblance at all). Family resemblance requires resemblance – agreement in use.

In other words, if Solove's point that privacy *is* a concept in disarray was well-taken, then the disarray *isn't and cannot be* dispelled by agreeing that privacy is a pluralistic notion and invoking family resemblance. If privacy *is* a family resemblance term, the concept is *not* in disarray, any more than the concept of games is in disarray. Solove's theory is attractive, *but only if we do actually agree in how we use 'privacy' and related terms.*

Wittgenstein's slogan 'meaning is use' is hard to square with Solove's statement that:

> a conception of privacy is different from the usage of the word 'privacy.' The usage of the word ' privacy' constitutes the ways in which we employ the word in everyday life and the things we are referring to when we speak of ' privacy.' A conception of privacy is an abstract mental picture of what privacy is and what makes it unique and distinct. (Solove 2008, 13)

Wittgenstein's later philosophy is dedicated to showing that such 'abstract mental pictures' have no explanatory power at all.

Does this entail that, contrary to my statements in Part I, the reference list, a description of the use of the term 'privacy', gives its meaning after all? No, for two main reasons. First, it was not developed in any kind of scrupulous way, and so cannot claim to be a rigorous account of use. More to the point, second, it does not and cannot describe the use of the term in novel areas. As we saw in the previous chapter, when new contexts arise, new uses may be required, which will be simple for competent speakers to navigate but hard to anticipate in advance. I will discuss this faculty in Part III, Level 1. However, I do maintain that the reference list is a sufficient explanation of observed uses of the term 'privacy'. If someone asked why a particular situation is spoken of as privacy, it would be enough to say 'it's an instance of attentional privacy from O'Hara's reference list'.

As Wittgenstein argued, this is all we need. 'Here we come up against a remarkable and characteristic phenomenon in philosophical investigation: the difficulty ... is not that of finding the solution but rather that of recognizing as the solution something that looks as if it were only a preliminary to it' (1981, §314). The agreement *is* the solution to the problem. There is nothing more of note to say.

This may seem like a counterintuitive result, given that virtually all the privacy literature of the past two decades has assumed disagreement and dispute. This means that this second explanation of privacy's semantics *doesn't* explain the disarray. However, the family resemblance theory seems to explain other things about privacy, such as (i) the failure of anyone to find necessary and sufficient conditions, (ii) the fact that 'privacy' functions perfectly well in everyday discourse with competent speakers of English and (iii) its plural nature.

From this, however, following Wittgenstein, we should conclude, not that disagreement is endemic, but that we tend to *agree* in our uses of the term (otherwise there would be no resemblance). In other words, we get the same outcome as we did when we interrogated the ECC theory. We therefore need a third attempt to provide the missing explanation for the disarray in the academic literature. If we can pinpoint such an explanation, that would make it possible to concur with Solove that uses of the term 'privacy' are connected by family resemblance, entailing that it is not a concept in disarray.

Explanation 3: privacy definitions are overburdened

The inquiries of the previous two chapters have been helpful. If 'privacy' is a family resemblance term, however, our dilemma remains unresolved. The metaphor of resemblance trades on agreement in use even in the absence of necessary and sufficient conditions, while the ground for looking for a pluralistic account of privacy in the first place was lack of agreement about it.

The ability to use a term does not presuppose the ability to define it. Very few language users regularly or even occasionally fashion definitions for their vocabulary. Agreement in the use of a term such as 'privacy' certainly does not require agreement in its definition, as argued by Wittgenstein, by Quine in his theory of indeterminacy of translation (1960) and others. Wittgenstein's point was that a definition doesn't help explain coincidence of use, while Quine's argument was that, for any utterance, multiple adequate translations will always be possible, even between speakers of the same language. Evidence of use will always underdetermine definitional theories.

However, it is possible to falsify an inadequate definition. With that in mind, I will revisit Solove's magisterial survey of privacy definitions (2008, 14–37), looking at the *reasons* he gave for rejecting them. Those reasons should be informative about what is expected of a successful definition of privacy, should one happen to come along.

Solove's critiques of privacy definitions

Some definitions simply failed to cover enough privacy territory. Privacy is sometimes defined as intimacy (Fried 1968; Rachels 1975;

Inness 1992), which Solove argued was too narrow: there are many breaches of privacy that don't impact on intimate relations, such as e-commerce records (Solove 2008, 36–37). More positively, intimacy seems to usher in aspects of value directly, and Solove maintained that: 'a theory of privacy should articulate why privacy is good or how it will further the good life' (2008, 78). Hence we have two criteria for successful definitions: they should be wide enough to cover the space, and they should connect privacy to the good life (and maybe to the bad life, where privacy is a cover for wrongdoing?).

Warren and Brandeis' right to be let alone (1890), as we have seen, was not a definition of privacy. However, many commentators take it as one; it was rejected by Solove as a definition because it is vague, and 'fails to provide much guidance about what privacy entails ... [and] does not inform us about the matters in which we should be let alone' (2008, 17). A similar critique did for claims that privacy is control over PII or personal data (Murphy 1996); there is plenty of PII that is not private, such as well-known facts about public figures that are legitimately in the public domain (the salary of the President, for example). Furthermore, 'the theory is too vague because it fails to define the types of information over which individuals should have control. ... Privacy is not simply a sub-jective matter of individual prerogative; it is also an issue of what society deems appropriate to protect' (Solove 2008, 25). Hence the definition must also encompass appropriacy. We now have two more criteria: precision and a normative steer about where to draw the line.

Another category of definitions is that of limiting access to the self: 'privacy is the exclusive access of a person (or other legal entity) to a realm of its own. The right to privacy entitles one to exclude others from (a) watching (b) utilizing (c) invading (intruding upon, or in other ways affecting) his private realm' (Van Den Haag 1971, 149). This failed because it 'omits any notion of the individual's power to make certain choices about revealing aspects of herself to others. ... Privacy involves one's relationship to society; in a world without others, claiming that one has privacy does not make much sense' (Solove 2008, 20). So (fifth criterion) the definition should include an account of someone's ability to negotiate privacy with the embedding society. If we define privacy as an 'existential con-dition', a state of limited access, the condition of being separate

(O'Brien 1979), we also need psychological and sociological accounts of how individuals can protect this state successfully when they choose to, and their capacities for imposing their choices.

Mere access is not sufficient to declare a breach. 'We are frequently seen and heard by others without perceiving this as even the slightest invasion of privacy' (Solove 2008, 25). Hence (sixth criterion) the definition cannot only be formal but must also be sensitive to our perceptions of privacy. Furthermore, 'it would be difficult to claim that something is a privacy violation if nobody viewed it as such' (2008, 71), so it must respect our preferences too (arguably a separate seventh criterion).

Gavison's attempt to narrow down limited access to 'three independent and irreducible elements: secrecy, anonymity and solitude' (1980, 354) failed because it was too narrow, excluding, for example, government interference in and regulation of sexual conduct, which does not affect any of these three elements (Solove 2008, 21). In general:

> Certainly not all access to the self infringes upon privacy, only access relating to specific dimensions of the self or to particular matters and information. ... In the continuum between absolutely no access to the self and total access, the important question is ... what degree of access should we recognize as reasonable? (Solove 2008, 20)

A definition must tell us not only what privacy is, but when it is reasonable (eighth criterion).

Our expectations are psychological, but what is reasonable is a social construct. 'Privacy does not turn solely on the individual's particular expectation, but upon expectations that society considers reasonable' (Solove 2008, 71). Hence a successful definition would have to straddle both the social and the psychological. Indeed, the law needs to be added to the mix, as it also has something to say about what is reasonable, so, for example, the Supreme Court was cited to show that it is not an invasion of privacy to reveal illegal activity (Solove 2008, 68). A ninth criterion, then, is that the definition must balance these diverse perspectives on reasonable expectations.

Sidney Jourard asserted that 'privacy is an outcome of a person's wish to withhold from others certain knowledge as to his past and present experience and action and his intentions for the future'

(1966, 307; Posner 1983). But privacy-as-secrecy doesn't work, as it falls foul of the first criterion: it misses most cases of privacy (2008, 23). A secret is the concealment of a piece of information, but informational privacy is only one of several types of privacy (cf. the reference list). People aim for seclusion, anonymity, intimacy and so on, none of which has informational content (Allen 1988, 8).

Privacy-as-secrecy also fails to take into account the obvious fact that 'individuals want to keep things private from some people and not others' (Solove 2008, 23). The 'secrecy paradigm' (2008, 111, 139) trades on the idea that if a piece of information has been revealed at all, it is to all intents and purposes in the public domain, but acts of disclosure are rarely intended to be limitless, and indeed rarely are. This fails to meet the fifth and seventh criteria, to do with preferences and how people achieve them.

Yet even if we ignore those criteria, privacy-as-secrecy will not work, because many facts, such as the people we associate with or the books we read, despite their not being secret 'we nonetheless view ... as private matters' (Solove 2008, 24) where it is inappropriate for another to intervene or interfere (Benn 1971). Hence (tenth criterion) a successful definition should take into account norms about which matters are private, independently of how far privacy has actually been breached.

Perhaps the most common alternative to privacy-as-withdrawal is privacy-as-control, whose hallmark is the individual's control over the flow of information, the better to determine one's identity and how one is seen by others (Westin 1967; Fried 1968, 209; Miller 1971; Rachels 1975; Scanlon 1975; Inness 1992, 47–53). For some reason, most of its advocates neglect anything other than informational privacy, but it can relatively straightforwardly be expanded to include other kinds, such as control of who is in one's space (Altman 1975), or protecting extrinsic privacy against distractions, subliminal influence, or obscenity (Solove 2008, 28–29). I will discuss this in more detail in Part III, Level 4, but it fails for a number of reasons in Solove's view.

Few definitions specify what they mean by 'control' (Solove 2008, 26). When they do, they tend to reach for the language of property rights, as if information about oneself was property (Westin 1967; Murphy 1996), but unlike physical property it may be shared without being lost, and its use may not easily be constrained. PII may provide information about others (genetic information expresses something about the genes of blood relations) and may be created, at some expense, by others as when one's Web browsing behaviour is tracked. Hence others also have interests in the information and might also expect to have some control. It may also have wider significance; that someone is a wife abuser may be private information about the husband that he may reasonably wish to be concealed, but equally it is private information about his wife, about which she may have preferences, and the public may have an interest in its publication. Luciano Floridi's information-theoretic point of view (2005), despite explicitly stating that privacy is of a high but ultimately negotiable value, was rejected because his account 'fails to provide guidance about when conflicting interests should prevail in the balance' (Solove 2008, 86). Hence (eleventh criterion) a definition of privacy needs to balance the interests of all concerned, and not simply the individual currently in focus.

Finally, privacy-as-control may be a social affair as well as a matter for the individual; power asymmetries between big tech companies and the consumers of their services mean that there arguably should be regulation and support from the state. So a twelfth criterion takes in power, covering 'an aspect of social structure, an architecture of information regulation, not just ... the exercise of individual control' (Solove 2008, 29).

Another view probed by Solove says that privacy protects individuality and personhood (Bloustein 1964; Benn 1971; Reiman 1976). Such theories fall short because they do not say enough about personhood itself. Personalities have public and private aspects, and the public aspects are often highly personal – opinions, for example, or creative works. On some accounts, the state determines the boundary, which makes privacy a matter of law (cf. Solove 2008, 54). Rubenfeld (1989) rejected such positions, as ceding too much power to the state to define what an individual identity should consist in, and himself adjusted the personhood view so that privacy is an anti-totalitarian measure designed to protect the person against the state. Solove argued that this was not enough to save privacy-as-personhood (2008, 33–34). Someone has to define what a person should be, because otherwise how would we know what to protect against the state? Without specifying this,

Rubenfeld's theory collapses into the vague right to be let alone. Furthermore, the state, while it clearly often infringes privacy, also protects it in many ways, not least through the administration of privacy law. A number of criteria are engaged in this series of arguments, including the fourth, fifth, tenth and twelfth, but we might discern a thirteenth in the need to define the legitimate activities of the state.

'Privacy is a condition we create, and as such, it is dynamic and changing' (Solove 2008, 65). This boundary will shift between cultures and over time, making the requirements on the definition even more complex. 'What it means for them to be private is different today than it was in the past and different for each subject matter' (Solove 2008, 50), giving a fourteenth criterion that 'a theory of privacy should leave room for cultural and historical variation, but not err by becoming too variable' (Solove 2008, 66).

This isn't an exhaustive analysis of Solove's work, but even this examination of some of the most common ways of defining privacy generated fourteen different reasons for rejecting them. The reasons are arguably valid, given the scope and ambition of the definitions critiqued. That puts enormous pressure on definitions, if they have to nail all these things down. Is it realistic? Is it even possible – if privacy depends on meeting these fourteen criteria (and most likely others), isn't it possible, inevitable even, that they will contradict each other at some point?

Note that this isn't anything to do with privacy's being a family resemblance term. Pluralism concerns the difficulties of finding anything in common in uses of the term, not the scope and intention of the definitions. Neither is it anything to do with the multidisciplinary nature of privacy studies, requiring the input of anthropologists, psychologists, biologists, physicists, historians, psychiatrists, philosophers, lawyers and laypeople (Westin 1967, xiv), and more, including computer scientists, sociologists and economists. Early classics, such as (Westin 1967) and (Altman 1975), were masterpieces of synthesis; the flip side was an increase in complexity, but why should this necessarily lead to incompatibility?

The definitions were developed by lawyers, philosophers, computer scientists, sociologists and political scientists, not to model ordinary usage, but primarily in order to nail down issues of scope, value, culture and so on, and to anticipate debates in which the definitions would be put to use. From their various perspectives, judgements of courts (especially human rights courts), public outcries, business decisions about data, governments' attempts to influence and shape the private sphere, technological developments, and media practices all loomed large, representing developments to be encouraged or resisted. Definitions skew toward aspects that seem particularly problematic. They also focus on particular discourses, so that, for example, someone writing about privacy law is basically interested in what might be defensible in court. The definitions critiqued by Solove are purpose-specific scoping measures for particular discourses, addressing different problems.

Kitchen sink definitions

Solove's criticisms are convincing; with their fourteen criteria they are demanding, but then those defining privacy are demanding too. But why are such strong demands being made at all? After all, in the days of the classic papers reviewed in Part I, Disarray 1, such ambition was absent. Explanation 3 is my own gloss on why things have changed.

Through the century, privacy became increasingly politicised and controversial, which led to more engaged argument, and inflated ambition. No longer were debaters and combatants prepared to leave to chance how their readers understood privacy. Definitions were provided to tilt the argument in the author's direction. If they (i.e. the author) thought that the value of privacy is that it helps autonomous individuals control their own destiny, then privacy would be defined as control. Conversely, if they were an apparatchik of a social networking company, they would hardly define privacy as control over the flow of personal information because that is what they manipulate. Privacy might instead become property that could be traded off for greater goods, such as the ability to use the wonderful services of a social network for instance. Interlocutors use semantics to fix the fight before it begins.

As a result, definitions cram a lot of material in, which has the perverse effect of rendering them susceptible to a wider range of criticisms. However, as Solove noted, none of them has wide adoption, and they don't represent ordinary usage, as captured, for example, by the reference list. There is disarray in this world of professional definitions because there are so many of them. As Solove demonstrated so devastatingly, it is remarkably simple to push them over, a matter of their being vulnerable to attack by trying to cram too much in, in order to fix the debate in advance. If privacy has to be reasonable *by definition*, then breaches are unreasonable, QED. If privacy has to involve control *by definition*, then a loss of control is a breach. If privacy is a necessary condition for personhood *by definition*, then a breach will deprive subjects of dignity and identity. The range of potential lines of attack for Solove on the privacy literature is indicative of the range of topics that commentators are inclined to cram into their definitions.

Of course, the opponents in the debate will hardly lie down and take it, and will in all likelihood come up with their own rival gerrymandered definitions, and so a substantive and possibly informative debate is replaced by a sterile semantic argument about what 'privacy' means. And suddenly, 'everybody is talking about "privacy", but it is not clear exactly what they are talking about' (Solove 2008, 5).

The concept therefore appears to be in disarray, and we now, at the third attempt, have our full explanation why: *privacy definitions have become theory-laden, overburdened with additional enhancements and superfluities designed to influence debates about it, which has prevented consensus forming about any particular definition.* Meanwhile, the word 'privacy' remains in perfectly consistent use in everyday English, and – despite over half a century of academic and legal wrangling – does not cause problems for English speakers in ordinary contexts.

In the definitions that Solove challenged in his book, axes were being ground. The disarray happens because various points about value, reasonableness, legitimacy, cultural variance, etc., are shoehorned into what we might call *kitchen sink definitions* (because, as the expression has it, they contain everything but the kitchen sink) in order to fix debates in advance. We saw that privacy is probably not an ECC, but sometimes it is rendered problematic by defining it using essentially contested terms, such as reasonableness, identity, intimacy and so on. Yet need it be this way?

Without wanting to insist on a fact/value distinction, it might be worth asking whether there is a way of looking at privacy which doesn't prejudge the debates about it. It certainly has its rights and wrongs, but they should not feature in our understanding of what it actually is. Like death, taxes, and genetic engineering, and unlike right, sin and justice, its *definition* need not appeal irreducibly to an ethical vocabulary. That is *absolutely not* to say that it does not feature in moral discourse – like death, taxes and genetic engineering, there is quite obviously a flourishing ethical debate about privacy. But like the other concepts, we can work out what it is and then worry about the moral issues. I am with Warren and Brandeis, Schoeman (1992, 11) and Nissenbaum (2010, 3, 148) that we can talk about privacy perfectly well without defining it.

An example: 'Few would contend that when a crime victim tells the police about the perpetrator, it violates the criminal's privacy' (Solove 2008, 48). Well, few would contend that the criminal's privacy is either here or there in such a case; by committing a crime, he has forfeited any *right* of privacy or confidentiality. But surely he has privacy *interests*, as in the statement of Joseph Pulitzer, who had obviously never met some recent politicians: 'there is not a crime, there is not a dodge, there is not a trick, there is not a swindle, there is not a vice that does not live by secrecy' (quoted in Solove 2008, 81). It may be that a victim does not tell the police, *precisely* to protect the criminal's privacy (they may be related). If the victim having no obligation to protect the criminal's privacy entails that there is no privacy to protect, then how can the victim protect it? What is being protected by their compassion? And what is the victim bargaining with if they decide to blackmail the criminal? Some crimes are more heinous than others. Homosexual activity used to be illegal, and gay men were sometimes blackmailed by their 'victims', but – at least from our present-day perspective – their privacy was hardly irrelevant.

This is weird. Victim tells police: no privacy violation, privacy not relevant. Victim doesn't tell police: no privacy violation either, but the criminal's privacy is preserved. Victim blackmails criminal: privacy is preserved unless the victim spills the beans, which isn't a privacy violation. Privacy cannot surely appear and disappear, like Schrödinger's cat, as the victim wavers between grassing and keeping shtum. If we can disconnect the *fact* of privacy from the *obligations* of others to protect it, the story becomes far simpler: the criminal has privacy interests, and prefers the information about the crime to be kept confidential, but the social norms around crime and lawbreaking are such that witnesses are expected to report to the police, so the criminal's privacy interests would normally be completely and quite properly disregarded. That does not mean they don't exist, just that they carry no moral weight, and there may be a legal duty for the victim to disregard them.

Let me state the thesis of Part II clearly and baldly.

1. The disarray Solove correctly detected was between kitchen sink definitions of privacy, *but*
2. Kitchen sink definitions are illegitimate; *therefore*
3. Neither the concept, nor the use of the term, is in disarray.

Separating what privacy is from our attitudes and discourses about it is not simple, but it needs to be done to free us from the claustrophobic tangle of current debate. These discourses veil the meaning of privacy from us, opaque gauzes obstructing a clear view. A framework for unblocking the kitchen sink definitions will be the business of Part III.

Part III

A framework for privacy discourses

Examination of the privacy debates within the well-understood frameworks of ECCs and family resemblance revealed not disarray but a surprising measure of agreement. Our disagreements tend to be about value and propriety, not meaning. The best explanation of the disarray in the academic field, we found, was that people have been tailoring their personal definitions of privacy to support moral or political positions.

There doesn't seem any reason why basic propositions about privacy can't be couched as neutral statements of a relation between oneself or one's group and others. They need not express whether and when such privacy is appropriate, valuable, insidious, desired, desirable, legal, enforceable, functional, anti-social, vital for democracy, self-indulgent, corrosive of security, essential for psychological well-being, good, bad or indifferent. These are additional factors, present in specific non-conceptual privacy discourses.

How can we capture this? We can think in terms of different *discourses* on privacy, some of which are about rights and wrongs, others about the law, others about how we enact privacy, and so on. These can be kept separate, at least to a degree, rather as a practical discussion of how to collect VAT need not invoke the morality of taxation or the minutiae of the law. I don't propose a specific formal theory, but let us take a discourse to be roughly a form of communicating that serves a social purpose, delimited by a more or less clear boundary (that may be disputed). Its purpose means that certain assumptions underlie a discourse, which therefore provide a perspective on its topic, rather than a complete account of the topic itself. Such assumptions are likely to include particular research or knowledge-producing methods, as well as the legitimacy and illegitimacy of certain voices. A discourse therefore *frames* a topic, and, in the set of discourses I set out in Part III, the frames approximate to the fairly wide ones adopted by different disciplines of science, social science and the humanities (cf. e.g. Messer-Davidow et al. 1993; Becher 1994; Hayes et al. 2021).

A discourse must be at least that, but this account may be stretched by someone who wanted to go the Full Foucault and critically question the relationships between all discourses through the lenses of negative genealogies of knowledge (Fraser 1981). In particular, we should be able to distinguish a *theory of privacy*, which explains what privacy is, from a *privacy discourse*, which is a type of discussion assuming a particular frame *vis-à-vis* privacy. Indeed, as will become clear, explaining what privacy is is one of many privacy discourses, and it is well to know when we are indulging in that discourse, and when we are not. Taking a discourse-relative perspective fully into account would increase the scope for cross-fertilisation and the sense of unity between the discourses, provide the basis of a mutual coherence that is currently lacking in privacy studies, and defuse the disarray and chaos that concerns so many commentators.

Nissenbaum motivated her theory of contextual integrity by suggesting certain *levels* of discourse: 'interest-brawls are conceived as taking place at ground level, [while] appeals to universal human values and moral and political principles take place in the stratospheres of abstraction. ... Between the ground and the heavens ... is the realm of the social' (2010, 10). Part II, Explanation 3 above shows she was absolutely right to want to keep these separate. Similarly, while they did not specify this in terms of discourses, Koops et al. wanted to separate the conceptual from discussions of value, social dimensions and management by individuals (2017, 489).

The next question is what relevant discourses there are; Nissenbaum's sketch is a good start. Rössler set out a range of discourses, some of which map directly onto my framework, but which she left unstructured (2005, 2–4), and noted that we can 'draw a distinction between legal, moral and purely conventional claims to privacy' (2005, 75). Gary Marx specified a set of questions to motivate a 'research strategy' that highlights some of the discourses of this section (2001, 167–168). I do not want to make a strongly reductive claim, but I will set out seven levels of discourse (O'Hara 2016). I call them levels, and number them, because there appear to be stronger connections between adjacent levels than between random pairs. The discourses veil the meaning of privacy, and – hey! – there are seven veils. How pleasing.

These seven discourses cover much ground, but I do not claim that they are complete or sufficient. I do claim, however, that we should work hard to keep them separate. They naturally interact and influence each other, and so work at one level should retain awareness of factors from other levels. In this Part, I will concentrate on the separate identities of these levels/discourses. In Part IV, I will consider ways of stitching them back together and understanding their mutual influence.

The seven levels are the following.

- *Level 1: conceptions of privacy*: different privacy conceptions, breaches and remedies. New conceptions emerge alongside new behaviours, technologies and other innovations. Different conceptions have a family resemblance to each other, and as a matter of fact we are pretty good at recognising these resemblances and agreeing when to categorise a conception as one of privacy.
- *Level 2: architectures and affordances of privacy*: the extent to which a person has (or people have) privacy on a specific (level 1) conception, relative to other persons. How is each kind of privacy implemented or facilitated in this context, if it is? Is the current state of the world liable to protect privacy, or to hinder its protection, as a matter of fact?
- *Level 3: phenomenology of privacy*: what privacy, or its breach, feels like. This often overlooked level includes questions about whether one even notices, or cares about, a breach of privacy.
- *Level 4: preferences for privacy*: desires to be concealed or visible to one's networks. It also includes questions of what privacy behaviour others want from one and one's preferences about others' behaviour (Nissenbaum's 'interest brawls').
- *Level 5: norms of privacy*: informal privacy-related regularities, conventions and expectations, which will vary across cultures, genders, generations and classes (Nissenbaum's 'social' level).

- *Level 6: regulation of privacy*: law, and other compulsory privacy codes, which the state (or other legitimate organisations) expend resources to enforce.
- *Level 7: morality of privacy*: justifications of privacy, questions of non-legal rights, and issues to do with the value of privacy and questions of power (Nissenbaum's 'heavens').

The levels are depicted in Figure 1. They are intended to suggest relatively self-contained discourses that more or less cover the major issues that privacy scholars wrestle with, and the numerical order is intended, roughly, to indicate relationships between them. The relations are correlative, rather than reductive or supervenient; we cannot 'read off' or deduce facts at one level from facts at another. In particular, as can be seen in Figure 1, the major axis is open-ended. It may well be that there are meaningful things to say prior to level 1. At level 1, the pluralistic nature of privacy conceptions is evident, and the family resemblance revealed. However, there is debate about whether there are deeper connections – the elusive 'concept of privacy' – and there may be some unifying claims that one could make, which could be the business of a 'level 0', tentatively discussed in Part IV, Commentary 3.

Similarly, the main axis is open at the top as well, beyond level 7. In particular, I have bundled together in that level a number of not necessarily connected fields, including rights, ethics and politics, under the broad heading 'values' and scholars in those areas might with justice argue that relatively pragmatic political or ideological considerations are distinct from the more abstract claims of morality. Rights, meanwhile, which stand between law and ethics, may be deserving of a level of their own. So level 7 itself may conceal a lot of complexity, and there may even be levels beyond, in the area of theology for instance, which currently plays a relatively small part in privacy debates and about which I am ashamed to confess I am utterly uninformed (Webb 2007; Dahl 2011; Walters 2011; Lockwood 2014; Sedley 2017; McPherson 2020, 166–180). And from a Godlike contemplative solitary level 10(?) or so, the axis might even swing right round and meet up again with level 0. I leave such questions entirely open.

Figure 1 also shows some of the gradations that connect the levels. We move from abstract philosophical and technical issues, to those concerning the individual, to the societal as we ascend from level 1

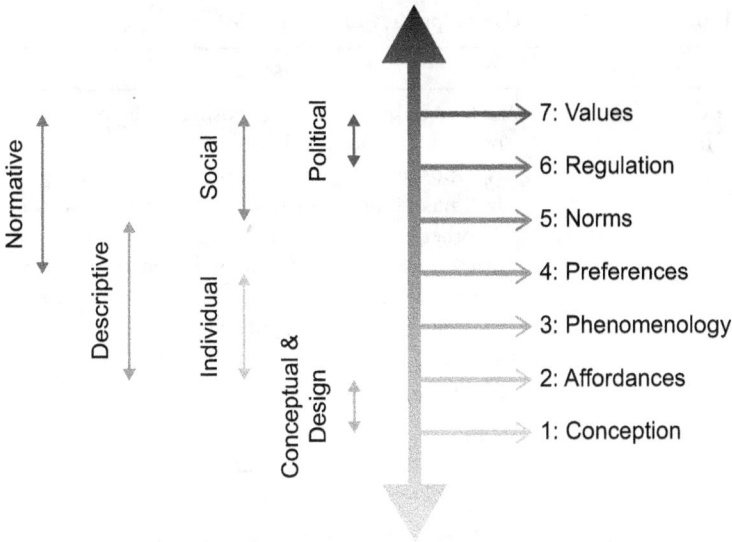

Figure 1: The seven levels of privacy discourse

to 7. On that route, we will also make a gradual progression from primarily descriptive issues to primarily normative ones. This means that, with regard to the perennial debate about whether accounts of privacy should be descriptive or normative, I am studiously neutral. However, having said that, normative discourses are at the upper levels on this diagram, while the descriptive ones are at the lower levels, and the definitions of privacy we work with are fundamental. I agree with Gavison (1980, 348–349) that normative accounts require descriptive accounts as inputs and with Warren and Brandeis (1890) that we can often rest normative accounts on an understood description. A normative account of privacy that affects to define it as well will produce a kitchen sink definition. As we shall see, levels 4 and 5 are where the temptation to be normative in the absence of a satisfactory description is strongest.

While this is an abstract characterisation, the remainder of Part III should put flesh on the bones. But to give a little spoiler of the distinctions I will describe in more detail, let us take an example of risqué photographs of a person X placed online, and partition some of the major issues about this activity across the seven levels, as in Table 2.

Table 2: Different levels of a privacy discussion

Level	Issues
1: Conception and breach	One type of breach is the exposure of the body to public view. Do the photos reveal intimate parts? Is X posing for the camera or taken unawares? Is X naked, in a state of undress or scantily clad? Another conception is that of access to private property; whose photographs are they? A third is the association of the body with an identity; do they allow X to be identified by the viewer, e.g. by showing a face or tattoo? Is the furniture in the photo recognisable by friends and family?
2: Architecture/ affordances	Are the photos behind a paywall? Are they encrypted? What format are they in? How many times have they been viewed or downloaded?
3: Phenomenology	Is X horrified? Excited? Unconcerned? Proud? Angry? Amused? Devastated and suicidal? Blissfully unaware that the photos have been uploaded? What about the feelings of those consuming them?
4: Preferences	Did X consent? Did X put the pictures up there, or otherwise expect them to be published? Is this an example of revenge porn, strongly against X's wishes? What are X's views if the pictures are seen or downloaded by strangers? By friends? By family? By their employer? By their children? What does X's spouse think? What does their boss think? And, with respect to the audience, how do we describe the demand for such content?
5: Norms	How are such photos generally treated in this culture? Is it a matter for the subject alone? Is nudity celebrated or frowned upon? Does publication contravene existing norms? Are different norms discernible across generations, or classes, or sexes? Is X's family dishonoured according to local norms?

Level	Issues
6: Regulation	Who has the rights to the image? Do the photos contravene obscenity law? Do they contravene data protection law? Is a data subject identifiable from the image? (When) is consent needed for the legal publication of someone's image?
7: Morality	Should we outlaw pornography? Revenge porn? Sexual images of women or minors? Is this a freedom of speech issue? Is there a public interest in publication? Is it bullying? Should we accept the existence of a market where there is much demand and willing supply? Are women's rights breached *tout court*? Is nudity a special type of exposure that deserves protection?

These are related but separate discussions demanding different methodologies for investigation. We should not confuse the levels, for instance by assuming that because X consented there was no breach of privacy or because the post was legal there was no harm committed. Yet many accounts do jumble these up. We can sketch a roughly ordered route map from level to level. Level 1 takes in the conceptions of privacy specific to particular contexts. Level 2 looks at the affordances of the environment with respect to particular conceptions of privacy for preserving them or supporting breaches. Individuals experience privacy in particular ways, depending on how the affordances of the environment are evident to them and shape their experience (level 3), and that pleasant or unpleasant experience may prompt particular preferences for or against privacy (level 4). If those preferences are broadly shared in a community, then social norms might emerge (level 5), and a strong enough state might even step in and regulate (level 6). Regulation informs and is informed by political and ethical considerations (level 7). So the levels are roughly ordered, although non-contiguous levels may also influence each other, so that, for example, a privacy breach may feel bad or humiliating (level 3) because it goes against prevailing social norms (level 5) or because it is just wrong (level 7). I will discuss the interaction of the levels in more detail in Part IV, Commentary 1. While I have drawn Figure 1 going down-to-up from level 1 to 7, there is nothing special about that direction.

A final thought: in this part of the book I will discuss these levels. This is a theory of privacy *discourse*, and I hope an aid to unravelling at least some of the confusions and arguments that bother people – an antidote to disarray. *It is not a theory of privacy*, and I do not try to say what privacy is (although I have a few opinions which I will chip in, especially in Part IV).

With that sketch of the overall conceptual scheme, let us consider each level of discourse in more detail.

Level 1: conceptions

The concept of 'concept'

The notion of a concept is a live one in philosophy. Are they abstract or fixed by linguistic facts? Mental representations or logical conditions? Grounded in abilities to discriminate between types of object or the means which make such abilities possible? There is even a debate about what the concept of 'concept' is intended to explain: cognitive development; the determination of referents of terms; the structure of ontologies; the generative properties of language (e.g. from the concepts of 'white' and 'cat', we generate the concept of 'white cat'); the success of science; or psycholinguistic phenomena such as defaults and typicality (for instance, the concept of 'bird' tends to evoke ideas of flight, even though by no means all birds fly). The privacy literature, so thirsty for a concept, has rarely plugged into these debates to determine exactly why it needs one. Solove came closest, arguing that it would improve legal reasoning (2008).

The sprawling privacy debates suggest that it may be profitable to think in plural terms. One idea is that concepts are Heath Robinsonesque devices with lots of components, each of which does a different explanatory job. A basic common core could explain logical inference, outlier recognition and language generativity, while discrete offshoots might encode basic paradigms and typical cases, and the whole might gradually evolve into a hybrid mental representation to underpin psychological abilities (Laurence and Margolis 1999). Another approach is to say that there is no overarching concept but mini-concepts of multiple representative kinds, each of which explains different things (Weiskopf 2009).

That would leave open the natural question of what makes these heterogeneous concepts all versions of the same thing? Another approach would focus on the evolution of apparent conceptual discrimination in the natural world – in other words, see how animals learn to tell types of things apart, rather than looking for phenomena that fit in with our sophisticated linguistic intercourse (Plotnik and Clayton 2015). The nuclear option is to do without concepts at all (Machery 2009, 242ff.). This eliminativist idea, which Solove ultimately adopted, is that the notion of a concept is botched together from a number of more useful ideas, such as theories, prototypes and exemplars, and we should just drop it. They aren't natural kinds, and they won't furnish cognitive explanations.

The public face of the concept, outside philosophy, is some kind of logico-semantic apparatus, such as necessary and sufficient conditions, which enables classifications to be made. We have already realised that we will struggle to provide these, and the family resemblance arguments undermine our faith in their existence. I want to accept that the global idea of privacy is highly pluralistic, containing or connecting many different ideas that live in different contexts (Weiskopf 2009), while emphasising that – for whatever reason, whether psychological or metaphysical – we have little difficulty connecting them, at least when we are not being academic, philosophical, lawyerly or otherwise over-thinking things.

What should we be looking for? Felix Oppenheim (1975) proposed a useful set of criteria that we can use as a lodestone in our inquiry. First, concepts should be operational. Second, they should ideally establish definitional connections with other terms. Third, they should draw attention to important aspects of the subject that might easily be overlooked. Fourth, they should not preclude empirical investigation by making true by definition what should be open to inquiry. Finally, they should largely respect ordinary language use. Let's keep these in mind. Whereas most authors are interested in their own agendas, and therefore the first three criteria, our particular focus will be on the final two – the constraints. How do we craft accounts of privacy that take their cue from standard usage (respecting the family resemblance argument), and don't prejudge the outcomes that we favour (respecting the moratorium on kitchen sink definitions)?

What is a conception?

Without speculating about the existence or nature of any overarching concept of privacy (for that, see Part IV, Commentary 3), I want to develop the idea of a *conception* of privacy, in the sense adumbrated by John Rawls (1971, 2005, 11–14), who discussed political conceptions of justice. His starting point was that citizens in a pluralistic society would need freestanding conceptions independent of their doctrines and ideas, a sort of political *lingua franca* about and with which they could debate. Conceptions' freestanding nature rules out precommitment to particular values or societal functionality (and therefore what we earlier termed kitchen sink definitions). For people to have endemic disagreements such as those in the privacy sphere, they must have settled on a family of conceptions in advance of their discourses (see also Waldron 1985, 333–340 for a similar idea, but which links conceptions to essentially contested concepts, while Solove's definition of a conception is entirely different from this – 2008, 13).

A conception inhabits the framework of basic institutions, principles, standards and precepts of the society in question, and the character and attitudes of its members, what Rawls called the 'background culture' of everyday social life. Our conceptions of privacy can cover technologies, practices, behaviour, and the affordances of the human body as a sensing device. As a conception is freestanding, it requires no commitment to a particular ideology, and so can be shared, not only within the society in question but in other contexts too. It also should give us enough purchase for fruitful description, in accordance with the principles of (Oppenheim 1975).

Privacy, as suggested by the reference list, is best seen as a *state*. In other words, a conception of privacy should express the relationships of a person who is private in that respect at a point in time, or over a short interval. Many commentators argue that privacy is a *process*, e.g. 'a central regulatory process by which a person (or group) makes himself more or less accessible and open to others' (Altman 1975, 3). This idea was intended to capture what Altman called the dialectical nature of privacy, that it is generally negotiated by the person/group within a social environment, that it may or may not be successfully achieved, that it is always in question, and that privacy-related goals are always in flux. His emphasis on the dialectics is absolutely on the money, but insisting that privacy *itself* must therefore be a process in his teleological account confuses action and goal, giving another kitchen sink definition. As a social psychologist interested in how people organise and control their relationships, of course he laid emphasis on the dynamic aspects. On the other hand, he gave separate accounts of the *mechanisms* by which privacy goals are pursued, and of the *goal-states* themselves (which, although subject to arbitrary change, are not always in flux).

Hence, it is not clear that privacy-as-process does more than complicate the picture. If a privacy conception describes a state, then nothing Altman wished to note is missed: people want to achieve particular goal-states, have various mechanisms for doing so, receive both pushback and aid from the social environment, and as their goals change they adjust their strategies. Their *privacy management* is indeed a process, but that is a *means* of achieving (desired levels of) privacy, not privacy itself. We will discuss this in more detail at level 4.

Each conception will include not only what privacy in that context consists in but also what counts as a breach and what might be a remedy. Remedies in this sense restore the privacy *status quo ante* following a breach, rather than compensating for harm. This may not be possible – once a secret is blurted out, out it has been blurted and it can't be unblurted. Breaches of spatial privacy can be remedied by removing the intruder from the space and breaches of attentional privacy by removing oneself from scrutiny. Once Peeping Tom saw Lady Godiva in her nakedness, she had been seen, and that could not be undone. However, when he was removed from the scene, she was restored to her privacy in the appropriate conception of not having her nakedness visible. In the legend, Tom was struck blind by the vengeance of Heaven, which restored the attentional *status quo ante* but left him with his memories (which may or may not have been sufficient compensation).

The same basic idea, e.g. being physically observed, might in itself include a range of privacy conceptions. For instance, one relevant distinction is that between happening to be observed, and being closely observed or singled out, targeted as a specific individual (Benn 1971, 225; Inness 1992, 35). Technology might add further refinements, such as the recording of events with cameras and the ability to search databases retrospectively. As the capabilities of those breaching privacy increase, so do the privacy conceptions involved.

I don't propose to hone this idea to make it philosophically or logically precise, with identity conditions for particular conceptions. This might be done, but the increase in semantic rigour would be bought at the cost of intuitive attraction. 'Privacy' is a word that is generally used consistently by accomplished speakers of English, who are comfortable with the association of different conceptions with a family resemblance (I will postpone the question of cultures remote in space and time, where English usage is no help, until Part IV, Commentary 2). What makes them *privacy* conceptions, as opposed to torture conceptions or conceptions of chocolate? We can lean on the observations of lexicographers. A privacy conception is one that has a family resemblance to other privacy conceptions, and they are characterised by agreements within a linguistic community on the use of the term 'privacy' or related terms. In non-English communities, then we look to words or phrases that translate 'privacy'. For a further guide, we can look at dictionary definitions, such as the *Concise Oxford*'s 'being withdrawn from society or public interest'. Given that we have agreement that something is a privacy conception, a corollary of the family resemblance account is that there is no necessity for further explanation.

Family resemblance is what links different conceptions, marked (across monolingual contexts) with the common use of the term 'privacy'. In the discourse on conceptions (level 1), we are not concerned with questions about what types of privacy people *want*, what they *don't* want, what they *ought to have*, what they *ought to allow others*, what is *legal/illegal* and so on (Gavison 1980, 349). It is a simple statement of what privacy, and its breach, consists in. At this level, the question of whether, or when, breach is desirable or permissible, is not relevant; we focus only on defining what it means to be private, or to have privacy breached, in a particular way.

The formation of conceptions

A particular situation or context may evoke some privacy interests of its participants or may lead observers to describe it using privacy vocabulary. We can phrase this as saying that it *subtends* some conceptions of privacy. I don't mean anything particularly complex or philosophically involved by subtending. I mean 'implying' or 'creating', in the way that an arc or line segment subtends an angle.

The practice of wearing clothes and taking them off again subtends a particular conception of privacy, that of being seen without one's clothes. Although interest in the naked form is what makes this conception important, it could be explained even to someone who did not wear clothes, to someone who never took them off, or to someone who was so grown up they didn't care whether people are nude or not. The practice of wearing a veil subtends a conception of facial privacy, unrecognisability, invisibility or inscrutability of the face. The practice of building on and occupying land subtends conceptions of private property and private territory. The practice of communicating some thoughts to one's fellows and concealing others subtends a conception of private thought. The practice of communicating to specific individuals subtends a conception of private communication.

A practice will subtend a range of privacy conceptions, some of which may be marked by a culture (through language, practice, attitudes or laws), while others will not register. What is considered relevant within a culture or to a person or group will vary. Outsiders may note other conceptions in play that those within the culture consider irrelevant or even frivolous (as for instance the desire of Muslim women to wear burkinis on European topless beaches, and the response of burkini bans – Nielson 2020).

The more sensitive an area is considered in a general sense, the more privacy conceptions tend to apply to it. For example, sex subtends a large number of privacy conceptions (not to mention other types of conception), including among others the ability to have sex in seclusion, to prevent others from gaining information about one's sex history, and to have sex unregulated by the government (Solove 2008, 54). These conceptions can all be discussed and considered separately or together, even when they don't actually hold, or if they are not desired, in society.

We can relate privacy conceptions to the reference list by understanding its heuristic categories as non-disjoint sets of conceptions. Conceptions are therefore more specific than the rough categories of the reference list. The conception of facial privacy is a kind of attentional privacy; landowning is a kind both of private property and spatial privacy; the privacy of thought is a kind of psychological privacy. They are all conceptions of privacy, divided and classified by the reference list.

Typically, a privacy conception will emerge when people have a concern about a situation which exposes them, or some aspect of their lives, affairs, intentions or relations, to unwelcome scrutiny, publicity or exposure. A conception of privacy will in all likelihood first be noticed in its absence or disappearance, although it might have been latent beforehand. For example, the conception of financial privacy, that others do not know how much money one has, was subtended by the invention of money, but may only have become pressing, and therefore noticed, with widespread and efficient collection of taxes, prompting incentives to conceal and the development of means to do so. Other conceptions may be felt as an unwelcome absence of exposure. St Ciarán, living as a hermit, found the notion of eating in solitude disturbing because no one else was present to say the responses to his Benedicite at mealtimes (Webb 2007, 36).

In these ways language grows organically to incorporate new situations and express new interests or ideas in new contexts, with terms connected by family resemblance – new ways of 'seeing as …' (in Wittgensteinian terms), perceiving similarity in dissimilars (Aristotle 1989, 80, 1459a) or using metaphor to redescribe reality (Ricoeur 1977).

The dynamics of conceptions

New technologies and new practices may subtend new conceptions of privacy. Indeed, the classic argument of Warren and Brandeis was prompted because at the *fin de siècle*, 'instantaneous photographs and newspaper enterprise have invaded the sacred precincts of private and domestic life; and numerous mechanical devices threaten to make good the prediction that "what is whispered in the closet shall be proclaimed from the housetops" ' (1890, 76). Before instant photography and the ability of the yellow press to publish and distribute such photographs cheaply, there was no need to theorise such a conception. A photograph of someone would take time, and the subject would have to cooperate for some seconds. Their facial expression would be composed with the observer in mind – it would be a 'public face', rather than an unconsidered expression that might reveal hidden thoughts or feelings (1890, 82; Sennett 2002, 16–24). A whole sociotechnical ecosystem had emerged to capture and broadcast the unguarded moment.

Even a traditional photograph might have been revelatory, so the relevant conception of privacy was already subtended by the older technology. Charles Dickens had mused in 1851 about a perfect way to kill someone, to find a secret about them and print it on a poster (Guffey 2015, 41), while Pinkertons started to include photographs on their wanted posters in the 1860s (Fifer and Kidston 2003, 7). But it played little role in social life, and there was no felt need to regulate – contract or trust would ensure that an old-style photo could not threaten the privacy of the sitter. Instant photography became a problem in a way that posed photography did not (Warren and Brandeis 1890, 84–85), as one's image could be grabbed and distributed without one's cooperation. The irritations of the 'photo bug', or candid photography enthusiast, became a trope in the US, as for example in Jack Rice's short comedy of 1937 *The Photografter*. The simultaneous invention of microphones and dictagraph recording subtended an analogous conception of privacy with conversation (Westin 1967, 378).

Another example of a privacy conception subtended by technology is the privacy of communications, beginning with letters, and then moving onto telephone calls and emails (within ten years of the invention of telephones, newspapers were carrying stories of telephone tapping – Westin 1967, 378). When the practice of remote communication began, it no doubt quickly became clear that there was a no-man's-land between sender and receiver under the control of neither, a space for a third party to intercept a message. A privacy conception emerged of security from third-party access, implicit already in Socrates' discussion of writing in the *Phaedrus* around 370 BC, although that isn't his direct point: 'When it has once been written down, every discourse roams about everywhere, reaching indiscriminately those with understanding no less than those who have no business with it, and it doesn't know to whom it should speak and to whom it should not' (Plato 1997a, 552, 275e). Privacy of remote communications might be preserved by envelopes, codes, special inks or – more typically as postal services grew – legal regulation. The conception was subtended by analogy by the telegraph, the telephone, email and instant messaging, and technological means to both breach and guard against breaches have always been explored.

Certain aspects of modern communications spawned still more conceptions – for instance, the metadata of an email can be gathered more easily and separately from the content of the message (with a correspondingly smaller but nonetheless real privacy breach), whereas gathering the same metadata about a letter would require reading it anyway (although you might find something from a postmark, or the handwriting on the envelope). Some have emphasised the parallels between paper-based and digital communications to imply that the same privacy conception is in force, to press the case against surveillance. 'If postal workers read our letters in the way that Gmail and third-party app developers have scanned our emails, they would go to jail' (Véliz 2020, 63).

Others sympathetic with industrial-scale gathering and processing of communications metadata for reasons such as counter-terrorism have in effect tried to reassure the public by arguing that there is a difference in conception between a human intelligence officer reading one's letters or listening to one's telephone calls, and the creation of a vast database that will only ever be accessed by machine learning systems. Westin found professional psychologists in the 1960s arguing that 'if a machine of some sort did the actual evaluation of [psychological] test results, there would be no privacy problems' (Westin 1967, 303). Richard Posner argued that machine analysis 'far from invading privacy (a computer is not a sentient being), keeps most private data from being read by any intelligence officer' (Posner 2005). And after the revelations by Edward Snowden of large-scale surveillance (Greenwald 2014), Sir David Omand, former head of the UK's GCHQ signals intelligence organisation, reassured the public:

This involves computers searching through a mass of material, of course, and that might include your and my emails and data on our web traffic, but it is only the legally requested material that ever gets seen by a human being. These computers are not conscious beings: they will only select that which they are lawfully programmed to select. (Omand 2013)

Such writers draw explicit attention to the lack of a human in the loop, often going so far as to say that it rules out a breach of privacy. Clearly big data analysis of telecommunications is a breach of privacy! But it is a breach different in kind from one where a human operator looks at content. Whether this is reassuring or not, it is surely correct to say that the big data/machine learning breach is of a different *conception* of privacy from the postal worker's. The questions of whether this new kind of breach is more or less harmful (after all, automatic scanning scales up, which human reading will not), and more or less acceptable to society, are put aside in a level 1 discourse that seeks only to define and characterise privacy conceptions.

Hypothetical and fictional cases

A privacy conception will most likely evolve alongside some kind of perceived problem or harm – these are, after all, the itches we are most likely to scratch, and where debates are likely to be most fraught. We typically develop privacy conceptions in areas that concern us.

Yet it need not always be the case; we can and do create and discuss privacy conceptions that affect nobody at all and whose breach causes no harm. In Wittgensteinian terms, if we can flesh out a hypothetical language game in which it appears intuitive that we should use the word 'privacy', then that will subtend a conception, although not necessarily a very practical one. For example, in a science fiction novel such as John Wyndham's *The Midwich Cuckoos*, we might describe the privacy breaches caused by a race of telepaths, but there are no telepaths and no privacy breaches have ever resulted from their reading our minds. Telepathy poses no problem to anyone, and even its believers seem unconcerned about the issue. Yet telepath privacy can be written and cogently theorised about just the same (Wasserstrom 1978, 321–323; Braude 2020).

One could imagine a privacy conception being subtended by multiple personalities contained within the same person (whether or not one thought this possible), whereby the different selves may or may not have privacy from the others. There has been a lot of thought about how multiple selves may interact (Braude 1991; Hacking 1995; Radden 1996; Rovane 1998) – do they witness or remember each other's episodes of control? Can they interfere? Can one personality consent to psychotherapy for another personality? But despite the potentially fertile ground, to my limited knowledge not much has been written about privacy relations between multiple selves. It hasn't seemed imperative either for scholars in the field, for patients who present for treatment, or imaginative writers and novelists. It might have. It wouldn't have been wrong if it had. But it hasn't.

Fictional privacy conceptions need not stretch metaphysical credibility. A classic example is the claim that the Victorian British covered up piano legs for the sake of decorum (Sennett 2002, 167), although apparently this is an urban myth with no documented cases (Mullen 2003, 549). This would not be to protect the privacy of the piano of course, but rather the extrinsic privacy of the household (especially the ladies and servants) from provocative imagery, sparing them the intrusion of marquetry coquetry into their refined lifeworlds. Bizarre, and a comic staple since Lytton Strachey, but perfectly understandable to all those who have disseminated or laughed at this *canard*. Anything, however ludicrous, could subtend a privacy conception to someone imaginative enough.

A breach of a privacy conception might be impossible but widely believed to be practical, even dangerous. If you thought your horoscope could breach your attentional privacy by telling others your future, it would be essential to protect the time and place of your birth to prevent its being cast (rather as you keep your mother's maiden name concealed nowadays). Another example is an invasion of decisional privacy: old beliefs credited witches with the ability to manipulate people, for example making them fall in love, by using their hair, fingernails or even excrement (Thomas 1973, 520). To avoid this kind of zombification, safely disposing of hair and nail clippings is a must (Frazer 1987, 233–237).

Even in those societies where privacy is less prized than other goods, privacy conceptions may be subtended, although perhaps overlooked or interpreted differently. In Plato's *Republic*, the character Glaucon introduces the myth of the ring of Gyges (Plato 1997b, 1000, 359d), an impossible situation in which the eponymous ring confers the power of invisibility upon the wearer. Clearly there is a privacy issue here, if only in supernatural theory. But Glaucon is concerned largely by the possibility of the wearer being able to get away with unjust actions if he had such a device. A more privacy-sensitive framing shows that it is the joint ability of the wearer to (i) breach the privacy of others, (ii) in total privacy himself, that opens up the possibility of injustice.

Boundary cases

It may be that the emergence of a privacy conception brings agreement on paradigms, but there may still be disagreement on edge cases. For instance, we can easily understand the conception of privacy as solitude, isolation from other people. It is generally conceived as a state created by separation, seclusion or banishment, a state that has to be maintained, not an equilibrium – others are always apt to intrude unless actively excluded. By default it is a temporary state. As Milton says in *Paradise Lost*, 'Solitude sometimes is best society, / And short retirement urges sweet return.' The boundary case is someone like Robinson Crusoe, stranded alone on an island for many years (and for all he knows, forever). Does Crusoe have privacy-as-solitude? I would say that he does (with Westin 1967, 44), but the majority contends that privacy is meaningless with no possibility of meeting anyone else (Inness 1992, 9; Rössler 2005, 7; Webb 2007, xv; Solove 2008, 20; McStay 2014, 5). I would only suggest that a privacy conception, to make sense as a conception, must not be *tautological* (Oppenheim 1975), and so must also include an idea of what a breach would consist in (in this case, the arrival on the island of others, which of course eventually happens). Those who would press the idea of privacy-as-control would, on the contrary, look for signs of Crusoe's control over his state; he has none, and therefore no privacy. Others might think of privacy as something one welcomes and seeks out, and on that measure he is not in private either. Not a great deal hangs on the resolution of these boundary cases, except to draw attention to the circumstances, usually quite specific, where agreement runs out.

Quite often, they degenerate into a clash of intuitions, partly because abstraction pushes us toward generalities and paradigm cases, omitting the detail of a real context. For example, let's consider the privacy or otherwise of someone in solitary confinement. Our intuitions may differ, but most people add flesh to the abstract picture to create a paradigm, perhaps thinking of Steve McQueen with his baseball in *The Great Escape*. If we take this image, and run through the reference list, we might be able to whittle down what *types* of privacy he has (if any). Informational privacy? Probably not much, and solitary confinement won't add anything to it. Decisional privacy? Zero. Private property? No – he has his baseball, little control over who accesses it, and will be subject to arbitrary searches. Psychological privacy? Maybe he can remain an enigma to the guards, but prisoners' mental health can be undermined by confinement (Rhodes 2005). Ideological privacy? Not if he is classified as having dangerous views. In general, even though some prisoners are able to establish a sense of agency through religious conversion, that often needs social support (Herley and Copes 2009). Spatial privacy? No, as presumably he will be liable to be searched at random intervals, including intimate body searches, and guards will be able to enter his cell at will. Attentional privacy? None, surveillance is pervasive. Extrinsic privacy? No: if the prisoner in the next cell has the heebie-jeebies all night he will be forced to listen. So when we boil down a specific case of solitary confinement with the help of the reference list, we find nothing. Steve McQueen may be solitary in his cell, but he is not in private.

However, with different flesh on the bones, it may be possible to make the case. In an episode of the prison-set TV sitcom *Porridge*, the main character Fletcher, driven crazy by the inane chatter of his cellmates, deliberately gets himself caught in a major infraction of regulations so that he is given 'solitary' and can get a bit of privacy. Of course this is a joke, but one we understand: spatial and extrinsic privacy from his eccentric cellmates, with whom he is already over-familiar, are his main goal. Denied agency as a prisoner, he games the rules in order to achieve his privacy preference.

Some make the assumption that privacy only applies to the living (privacy-as-control entails it). However, there are certain privacy conceptions that appear to apply to the dead, at least in some circumstances (Scarre 2012). Many writers and artists have destroyed not just immature or unpublished works (an intellectual property issue) but also their private letters (e.g. Somerset Maugham, who prevented his secretary from pulling them out of the fire, and Dickens, who lamented 'Would to God that every letter I had ever written was on that pile' – Hartley 2012, xx). Those who merely restrict access to their letters for twenty-five or fifty years after their death may be chiefly concerned about the privacy of the living (Robinson 2013), but they might wish to preserve their own *post mortem* privacy until potential readers about whom they cared would also be dead. Some have argued that the sheer size of data stores demands posthumous legal privacy protection (Banta 2016), although I don't see that the quantity of information involved changes the principle.

Ancient Egyptian Pharaohs' practices of concealing entrances to their tombs, and later the tombs themselves, had a lot to do with protection against grave robbers. However, their elaborate ideas of the soul – particularly the importance of the survival of their body and name, and the vulnerability these caused for the dead (David 2002, 116–118) – may have subtended conceptions of *post mortem* privacy. Many indigenous peoples have demanded return of long-dead remains from museums and universities (Woodhead 2002), and many curators are uncomfortable with the practice of displaying bodies, even from long-extinct cultures (Jones and Whitaker 2013).

Whether or not the privacy interests of the dead strike anyone as particularly pressing, that does not mean that we don't form conceptions about them. For instance, I recall feeling mildly embarrassed to read a letter in a history book from a German Landgrave to his wife in 1675 that began 'Beloved Fatty'. This salutation betrayed a combination of fondness, intimacy and informality that made me feel like an intruder, and while the letter was of historical importance (it described military tactics), the salutation was surely not (Blanning 2007, 531–532).

We can go further, to privacy conceptions that apply to animals (Westin 1967, 7–10). Cats, for instance, hate to excrete before an audience, preferring solitude, often behind the wardrobe. It seems reasonable, if not compulsory, to read this as their preference for privacy, albeit a primitive and hard-wired one (cf. Roquet 2013, about the cat stories of Yoshiyuki Rie). Online webcams of nature reserves have been used by poachers to identify vulnerable animals, leading to a (human) movement advocating 'privacy for tigers' (Anderson and Berger-Wolf 2018). We may or may not take such conceptions very seriously, but if they are held by people observing animals, then they add to the global semantics of the term. Neither animals nor the dead are central to privacy conceptions, but they are still interesting boundary cases. Indeed, this may be a parochial view: in some non-Western cultures, animals' privacy may be far more central.

Systems or constellations of conceptions

While Inness was correct to say that 'any exposure of a person's self to a "public" ... necessarily detracts from her privacy' (1992, 42), she appeared to take the view that privacy is a continuum from zero to total. Conceptions are, however, plural, and do not necessarily stand alone, or work independently of others. Neither do they integrate into a single parameter, although some might work as an interlocking *system* of conceptions, each affecting the other in context. Any moderately complex social situation is likely to invoke a range of conceptions.

I want to resist the idea that privacy conceptions can easily be structured relative to each other, as with Inness' linear view, or Rössler's 'onion' model, where privacy is layered – first the personal realm, then the group, and third a wider private sector (2005, 5–6) – or Cynthia Dwork's proposal that complex policy challenges can be addressed by computing a quantitative measure of privacy (2014, 317). Even Gavison's suggestion that it 'may be broken into three independent components' (1980, 350) of informational, attentional and spatial privacy seems too coarse; while it gets away from a linear model, each of the components can be decomposed much further.

A constellation of privacy conceptions will be finer-grained than this. One can be private in some respects and not in others, with many conceptions in play in a particular context, some related and some incommensurable. For example, if one is travelling on a bus (i) one is not 'in private', as one is in a recognised public space. However (ii) if one was being stared at by another passenger, that would be an extra and separate breach of privacy (even in public). (iii) One's personal space may be invaded by another passenger squeezing onto the seat – particularly galling if it was not crowded. (iv) If the bus was under surveillance with closed circuit television (CCTV), that would be an additional breach. (v) And if one was directly and explicitly linked to the surveillance footage by the use of face recognition technology, that would be yet another. (vi) If one paid with an automatic travelcard, then the starting and stopping points of the journey would be logged on a database, linkable back to one's card and possibly credit card. And finally (vii) one might be sitting next to someone having a loud mobile phone conversation, a further breach. Here we have seven different conceptions of privacy, all coexisting, and all of which may be invoked in the question of whether and how far one had privacy on that particular bus. Some demand particular technologies to be in place, others might have happened when buses were drawn by horses. Exposure will take a certain form, which will breach some conceptions of privacy, and leave others unaffected. This constellation of conceptions illustrates that being 'in public' doesn't mean that your privacy has gone and everything is up for grabs.

Conceptions may turn on the way in which the breach interferes with the person's life, if at all. The 'Dark Lady' of Shakespeare's sonnets might have been mortified by the revelations of her erstwhile chum, especially as he was on occasion rather rude about her (Richmond 1986), but Shakespeare successfully concealed her identity, rather than exposing her to the public gaze. Analogously, someone photographed in a compromising position has clearly had their privacy breached, but are they identifiable from the photo, perhaps by their face or distinctive tattoos, or by tagging of the photo with their name? Here, there is a basic conception/breach of privacy in the sense of being seen unclothed, and a second conception/breach where the image is linkable directly to the subject. Consider a film star, required to perform a nude scene, who employs a body double. The star's privacy is not breached by the filming, although that of the double is, with their (i.e. the double's) consent. The editing of the film, however, strongly implies that the body on the screen is that of the star, so the sequence is directly linkable to the star (incidentally protecting the identity of the double). Is that a breach of the star's privacy? Yes, also with their (i.e. the star's) consent.

A particular situation may expose one to a privacy breach on some conceptions, but not across the board. Suppose Peeping Tom drills a hole in my shower wall. If I do not know he is there and take a shower, he breaches my attentional privacy by scrutinising my nakedness. If I know he is there, and forego my shower, then my attentional privacy is saved at the cost of a breach of my decisional privacy – he has stopped me doing what I wish. If I take my shower knowing he is there, but am inhibited and self-conscious as a result (not launching into my usual full-throated version of 'I Will Survive'), my decisional privacy is still compromised along with my attentional privacy (Wasserstrom 1978, 324). My decisional privacy when I don't know he is there depends on how we describe the decision; Tom clearly has not interfered with my decision to *take a shower*, because I wanted to take one and did, but he did interfere with my decision to *take an unobserved shower*, even though I was unaware of it.

However, many other conceptions are unaffected. Tom has no access to my financial records, cannot prevent me from willing my property to the cat's home, doesn't know what I am thinking, and though he can see through the spyhole he can't actually get into the bathroom so even my spatial privacy is arguably intact. His invasion of my privacy is serious, but the context subtends so many conceptions that it can only be partial.

This is therefore not a parsimonious account of privacy, but an extravagant, open, fine-grained one with plural conceptions, generated by both cultural insiders and outsiders, associated by family resemblance. In specific circumstances (such as a law court), we might be more prescriptive, but outside such constrained contexts, the set of privacy conceptions is open-ended (although at any particular time we are only likely to be concerned with a few). In particular, new technologies, behaviours or interests can subtend new conceptions unpredictably at any time.

The key thing is that level 1 discussion is to enable precision in any specific context about the conception(s) in play. The flip side is that, because 'privacy' is a family resemblance term and there are many conceptions, it is impossible to give generic accounts, write generic rules, or generate generic principles. A loss of privacy on one conception may well accompany a gain on another.

Level 2: architecture and affordances

Suppose a particular privacy conception is in play in a context. That context, which might be real or virtual, immediate or extended over time and/or space, will facilitate the preservation and/or breaches of that conception for people and groups to an extent with respect to relevant others. A complete description of the affordances of the structures that make up the environment may include such aspects as its physical construction, such as screens or windows, devices such as modesty panels for desks or two-way mirrors, and technologies present, such as bugs or hidden cameras. There may also be symbolic markers, such as signs saying 'Ladies Only' or 'Keep Out: This Means You!!!'

The environment may have been designed to support or to undermine privacy, sometimes to make it easier for people to achieve a state of privacy, sometimes to facilitate observation. The effectiveness of the factors and affordances will depend on the likely set of people in that context, norms and rules of behaviour, and the incentives for privacy breaches. People change and are changed by environments, so we can think of them together forming a social ecosystem (Altman 1975, 205–206), so that 'the environment can be viewed as the behavioral extension of an individual or group – for example, when people establish territories through the use and arrangement of areas and objects or when people move closer to or away from one another' (Altman 1975, 5). People adjust environments to make them more convenient – they move chairs around, prop open doors, publicise passcodes and so on. Devices may be badly designed or unusable (those of us of a certain age remember Max and the Chief's hapless attempts to talk within the Cone of Silence in TV's *Get Smart*). In all these ways environments may become more or less privacy-preserving. Discourse at level 2 concerns the affordances of the environment, and the privacy (breaches) that it enables, and at the limit, the actual breaches that have happened.

The questions we ask at level 2 are about how (a particular conception of) privacy is implemented or facilitated in a context, if it is. For instance, has a dataset of PII been encrypted? Are there curtains in the window, and have they been drawn? Is private property secured (is the bicycle locked)? Is there a serial number and a record of ownership? Is there a camera concealed in the room? Does a diary have a lock on the front? Is its function made clear (for example, by a prominent notice on the cover like 'My Secret Diary')? Is it kept out of sight in a drawer?

Note that these architectural questions do *not* equate to any of the following: Have the subject's rights been breached? Has the law been broken? Has harm been incurred? Has the subject noticed anything untoward? Has anything happened that the subject cares about? These questions are separate. The level 2 question is about what privacy breaches are *possible* or *happening*.

The architecture of privacy

Conscious, intentional designs will usually be made with specific regulatory backgrounds or social norms in mind. For example, a children's classroom may have a great deal of window space to allow plenty of natural light for them to work in, but the windows might not be visible from the street, partly so the children aren't visible to the public and partly to minimise distraction. In contrast, strong sensitivities mean that the school changing rooms are closed in, with no visual access from outside. Different situational aspects, such as familiarity or strangeness of environments, formality or informality of contexts, or public accessibility or inaccessibility will alter expectations and preferences (Altman 1975, 84–85). Roman houses were designed with a hierarchy of spaces, some reserved for the master and his family, others more open to visitors and outsiders (Webb 2007, 8–9). This practice declined in medieval times (except in monasteries and manors – Webb 2007, 34, 54), before gradually reviving in modern times (Pardailhé-Galabrun 1991).

Only some of the affordances of an environment are designed with privacy in mind. Windows are vulnerabilities from the point of view of privacy, but they are there to provide light and sometimes agreeable views, which may have to be traded off against problems of sound disturbance and confidentiality of speech, informed by the architectural contributions of sciences such as acoustics (Gover and Bradley 2004; Bradley and Gover 2010). Such trade-offs have always been a factor in architecture, and we find obvious compromises such as placing the rooms where more sensitive activity takes place on higher floors, and the development of frosted glass. A trade-off in the workplace is between the individual office versus open-plan space; the advantages of the latter are supposedly that people mix and collaborate more, while their privacy recedes, and they can be monitored and managed more easily. Slaves and servants, required for the running of households in some societies, provide an obvious intrusion vector to be bribed to tell what they have seen. The amount of privacy one receives in economy class on an aeroplane (at least pre-pandemic) is absurdly tiny, not because the airline thinks that passengers should have little spatial privacy, but rather because privacy is not as salient as the need to reduce space to allow lower fares. In such contexts, those who wish to be private have to struggle against the environment to get the desired or appropriate level (Altman 1975, 211). Altman pointed out that environments get changed by their occupants independently of designers' intentions, and supported the idea of responsive environments open to adjustment (1975, 207–220).

One of the most famous architectural interventions to manipulate privacy affordances was Jeremy Bentham's panopticon (Bentham 1995), an eighteenth-century design for a prison intended to be more humane and less brutal than the norm at the time (although influential on penal thinking, it was never built). Each prisoner was observable from a central point by a guard at all times. Bentham reasoned that the lack of privacy afforded by the environment would suffice to induce good behaviour in most prisoners, because, although at any point in time they may be observed, they could not know when, and so would moderate their behaviour perpetually (cf. Wasserstrom 1978, 324). A similar arrangement motivated the two-way telescreen in George Orwell's *Nineteen Eighty-Four*.

In neither case did the architecture include arrangements for recording – Orwell anticipated automatic writing but not automatic listening/reading. Both the panopticon and the telescreen could be augmented with modern recording technology to render behaviour not only permanently observable but also reviewable and maybe even searchable. The lessons have been learned. The Chinese Communist Party has been likened to 'a giant anaconda coiled in an overhead chandelier' that rarely moves or acts, but 'everyone in its shadow makes his or her large and small adjustments – all quite "naturally"' (Link 2002). Buoyed by input from social media, the Party is experimenting with 'social credit' systems, 'grid management' of groups of households or university dormitories by designated monitors, face recognition and Party cells within private enterprises (Liang et al 2018; Miles 2021).

Not all privacy-related affordances pertain to physical architecture. An important set is provided by the clothes we wear, which may be designed to conceal, reveal or hint at a revelation, either through covering/showing or by manipulating fabric to emphasise/disguise body shape (Frith and Gleason 2004). In the West, women's fashion in particular plays with such ideas, sometimes revealing, sometimes falsifying the body to suggest an 'ideal' shape, whether through stays, bustles or underwired bras. Clothes can also deliberately conceal, as with some religious dress or today's 'modest' fashions, designed to look attractive without inviting attention to the body underneath (Patel 2012; Lodi 2020). The introduction of technologies such as CCTV and face recognition subtended clothing designed to protect identities, such as hoodies (Turney 2019), camouflage designs (Nagenborg 2017) and face masks (a conference in China recently sponsored a competition 'designed to motivate solutions aiming at enhancing the face recognition accuracy of masked faces'; no totalitarian implications there – Boutros et al. 2021). Clothes do unrelated things of course, such as keeping their wearers warm or signalling social status, but, like physical architecture, they provide affordances for both wearer and observer, facilitating or hindering privacy breaches.

Technology is another type of architecture, a key driver of today's interest in privacy. All media subtend the privacy conception of what a subject consumes: what papers does each individual read? What programmes do they listen to? This has often mattered in totalitarian and religious states. The Catholic *Index Librorum Prohibitorum*, which listed books too dangerous to be read ('After Rome has spoken, the matter is in no way left to our own estimation and choice, and such books may not be read by anyone, whatever be the position he holds' – Betten 1925, 285), was not abolished until 1966, and even now is regarded as having moral authority, even though it is a matter of individual conscience whether a Catholic reads a book named within it. In more recent times, the development of the World Wide Web subtended the same issue – what websites have been visited?

To begin with, this was hard to discover, because the Web's information transfer protocol HTTP includes no way of finding out who is downloading content. However, this was awkward for many purposes – if you moved between pages on an e-commerce site, it was impossible for that site to know that it was the same person who wanted to buy product X and product Y, still less to connect that person with a credit card. Hence the invention of cookies in 1994, which the site would place on the buyer's computer to identify it through a series of visits, even on different days. This made life on the Web infinitely more convenient, but by creating this valuable data it subtended the conception of *tracking* – the collection and amalgamation of data generated by a person's behaviour across all the sites they visit and their downloads. This became increasingly possible as webpages evolved from being creations of their owner, to 'complex tapestries of third-party code and content woven together and served from different places' (Binns 2022), so the rendering of a page on one's browser required the cooperation of several sites, all of which could get access to details of the transaction. Cookies, incidentally, can be encrypted so it is impossible to find out who placed them, thereby protecting the privacy of the surveillant. Tracking enabled the advertising industry to target its ads to those users that were more likely to be susceptible to their product, which broke the ground on the tech giants' gold mines (Zuboff 2019). With the accelerating addition of such technologies, the Web architecture's affordances for privacy breaches increased dramatically.

Not all affordances are designed in. A lake in a remote area may be perfect for skinny dipping but not by design. Open windows can allow others to overhear conversations or arguments; traffic noise tends to conceal them. The owner of a large granite sculpture might have fewer worries about the misappropriation of their private property, since it weighs several tons, than they do about, say, the painting on their wall. But this does not mean that Henry Moore was more respectful than Rembrandt of the private property of his patrons.

Using the notion of affordances, we can distinguish between privacy that has been breached and privacy that is at risk, even if it has not actually been breached by any individuals, i.e. between actual and potential. For instance, if some piece of private information goes online where it can be downloaded by anyone, it is no longer private in the potential sense, even if it has not actually been downloaded; ditto a compromising recording of a conversation that has not yet been listened to. Hence we can already describe a lack of privacy, even in the absence of a direct breach. If a piece of revenge porn has been posted on a website, it will be of little comfort to the victim to know that it has not yet been downloaded.

Inness argued that the gap between the potential and the actual was fatal for any account of privacy as a state of separation or withdrawal (1992, 46–47). One of her examples was 'I realize that a peeping Tom is coming to my window, so I evade him by ducking under the bed'; on the withdrawal thesis, this is only a threatened privacy loss rather than a real one. It is undeniable that Tom has failed to achieve his intended goal, and that attentional privacy is preserved in that case. Clearly, however, privacy has been breached in other ways – decisional privacy (who wants to dive under the bed?), the attentional privacy of the household (the room is being spied on, even if its occupant is now invisible to Tom), and probably spatial privacy (the wretched fellow is standing in the flower bed). Even if a threat is not actualised, it can be highly potent – as Orwell's Winston Smith would testify. The affordances of the environment may present or encourage a threat, a relevant topic at level 2.

The costs of privacy and its breach

Many technological developments begin with a marginal link to privacy issues, to solve evident social problems, but it is later discovered that they can be used for surveillance (the Internet was of this type, a data transport infrastructure only later discovered to be useful for surveillance of all kinds of behaviour and interaction – O'Hara and Hall 2021, 92–102), or alternatively, it is discovered that surveillance for one purpose can be adapted for others.

Even when intended to protect privacy, new technologies may usher in new vulnerabilities; putting a lock on a door makes it more secure but also creates a keyhole through which activity in the room may be observed unnoticed. Of course, the keyhole is less of a privacy problem than the open door, so we tolerate it; we could also address the new vulnerability by adding a piece of metal (called an escutcheon, if you're interested) that covers the lock. The risk of a breach of privacy is connected to the cost of breaching it, which can be manipulated up or down by the design of the architecture.

The adaptation of technologies in this way is related to 'their relatively low cost in relation to the resources of those wishing to employ those techniques for surveillance' (Westin 1967, 411), i.e. the *transaction costs* (Hartzog 2018, 28–30) that accrue to someone undertaking an enterprise, including the costs of gaining information – in this case, access to the private person.

For example, Megan's Laws in the United States mandate community notification of the presence of a registered sex offender at an address, to enable a community to protect itself and its children against potential reoffenders. A natural counter-concern is vigilantism or other action against the offenders (who have after all served their time) preventing them from reintegrating and becoming useful citizens (Logan and Prescott 2021). In considering the extent of the breach of offenders' privacy, Amitai Etzioni argued that, although the information was sensitive (often including addresses and photographs), the high transaction costs of searches would deter merely vindictive investigations, while those with serious concerns, prepared to devote more resources, could find the information they wanted. He considered this an equitable balance between the privacy interests of offenders and the security interests of communities (1999, 66–67). However, America's generous freedom of information tradition combined with the Web enabled easy and cheap access. Within a few years, free websites, often locating offenders' addresses as flags on street maps, popped up, their affordances dramatically reducing search costs, tilting the balance against offenders' privacy (O'Hara and Shadbolt 2008, 152–153; Nellis 2012).

Transaction costs also apply within an organisation, affecting the efficiency with which it accesses information, such as this description of the affordances of a computer system for a welfare program.

> The extent to which this transforms the system cannot be overstated. Previously the time and space obstacles to case management and client control were insurmountable; paper records were in thousands of filing cabinets spread out across Ohio's eighty-eight counties. The possibilities for centralized surveillance and control were sharply limited by the simple facts of physical distance and the resulting information fragmentation in the system. (Gilliom 2001, 35)

Obscurity

The growth of information technology subtended all sorts of new and tricky privacy conceptions and breaches, affording instant access, aggregation of information and fast inference. It was not ever thus. Dickens' classic *Bleak House* (1853) turns on the revelation of information through painstaking search and analysis. In that novel, the sudden and surprising collapse of Lady Dedlock upon sight of an apparently uninteresting legal paper is investigated by a number of interested parties, but their search through written records on paper, badly curated (one key set of papers is in the care of the illiterate Krook who cannot keep them in order or even understand what they are) is hardly a trivial matter. Eventually, the secret is revealed (after several hundred pages and a large cast of characters).

Compare that to the recent exposure of a British couple who had absconded with insurance money after faking the death of the husband; later, he returned, feigning amnesia. This made the newspapers, and an interested person simply Googled their names, to find pictures of them buying properties in Panama together at a time when the husband was supposedly lost at sea (Cohen 2008). Thanks to Google, it took milliseconds to find them – a decrease in privacy from *Bleak House* of several orders of magnitude, although structurally there is no difference between the cases, both searches through public records.

Public records in paper files, possibly in different buildings, didn't present the overwhelming privacy issues of digital technology. They couldn't be searched for individual terms, and if a file was put back in the wrong place, it was as good as lost. The conception of privacy at risk from meticulous bureaucratic records is as old as record-keeping, but until the affordances of digital technology, it was protected by *obscurity* (Hartzog 2018, 108–116). Digital technology has the effect of accelerating search, aggregation and inference so that information about someone can be revealed dramatically quickly and at scale (a perceptive early warning was sounded by Wasserstrom 1978, 325–329). As a result of the widespread deployment of these technologies, the salience of this particular conception of informational privacy has grown out of all proportion, and it is fair to say that the increased interest in the politics and law of privacy has been prompted by the new affordances of digital technology.

Obscurity, which trades on practical difficulties and high transaction costs, is unprincipled and contingent. It is hard to predict which information will disappear, and which will be easy to find (so it can't protect the most important information more securely). It offends the neat-minded, who would prefer privacy protection to be predictable and designed. However, merely because obscurity is not predictable does not mean it is not effective across a population. It can also deter an intruder who does not know in advance how open to access a particular piece of information is, and who must therefore make a probabilistic estimate of the costs. The costs of non-specific fishing expeditions for incriminating information are particularly hard to estimate, and therefore they are easier to deter. Whole industries of prying open up when generalised access to information is facilitated.

Level 3: phenomenology

Given a conception of privacy, and an environment which facilitates or inhibits it, we can people the environment and ask what it is like to be there and to inhabit it. What does it feel like to be exposed or protected in these ways? What is the phenomenology of privacy, in the philosophical sense of lived experience, the subjective, first-person dimension? This is a neglected area of privacy research (Arendt 1998 and McStay 2014 are exceptions), although privacy and phenomenology are connected; feeling private liberates one to do silly, offensive or disgusting things that one would feel bad about doing in public, where we are 'on stage' (Goffman 1959). Phenomenology brings privacy down from the august debates of lawyers and philosophers to the banal and personally significant. 'The imagining of privacy in experiential terms produces consequences quite different from those of what one might call theoretical imaginings of privacy' (Spacks 2003, 9). Much regulation of privacy in social settings depends on managing feelings of guilt, embarrassment, coyness, shame and self-consciousness.

Phenomenology as evidence of privacy status

Before we get onto the *character* of experience, let us begin with the relationship between subjective experience and the objective world, and in particular how experience is world-disclosing. Much of the phenomenology of privacy turns on the subject's awareness of the observer. There is a big difference between mutual and one-way observation. How privacy feels varies dramatically across these two conditions, while a sudden discovery or realisation that one didn't actually have the privacy one thought one had itself has significant phenomenological effects.

A moment's reflection shows that what privacy feels like can only be a rough guide at best to the question of whether we actually have it. Let's take four types of case. First of all, back to the shower, with an undetected spyhole, behind which is our old adversary Peeping Tom, breaching our attentional privacy. But the *experience* is identical to that of taking a shower in private. Phenomenology alone does not allow us to distinguish between privacy and intrusion.

Conversely, one can feel like one's privacy is breached without it being so. This can happen trivially to anyone, but as a pathological example, one group of symptoms of schizophrenia is transitivism, a feeling of permeability of the boundary between one's self and the world. This can take the form of losing the sense of psychological privacy and the boundary with other minds, so the patient is unable to tell whether their thoughts are their own or those of the interlocutor, or whether their own feelings are being felt by the interlocutor. The experience of decisional privacy can be affected, and the patient may feel at the mercy of the world. Breaches of spatial privacy become unbearable, with 'feelings of inadequate bodily demarcation (also versus inanimate objects), a pervasive feeling of being somehow "too open or transparent" or having extraordinarily "thin skin"' (Parnas et al. 2005, 254–255). These problems of self-formation are troubling delusions; although privacy seems absent, it is not.

The same case can also relate to the privacy of others. For instance, the facial expression of another breaches their psychological privacy, revealing thoughts and moods which they may prefer to conceal, but *only* if the expression is candid and undisguised. If the expression is adopted to *camouflage* their mood, then it will *preserve* privacy. In the absence of any other evidence (such as excess theatricality), the observer of the expression cannot know which applies. Recall King Lear's failure to read the intentions of his three daughters.

A second kind of example illustrates the phenomenological salience of social variation. Imagine the identical action of removing one's clothes in different environments: alone; in front of one's spouse; in front of one's children; in front of one's mother; in front of one's nephew; in front of one's doctor; in front of a customs official searching for drugs; in Grand Central Station at the rush hour; on a stage for money; at a well-populated naturist beach; while giving a lecture; as part of a protest; as a dare at a party; reluctantly giving in to unwanted peer pressure; immediately prior to a long-anticipated sexual encounter; after a game of football in the changing room with one's teammates; at gunpoint. Although there are no differences either in narrowly described behaviour or the conception of privacy in play, clearly these various experiences of exposure *feel* very different to the subject, from terror to excitement to embarrassment (which itself ranges from mild to extreme) to the utterly routine. And let's not assume a 'standard' subject. The gender of both subject and audience will make a difference, especially in sexually charged cases. I write flippantly, but we also tend to consider cases from the point of view of someone in a secure environment; imagine how a vulnerable or recently traumatised person would experience such a scenario.

Third, there are cases where privacy, or its breach, is hardly noticed (Rachels 1975, 297). To an argument that 'control over who can sense us, is the core of privacy' (Parker 1974, 280), Solove replied that 'We are frequently seen and heard by others without perceiving this as even the slightest invasion of privacy' (2008, 25, and cf. also 86). Yet (without buying into Parker's privacy-as-control definition) Solove's criticism rather begs the question of the relation between breaches of privacy and our perceptions of them.

We have seen that deceptive spying can be phenomenologically null; are there other types of privacy breach of which we can say this? Yes: one example is when personal data is processed (e.g. by a third-party advertiser), which we tend not to perceive at all, or if we do it is so indirectly (e.g. by the ads we receive) that it is hardly salient. As another, the UK is one of the surveillance centres of the world with its ubiquitous CCTV cameras. Yet, despite vociferous debates about the privacy rights and wrongs of this, few British people actually notice that they are there (Goold et al. 2013). It's not that they don't know they are there, it's just not very salient at the point of breach, even if people's more reflective opinions might be somewhat more negative.

However, Solove's point was not that there can't be privacy breaches that we don't perceive but rather that there can't be breaches that we perceive but don't perceive *as* breaches. Is he correct?

Let us consider the example of a facial veil, supporting the attentional privacy conception of the face being unavailable for scrutiny by others. A high-status Tuareg male (Murphy 1964), a lady in a Middle Eastern country (El Guindi 1999), a European lady in early modern times (Sennett 2002, 167; Burghartz 2015) or more recently mourning at a funeral (Baker 2014), might keenly feel the lack of a veil and consequent exposure. In contrast, a typical group of unveiled Western people at a (pre-COVID) business meeting would not register that their facial privacy was breached in an analogous way, although they would be fully aware that their faces were on show and observed. How do we describe this divergence? I would argue that it is more parsimonious to say that all cases are breaches of (facial) privacy, but that in the first group the subjects care and notice, and in the latter case they do neither. While the different reactions inform the *seriousness* of the privacy breaches, they do not affect their classification *as* breaches.

The unpalatable alternative is to say that the former group are privacy breaches and the business meeting not. At that point we necessarily import some notion of the psychological reaction to its breach into our definition of privacy and thereby complicate it in ways that we were hoping to resist (i.e. we turn it into a kitchen sink definition). For instance, suppose someone, an unremarkable man, at the business meeting who for some reason had formed a particular aversion to his (perfectly average) face, did not want it to be seen. Do we count his unveiled public state as a breach of privacy, or not? If we do, then we understand that man to be in a *conceptually* – not just attitudinally – different situation to all the other people at the meeting, which seems odd, because he isn't. If we don't, then we have to treat him as being under some kind of delusion in which he believes he wants privacy and doesn't have it, whereas actually there is no privacy to be had in that situation. But that also seems false, since he could wear a mask or veil and provide himself with privacy.

Surely it is conceptually simpler to count all the cases, including the business meeting, as breaches of privacy, to which people react in different ways, or don't react at all (Wacks 2010, 42–44, takes a similar line to Solove against this manoeuvre, claiming it is a 'distortion' of the notion of privacy, but does admit that avoiding it 'presents difficulties' too). And if we take this route, then the failure of some people in the examples even to notice their privacy is being breached means only that the breach of that particular conception leaves no phenomenological mark.

Fourth, many types of privacy breach would not be expected to produce phenomenological capta under any circumstances. The idea of universal surveillance was not invented by Facebook; those who believe in an omniscient God must also believe they are constantly being watched (or at least could be, if He chose to – Russell 1950, 75–76; Arendt 1998, 74–75; Lackey 1985), in such a way as to leave no immediate traces in consciousness. John Wesley apparently believed just that (Spacks 2003, 182). The Devil too has been thought to have this power (Thomas 1973, 561). It is a matter of faith that this is happening, not consciousness.

Phenomenology as evidence of autonomy

Phenomenology can furnish a useful corrective to essentialist arguments about what is possible with or without privacy. For example, consider Charles Fried's powerful and attractive argument that:

> ... privacy is not just one possible means among others to insure some other value, but ... it is necessarily related to ends and relations of the most fundamental sort: respect, love, friendship and trust. Privacy is not merely a good technique for furthering these fundamental relations; rather without privacy they are simply inconceivable. They require a context of privacy or the possibility of privacy for their existence. (Fried 1968, 205)

Fried defended privacy not just instrumentally, as a handy tool for some useful things, but intrinsically valuable, and there is much to admire in his picture. His argument is that intimacy involves the sharing of information with the intimate other that one does not share with (many) others, and which one need not share with anyone (1968, 211; Wasserstrom 1978, 325; Bauman 2010, 12), a view of long standing – for instance, a household management manual of 1612 advised 'It doth greatly increase Love, when the one faithfully serveth the other: when in things concerning marriage, the one hideth no secrets nor privities fro the other, & the one doth not utter or publish the frailties, or infirmities of the other' (quoted in Vincent 2016, 22).

One immediate response would be to note that while intimacy no doubt involves information management, its nub is more to do with closeness, caring, tenderness, empathy, and so on, but it is arguable that privacy is quite likely to be needed for these attitudes too. Nevertheless, might it be overstated to say that respect and love are *inconceivable* in its absence? There are plenty of examples of the achievement of intimacy despite restricted autonomy and freedom of action, ranging from the pathological, such as Stockholm syndrome (Adorjan et al. 2012), to the socially sanctioned, such as successful arranged marriages (Epstein et al. 2013), to the joyous, as with unplanned children (Inness 1992, 99). In surveillance societies, such as Stasi-dominated East Germany, intimacy adapts (McLellan 2011).

As an extreme case, the 1998 film *The Truman Show* portrayed a character who lives his entire life on a reality TV programme. Truman has no privacy, although this is not evident to him. Are we to say that he cannot fall in love, trust or respect anyone? Granted, he pursues his lost love in secret, but equally he fell in love with her in plain sight of the TV audience. What is his phenomenological position? Truman has illusions of privacy and control. Granted Fried's premise that an intimate relationship will involve a deep commitment to sharing information (and space, decisions, attention, etc.), the intimate's *intentions* to play his hand *as he sees it* is a mark of the intimate relationship. The sincerity and rationality of his intentions cannot be judged except against the phenomenological background – it is not a betrayal to fail to take into account something of which one is unaware.

As phenomenology is a fallible guide to privacy, that is sufficient wedge between privacy and intimacy. While we can hope to put our control of information to the service of our intimate relations as Fried urged, a space opens up for intimacy to flourish even in conditions of limited privacy. Fried suggested that a paroled prisoner being monitored 100 per cent of the time 'cannot be private' because he does not have control over his environment and so cannot be fully autonomous (1968, 217–218). This is certainly true, and I don't want to deny that (i) the monitored prisoner is in a pretty dubious place, ethically speaking, (ii) the state shouldn't do this to people, and (iii) I would not want to be in the prisoner's shoes. However, does it follow that human ingenuity, plus sympathy on the part of friends, trusted others and loved ones, plus the ability to make the best of a bad situation, cannot overcome these problems? In this case, the prisoner does not have the misleading phenomenological background that Truman has; he is fully aware of the monitors, which enables him to reason about and around them, which is better perhaps than suspecting they are there and not knowing (Wasserstrom 1978, 324). As Cole Porter reminded us, 'goldfish in the privacy of bowls do it'.

Robert Gerstein supported Fried's contention with the different observation that, while outside attention is deleterious for intimacy, at least as bad is a breach of *extrinsic* privacy, the intrusion of others outside the intimate relationship into their lifeworld. 'The fragile unity of the experience is broken. The intensity with which such experiences involve us shields us to some extent from such distraction, but once it occurs the experience dissolves' (1978, 266). The observer prevents the intimates from devoting their entire attention to the experience and each other. However, this doesn't rescue Fried's essentialist point, because in order for their phenomenology to be disrupted, they still have to be aware of the intruder.

Conversely, intimacy may struggle to flourish when privacy and control are both strongly supported. Dean Cocking (2008) argued that in an online environment, where one can curate the self with a large degree of control, intimacy will still be problematic, because the self presented is so carefully constructed (cf. Baruh and Cemalcılar 2015, and for a parallel argument about the nineteenth century, Sennett 2002, 177–183). Intimacy involves not just revealing deeply personal facts but also a 'true' or 'truer' self, a more objective view including the imperfections that perhaps only the intimate other can see, or alternatively, forgive, but which may only be revealed by interactions outside the intimates' control. To deny the intimate other the dubious benefits of seeing oneself 'warts and all' is to be controlling – controlling not only the information flow but also the intimate other's view. It may be that true intimacy requires periods without privacy, so that the intimates are able to see each other reflected in a range of social situations.

The phenomenology of surveillance

That is not to say surveillance leaves no mark. There is a phenomenology of feeling under observation, as evinced by the line in thousands of Westerns, 'Hey Cody, I got a feelin' we're bein' *watched*,' just before an arrow thwacks into the speaker's back. This has been the subject of investigation since the nineteenth century; psychologist Edward Titchener argued that this feeling, though real, provided no evidence or guidance as to the question of whether we are in fact under scrutiny, ending his essay with the splendidly defiant rallying cry:

> If the scientific reader object that this result might have been foreseen, and that the experiments were, therefore, a waste of time, I can only reply that they seem to me to have their justification in the breaking-down of a superstition which has deep and widespread roots in the popular consciousness. ... At the same time, the disproof of it in a given case may start a student upon the straight scientific path, and the time spent may thus be repaid to science a hundredfold. (Titchener 1898, 897)

Hear hear!

On the other hand, phenomenology is hardly irrelevant to surveillance. Surveillance *depends* on awareness, or its lack, for its effects (Solove 2008, 108–109; Wacks 2010, 1–5). One of its uses is to study, order and optimise behaviour – for example, surveillance by a smart meter for monitoring energy use. Here, the aim is to eavesdrop on natural behaviour, and try to influence it through feedback; the surveillance therefore shouldn't be too intrusive or evident (Zuboff 2019, 424). A second use is to control crime, such as theft or vandalism in city centres or speeding on roads. While surveillance footage is of some value in solving crime (Coupe and

Kaur 2005; Ashby 2017; Morgan and Dowling 2019), its main function is deterrence, so cameras being visible and evident parts of the environment is important. Third, there is intelligence gathering, where officers attempt to understand plans and conspiracies, and to produce evidence that can be used in court. Here the surveillance needs to be unobtrusive. A fourth use is political control, to suppress activities such as protests and demonstrations. The prominence of devices is required to produce a chilling effect, but they need to fade into the background if they are to be used to entrap.

Surveillance also raises the question of knowledge versus awareness. For instance, in social media, surveillance is on, and known by users to be on, 100 per cent of the time. Whatever you do is captured, and this is hardly a secret. However, those companies that make their money from surveillance ('surveillance capitalists' – Zuboff 2019) want to *avoid* chilling effects because they want to capture behaviour to support their advertising and personalisation models. Hence, despite widespread knowledge of surveillance, it is in the interests of companies to render its *experience* negligible or invisible.

In the panopticon and Orwell's telescreens, the calculation is very different. Those under surveillance, like Winston Smith, are *aware* that the architecture renders them visible, but they do not *know* whether they are being watched. Indeed, the authorities go to some lengths to ensure awareness, because it is essential to the cost-benefit calculation. Winston does not know whether he is being watched, but if he estimates that the probability is low, this has to be compensated for by the extreme consequences that will follow a discovered transgression. Only a high expected cost can ensure that the risk is internalised by people under surveillance, who therefore police themselves – and as a result reduce the cost of the system.

The strong surveillance of welfare systems by technocratic bureaucracies, diligently searching for proof of eligibility and evidence of fraud, can have this effect. Those in extreme need are often faced with baffling, complex systems with which negotiation is impossible, and can easily (and understandably) be tempted by minor employment opportunities in the cash economy (e.g. labouring, babysitting, taking a lodger) that might be penalised if discovered (Swan et al. 2008). So complex are such systems that it can be hard even for officials to work out the hypothetical effects of declaring such employment (Gilliom 2001, 85–87). The fear of losing the welfare payment reveals itself phenomenologically as degradation, even like being jailed.

> Someone is watching like a guard. Someone is watching over you and you are hoping every day that you won't go up the creek, so to speak, and [that you will] get out alive in any way, shape or form. You know, 'Did I remember to say that a child moved in?' 'Did I remember to say that a child moved out?' And 'Did I call within that five days?' You know ... making sure all the time. ... It's as close to a prison as I can think of. (quoted in Gilliom 2001, 51)

Furthermore, the phenomenological effects of aggressive surveillance don't disappear with the surveillance – even though *privacy* is restored when surveillance ceases, relative well-being may not recover so easily. The phenomenology of intensive surveillance itself has effects – sleepless nights worrying about whether information was properly supplied, shame of having secrets exposed, often groundless guilt, fear of being punished, constant working to rationalise, disguise and conceal minor infractions of the rule. The demeaning feeling of being pushed, filed, stamped, indexed, briefed, debriefed and numbered (as Number 6 put it in *The Prisoner*) not only disincentivises defiance of the system, but is also apt to affect future confidence and self-image (Gilliom 2001, 122).

The creepy line

Earlier I said that data processing had little phenomenological salience. That was too sweeping, as evinced by the growing psychological topic of *creepiness* (Tene and Polonetsky 2013; Shklovski et al. 2014; Langer and König 2018), a feeling of discomfort and unease that accompanies a perception that one is the object of unwanted or unanticipated attention or activity, even for one's benefit, or, in a Marxist analysis, 'the reification of subjectivity in the object' (McStay 2014, 131). Creepiness is related to informational and attentional privacy via the sudden intrusion of app outputs clearly related to users' recent behaviour, such as receiving an advert for a restaurant one is just passing or for a medical remedy immediately after Googling a condition (Torkamann et al. 2019). The very fact that one is under surveillance from devices such as voice-operated intelligent virtual assistants can also be eerie (Pierce 2019).

As a classic contribution to the venerable tradition of Silicon Valley bigwigs saying ludicrous things betraying their complete lack of empathy and psychological insight, in 2010 Google's then-CEO Eric Schmidt said that 'There is what I call the creepy line. The Google policy on a lot of things is to get right up to the creepy line and not cross it' (Saint 2010). This policy of being as creepy as possible without actually being classified as creepy is, in itself, creepy. The net result is to render *all* Google's policies creepy, as you know they are trying to be creepy without creeping you out, like a stalker persistently on your trail but not so intrusively that they are classed as a stalker.

A related topic of research is the *male gaze*, the idea that many media are structured so that women become passive objects of audience voyeurism, inclining the audience to a male perspective (Mulvey 2009; Oliver 2017). Online, there is hardly a shortage of objectification, ranging from creepshots (photos of women taken without consent) to upskirting to revenge porn, not to mention celebrity culture, but a woman's experience of the Internet does not always include these types of content. Socially, the male gaze manifests itself as a generalised and endemic heterosexual-male-oriented surveillance of women conceived as objects of desire imposed as a standard (e.g. Gervais et al. 2012, 2013) – one author writes of women's 'minds and bodies colonized by the male gaze – symbolically, affectively and physically', even while considering them not 'as solely *exposed* to men's looks, [but rather] as *engaged* in the gendered relations of looking' (Glapka 2018, 99).

The phenomenology of intrusion

We should also note that there is a phenomenology of *intrusion* as well as of privacy. It *feels like something* to be Peeping Tom, just as much as it does Lady Godiva, a feeling sought out by voyeurs (Hopkins et al. 2016). What is watched is less important to the voyeur, than that he is not *supposed* to see it. The bodies are less important than the undetected intrusion. Voyeurism, of course, is not always a sexual impulse, and has been associated with reality television (Baruh 2010), disaster tourism (Lisle 2004), poverty tourism (Selinger and Outterson 2010), 'emotional rubbernecking' of online grief (DeGroot 2014) and congestion around traffic accidents (Chung and Recker 2013).

Rössler takes the voyeur as the paradigm case of a breach of informational privacy (2005, 112), but the phenomenology of intrusion tells us this cannot be correct. Tom may discover some information from watching me shower, such as whether I have prominent scars or tattoos, but although he will get all the information he is going to within thirty seconds, he won't stop looking when he has got it. And tomorrow, he will be back, even though he knows there will be nothing further to learn. His interest lies in the voyeuristic experience, which is why it makes sense to block up the spyhole once it is discovered. Voyeuristic privacy invasion can be enjoyed over and again. This contrasts with the discovery of information, which is a one-off, so that future protection against it is shutting the stable door after the horse has bolted. If Tom sets up a miniature camera to record my ablutions, there is a technical sense in which he has some information about me, as the MP4 file is data that can be bought or sold. But that technical sense is uninteresting compared to the pleasure of consuming the video afterwards at Tom's or his customers' leisure.

More mundanely, we often feel embarrassed when we burst in upon someone or otherwise witness something we shouldn't. Vicarious embarrassment is a type of empathy, felt whether or not the third party is aware that he has been observed (Krach et al. 2011). The connections between embarrassment and empathy are complex; for instance in Robert Louis Stevenson's story *Olalla*, the narrator, exploring the residence of the family he is staying with, feels embarrassment and mortification when he accidentally enters the room of the poised, intelligent and beautiful Olalla, finding her sensitive poetry, but has no compunction in breaching the privacy of her stupid, slothful brother, with whom he feels no connection or affinity. It has been argued that those who are particularly self-conscious and easily embarrassed in public can mitigate their fears by putting themselves into the position of an imaginary observer (Jiang et al. 2018).

Level 4: preferences

Being private feels like something, which brings it into the mental realm. The next important layer of discourse concerns the *cognitive psychology* of privacy, the mental processes that influence behaviour, including attention, memory, problem-solving and planning, linguistic functions and reasoning.

Much of this discourse concerns the *preferences* people have about their privacy: in a particular context, does someone wish to be more or less private? Preferences have a natural link to phenomenology – if exposure feels unpleasant, embarrassing, shameful, then one generally prefers to avoid it – but it cannot be their only determiner. Privacy is often either not desired, or desired less than a competing good. Most people are well aware that social media hoard information about them, but they prefer the free services that they receive as part of the bargain to their informational privacy. Receiving medical treatment may require sharing embarrassing information about lifestyle or behaviour. A loan from a bank may require giving it access to detailed financial records. Such preferences can undermine defences of privacy. For instance if privacy is a necessary condition of human flourishing, social networks' users could not flourish, but the users themselves might beg to differ (Rössler 2005, 120).

A more wide-ranging concept, which could have been used to label level 4, is *utility*, an abstract measure of value from economics (Posner 1978, 334–335; Moscati 2019). X prefers option A over option B if X expects greater utility from A than B, and X's choice of A over B is sufficient reason to declare that A's expected utility is higher than B's for X at that time. I don't find utility helpful to characterise the cognitive psychology of privacy. In the first place,

I am trying to develop as broad a framework as possible, an aim which will not be well served by the technicality and abstraction of economics, which tends to treat privacy in terms of trade-offs associated with concealment or revelation, e.g. of personal information (Acquisti 2014, 78), certainly important but a narrow focus nonetheless. Second, the idea of a utility function implies something relatively fixed and rational in structure, whereas our privacy-related behaviour is as often as not more emotional than rational (Schoeman 1992, 19–20) and may also evolve fairly speedily.

Preference is also connected with *choice*; if I choose A over B, I generally prefer the former to the latter. Hence choices are overt evidence for preferences (Samuelson 1938) that are easy to spot, record and aggregate, which may be why there is far more research and debate at level 4 than the phenomenological level 3. However, I don't use 'choice' to label level 4 because preferences change, may not be revealed through choice, and indeed our choices, particularly our misguided ones, often help inform us about what our preferences 'really' are. Our preferences are present, if latent, whereas choices happen intermittently.

Hence I characterise level 4 in terms of preferences, but the key topic is individuals' models of and action in the world. If you prefer 'utility', 'choice' or something more esoteric such as 'being-in-the-world' as a label, then that's fine.

The nature of preferences

In any particular context, more than one conception of privacy may be in play, and for different people, different conceptions may be salient. To take one contrast, a European man's Android smartphone with its promiscuous data collection and chaotic data-hungry app ecosystem may represent a threat to his private world. To a young woman in South Asia living in a crowded home, in close proximity to neighbours and under relatively strict parental authority, the data gathering may pale into insignificance compared to the *increase* in privacy she gets from being able to watch without interruption TV shows and short form videos with the latest stars, and being able to talk to her friends without others knowing or overhearing. Both undergo identical breaches of informational privacy and gains of attentional privacy, but for the man, the latter are negligible, while for the woman, the former are irrelevant.

Preferences need not be constant through time, nor rational, nor reasonable, nor consistent with other preferences (Solove 2008, 70–71). And although we may be able to generalise across groups – for example it is often hypothesised that women are more concerned about privacy than men (Sheehan 1999; Park 2015), or the old more than the young (Palfrey and Gasser 2008, 53–82; Steijn and Vedder 2015; Van den Broeck et al. 2015) – these can be no better than probabilistic. Nissenbaum wanted to 'put to rest the frequent insinuation that privacy preferences are personal and idiosyncratic' (2010, 151; Raab 2005, 285), but even if there are regularities, some people conform more than others, and attitudes change through time, so I will resurrect the insinuation.

Preferences are subject to external influence; the environment described in Aldous Huxley's *Brave New World* was designed to adjust people's preferences against privacy. This was science fiction when it was written in 1931, but by 1958, Huxley was able to write a non-fiction account of preference-altering technologies actually in use in *Brave New World Revisited* (Westin 1967, 319–320; O'Hara 2012, 172–174). The architecture of surveillance capitalism described by Zuboff (2019) is, on her account, intended to perform the same trick, while many social networking sites have been accused of creating an addictive environment, so that the user needs the rewards that only they provide (Brailovskaia et al. 2018; Saura et al. 2021). Knowledge about the underlying processing can affect preferences and feelings – subjects told how often their data is used by an app become more inhibited in its use, while those told the percentage of other users who approve of such use are reassured, and their app use more relaxed (Zhang and Xu 2016).

One can even have preferences about one's preferences. A first-order preference is what one wants now, while a second-order preference is more reflective and indicative of the kind of person one aspires to be (Frankfurt 1971; Jeffrey 1974). For instance, one may always prefer a drink before dinner, but one may also have a second-order preference that one did not drink every day. To achieve the second-order preference, one has to resist at least some first-order preferences, which is easier said than done. One's privacy preferences may also be subject to weakness of the will; for instance, one might enjoy social networking or e-commerce (first-order preferences) but may also have the second-order privacy preference to avoid overexposing one's data to third parties. The commercial incentives of the sites themselves are to entice individuals to give in to their immediate first-order preferences, even at the cost of regretting it later. In short, the individual works to exercise the will, while the social networks work to exorcise it. Some have argued that an *authentic* life is spent following second-order preferences, as opposed to one influenced and swayed by others (e.g. Rössler 2005, 53–60).

Privacy preferences may be other-directed. We tend to focus on preferences about one's own privacy, but one typically also has preferences about others'. Most obviously, we are concerned with our loved ones; spouses have preferences about their partners' privacy, and parents about their children's (Lwin et al. 2008; Wacks 2010, 66; Hancock 2016). Parents may wish their children to be kept private from outsiders but transparent to their own watchful eyes (Boesen et al. 2010). Voters may want to be private but prefer their politicians transparent (Macmanus et al. 2013). Curiosity about others – a preference for their reduced privacy – helps 'to provide vicarious experience, to circulate information, and to promote group and community norms' (Westin 1967, 60). Curiosity, surveillance and voyeurism are strongly connected, a theme in many works of art, from Hitchcock's *Rear Window* to José Saramago's *All the Names*. Retailers may prefer their customers to surrender personal information, to improve services, target advertisements and set prices optimally – in short to create an advantage in their bargaining. In patriarchal societies, men may wish to ensure and protect the privacy of their female relations to outsiders, possibly against the preferences of those women themselves (Sunder 2003, and Mancini 2012 for pushback against narratives of non-Western patriarchy). The preferences of many men for reducing or removing women's privacy sustains an enormous pornography industry (D'Orlando 2011; Lykke and Cohen 2015). Preferences can become quite tangled; a voyeur, for instance, requires privacy for himself as an essential precondition for achieving his preference of breached privacy for others. While bearing such complexities in mind, in this chapter I will focus on the preferences of individuals for their own privacy.

Harm

Getting one's preferences does not mean avoiding harm (although it does reduce the ability of others to harm one), but to the extent that one is the best judge of one's own interests, it is one of the most efficient ways of reducing harm. Preferences before the fact may be different from preferences afterwards (I really wanted that last drink, but now I realise it was a stupid thing to do, and I can't drive home). Harms may be tangible, like loss of money or reputation, or intangible, such as chilling effects (Calo 2011). One may sacrifice privacy for an anticipated benefit that disappoints: Benedetto Croce defined a bore as 'one who takes away our solitude and does not give us companionship' (quoted in Ortega y Gasset 1961, 131n).

Many argue that leaving privacy to individual choice is a hallmark of a liberal society (Westin 1967, 46; Inness 1992, 47–48; Rössler 2005, 116; McStay 2014, 22–35). However, individuals' preferences may also result in social harm, for example reducing the amount of information available to judge economic agents in the marketplace, reducing the market's value as a signalling system (Posner 1978, 1981; Stigler 1980).

Many privacy breaches cause no, or negligible harm. That does not mean they are not privacy breaches, they are just harmless. If they are harmless, I may have no preference whether privacy was breached or not. Or, if I do have a preference, on principle as it were, it might seem fussy or preposterous.

> For example, if a friend examines a pen sitting on my desk, she usually does not violate my privacy despite the fact that it is *my* pen, but if she examines my open diary on my desk, a privacy violation occurs. In the first place, a privacy claim on my part would be unreasonable (despite my property claim). If I made such a claim, perhaps telling my friend, 'You violated my privacy – it's *my* pen!', she would not question the fact of my ownership; rather, she would point out, 'It's only a pen!' (Inness 1992, 33–34, her emphasis)

I would argue it is more parsimonious to classify *both* as privacy breaches, one trivial, one less so (the complicating 'despite' clause would not then be needed). Most people would care much more about the diary, unless it is merely a desk calendar (Kelley and Chapanis 1982; McKenzie 2020), than the pen, even if they silently and impotently resented unauthorised fiddling with the latter, while being too abashed to say anything. Inness' example resonates with me, if I might be permitted a reminiscence. In my early career, I, like many others, was in the habit of chewing the end of my pen when deep in thought. One day, I returned to my office from lunch to find a colleague waiting to speak to me. He was sitting on my desk (another privacy breach, incidentally, which I didn't mind), with my pen in his hand, using it to clean out his ear. I have never chewed another pen to this day. While visitors might not expect me to have a strong preference about my pen, it *is* my property, and as such I *might* prefer that they kept their hands (and ears) to themselves.

The privacy paradox

The complex nexus between first- and second-order preferences, self-directed and other-directed preferences, and preference and harm, have led to what is known as the *privacy paradox* (Acquisti et al. 2015; Kokolakis 2017), that people express strong concern about privacy risks, particularly to do with online data, while still behaving in highly risky ways. In typical studies, people who declare that they would keep sensitive information to themselves without good reason to blab it, still blab it to experimenters for trivial rewards (Spiekermann et al. 2001; Norberg et al. 2007).

That we behave paradoxically shouldn't be too much of a surprise, and it is partly explained by conflicts between first- and second-order preferences creating a so-called *intention-behaviour gap* (Hassan et al. 2016). Psychologists also point to general explanations for lack of rationality (Acquisti 2014, 86–89) such as having to reason from incomplete information, imperfect or bounded rationality, confirmation bias (the tendency to interpret information consistently with prior beliefs), hyperbolic discounting (a preference for early rewards over later ones) and immediate gratification (downplaying future risks for present rewards). Other common sense explanations are: that people's self-knowledge is not high; that the salience of long-term risks is artificially raised by the studies' pointed questions; that people answer surveys as they feel they 'ought' to, not honestly; that ideological or moral beliefs are rarely powerful enough to influence behaviour (Sennett

2002, 33–34); and that individuals' preferences change even over short periods of time, as they move from intriguing prospect to intriguing prospect, so that the whole theoretical frame of fixed general attitudes informing a mutable but stable utility function is misguided (Nissenbaum 2010, 150–152). Quite likely all of the above. It may be that the privacy paradox and other difficulties in surveying privacy accurately undermine empirical survey-based methodologies altogether.

Some have promoted market solutions to privacy (Posner 1978, 1981), arguing that secrecy brings costs to others that subjects do not have to pay, an unjustified externality. Privacy should be purchased by subjects for the amount that such secrecy is worth to them, thereby rationing it and mitigating its cost by the exchange. However, such markets have not taken off, and apart from the exceedingly wealthy, most seem relatively apathetic about paying for privacy protection or privacy-enhancing technologies (Acquisti 2014, 90). It has also been argued that even a well-functioning market would undermine privacy, thanks to difficulties of coordinating defensive responses, and the value of information to outsiders would still produce excessive information gathering (Cohen 2000; Choi et al. 2019).

In any case, privacy is only sometimes the most salient aspect of a situation. One might have privacy concerns that go unaddressed, because other benefits are in the offing, as with social media (Edwards 2013, 313). Many people have a preference for personalised online services, which trumps their privacy preferences because the provider needs to know more about the customer, not less (O'Hara 2021a). Asserting privacy interests may be expensive. Someone who discovers that their bank has been subject to a data breach may initially wish to transfer to another bank with a better reputation, but would this really help? It is an extremely tedious process with uncertain gains that will disclose personal information to a second firm and so make a future data breach more rather than less likely (Romanosky and Acquisti 2009).

Preferences can anyway only convert into action if one has agency and choice. In general, the physical environment will afford privacy to a degree, and if this is not the degree desired, one has either to adapt it, or to adapt to it, or some combination of the two (Altman 1975). People who bought expensive flats in London's

Neo-Bankside development found themselves extremely visible from an art gallery's viewing platform, but after losing a court case found that all they could do was draw the curtains (Lees 2021), although in 2023 they finally won their appeal as the UK Supreme Court judged in their favour. Online, there are high costs involved in leaving social networks in which one is invested (Hartzog and Selinger 2013).

Control does not define privacy

Whether or not one gets the privacy one wishes is a complex matter, important for the individual, but hard to generalise, which has led many commentators to posit a strong internal connection between privacy and control: 'privacy will be defined as *selective control of access to the self or one's group*' (Altman 1975, 18, his emphasis), or as 'the claim of individuals, groups, or institutions to determine for themselves when, how, and to what extent information about them is communicated to others' (Westin 1967, 5). This is a very influential theory, and the rest of the chapter will be devoted to examining it.

Voluntarism

Control is central to many of our privacy-related practices (whether they encourage or intentionally thwart individuals' control). Many privacy-as-control theories may have begun with the observation that individuals and groups tend to seek rather than reject it, leading to voluntaristic claims such as 'privacy is the *voluntary* and temporary withdrawal of a person from the general society' (Westin 1967, 5, my emphasis), or 'the protection of privacy means protection against *unwanted* access by other people' (Rössler 2005, 8, my emphasis).

Volition certainly influences our use of the term 'privacy', yet voluntarism only goes so far. As it is usually left to the subject to decide whether or not he is private, he is able to make the distinction between (desirable) privacy and (undesirable) solitude or loneliness, which is what makes voluntarism compelling. From the outside, the subject's intentions are invisible, so for instance we do not know whether the solitary figures in an Edward Hopper painting have sought privacy or had it thrust upon them; on a voluntarist reading, are they in private (voluntary), or merely lonely (involuntary)? But not all decisions are down to the subject. Certain forms of exposure are repressed in many societies, ranging from the harmless, such as breastfeeding (Grant 2016), to the threatening, such as indecent exposure (Lindsay et al. 1998; Hayes and Dragiewicz 2018; Oswald et al. 2020), to the intrusive, such as annoying mobile phone conversations (Monk et al. 2004a, 2004b; Turner et al. 2008; Emberson et al. 2010; Sutter and Holtgraves 2013), to the challenging, such as women's expression of their sexual and romantic hopes in the eighteenth century (Spacks 2003, 68), so that agents are *forced* or incentivised to do things in private – hardly a voluntarist stance.

Such cases may or may not be convincing against voluntarism, but if volition is characteristic of privacy, paternalism must be impossible, yet it has its supporters. Allen (2011) argued that some privacy should be compulsory to prevent self-defeating bad choices, and others have advocated paternalism in data protection (Alemany et al. 2019). Despite his voluntarism, Westin described people whose privacy is involuntary (1967, 44), argued that 'neither law nor public pressure should force anyone to have privacy if that person … wants to give up his privacy for psychological, commercial, or humanitarian purposes' (1967, 419), and also considered individuals' own failures to 'observe [their] own minimum boundaries of privacy' (1967, 57–59). If privacy is essentially voluntary, it is hard to see how one could be forced to be private, or voluntarily breach one's own privacy (the cases concerned are not mismatches between first- and second-order preferences).

How can we describe those who would attempt to force privacy on people, when that very formulation would be contradictory? Far simpler to disconnect privacy and the will, and theorise about variations in privacy preferences.

Control and empowerment

To make control a constitutive aspect of privacy produces another kitchen sink definition – just because control is important to the individual, that does not mean that *control over privacy* equates to privacy. If it does, we are in danger of a regress.

To avoid this, privacy-as-control theorists play up the importance of the active pursuit of privacy. Control speaks to the liberal vision of the empowered individual, while Rössler saw the passive desire to be let alone as too weak to underlie an account of privacy (2005, 7). She hedged privacy-as-control with studied ambiguity: 'something counts as private if one can oneself control the access to this "something", with "can" glossed as "can and/or should and/or may" ' (2005, 8). She was keen to include a normative element alongside a descriptive part, to cover both where one shouldn't have privacy but as a matter of fact does, and where one as a matter of fact does not but should. Normative accounts can have the unfortunate effect of problematising privacy for children, the severely injured and the dead but (Rössler 2005, 214n.117) sketches how these cases may be dealt with. The resulting definition is a complex grouping taking in abilities to achieve preferences, rights to do so even where such abilities are absent or thwarted, the affordances of the architecture and the actions of others in helping or hindering. A definition that eschewed the ambiguity and focused on the normative sense that was Rössler's chief interest would have had cleaner lines, but would have lacked plain descriptive capabilities.

Inness raised the dilemma that 'privacy may work by separating a realm of the agent's life from the access of others, or it may work by providing the agent with control over a realm of her life' (1992, 23). Actually, neither is the case. Privacy doesn't 'work' at all (see McStay 2014, 98–99 for a contrary view of privacy as an actor in its own right); once an agent has separated a realm of their life from others, they simply *have* it. It has done no work, but is the outcome of some purposeful activity of withdrawal by the agent. It cannot *provide* an agent with control, although once they have control via some mechanism or practice, then they can use it to achieve privacy to the level they desire. But this is hardly the whole story – they may get privacy accidentally, or through the agency of others; it may be thrust upon them unsought.

The empowerment story, superficially attractive, is less endearing in detail. Empowerment – the imposition of one's will on the world to mould it into a desired form – has a strong association with meritocracy. It converts privacy into a personal responsibility: one is given the technological and legal tools to protect it, and then has to work hard to achieve it. Privacy is the reward for diligence about privacy. Meritocracy is somewhat tarnished as an ideal (Sandel 2020), while its collateral demands of constant alertness and sedulousness are unattractive. Posner added the sinister spin that people 'want to manipulate the world around them by selective disclosure of facts' (1978, 338), so that the law should really support the rights of others to obtain the full picture.

The constant tension that meritocracy's scrappiness demands may simply produce stress. In her critique of the data industry, pointedly entitled *Privacy is Power*, Carissa Véliz discussed the power that tech companies have over us (2020, 50–71). On a well-known definition of power such as 'the capacity of A to motivate B to think or do something that B would otherwise not have thought or done' (Forst 2015, 115), the companies often have power over us in that sense. However, our privacy doesn't win us this kind of power over anyone, except in the trivial sense that B has to leave A alone, which B wouldn't otherwise have done. Empowerment is neither here nor there, but privacy enables *resistance* to the power of the surveillant, which is far more useful. The welfare recipients described by Gilliom (2001) resist by using or engineering privacy to earn money in the cash economy, but the result is not always positive, sometimes shame, and always fear of discovery. Privacy is *not* power in any meaningful sense.

Empowerment and privacy-as-control contrast with the ideal of being let alone, which has its own attractions, whether from a position of Bostonian patrician loftiness (Warren and Brandeis 1890) or from the perspective of poor welfare claimants in Ohio (Gilliom 2001, 69–71). However, it may leave those in the middle with less protection; Westin argued that the right to be let alone was something that appealed largely to those in a good position (e.g. property owners), and less to those behind the eight ball, such as employees and customers (1967, 388–389).

Empowerment is a drag. While Posner's cynical view was that 'few people want to be let alone' (1978, 338), Warren and Brandeis were closer to many people's ideals with their plan to rid the world of Buttinskis. However, the value of empowerment might be to *make others let you alone*, in which case it is derivative from, a means to, the Warren and Brandeis right.

Exhibitionism

Some people want to be seen, to be affirmed and socially significant, perhaps to liberate themselves from shame or simply to rebel, in what has been called *empowering exhibitionism* (Silverstein 1996; Koskela 2004; Munar 2010; Jarvis 2011, 11; de Vries 2019). We find this idea in the division between the boring private sphere and the exciting public sphere in Aristotle's *Politics* (1995, 10, 1253a2; Arendt 1998, 28–37), and it is still a common thought. As Oscar Wilde said, 'There is only one thing in life worse than being talked about, and that is not being talked about.' A specifically modern twist is celebrity culture, where some individuals expose themselves to public view via mass and social media so that their every move and thought can be consumed by their 'fans'. There used to be a barrier to entry to celebritydom, which was that the celebrity needed to have done something to 'deserve' attention (flown across the Atlantic, scored the winning goal, topped the charts). Nowadays, one can become famous purely for being famous; the achievement *is* to be an object of consumption (Aspinall 2006; Barron 2010; Gamson 2011; Driessens 2013).

A pathological variant of celebrity is *notoriety*. Certain individuals commit prominent crimes or outrages in order to be the subject of attention, sometimes against celebrities themselves, as for example with the murder of John Lennon (Stashower 1983) and the attempted murder of Ronald Reagan (Fuller 1982). If notoriety is to be achieved at the expense of unknown citizens, one tactic is to murder many of them in a spree, perhaps one of the most depressing and dispiriting tendencies in our rampant celebrity culture (Meindl and Ivy 2017; Raitanen and Oksanen 2018; Lankford and Silver 2020). Media coverage of these outrages must surely be modified to give less exposure to the barbaric killers, thereby reducing their notoriety and incentive to murder (Schildkraut 2019). How much effect that will have on incontinent social media is unclear.

Note a paradox: for exhibitionism to be empowering, the exhibitionist must have at least *some* privacy. This kind of (over-)sharing cedes attentional privacy – e.g. naturism (Jarvis 2011, 33–34) – or informational privacy – e.g. revealing one's medical details (Jarvis 2011, 34–41) – but if it is to be genuinely *empowering*, the decision to share must be authentically that of the individual, not influenced by others. The individual in question must have decisional privacy at a bare minimum. The people in *Brave New World* did not have decisional privacy over their exhibitionist sex lives, as their preferences were being manipulated.

When control does not lead to privacy: the Jennicam

Yet there is a stronger reason to resist the privacy-as-control thesis, which is quite simple: if I have control over access to my self or my territory or my property or my data or whatever, then I may use it to grant unlimited access, in which case I am in control *but not private* (Gavison 1980, 349–350).

This is not simply a thought experiment. The pioneering lifecaster Jennifer Ringley set up Jennicam, a webcam that posted candid pictures from her bedroom every few seconds on the Internet between 1996 and 2003, initially available for free, but then behind a paywall (Jimroglou 1999; Smith 2005). It was a real-time depiction of her life, including long periods without motion punctuated with action, but also mooching around, reading, watching TV, doing laundry and taking care of her ferrets, which became minor celebrities in their own right. She sometimes acted up (even stripping) for the audience, aware of the voyeuristic gaze, but in general ignored it.

She clearly had control, and surely every one of our intuitions screams that she (through choice) had no privacy. For her, the value of control and privacy were inversely correlated, because her preference was to have no privacy. Suppose that the Internet in her apartment died for an hour or two. At that point, the Jennicam would go off, and Ringley would therefore *not* be in control of the flow of information; the screen would be blank. So if privacy was control, we would have to say at this point that Ringley, not being in control, therefore had *no privacy at all*. This is doubly absurd – it seems far simpler to say that when Ringley had control she had no privacy, and she only had privacy when she had no control, and to be able to say that, we have to admit that privacy is not control. Control allowed her to achieve her preference for zero privacy.

The privacy-as-control idea no doubt seemed more plausible pre-Internet, when it was pretty well unthinkable that anyone would do anything this daft. If you had control you would ensure you protected your personal space, because 'opening' the self wouldn't mean allowing unlimited access to all comers, right? We know better now. The Jennicam was ludicrous science fiction (if still a conceptual challenge), until it became science fact.

The focus on the Internet highlights attentional and informational privacy, but similar considerations about privacy-as-control apply across the reference list. With spatial privacy, control is over who you allow into your territory, and you can throw your doors open. Decisional privacy has a stronger internal link to control and autonomy, but it is still possible to outsource decision-making, for instance employing an agent, assigning power of attorney, or even by deciding on the throw of a die, as in Luke Rhinehart's novel *The Dice Man* (whose protagonist retains some decisional privacy as he decides the range of options, but one could imagine a sequel in which others decided the options, and even rolled the die for him).

Using the reference list, one response is that Ringley had abandoned her attentional and informational privacy in favour of decisional privacy over the Jennicam. While this, I believe, is the correct characterisation of her project, it is not available to privacy-as-control theorists. Their claim is either that privacy is *characterised* by control, in which case it should apply across the reference list, or the weaker idea that control characterises informational and/or attentional privacy only, and hence they can't substitute another kind of privacy for it.

Insisting that privacy is control over access comes at the cost of jettisoning the basic intuition that if one's day-to-day activity is observed by a large audience, one is not in private. Some are prepared to take this heroic step. Inness (1992, 51–53) argued that someone who passes their personal information onto millions (an example of Gavison's – 1980, 384n.23) actually *relinquishes* control (and therefore cannot have privacy-as-control). This is arguable in the special case of passing on a secret, of which one loses control when it is blurted out, but fails to deal with Jennicam's live stream, which was perpetually under Ringley's control.

Conversely, Inness also wrote that someone trapped in her bed-room out of sight or hearing of anyone else 'would presumably describe her situation as characterized by an undesirable lack of privacy' (1992, 43). It is odd to suggest that anyone in that situation would complain of the *lack* of privacy upon release; surely the problem is too much privacy, and not enough publicity.

Altman too de-emphasised what he called the ' "keep-out" character and emphasize[d] the idea of control – opening and closing of the self to others and freedom of choice regarding personal accessibility' (1975, 17) as he focused on privacy's dialectical balance of withdrawal and exposure (1975, 23). But he struggled to keep the 'keep-out' character out of his account. Privacy-as-control involves aiming for a desired level of exposure, which requires control mechanisms to adjust it. If the ideal is achieved, then success, but a disparity either means isolation or overcrowding (1975, 7). Altman struggled to express these disparities without contradicting himself: he defined social isolation as achieving more privacy than desired, and crowding as less privacy than desired (1975, 7): 'too much or too little privacy is unsatisfactory, and … persons or groups seek optimal levels of social interaction' (1975, 25); 'more achieved privacy than desired creates a situation of being isolated from others; less achieved privacy than desired creates a state of being crowded or intruded upon' (1975, 43). Yet if privacy is control, 'less achieved privacy' cannot equate to 'being crowded', because it must mean 'too little control'. 'Too little control' may equate either to isolation or overcrowding depending on the ideal aimed at. Is it even possible to achieve more privacy-as-control than desired? Who would want more than total control? Altman found himself switching between his preferred definition of privacy and the intuitive sense of withdrawal I defend here, at one stage even appearing to misread his own explanatory figure as a result (1975, 26).

Inness and Altman were writing before the growth of the Internet. Rössler was able to take its challenges into account, more subtly discussing someone who 'deliberately gives up *certain aspects of* her privacy' (2005, 74, my emphasis). Her idea of different 'areas' of privacy where control can, should or may be exercised, gave her some resources to sidestep the Jennicam problem (2005, 8). Ringley could control access to her bedroom and the images taken, and so this marked out a private domain, even though she chose to publish the images. Ringley's behaviour in it is irrelevant; although she chose not to, she *could have* limited access to others, making it a private area.

Rössler can perform this sleight of hand, saying that Ringley has privacy despite every intuition saying the opposite, by means of the ambiguity of her account of control discussed earlier in this chapter (2005, 8). Ringley has privacy-as-control, on this ambiguous descriptive/normative account, if she can restrict access, or if she should restrict it, or if she may restrict it.

But this won't do the trick. Imagine someone else set up a webcam in Ringley's neighbour Mr Smith's apartment to broadcast without his knowledge. Using Rössler's ambiguity, we can say that this is a private domain too, because Mr Smith *should be* able to control access, even though he *cannot*. The problem is that while the ambiguity enables us to classify both domains as private, it doesn't tell us why the two situations are different.

Why not? Rössler would presumably want to claim that while Ringley has privacy, Mr Smith does not. This response trades on the obvious difference between the two – she has control and he does not. On the ambiguous account, Ringley has privacy because she can/should/may restrict access. But while this suffices for Ringley, it obliterates the distinction from her neighbour, who *also* can/should/may restrict access. Ringley *can* restrict it, and the neighbour *should*, both disappearing into the black box of Rössler's ambiguous account.

My own account, on the other hand, banishes the *similarities* of their positions to level 2 – their actions are being posted online by the webcam architecture, meaning a breach of the relevant level 1 privacy conception for both of them. The key *difference* between them appears at level 4, because Ringley *is* achieving her preferences, while the neighbour emphatically *is not*. The fact that Ringley has control and Mr Smith has not is a central level 4 idea, and not a major focus of the other levels.

While it is fine to talk about private areas, the ambiguous account (which we now see as a level 4 account) seems to have sacrificed the ability to point out the obvious (level 2) fact that neither Ringley nor her hypothetical neighbour *actually has* privacy

(Rössler would deny this was a fact, of course, never mind obvious, because she does not make the distinction between the levels). Neither, thanks to the necessity for ambiguity to bring the cases under a single idea of privacy-as-control, can we easily explain the difference that Ringley's situation is perfectly above board, but the neighbour has been violated, as will be clearer once we have explored levels 5–7.

The paradoxes of privacy-as-control

If we step through the dialectic of privacy-as-control, what does it mean to want more privacy? Privacy = control, so if one wants privacy, one therefore wants more control. This seems natural. But what does one want the control for? It can't be to adjust the level of privacy, because privacy = control, and it is not informative to say we want control in order to adjust the level of control. What does it mean to want less privacy? It must mean one wants less control. But how will that serve one's preferences, unless they are quite complex and second-order? Far more straightforward, surely, to say that one may want more or less privacy-as-withdrawal, and one will use whatever control one has to achieve these preferences (unless they are outweighed by others).

A parallel: suppose we are designing an audio speaker system and we are concerned with how loud a noise it makes – we call this the *volume*. But then someone says 'look, although the better the speaker the louder it can go, what really matters to customers is control to achieve the appropriate level of noise. They don't want to be deafened, or to cause the neighbours to complain, but equally they want to be able to hear the sound. So when it comes to volume, what matters is not quantity, but appropriacy, and customer control.' This is true: we admit it. 'So what we mean by "volume" is not the *level* of noise, but *control over* the level of noise.' This is false, and quite possibly mad. We can keep the traditional meaning of 'volume' as noise level, and still create a volume control, which allows the user to turn the volume up when it is too low and down when it is too high. This is what audio equipment makers do. If they tried to persuade their customers that 'volume' meant control, that a high volume meant a sensitive noise level control and a low volume meant that it was less so (perhaps with only 5 settings), that zero volume meant the speaker could never be changed from factory settings (and therefore zero volume could mean a substantial quantity of noise), and that a high volume might be quieter than a low volume, confusion would reign, for no obvious benefit.

Granted, privacy is more complex than a linear scale, so the privacy-conscious can't just turn it up to eleven like Spinal Tap, but the point of the analogy is that it is very difficult to keep up this non-standard usage. Altman's focus, as a social psychologist, was on coping strategies and behavioural mechanisms, which is why he saw privacy as a process with its own dialectics. Outside the 'official' statements of his theory, however, he often relaxed into the intuitive but incompatible idea that more (less) privacy means fewer (more) others around. He could have got round this awkwardness with a new coining of vocabulary (e.g. using 'withdrawal' to mean what the rest of us mean by 'privacy'), but surely far simpler to admit the force of the paradox that privacy-as-control may mean no privacy despite total control, and drop the definition.

We avoid the paradoxes if we say that privacy is a state of withdrawal of access, of which people have preferences for more or less, and control means that they can get their preferences. All things being equal, control is good for the individual, but not everyone acts effectively in their own interests, second-order and first-order preferences may clash, there may be collective action problems, and others have preferences that may be at odds. Control is not a state of withdrawal. It is a level 4 discourse about whether there are means to allow individuals to achieve their preferences. The major split in the literature between control and access accounts can now be seen as a non-issue – 'control' precisely means 'control of access'.

Privacy is not all about preferences, and its social and moral weight may mean that preferences have to be overridden (Nissenbaum 2010, 66). Further privacy discourses must cover these aspects, and hence we move to further levels, from the psychology of the individual to think about social matters in levels 5, 6 and 7.

Level 5: norms

Interaction requires more than simply following one's preferences; one needs to take into account the likely actions of others. The fifth level of privacy discourse concerns the expectations, standards, conventions, regularities or norms that allow people to plan their own behaviour and anticipate what their fellows will do. They specify what behaviours are allowed, frowned upon, and expected (Hetcher 2004, 17–146). They are therefore as much descriptive as normative – that is, they have normative *content*, but should be *descriptive* of the norms that actually hold in a specific society; one cannot make them up, they are not ideals, they must be detectable and understood to hold in real societies by their members. Some require obedience – not littering someone else's garden – while others are mere regularities – serving pudding after the main course. Schoeman distinguished between norms that liberate (enabling one to act as one chooses) and those that control (constraints that express 'respect for human dignity by protecting us from public association with the beastly, the unclean' – 1992, 17). They are generally informal, although some prefer to formalise them into rules or 'protocol' (McStay 2014). However they are described, they must be *shared*.

Normative versus descriptive accounts of social norms

Many areas related to privacy are governed by more or less strict norms. Georg Simmel argued that social interaction requires a balance between self-revelation and self-restraint, and norms about privacy and reserve specific to particular societies guide behaviour and help relationships perdure (Simmel 1950). Nissenbaum described privacy resting on 'finely calibrated systems of social norms, or rules, [that] govern the flow of information in distinct contexts (e.g. education, healthcare, and politics) … [and] define and sustain essential activities and key relationships and interests, protect people and groups against harm, and balance the distribution of power' (2010, 3).

Norms are structured around conceptions of privacy regarded as socially salient. There are no norms governing the veiling of the male face in a Western workplace in the 2020s (other than you don't do it, except in a pandemic, and then not for privacy reasons) because the breach of facial privacy is not salient in that context. On the other hand, there are several privacy conceptions in play when one travels on a bus, and unsurprisingly, given the prevalence of buses, plenty of norms have evolved around them. For Schoeman, privacy is of little value in the absence of norms; norms make it actionable (1992, 137).

Situations where intimate goings-on are evident to others (for example, in crowded houses, thin-walled apartments or dormitories) are often managed by norms where architecture can't do the job. If the architecture cannot guarantee privacy, one still might be able to engage in intimate relations confidently if one knows that others will disregard what is happening, avert their eyes, never mention what is seen or heard. If appropriate (reciprocal) norms are in operation, things can proceed *as if* one had privacy (in that level 2 sense), even if it is evident that one does not. We don't stare into lighted windows, or step over low fences into private property. Medieval peasants, or denizens of modern *favelas* or slums in the global South's megacities have hardly any privacy that would be considered suitable among the Western bourgeoisie – yet trust and friendship were/are surely possible, because people, as the saying goes, 'turn a blind eye'. Chang and Eng Bunker, the famous Siamese twins of nineteenth-century freak shows, married and had twenty-one children between them. Norms can be leveraged to compensate for the absence of privacy.

Many norms facilitate navigation of the complex lifestyles of individuals occupying several different roles, some public, some private (Goffman 1959). On this view, each role demands a certain amount of signalling (for instance, a bank manager needs to communicate sobriety and respect for customers, which is done using clothing, facial expressions, some deference, some confidence and power, etc.), while restricting access to signals from other roles (the manager may store a finger painting by their young child in their desk, rather than mounting it on the wall, even though it gives them pleasure to view it). Composer Charles Ives was also a successful insurance executive and had great difficulty combining the roles, only venturing into the artistic limelight after retirement; he seems to have thought that being one of America's greatest composers would be perceived as an effeminate weakness by colleagues and clients (Swafford 1996). We coordinate some role-playing with role-sets, suites of interlinked roles each of which rests on the others – for example, the bank manager, clerks, customers and security guards each have an elaborate repertoire of behaviour, which will help them interpret their necessary interactions (Murphy 1964, 36; Rachels 1975, 293; Schoeman 1992, 14–19; Sennett 2002, 28–44; Nissenbaum 2010, 133, 141–143).

It is less a question of dividing things into private and not, than of sensing which information needs to be released and when. Our privacy antennae are sensitive to the importance of role in determining the seriousness of a privacy breach (Nissenbaum 2010, 142). Is one to be treated as an impersonal occupant of a role, or personally as the individual who happens to occupy it? This will vary with context, and brings risk. 'Being treated as an individual rather than as a fungible abstraction leads to a loss of anonymity and, in some contexts, to a loss of self-respect' (Schoeman 1992, 17); fungibility allows a measure of dissociation and distance between oneself and other people and objects because things and people are interchangeable. Distance is essential for role-based selective disclosure, especially if a relationship will be perpetuated; so interconnected is society that two people might meet one day in one role-set, and another day in another. The TV comedy *Dad's Army*, about Britain's wartime citizen militia, made great play with the characters' reluctance to separate their distinct roles – the platoon Captain was also the bank manager, the Lance Corporal was the butcher (and therefore, in days of rationing, with sausage-distribution powers beyond his rank), one of the private soldiers was also the local black marketeer and so on. Their deep familiarity with each other, all residents of a small town, made a mockery of supposedly impersonal military relationships.

Norms, roles and role-sets apply in contexts, and need not stay constant across them. A context – for example, healthcare, education, policing, sport, shopping – will have a structure and history which partly determine the expectations and regularities that it displays (Nissenbaum 2010, 130). Schoeman developed the less formal notion of a 'sphere of life' (1992, 151–164), and ultimately the behaviour supported in such contexts is reminiscent of Wittgenstein's language games embedded in, and limited by, social settings (1953, §19, §240, §363, 1969, §618, 1981 §350, §387). Contexts may be nested, so that for example in a supermarket there will be supermarket-specific norms, and others inherited from the wider shopping context (Nissenbaum 2010, 136).

The passage of time reveals which practices are effective and which maladapted to their contexts. As these evolve, there will be debate or even conflict about what norms hold, where and when. They needn't be consistent – norms governing gossip sometimes deter one from sticking, sometimes encourage one to stick, one's nose in (Schoeman 1992, 136–150). When contexts are nested, the sub-context may introduce norms that conflict with those inherited from above. The norms, regularities and rules form a loose system in which change to one rule will have repercussions across the set; privacy is not 'an independent principle that either succumbs to or overrides other considerations' (Schoeman 1992, 137).

Reasonable expectations

Norms engender conformity and regularity, working to reduce the complexity of behaviour choices for individuals, and their interactions with others. This has led to the notion, which has become an important means of representing social mores in law, of *reasonable expectations of privacy* (Jones 1997). Though it originated in law, it is intended to be a description of the norms currently *recognised across society*, and hence is an empirical concept (Slobogin and Schumacher 1993). It prioritises a privacy complaint, when someone expects privacy in a particular context only to find it breached. For instance, on a telephone call with a friend, one does not expect the call to be bugged (Nissenbaum 2010, 152–153). One does not expect information given in confidence to be passed on. Different expectations apply to people in the public eye. However, expectations must be *reasonable*, that is, must express existing and recognised norms; an expectation not to be stared at while doing something outlandish in public might be real but would not be reasonable. In this way, legal judgements can respect changing mores, or the different status of different people, without having to update laws on a regular basis.

Should one expect that one's emails be read if sent on one's work account (McArthur 2001)? Should one expect that one's privacy preferences be respected by the social networks one is a member of (Newell 2011)? Should we give inexperienced young people more latitude, even though they are more tech-savvy than the rest of us (Leary 2011)? Should someone who has passed on their information to another expect their confidence to be respected (Scott-Hayward et al. 2015)? Should one expect one's mobile phone to be used for surveillance upon one (Smith et al. 2016)? Should one expect one's virtual assistant to work for oneself, or for the service provider (Lee 2020)? Subjects will doubtless have genuine expectations about such matters, but these must be tested against wider social understanding.

Considering how norms might change, or apply, to new technology is an important sociological and legal task. For instance, one's house is visible, in normal light, from the street and one should therefore be prepared for it to appear in photographs. What if the photographer used a device in the street to capture infra-red light, which shows patterns of heat and therefore activities *inside* the home (Julie 2000; Penney 2007)? The use of thermal imaging technology to detect abnormally hot dwellings that might be being used for cultivating marijuana has been a contested issue, as we have already seen in the *Kyllo* case discussed in Part II, Explanation 1. Are our reasonable expectations about photography inherited by thermal imaging devices? All the operator is doing is capturing the light emanating from the building, just like the conventional photographer, except on different wavelengths, yet the very novelty of thermal imaging and its limited function inclines me to answer negatively.

Many commentators worry about a ratchet effect of reasonable expectations under digital modernity. As more and more objects come online as part of the Internet of Things, and more services become 'smart' and connected, then – while they don't know a great deal about what happens to their data trails – people's expectations about the use of that data will naturally tend to encompass fewer and fewer restrictions. As early as 1978, Wasserstrom worried that 'we might ... become so used to being objects of public scrutiny that we would cease to deem privacy important in any of our social relationships' (1978, 328–329). Without a halting condition, reasonable expectations of privacy will naturally diminish as surveillance gets increasingly pervasive, all things being equal, unless a stand is taken.

Contextual integrity

Nissenbaum's theory of *contextual integrity* was developed as a means to take that stand. One of the most successful theories of privacy of recent years, it traded heavily on the importance of norms in understanding privacy practice and preferences, to explain why 'the huge and growing set of technical systems and technology-based practices ... provoke anxiety, protest, and resistance in the name of privacy' (Nissenbaum 2010, 3). By focusing particularly on informational norms (i.e. how information should flow, to whom, and when), Nissenbaum's technology focus led her to restrict her account to informational privacy alone, although it wouldn't take much tweaking to cover more items on the reference list.

She defined contextual integrity as the preservation of the information-related norms within a context as it changed (2010, 140). The notion of 'integrity' cleverly brings out the importance of the condition of remaining intact in essential aspects through time, implying the possibility of damage through change. If an innovation in technology or practice damaged or replaced existing privacy-concerning norms, this would cause further deterioration to ripple through the network of norms of the context. This would cause dislocation for those within the context, and disputes and conflict over privacy (cf. Wittgenstein 1969, §617).

Conversely, protecting or respecting norms helps cement social cohesion (Peters et al. 2017).

Norms were characterised in terms of the actors/roles involved, the types, importance and sensitivity of information concerned, and the principles of transmission (e.g. is the transfer of information compulsory? Reciprocal? At the discretion of the subject?). Specifying these is often intuitive, based on hermeneutic understanding of the context (2010, 144). Relevant types of norm include moral norms, etiquette, formal procedures (such as the Chatham House rule), religious injunctions and fleeting fads (Nissenbaum 2010, 139). They are rarely reflected upon, at least when very familiar; some may be observed largely in the breach, and others may be so internalised that if they manifest themselves at all they appear as 'common sense'.

While privacy norms may help shore up other norms (for instance, kinship norms may require careful restriction of the flow of information – Westin 1967, 14), they may also clash or conflict. Most norms of spatial privacy allow people to eject unwanted (non-official) visitors from their home, but some societies also feature powerful norms on providing hospitality to strangers (Shryock 2004; Young 2007). These may clash when unexpected visitors arrive at the door. Norms across society might conflict with those within specific groups, such as religious groups (Solove 2008, 94). Privacy norms might be used to resist the application of other norms in the wider society; this can have positive effects allowing the development of the individual free from social pressure (Gerstein 1982) but may merely allow resentment at and resistance to outsider interference. Nissenbaum was optimistic that her method for specifying contextual integrity would allow most conflicts to be defused, so that the 'appropriate flow' of information would make allowances for other relevant norms (2010, 238–239). If not, we would have to examine closely on a case-by-case basis (2010, 239).

Nissenbaum's account sometimes confounded levels. She characterised contexts by all the implicit or explicit rules within them (2010, 139), which unfortunately meant that her 'norms' often shaded into regulations and laws (2010, 135), which are properly held separate – indeed, some laws are crafted in order to *suppress* social norms (Bicchieri 2017, 106–162). Her own example, the injunction that 'law enforcement agents are entitled to information about gunshot wounds' (2010, 146), is a law and not a norm. In many circles, the norm is to *conceal* gunshot wounds from the police, as evinced by innumerable heist films from *Armored Car Robbery* to *The Asphalt Jungle* to *Reservoir Dogs*. The legally mandated information flow in that particular example *threatens* the integrity of the deviant norms that sustain criminal gangs (as, of course, it is intended to). Even in non-criminal contexts, law (for example, contract law in privacy policies) threatens contextual integrity, rather than constituting it.

If we are to explain privacy concerns by the subversion of contextual integrity, then we need to account for individuals' resistance in well-regulated contexts, including types of resistance Nissenbaum herself has written about, for example against privacy policies (Barocas and Nissenbaum 2009) or using technology to skew the data that online services produce (Brunton and Nissenbaum 2015). The point is not that laws play no part in the context – of course they do – but they are an exogenous imposition, rather than the organic working-out of expectations and preferences in a social setting, although they may be internalised over time. Sustainable norms can lead to a rough-and-ready fairness (Bicchieri 2006) but won't implement regulators' agendas. Hence it behoves us to keep them separate.

Contextual integrity as a moral theory

This shows us that privacy norms can be divisive – one person's 'maladaptive' norm (Bicchieri 2017, 1) is another's familiar lodestone. Furthermore, many are discriminatory. This does not mean they are therefore intrinsically bad, but it is not a good look. Class is an obvious fault-line. Westin wrote that we should try to avoid the wealthy getting more or higher-quality privacy (1967, 389), though he also wrote rather snobbishly about the regrettable tendency of the masses to focus on crude exhibitionism and voyeuristic television programmes (1967, 61).

There may be different norms about how ethnic minorities are treated, while some minority communities may adopt divergent norms, leading to different treatment and expectations (Liversage 2014). Genders are treated differently – norms around the visibility of nipples or body hair vary (for example, in social media censorship – Faust 2017; Are 2021), and women's bodies generally are more likely to be sexualised and subject(ed) to more stringent privacy norms (Hasinoff 2014; Matich et al. 2019). Kissing or holding hands in public is fine for heterosexual couples but gay canoodling frowned upon (Hubbard 2013; Buck et al. 2019). Considerations of the egalitarian or just distribution of privacy are relatively lacking in the privacy literature (Raab 2005, 289ff.).

In consequence, those who set out to describe privacy norms will be tempted to moralise. There is a philosophical debate about how critical one should be when one engages with social norms (Nissenbaum 2010, 138; Rössler 2005, 16–17; Bicchieri 2017, 18–21), or how aligned they should be with moral or political norms (Schoeman 1992, 2), but I would argue that the temptation is best resisted. Nissenbaum was concerned that her own account was too conservative, but if one's *aim* is to change existing social norms (Bicchieri 2017), rather than to understand and respect them, then it is important to realise that one is not *describing* social relations, but making a moral claim. An objective (level 5) description of privacy norms ought, as good practice, to precede a morally or politically committed critique and programme of social change.

Nissenbaum's worries about conservatism led her to go down the opposite route and introduce moral content directly into the mix: 'more is needed from contextual integrity if it is to serve further as a moral concept' (2010, 165). At that point, contextual integrity theory ceased to specify what norms and expectations people *had*, and morphed into a theory of what they *ought* to have.

Nothing wrong with this, except that if contextual integrity is a *moral* theory, it cannot do what it was advertised to do, which was explain 'anxiety, protest, and resistance' about privacy (Nissenbaum 2010, 3). To be explanatory, it must be descriptive. It cannot be moral, because the moralist's ideals may not be widely shared, in which case it will not explain the anxiety. The moral overlay is the opinion of the theorist, who, even if they (i.e. the theorist) are somehow representative of or have authority over the community under study, may not have the right to impose their opinions upon it.

Nissenbaum wanted to have her cake and eat it – a moral theory that simultaneously explained public attitudes. But with such a theory, failure to be moral leaves an unpalatable dilemma. 'One path forgoes any significant role for contextual integrity in the moral evaluation of controversial socio-technical practices. ... A second path ... [is] that contextual integrity carries moral weight, committing us to a justificatory framework with a rigidly conservative bias' (2010, 161). But is this as problematic as it seems, even for a non-conservative?

To say that social norms are inherently good goes well beyond a respectable conservative position. However, even if a norm is apparently arbitrary or counterproductive, there is still reason to respect the stability of the norm system, as it contributes to the legibility of a context to those within it (Scott 1998; O'Hara 2011; 2021b; Peters et al. 2017). A stable norm system may be referred to in the aggregate as 'custom', and while it may be influenced by legal arrangements (Hetcher 2004, 149–214), it must be such that imperfect people are able to follow it (Schoeman 1992, 54–55). Practically, there is some evidence that behaviour with moral implications aligns more easily with expectations about others' behaviour and reactions, than with political or religious commandments (Bicchieri and Xiao 2009).

Given that one has mapped and described social norms (which clearly does not entail endorsement by the mapper), a *separate* theory is needed to work out their moral significance. That should typically be insulated from the norms and cultural specifics of the society under consideration (cf. Schoeman 1992, 37–52). We describe the privacy norms, and then use our favourite independent moral theory either to decide whether they are morally good or bad, or whether an innovation is an improvement or otherwise, if it is appropriate for the researcher to be judgemental.

Understanding norms need not box the researcher into a conservative position. It is probably standard academic dogma that conformity to norms is a moral failing, but this is based on the false assumption that norm-following is equivalent to acting robotically. On the contrary, norms need interpretation, hermeneutic engagement, adaptation to context, resolution of conflicts, and so on – the intuitive, prudential thinking that Aristotle called *phronesis* or practical wisdom (2011, 130–134, 1143b20ff.) – which makes them adaptable and open to evolution (Schoeman

1992, 80). They can usually be worked around when they threaten to become inhumane (Sennett 2002, 23–24). In the afore-mentioned *Dad's Army*, the widowed Mrs Pike has been having a long-term affair with Sgt Wilson, whom her son Private Pike has been brought up to call 'Uncle Arthur'. Everyone in the platoon but Pike is well aware of this, but nobody ever mentions it. By not forcing the issue, they honour the norm against extra-marital relationships (in the breach, as the saying has it) without challenging Pike's naïve model of his domestic arrangements or disturbing the happiness of their friends.

In any case, norms adapt to new circumstances, practices or technologies. There is inevitably a lag, and new behaviours may appear deviant and transgressive. Entrenched norms may indeed resist some changes, which then look like fads before they fade out. Entrepreneurs disseminating new technologies, products and services may challenge norms: *productively*, by innovating to create fresh sources of value; *unproductively*, rent-seeking to misallo-cate resources, for example, by imposing costs on those seeking privacy; or *destructively*, by subverting norms with transgressive behaviour that may even be criminal, for example, through identity theft and data misappropriation (Baumol 1990). Even if these tech-nologies end up reinforcing existing norms, innovation will require transcending existing biases, bending rules, being creative and negotiating the liabilities of novelty, while incumbent competitors will defend their own positions and criticise the upstarts' legitimacy (Hall and Rosson 2006).

The dilemma, then, is not a dilemma at all. We describe social norms to understand current behaviour and contexts. Given that account, we may wish to obtrude and decide whether they are eth-ical, but we are likely to find, given the adaptability of norms to contexts, that they will generally be acceptable to the inhabitants of the context (Schoeman 1992, 80–83). Conservative privacy norms might also help people defend themselves against interference (Gerstein 1982), and so conservatism with respect to privacy might *support* more radical positions in other areas of life.

Adding moral judgement to the theory of contextual integrity elides two discourses – the description of social norms and their ethical evaluation. This is why Nissenbaum introduced two stages of evaluation, one based on the needs of the context itself, and one external to it (2010, 182), while Rössler also split her account of the 'fundamentally contradictory' (2005, 20) liberal concept of privacy into a 'quasi-natural' meaning and a 'legal-conventional' meaning (2005, 21–22). Her problem was that the social norms of privacy (specifically in the household) are discriminatory against women, but that the moral norms of liberal privacy are intended to leave these untouched, a conclusion that she could not accept (2005, 20). There is no contradiction in this, as of course Rössler was entitled to reject social norms incompatible with her own moral principles, but we should always bear in mind that critical interference has two components: understanding the behaviour of people within a context, and meddling in it.

Similarly, one can only claim that contextual integrity can 'serve usefully not only as an indicator of breaches of entrenched informational norms, but [also] as a guide to the moral legitimacy of such breaches' (Nissenbaum 2010, 165), at the cost of using the label 'contextual integrity' to yoke together two separate things, rather as a boat-train is not an amazing mode of transport over both water and rails, but instead signifies that one will travel in a boat over water, and then on a train over land. Notwithstanding its decision heuristic (Nissenbaum 2010, 182–183), the evaluation of practices is *not* performed by the theory, but is an add-on once the theory has described the entrenched norms and the threats to them.

One can produce a basic minimal evaluation, by referring not to independent value-frames but instead with reference to the values of the particular contexts under examination via teleological accounts of them (2010, 166–178; Walzer 1983; MacIntyre 2007, 148–152) – i.e. what sort of value is necessary for the contexts to function at all. Some norms are preconditions for a practice even to take place (2010, 175; O'Hara and Robertson 2017), so if the norms are upended, the practice will cease and the context collapse. But even the focus on the essential values of the context won't turn contextual integrity into the moral tool Nissenbaum wanted. Contexts where the 'entrenched normative practices' are helpful for 'relevant contextual values' (2010, 166), can create rather than resolve ethical problems – for example, norms of *omertà* in criminal gangs, which enable them to flourish in certain societies despite the best efforts of law enforcement agencies (Travaglino and Abrams 2019; Vveinhardt et al. 2019; Nissenbaum 2010, 180–181).

In short, however the theory is packaged, there are three things going on when contextual integrity is used to describe a context: (i) conceptions of privacy are subtended by the context; (ii) the norms that concern them are described (and where there is a new norm-breaking practice, the context description can be used to help determine whether the new practice will support or disrupt the existing context); and (iii) the norms are evaluated against external criteria to see if they are good or bad, or alternatively whether improvements are possible. Only (ii) concerns contextual *integrity*, providing input to (iii), whose criteria depend *not* on the theory of contextual integrity, but rather on the *researcher's* moral stance and prejudices.

Contextual integrity does not define privacy

The first proposition in the previous paragraph (i) entails that privacy is not contextual integrity. To claim that it is, to mix metaphors, is to turn the boat-train into a kitchen sink definition. To be clear (Nissenbaum 2010) did not assert that contextual integrity is definitive (although she has occasionally – possibly for a shorthand – written elsewhere as if it is – e.g. Barocas and Nissenbaum 2014, 47).

Contextual integrity, *qua* description of norms subsisting in contexts through time, can't define privacy, for more or less the same reason that control can't be a definition – it may be that the norms of a context are not privacy-preserving. The norms of a prison include perpetual surveillance, random searches of property, cells and beds, routine censorship of incoming and outgoing mail, drastically reduced capacity for making decisions, and highly rationed intimacy with visitors. Contextual integrity in a prison means perpetuating lack of privacy. Nothing about the theory enables the theorist to distinguish between norms that increase information flow from those that decrease it. Nissenbaum wrote as if a loss of contextual integrity will automatically decrease privacy, but there is no reason to think that, nor that a decrease in one conception of privacy can't accompany increases in others. For instance, in 2021, Apple made it easier for iPhone users to prevent app developers' access to their IDFA (Identity for Advertisers) identifier, thereby preventing them from recognising the same phone across different encounters (Burgess 2021). The norm is that smartphones create and provide data, so Apple's privacy-preserving move *violated* the integrity of the familiar smartphone context (though, as Martin Kraemer pointed out to me, it also partially restored the older context of analogue communications).

Furthermore, privacy-related norms are not always complied with. They bring with them a degree of social enforcement, which, for some, makes breaking them attractive (in other words, the existence of norms at level 5 can affect level 4 preferences in either direction). For example, streakers streak precisely because this flies in the face of norms about being publicly clothed (Heckel 1976, who amazingly managed to find ninety-nine streakers at a single university to interview – I may be in the wrong job). Conversely, no one streaks on a nudist beach. People have revealed extraordinary things about themselves so often in online blogs that they may collectively be undoing norms of reserve (de Laat 2008). Girls of North African heritage have proudly adopted the veil, using their privacy to resist Western norms of openness and freedom, from colonial Algeria (Fanon 1965) to the Parisian *banlieues* today (Hancock 2017; Najib and Hopkins 2019). Norms can help people bridge the intention-behaviour gap characteristic of the privacy paradox (Godin et al. 2005). Norms make behaviour predictable to a degree but not in detail; they frame behaviour, which becomes explicable whether it is in conformity with or reaction to social regularities. We understand both the conformist and the rebel on the same terms.

To insist on contextual integrity's moral content only puts further strain on it. How would we describe a norm that appeared to decrease privacy? What about a bad norm? What about something that appeared to be an instance of privacy that was not a norm or convention?

If one wants to argue that the norms in a society are thus-and-so, then one is at level 5 using the methods of sociology. If one wants to argue that the norms in a society are morally wrong or politically incorrect, then one is producing an ethical, not a sociological, argument. There is nothing wrong with this, except that they are two different projects requiring two different methodologies. The framework of this book is intended to highlight these differences, to help prevent people talking past each other. Nissenbaum's contextual integrity theory is the best developed attempt to understand privacy level 5 – in fact, probably the best attempt to drive privacy policy at any level. In her own words, 'it models intuitive judgements better than existing predominant theories and approaches to privacy, particularly in light of challenges from radical alterations of information flows due to socio-technical systems' (2010, 181). That is precisely what is needed at level 5.

Level 6: regulation

The informal restrictions of social norms are not always perceived as adequate. At that point regulation and law come into play. The government steps in, sometimes to preserve norms, sometimes to challenge them, sometimes to support its citizens in achieving their preferences, sometimes to prevent them. Lawyers work with those wishing to defend their privacy, using the regulatory tools at their command to carve out and defend a space for private action. Solove's work was mainly focused on this area.

At level 6, we place discourse about legitimate authority to address felt needs in the realm of privacy. Although in this brief review I will focus on legislation and common law, following the bulk of academic research, level 6 does include regulation by non-governmental bodies – for example, regulations within a firm about the surveillance of employees, or the publicity appropriate for internal processes (Westin 1967, 46–56). Such internal rules may of course conflict with the law (Vaux-Montagny 2021). In theocratic states, the ability of ecclesiastical courts to compel, for instance in relation to confession and the sacrament of penance, brings them into level 6 (Thomas 1973, 183–184; Gerstein 1970, 251–252). Other authoritative rule-sets include professional codes of practice (e.g. Francis 2021), principles such as privacy-by-design (Cavoukian 2011), and methods for implementing accountability for privacy breaches (Raab 2012).

It also includes privacy rights created by legislation, constitutions, treaties and conventions, backed up by courts. These are legal rights as opposed to natural rights, artificial rights that did not exist prior to their creation, whose meaning depends on the interpretation that courts give them. They cease to exist when the courts cease to protect them (Hart 1955, 175).

Further, there are regulatory matters that, though not directly connected with privacy, impinge upon it. As Robert Post put it, 'the pertinence of ... information for public deliberation ... is independent of the privacy of the information' (2001, 2089), so private information may need to be suborned for administrative purposes. But that does not mean that private information is always pertinent when demanded. In July 2021, digital rights expert Michael Veale tweeted that, as an academic peer reviewer for a proposed EU project *on data and privacy*, he had been forced by the review software to download the identity cards and birth certificates of the proposal's authors! You couldn't make it up. As Veale tweeted, what kind of review was expected? 'The proposal is very solid, but I have unresolved concerns that the investigators had never been born!'

Conversely, level 6 does *not* include non-regulatory matters, such as whether a law is morally supportable, an ethical issue. Keeping level 6 insulated from such questions does not mean that I endorse legal positivism, of the kind espoused by, say, H.L.A. Hart (1983), or that we can't take into account more expansive views such as that of legal integrity (Dworkin 1986, 94–96). Lawyers do not heedlessly follow rules but instead work in the light of coherent, but nonetheless jurisprudential, principles developed by a legitimate politico-legal community. Law is a hermeneutic procedure that needs to remain explicable to itself, and continuous with its history. It changes social reality by its prescriptions, by suppressing norms, by altering reasonable expectations, and by constraining the state to defend some rights and not others. Legal reasoning may involve input from level 4 when it supports (or suppresses) the ability of people to make their own choices, from level 5 when it supports (or suppresses) social norms, and so on, and we would expect the different norms and values of jurisdictions such as Europe and the US to delineate different styles of privacy law (Whitman 2004; Rössler 2005, 14). Raymond Wacks (2010, 51–71) gives a useful survey of privacy law across jurisdictions.

The law does not define privacy

Just because a legal right of privacy may have been defined in law, that does not make it definitive of privacy, though it can define the types of privacy that the state is prepared to defend. While Koops et al. were correct to argue that privacy is not the same as rights to privacy, their claim that 'the right to privacy aims to protect privacy and that therefore the overall set of rights to privacy should ideally cover all types of privacy' (2017, 490n.17) elided the two once more. Some types of privacy are simply too trivial or too wrong to be covered, so that 'not every threat to privacy is of sufficient moment to warrant the imposition of civil liability or to evoke any other form of legal redress' (Bloustein 1964, 188–189; Gavison 1980, 370–372). *De minimis non curat lex.* Two people sitting on the bus converse, their heads close and their voices low. An eavesdropper in the seat behind tries hard to hear what they say. Has he invaded their privacy? Surely he has (even if he has heard nothing and even if the conversation ceases because he has been noticed – Inness 1992, 34), but what he is doing is not illegal, just anti-social.

The major issue at level 6 – which is what underlies much of the 'disarray' and 'confusion' about privacy – is that the family resemblance between the myriad conceptions we uncovered at level 1 doesn't lend itself to a straightforward set of applicable principles that the state can clearly and unambiguously enforce. What is called 'privacy' can be good, bad or indifferent, can take the form of a major matter that profoundly affects lives or something totally trivial such as the desire not to be spotted picking one's nose. How on earth do you craft laws to regulate such an area? General definitions are too vague, while viable legal rights must be limited, tractable and enforceable (Gerety 1977; Post 1989; Nissenbaum 2010, 98). Such is the problem that Solove addressed.

The law is one of the disciplines with a hegemonic attitude towards privacy, and we find philosophical discussions often swerve into legal literature and back again promiscuously, as if the pronouncement of a judge will settle a semantic matter. For instance, Inness gave an example of the 'intense disagreement' characteristic of privacy discourse: 'one person contends that the state would violate her privacy if it compelled her to wear a seat belt, yet the state argues that privacy has nothing to do with the wearing of seat belts' (1992, 3). Actually, the state argued nothing of the kind; it merely noted that seat belts are compulsory, and the court (the Supreme Court of Illinois) found no reason to consider seat belt wearing as one of those private matters covered by the Constitution 'We are unwilling to graft onto the Constitution a right of privacy to decide whether or not to wear a safety belt where there is no textual basis or a clear historical precedent for such a right in the language of the Constitution or the opinions of the Supreme Court' (*People v Kohrig* 1986). The assumption that 'both a definition and an explanation of privacy's value undergird privacy law' (Inness 1992, 15) collapses, as Inness noted, on contact with legal reality. The law only defines what aspects of privacy fall under its scope (and, as Warren and Brandeis established, it could do that without using the word 'privacy' at all).

Solove's discussion was ambivalent between defining privacy *tout court*, and merely thinking about its regulation: 'the focal point for a theory of privacy should be the problems we want the law to address' (2008, 75). But that is surely the focal point for a *legal* theory of privacy. If I am to define *privacy in general*, then I also need to cover aspects that are not protected by law.

Privacy is not *defined by* law but is *regulated* by it. When it is *defined in* law, that is merely a specification of the aspects of privacy covered by the regulation. As an extra-legal concept it precedes regulation. Compare: death features strongly in law, and is defined in it, but ultimately it pre-exists it (Halley and Harvey 1968). If it didn't, we might ask for a judicial review to see if it might be abolished. On 3 February 2016, the 7th Earl of Lucan was declared dead, and his title passed to his son. Infamously, Lord Lucan went missing on 8 November 1974 and has not been seen since. It is often supposed that he died at his own hand shortly after the notorious murder of which he was accused, but he could have died any time afterward, and it is just possible at the time of writing that he is still alive. One thing is almost certain: he did not die on the day the law declared him dead, and if he did, that was an amazing unconnected coincidence. The law needs procedures to determine when estates are inherited, insurance paid out, etc., but these have no effect on whether a person is breathing or decomposing. If I want to know if someone is dead, I ask a doctor, a relative, a historian, or sometimes use common sense (Bach, born in 1685, must be dead by now) but hardly ever a lawyer. Similarly, if I want to know, say, whether a room is private, I might ask the person who hires out the room, the person I am meeting, someone who has used the room before or an expert in electronic surveillance, but rarely would I go to a lawyer. On the other hand, if I have a specific legal question – when can I execute my missing brother's will? Can I sue someone if they bug my meeting? – then of course the lawyer is my first port of call.

The law varies across jurisdictions, but concepts of privacy do not (though they may be valued differently). The law also varies over time and is modified according to public values. Upskirting, the practice of taking a photograph up a woman's skirt without her consent, is as clear a breach of privacy as one could find wherever and whenever it happens, but its legal status is inconsistent (Najdowski 2017). In 2015, prosecutors in Oregon were horrified to discover that a sixty-one-year-old man who had upskirted a thirteen-year old girl had done nothing illegal; the judge regretted his decision to acquit him but that was the law as it stood. Clearly legislators had not anticipated this particular type of reprehensible behaviour until the courts were confronted with it, but the judge's shock and the resulting media outcry are clear evidence that it was indeed a breach of privacy. The legal lacuna was soon filled by legislation, and an offence it became. It would be heroic to argue that it only became a breach of privacy at *that* point, and not before.

I would add that upskirting with the lady's consent is *also* a breach of privacy, although this is rightly a defence in law. Consent means that we conceptualise the harms done (if any) very differently, but privacy in the relevant respect is still absent (see Part V, Level 4). The fact that the lady is not bothered by the intrusion, and may even welcome it, does not affect the sacrifice of her privacy (Bloustein 1964, 177 makes a similar point about unconsented but welcome use of images). It is of course sensible that the law focuses on non-consensual breaches of privacy, but one could imagine highly patriarchal societies where the woman's consent was not deemed legally relevant, but a husband's or guardian's consent had to be obtained instead, however deplorable such arrangements may seem to outsiders.

Furthermore, law is shaped by irrelevant or idiosyncratic political considerations. One type of information given special protection in the US is PII pertaining to video rentals, via the 1988 Video Privacy Protection Act, brought in after Robert Bork's video rental records were published during the campaign against his Supreme Court nomination. Not to say that such records are not worth protecting, but are they *especially* worth protecting, deserving of their own act to boot? Such quirks are local in nature with no conceptual justification.

US law does not define privacy

Nevertheless, many authors go straight to privacy law to find out what privacy is, often to US law (e.g. Inness 1992, 16). So common is this tendency that Schoeman felt he had to apologise for not doing it (1992, 21–22). Etzioni even argued that 'America needs a new conception of privacy' (1999, 183), thereby extending American exceptionalism to the Platonic Realm of Ideas. In more recent years, as the EU's data protection laws and privacy rights have been fleshed out and become more important (Bradford 2020), many commentators have looked there for a steer. However, surely no single jurisdiction is uniquely equipped to tell us what privacy is (Koops et al. 2017, 488–489). If, on the other hand, we still believe law to be an authoritative source for conceptual truths about privacy, it appears to follow that it must be different in every country, and changing as the law changes.

One specific handicap for US law, if it is to be a privacy oracle, is the distribution of privacy regulation across the different areas of tort and constitutional law. Tort covers the separation or withdrawal of the subject (informational privacy, attentional privacy, spatial privacy, etc.), while the Constitution is more about freedom of action (decisional privacy) and privacy-as-control. To some this seems *ad hoc*. 'Given these different accounts of the function and content of privacy, which give rise to different definitions, our problem emerges. We cannot accept both definitions as it appears that they differ on a fundamental level, yet we cannot abandon either, since they both plausibly claim to define privacy' (Inness 1992, 17–18).

Some have tried to analyse the difference away. Legal scholar Edward Bloustein found a common thread between the torts and the Fourth Amendment via their protection of human dignity and personality (1964, 181). Westin argued for a protected internal privacy sphere demarcated by the Constitution holding people responsible for their actions but not their thoughts and beliefs (1967, 264). Inness concluded that the privacy torts allowed 'the agent to control her sphere of intimacy by separating herself' (1992, 134), thereby making them corollaries of the constitutional rationale, and endorsing privacy-as-control.

Inness' hierarchical move feeds into a narrative about the Supreme Court's focus on 'activities protected by constitutional privacy law due to their intimacy: child rearing, family relationships, procreation, life in the home, marriage, contraception, and abortion' (1992, 118–120). After the anomalous *Olmstead v United States* (1928), a bizarre ruling that tapping a phone was not a search restricted by the Fourth Amendment, came a skein of cases where the Supreme Court laid out:

> many of the basic elements of a functional definition of constitutional privacy ... for the person and the group [in which it] is not a 'negative' concept at all; it has been perceived as a protection of the positive needs of individuals and organizations in our society ... as ... threatened by scientific and social pressures. (Westin 1967, 398)

Olmstead was overturned by *Katz v United States* (1967), which developed the reasonable expectations of privacy test (critiqued by Etzioni 2015, 49–59). *Loving v Virginia* (1967) established interracial marriage, *Griswold v Connecticut* (1965) asserted the liberty of married couples to buy and sell contraceptives, *Eisenstadt v Baird* (1972) extended that to unmarried couples, and *Roe v Wade* (1973) was the famous abortion case. *Bowers v Hardwick* (1986) bucked the trend by declaring a Georgian anti-sodomy law constitutional (for the minority opinion, Inness 1992, 124–126), but *Bowers* was overturned by *Lawrence v Texas* as late as 2003. *Obergefell v Hodges* (2015) established same-sex couples' rights to marry.

Neat as this narrative is (and it was of course developed prior to the repeal of *Roe* in 2022, so we may already be in a different phase), tort and the constitution each specify different aspects of life where the state will step in to protect privacy. Neither reduces to the other; sometimes plaintiffs want their separation from others to be confirmed and supported (tort), and sometimes they want control over their business, and to deny access to the authorities (Constitution). In both cases, law brings in the power and legitimacy of the state to help protect privacy. They complement each other. The participants in a dispute in the private sector are roughly equal antagonists. Social norms are usually effective, leaving tort as a last resort to claim remedy for losses or harm. However, where the state is involved, the power imbalance between it and the citizen means that the rule of law is essential for achieving just resolutions, and the state is properly constrained by the Constitution (Schoeman 1992, 22–23).

Theoretically, that division works nicely. Whether it is sustainable in the long run is less certain. The fly in the ointment is the waxing of the power of private-sector technology giants. Even before their growth, Etzioni had argued that the state would be a better guarantor of privacy than the private sector, despite the lack of trust of Americans in the former (1999, 9–10; cf. Gavison 1980, 357–358). It is also not going to apply where the law cannot be used to limit government action, such as China (O'Hara and Hall 2021, 125–140).

Ultimately law is mutable, and if trends can be discerned, it is subject to fashion; restrict focus to US law and it is still more hostage to contingency. To contemplate it as the basis for an account of privacy of global scope is to note its lacunae. When Supreme Court judgements are involved, the law's treatment of intimate actions doesn't evolve incrementally at the pace of social change – behaviour becomes legal without limitation 'overnight' (Etzioni 1999, 192–193), and as the 2022 reversal of *Roe* showed, can lose that protection just as suddenly, for no better reason than the political make-up of the Supreme Court has changed. Until *Griswold* and *Roe* the US Supreme Court didn't protect contraception or abortion at all.

This is not to say that ideas about morality can't be used to critique court judgements – of course they can (Inness 1992, 135n.6). It is, however, problematic to *derive* ethical positions from the court's history, although during the period between *Olmstead* and *Obergefell* the trends might have seemed irreversible. James Whitman opined in 2004 that 'The prospects for the kind of dignitary protections embodied in a law of gay marriage, we could say, are remote. After all, protecting people's dignity is quite alien to the American tradition' (2004, 1221), but *Obergefell* did provide such protections by 2015, and there is evidence that Supreme Court judgements can affect public opinion proactively (Tankard and Paluck 2017).

However, President Trump and Republican Senate leader Mitch McConnell worked to reverse liberalising trends and to pack the Supreme Court for a generation, leading to the eventual achievement of the aspiration of many of their supporters to overturn *Roe v Wade*, by foul means or fouler, at whatever cost to settled law (the foulest, in terms of the affront to the rule of law, was the 2021 Texas Heartbeat Act, which effectively banned abortion consistently with *Roe* by relying on private citizens for its enforcement through civil lawsuits – thereby making abortion a *de facto* public matter by privatising its policing). I am not judging the quality of the original *Roe* decision or its reversal, only noting that both judgements politicised the court as protector and interpreter of the Constitution. There are ways round Trump-style manipulation of the court, for example the use of term limits, but an unintended side effect of this is to *erode* doctrinal stability still further (Sundby and Sherry 2019), and open up the court to still more political interference.

Has abortion ceased to be a private matter since *Roe*'s reversal, any more than it came to be one at the date of the original judgement? Many states have considered the possibility of making it harder for their residents to leave the state and travel to another (to procure an abortion in a more liberal state), which if enacted will certainly limit (not redefine) their decisional privacy (perhaps only for pregnant women). Surveillance may have to increase in order to keep track of pregnant women's whereabouts.

American law, especially in the polarised, politicised mess it currently finds itself, will not tell us what privacy is. The focus on the Supreme Court may be less useful than following in the footsteps of Warren and Brandeis and Prosser. 'Privacy' only featured, unnamed, as defensible under various torts (Westin argued that it had always been defended in US law, consciously distinct from more intrusive European regimes – 1967, 369–378). Common law, the medieval system imported from England based on precedent, is handily indicative of real-world issues that genuine plaintiffs are interested in resolving, exposing existing social needs and tensions in the nexus of individual preferences, norms and morality that might otherwise be hidden behind elite preoccupations (Post 1989; Solove 2008, 102). That foregrounded history is extremely valuable (if local) but not a conceptual discovery. Indeed, as Warren and Brandeis assumed, the knowledge of what privacy is is a precondition for recognising privacy-related judgements.

Expansive versus restrictive views of privacy in the law

However, that in itself is not sufficient to determine how comprehensively privacy will be protected in law. The significance of the right to be let alone is that it is an *expansive* view of privacy, a principle such that, were it agreed to be operative, would tend to support the *growth* of privacy rights to fill gaps in its coverage. Many lawyers have resisted the demand for an expansive view, arguing that it will create temptations to regulate more widely and inappropriately. Prosser's view of four discrete privacy-related torts (1960) had the practical effect of creating a *restrictive* structure that failed to provide much cover, and furnished no grounds for expanding it (Richards and Solove 2010). Chief Justice Rehnquist went further, complaining even about the misleading practice of labelling discrete elements as 'privacy', which created unreasonable expectations about its regulation that couldn't be fulfilled, both practically and because it was 'coming at the expense of other competing values' (1974, 21). Harry Kalven agreed that 'privacy', lacking definition in law, was not a good label, preferring ideas that were more precise and theorised, such as freedom of speech or of association (1966). This does not mean that they were sceptical of either the existence or the value of privacy (*pace* Richards and Solove 2010, 1915), only that they denied that (i) the law as it stood was an informative guide to privacy, and (ii) it should support privacy *tout court*.

The concern of these lawyers that privacy, if not restricted, would expand to encroach on other fields, has been borne out in the area of human rights protection. *Contra* Thomson (1975), it seems that people have found other rights more defensible by recasting them as privacy rights rather than the other way round, at least in the courts. For instance, the right to marry and found a family is explicitly protected by Article 12 of the European Convention on Human Rights, but courts have interpreted it narrowly. On the other hand, the right to a private life, protected by Article 8, has been given wide scope, and so people with claims relating to gay marriage, artificial insemination, adoption and other non-traditional forms of family tend to make a complaint in Article 8 terms rather than using Article 12, because they are more likely to win (van der Sloot 2017a, 26; Sumption 2019, 57–61). Linnet Taylor argued explicitly that resistance to algorithmic analysis of groups using big data should be couched in privacy terms precisely because the defence will be stronger (2017, 32).

In the US, the Fourteenth Amendment plays the same role as Article 8 (Sumption 2019, 83–87); it is so flexible that at different times it has been the ground for upholding child labour and same-sex marriage. The much-disputed *Roe v Wade* used it to declare abortion constitutional; the judgement in effect framed it as an issue of women's decisional privacy, whereas its opponents saw that as subordinate to the question of whether the foetus is a person and abortion therefore murder (Coker 2017). 'In Germany and Europe by contrast, it is inconceivable that a right to terminate a pregnancy be grounded on a right to privacy' (Rössler 2005, 14, 96–98, who is not an opponent of abortion). Whether the possibility of pursuing arguably non-privacy issues more successfully as privacy actions is a good thing isn't in the scope of this inquiry, but some have lamented that 'privacy has become the over-burdened camel of much individual rights (and wrongs) litigation' (Gerety 1977, 296).

While expansive views, such as the right to be let alone or the right to protection of personal dignity (Bloustein 1964, 186), cause nervousness in the profession, Prosser's buttoned-up account has undoubtedly proved too constraining to adapt to new technologies and harms in our own period. Prosser described his method of finding commonalities in the apparent variety of common law tort judgements as passive description, but Richards and Solove showed that it was an actively restrictive methodology, with feedback loops where judges referenced Prosser in their judgements, which then became confirming evidence for the next iteration of his theories (2010, 1901). They regretted his zeal for organising the 'energetic chaos' of the privacy tort into a 'rationalized, refined and harmonized' taxonomy that has ossified since his work: 'today, the privacy torts stand at the four Prosser identified, and no new privacy torts have been created since Prosser's death' (Richards and Solove 2010, 1906–1907). They also argued that he overlooked other torts with privacy dimensions, such as breach of confidence and intentional infliction of emotional distress (2010, 1907–1912). Breach of confidence in particular overlaps with privacy, is a developed tort in English law (Aplin et al. 2012), and was an important topic in Warren and Brandeis' paper (1890, 83–86).

Solove's twenty-first-century view, prompted by digital modernity's assault on privacy, was that the law cannot take a restricted view. Earlier scholars made the possibly complacent assumption that we can recognise it when we see it, but for Solove, without an independent, coherent and motivated account of privacy available to law, even one that is inherently pluralistic, it cannot be properly protected. The law needs to drop its binary view of privacy as present or absent, take into account individuals' expectations, and modify and expand its understanding of harms (Richards and Solove 2010, 1921–1924). On the other hand, when Solove did describe what he saw as privacy, he produced an impressive and rich taxonomy of activities, problems and remedies that looks very like a description of the resources the law holds, or might reasonably hold with a little creativity, for protecting subjects from privacy invasion (2008, 101–170). Similarly, Gavison's suggestion that the law should make an explicit commitment to privacy, not as a convenient label, but as a central value and a principle of interpretation, without necessarily spelling out in detail new laws or protections (1980, 377–381), was aimed at transforming the *performance* of law, rather than the law itself.

Whether such an approach will be able to square the circle, avoiding unreasonable rights expansion while supporting reasonable privacy protection in a period of sustained technological innovation is moot, especially as decision-making in the US is intractable, and in Europe painfully slow (the General Data Protection Regulation, or GDPR, will be the standard there for some time).

In the 2020s, those concerned about the unrestricted powers of the tech giants have begun to reach for other legal instruments, particularly competition law, rather than privacy (O'Hara and Hall 2021, 117–124). Gavison's call for a commitment to privacy may be welcome, but is it realistic in the context of data-driven policymaking and the digital economy?

Level 7: rights, morality and politics

At level 7, we finally come to wrestle with the value of privacy, where most of the debate, variation and excitement are focused. We are in the region of ethics, politics (Westin 1967), rights (Thomson 1975), the contribution it makes to a functioning society (Rössler 2005) and its costs (Etzioni 1999). When I mention rights at level 7, I specifically mean moral rights. Judicial rights, backed by law, inevitably shaped by compromise and arbitrariness, are discussed at level 6. Moral rights are inalienable, but are pragmatically only as strong as the backbone of those who undertake to enforce them.

The question is often posed as 'why do *we* value privacy?' (e.g. Rössler 2005, 66, Solove 2008, 48). That 'we' builds complicity between author and reader – the author is probably an academic or jurist in a Western democracy, and the reader probably a graduate with political concerns and possibly a professional interest: *haut bourgeois* calling *haut bourgeois* like mastodons bellowing across the primeval swamp. That is an important conversation to have, but others have a view as well, and what looks sensible from the perspective of the ivory tower may well appear insular to others. Even in wealthy democracies, privacy is not a major concern (a 2021 British survey showed that 14 per cent picked it out as one of their top three concerns – CPS 2021).

The relatively comfortable and ordered life in Western democracies – from which I benefit and for which I refuse to feel guilty – is unusually serene. Many people across the world, perhaps a majority, are vulnerable to abuse, trauma, insecurity, sexual or other violence, or oppression on a regular or even daily basis, and privacy will have very different meanings for them than it does for autonomous self-confident individuals in safe cities. I don't have the expertise to report such experience with any kind of fidelity, but we should remember that the 'we' who discuss the value of privacy are a fairly parochial group. That does not mean that 'we' should not try to protect the privacy of 'our' liberal and prosperous lifestyles.

A couple of caveats. First of all, this chapter is a survey of a very large literature, so it has to be selective. It will focus on the interests of the 'we', since I am one of 'us'. Second, when I argue about values such as autonomy and intimacy, my point is not that they are bad (they are certainly not), nor that they are not aided by privacy (they generally are), but rather that they shouldn't be read as *the* value of privacy, *the* reason we should protect it, *the* nub of any proper account. My position, as I hope will be clear at the end, is inclusive rather than exclusive.

The value of privacy is not always positive

The moral discussion about privacy concerns the conditions under which it ought to be protected, and the types considered important. In any particular context, it is influenced by a range of factors, including live ethical and professional debates, the role of mass media, social media and interest groups in framing the issues, the extent of interest group and political activity generally, the wider technological and ideological scenes, and conflict between privacy claims and other social values (Westin 1967, 187). We can expect to criticise law, norms or personal psychology, but we shouldn't expect to read moral or political truths directly from these discourses. I don't go as far as Hume in saying that it is impossible to derive an ought from an is, but we should at least be aware which one we are speaking about.

The plumbing-in of kitchen sink definitions often happens at level 7, where commentators try to define privacy as a normative good, thereby getting into the pickles that (Solove 2008) described. Trying to restrict the definition to those types worth protecting can only mislead. 'Privacy is usually considered a moral interest of paramount importance. Its loss provokes talk of violation, harm, and loss of agency. Paradoxically privacy is also described as a condition that we should flee, promoting isolation, deprivation, separation' (Inness 1992, 7). Both of these 'paradoxical' sentences are true, at least sometimes.

It follows that there can be no categorical statement that privacy is normatively good or bad in general (Allen 1988, 18; Spacks 2003, 3), without illicitly reducing its scope. Inness, for instance, rejected the idea that privacy covers all information about someone, from grocery lists to love letters, and instead argued that because it only covers intimate information (as per her theory), the grocery list isn't private after all (1992, 6). This is a misdescription; the grocery list *is* private, though no big deal (it's certainly not public). If someone caught a sneaky glimpse of my list, I wouldn't care, unless (for example) it contained something embarrassing, like anti-flatulence pills. We could take that to mean that the presence of anti-flatulence pills on my list made it an intimate piece of information, but that would not accord with Inness' definition of 'intimate', which is to do with caring and loving (1992, 10). Perhaps I love my wife and do not wish to subject her to my flatulence, but more likely the real reason I care is self-directed embarrassment (I could be buying the pills for my neighbour, and love may not come into it). Well, we can get deeply into flatulence and intimacy but isn't it easier just to say that grocery list intrusion is a privacy breach that I wouldn't ordinarily bother about, but occasionally I do? People can be embarrassed by what they need to buy; in one focus group a participant admitted, to the amusement of the others, 'I used to feel really weird about buying toilet rolls because I think people would know that I go to [the] toilet' (Tsaousi and Brewis 2013, 11).

Note in passing that Inness was writing before the growth of e-commerce (Etzioni 1999, 211, is similarly dated). Now the contents of one's shopping basket, shopping lists and even the amount of time spent looking at a product are of immense importance for predictive analytics and other wheezes to increase revenue, and with more at stake privacy concerns have indeed reared their heads, even about shopping lists (Zuboff 2019; Baumann et al. 2019; Bandara et al. 2020).

Basing an account of privacy on rights or positive consequences reintroduces parochialism. For example, in early medieval Europe, rights and utilitarianism were alien at best, and yet there were certainly discourses of privacy and secrecy, and an all-seeing 'divine witness' gave a different moral landscape. At that time, the goodness or badness of privacy and secrecy were thought to follow from the intentions or mindset of the subject, leading to 'moral and sinful modes of concealment' (Saltzman 2019, 11). This may be a lost moral perspective on privacy that could reasonably be restored, and its loss may explain why trying to understand privacy through the lens of rights is so difficult.

Occasionally, the perspective resurfaces. Aldous Huxley's final novel, *Island*, written thirty years after *Brave New World* (*BNW*), depicts a utopia, Pala, governed by the use of more or less the same techniques but for human flourishing rather than decadence. Both societies used hypnotic and subliminal learning and constant broadcasting of slogans. In both places, familial relationships were suppressed because of their inappropriateness for rational child-rearing, sex was divorced from guilt and reproduction technologically managed. On Pala, privacy, individuality and autonomy were restricted, not to create the illusion of well-being via manipulation of preferences and the cultivation of superficiality as in *BNW*, but to prevent individual autonomy undermining social rationality, and to stop children being afflicted by the neuroses of their parents. *Island* invited the reader to reconsider the dystopia of *BNW*, arguing that the same techniques could be used for good ratified by science augmented by the mystic tradition that impressed Huxley so much. *BNW* was a dystopia because it suppressed privacy *for the wrong reasons* (O'Hara 2012, 174–176, 186–190). But Huxley's position remained a twentieth-century outlier outside the totalitarian ideologies (Arendt 2017).

Hence, given the plethora of privacy conceptions related by family resemblance, the level 7 question is: which ones are morally justifiable, which unacceptable and in what circumstances? This involves describing the value it provides when justifiable, which may be intrinsic or instrumental.

Intrinsic value

In one sense the intrinsic value of privacy is straightforward to argue. I value it very strongly, for its own sake. I like it, and want it. It might be countered that in a liberal society, freedom is all, and so people should be able to look, gossip, collect data or whatever unless the subject gives a good reason why they should refrain or be restrained (Rössler 2005, 125). Very well, my response is that I desire moments of withdrawal, solitude, intimacy and contemplation, and should be free to have those too. Won't that do? There is no contradiction between privacy-as-valuable-intrinsically and privacy-as-valuable-functionally; even an unconditional fan of privacy sometimes wants it for more practical purposes (a deadline approaching, a difficult conversation to have, a kiss to bestow, egg yolk to scrape off the tie). As Martin Kraemer pointed out to me most people's demands about privacy are rooted in relatively mundane concerns (Crabtree et al. 2017), but sometimes there may be no reason beyond preference. Indeed, rationalisation of such feelings and reduction to other terms, even if possible, may distort them. 'Even where a given habit of concealment is reflective and deliberate, its motive is far less often definite prudence than a vague aversion to having one's sanctity invaded and one's personal concerns fingered and turned over by other people' (William James quoted in Schoeman 1992, 20). The welfare recipient who said that 'It's not right. I have nothing to really hide, but it's just I don't think it is right that they have to know everything about you instead of just your income part' (quoted in Gilliom 2001, 50, see also 76) probably felt just that, and why is further justification required?

This may be a parochial attitude, not shared for instance in some Asian cultures that prize social harmony (Ess 2005, 2; O'Hara and Hall 2021, 128–129). Simmel's speculation of 1907 whether 'modern man can, under favourable circumstances, secure an island of subjectivity, a secret, closed-off sphere of privacy – not in the social but in a deeper metaphysical sense – for his most personal existence, which to some extent compensates for the religious style of life of former times' (2004, 469) placed intrinsic privacy centre stage of secular modernity, while noting its Christian ethical heritage. Jesus commanded 'Take heed that ye do not your alms before men, to be seen of them' (Matthew 6:1), because good acts may only be purely good when done in private; a public dimension opens up the possibility of social motivation (Arendt 1998, 74–78). This Christian ideal may have evolved into a Western intrinsic preference for privacy.

Parochial or not, there are people who have this preference, and I am one of them. The problem is that privacy's value relates to one's preferences, but one will struggle to make an impartial case that will convince governments, Mark Zuckerberg or nosy social scientists to leave one alone. It might even be said that the intrinsic view is an aspect of cognitive psychology, level 4 fodder, nothing to do with ethics (Solove 2008, 84–85). Reasons quickly give out if privacy is an intrinsic good: *de gustibus non disputandum est*. Can I give a non-tautological answer to the question 'what do you lose when you lose your privacy?' (Rössler 2005, 69)? This will matter in conflicts with other goods and values (Solove 2008, 87–88), which is perhaps why the right to be let alone has its attractions, even as an incomplete account of the moral rights of privacy; leave me alone and let me get on with it. For wider society devising a moral code, this isn't terribly useful (Benn 1971, 231–232).

It is of course possible to devise tiebreaks – for example, in the rules of a context as described by Nissenbaum's method, or within a legal taxonomy such as Solove's, or perhaps in the economic comparison of preferences – but these abdicate the moral ground and descend into more pragmatic discourses, always an issue with moral reasoning (Schueler 1995). There are good reasons why we need to be able to decide objectively between values in law courts – decisions have to be taken, and justice applied in such a way as to create precedent and so on. Politically, a question of privacy may ultimately be resolved by the power that each side is able to bring to bear, but morally, the question of how right prevails is not as simple. Even if I trounce opposing interests by argument and establish my moral claim, I can't guarantee that others will carry out their obligations to me. The problem with moral as opposed to legal rights is that it is everyone's duty, but no-one's job, to defend them.

Hence, if privacy is valuable intrinsically, we will be on a collision course with those who want to breach it, because we lack a potent means to dissuade them. It may simply involve the will to power, or smaller-scale rebellions and everyday resistance (Gilliom 2001, 96). No big reforms, debates in moral philosophy or long marches to Shaanxi but mini-dodges from 'all the law-bending, radar-detecting, tax-dodging residents in the land' (Gilliom 2001, 13), reaffirming their agency with trivial, even petty (if satisfying) disobedience.

Social functional value

To avoid privacy's value ultimately collapsing into a matter of taste, Solove argued that it should be assessed with respect to the contribution it makes to social goods, making it a constitutive element of civil society (2008, 90–93; Gavison 1980, 360). 'Privacy certainly protects the individual, but not because of some inherent right of respect for personhood. Instead, privacy protects the individual because of the benefits it confers on society' (Solove 2008, 98; O'Hara 2013). For example, protections against disclosure are supportive of democracy and free speech (Solove 2008, 143).

Democracy

Privacy may facilitate plural democratic politics. On this view, it characterises a private sphere that can be left behind during political engagement (Arendt 1998). Distinctive preferences and prejudices can be parked, allowing political actors to foster the outward-facing aspects of their selves and foreground the commonalities that enable the political community to function (including rationality, enabling diverse groups to interact critically in a discursive space – Habermas 1987). Thinking and reflection (the life of the mind) require privacy, and achieve maturity and practicality when brought out of the private space into public expression. This in turn adds substantive meaning to the public (political) sphere, thereby enhancing public discourse (Arendt 1978). The erosion of boundaries between the public and the private characteristic of modernity have been seen as troubling, leading to a conformist public space and hedonistic consumerism in private (Arendt 1968; Sennett 2002).

Information is raw material for discrimination, so privacy helps ensure equal treatment – 'privacy is justice's blindfold' (Véliz 2020, 86). 'Freedom ... flourishes in the indifference of privacy' (Shils 1956, 22), implying a world in which neither government nor fellow citizens pay too much attention to the affairs of others in the ordinary run of things, allowing colour/gender-blind governance, unfettered action and freedom of association – the last important because individual influence is multiplied by group action (Westin 1967, 26–27; Bloustein 1977, 279; Schoeman 1992, 156).

Democracies tolerate groups to act as counterweights to the power of the state, but totalitarian states demand absolute fealty, and cannot stomach 'factionalism' (Arendt 2017). Extremist groups and cults reduce privacy; everything is 'their business', and 'alternate relationships or beliefs' are not tolerated, 'locking daylight out of the picture' (Stein 2021, 13; Banisadr 2004). Links with wider society are deliberately diminished, creating a life spent in great tension with the surrounding culture (Stevens and O'Hara 2015). Charles Fourier's theoretical utopia Harmony, from the early nineteenth century, demanded communal education and living, with work allocated by groups of 'friends' depending on their assessments of skills and tastes (choice did not come into it). A sympathetic commentator wrote of Harmony that 'Communal life is so well-organized that to some it might appear more like a prison than a paradise' (Marshall 1993, 151–152).

On the other hand, the vision of democracy presented as a meeting of equal citizens in the public sphere may exclude groups which don't have the skills or connections to present their cases in ways acceptable to dominant groups, if the causes of difference and diversity are seen as matters of private relevance only. Habermas emphasised rationality, but 'in other ways, the ongoing editing of … political discourse can work to exclude marginal perspectives and undercut creative analysis as our language calcifies around fixed terms and categories' (Gilliom 2001, 79). Raab (2005) also pointed out that, where privacy is a means of achieving social goods, questions of its just distribution across genders, ethnicity, classes and income levels arise. For instance, social services oversample the poor, and so have more access to data about their vulnerabilities, a publicising of private matters that can work against them (Eubanks 2019, 157).

Conservatism

A less goal-driven ideological position, conservatism, claims that if an existing institution or social norm has been widely respected for a period of time, this in itself is reason to think that it serves some (possibly non-obvious) social function, and innovations that threaten it need careful scrutiny in order not to impair this function as an unintended consequence (O'Hara 2011). This does not mean that all aspects of current society get a free pass, only that an existing norm has value in a complex, dynamic world that may not be captured by the models of rationalist social engineers. Conservatism recognises that a familiar, legible society is a prerequisite for individuals to flourish (O'Hara 2021b).

Norms often encode practical moral wisdom learned over generations. 'We are afraid to put men to live and trade each on his own private stock of reason; because we suspect that this stock in each man is small, and that the individuals would be better to avail themselves of the general bank and capital of nations, and of ages' (Burke 1968, 183). Norm-following can be effective as a means of instilling moral behaviour (Peters et al. 2017); the liberal preference for autonomous beings rationally working out the right thing to do is less compelling. Hence if we see 'the practice of privacy, not as a right but as a system of nuanced social norms' (Schoeman 1992, 6), it will in turn support and be supported by other positive norms, giving a pertinent, predictable and conventional steer. The switch from the language of rights (what does society owe me?) to norms (how should I behave so that my fellows understand me?) helps to promote other-directed over self-directed behaviour.

Nissenbaum was nervous of the undoubtedly conservative implications of her theory of contextual integrity. We have 'a right to *context-appropriate* flows' of information (2010, 187, her emphasis), and 'a right to live in a world in which our expectations about the flow of personal information are, for the most part, met; expectations that are shaped not only by force of habit and convention but ... confidence in the mutual support these norms accord to ... social life' (2010, 231). The introduction of rights talk alongside the descriptive account of norms produced a clear level 7 statement of a conservative position that might have come from Burke.

But contextual integrity was only one input to her level 7 account. 'Although there is a presumption in favor of entrenched norms, the framework allows that novel flows ... might trump entrenched [ones] when these ... are more effective in promoting general and context-relative values, ends, and purposes' (Nissenbaum 2010, 232). On Nissenbaum's considered view, context-relative values require augmentation with a universal account of value in order to be sufficient for a moral theory; similarly, Rössler argued that while social philosophy needs to take existing norms into account, it should be critical of them (2005, 16–17). No serious conservative position includes uncritical support of the *status quo*, but when thinkers are more committed to their own ethical positions than settled social morality, values are imposed upon society from the top down – a attack on both pluralism and conservatism. Nissenbaum's official theory of contextual integrity fails as a theory of privacy's *value*, because of the prominence of the general ethical principles that she wanted to plug in. A purely conservative view would relegate any supposedly universal account to a subordinate role.

However, Nissenbaum and Rössler assumed too quickly that eschewing universal rights-based morality is necessarily an anti-progressive or pro-establishment position. Welfare claimants' vernacular critiques of rights make the point effectively; the account below juxtaposes what is given up by renouncing progressive philosophy with what is gained by preservation of context-relative norms and practical wisdom.

> [Claimants] advance arguments that make sense of the world and lead to agendas of action by centering attention on particular needs that emerge out of daily life and particular actions aimed at fulfilling their needs. While there is clearly much to be lost in the departure from the conventional languages of public conflict, what these claims and critiques based in particular need bring as an alternative to rights is important. What they may give up in nobility, they may gain in accessibility. What they may give up in their capacity to unite and universalize, they may gain in personal relevance. And what they may give up in their potential to lead to widespread demands for fundamental change, they may gain in the realization of short-term and much-needed little gains in the effort to get through the day. (Gilliom 2001, 12)

As the conservative novelist Joseph Conrad wrote, 'the world, the temporal world, rests on a few very simple ideas; so simple that they must be as old as the hills' (1912, xxi). The complexities, abstractions and casuistries beloved by academics and lawyers are no more worthy of respect than intuitive principles that have emerged from everyday practice, are practically applicable and easily recognisable in a colloquial idiom.

Virtue and practice

One further collective value for privacy worth mentioning stems from the Aristotelian idea that value derives from practice, so that if one is engaged in some professional behaviour or task, then certain positions with respect to privacy may be dictated by best practice in that profession. Most obviously, it is difficult to imagine the practices of medicine, accountancy or law functioning at all if there were not important guarantees of client confidentiality. The Hippocratic Oath, written three centuries before the birth of Christ, promises 'And about whatever I may see or hear in treatment, or even without treatment, in the life of human beings – things that should not ever be blurted out outside – I will remain silent, holding such things to be unutterable [i.e. sacred, not to be divulged]' (von Staden 1996, 407). The demand for privacy is often a key component of ethical sub-disciplines such as medical ethics or business ethics.

Such principles increase trust in practices and professions, and their motivations may be quite profane; they simultaneously (i) increase the profession's social standing, (ii) increase its political power, (iii) increase its earning potential, (iv) raise barriers to entry into the profession, and (v) help cover the backs of practitioners in the event of failure (Hughes 1958; Carter et al. 2015; Gallois et al. 2017). Additionally, however, there is often an internal connection between the conduct of a profession and respect for privacy within it – in other words, it would not be possible to be a doctor, accountant or lawyer (for instance) without protecting confidentiality. This is less an ethical judgement than functional; confidentiality is a *precondition* for receiving the information necessary to do the job. If clients did not trust that their sensitive information would be protected, then they would not volunteer it, which would impair the ability of the professional to provide the requisite services. This fits into a more general account of the virtues of valuable social practices and can be extended to cover less formal practices or group activities (MacIntyre 2007; Nissenbaum 2010, 166–178; O'Hara and Robertson 2017).

Individual functional value

Privacy is a prerequisite for a liberal society (Westin 1967, 26–28). Even if it does have social functional value, it must also be valuable to self-interested individuals. Hence, it is often defended 'by linking it to other values with long-standing moral, political, and legal pedigrees. ... [Privacy is] a form of and expression of self-ownership, an aspect of the right to be let alone, a cornerstone of liberty and autonomy, or a necessary condition for trust, friendship, creativity, and moral autonomy' (Nissenbaum 2010, 9). Empirically, Pedersen's survey uncovered several important goals for individuals who seek privacy. Contemplation is needed for planning and self-discovery, autonomy for experimentation, and for socially undesirable or disapproved-of behaviour. Recovery from adverse social experience required isolation and/or solitude. Confiding with others (including praying) also required isolation of confider and confidant together. Solitude was important for creativity, while isolation facilitated 'disapproved consumption' (i.e. eating and drinking those nice things that we get shouted at for enjoying). Other goals that could be achieved in the midst of other people under conditions of anonymity and/or reserve were recovery from serious social harm, catharsis (sharing emotions and new behaviour) and concealment (Pedersen 1997, 151–154).

Most straightforward is the libertarian view that people should be allowed to achieve their preferences when they are feasible, except where they might materially damage the interests of others (Berg 2018). For the libertarian, the job of the moralist is to try to ensure that preferences can be converted into actuality, for example via mechanisms of control. However, merely positing control does not automatically 'bring to light' an 'inherent normative moment' *contra* Rössler (2005, 8). Where privacy is cast as an individual right, the individual will always struggle to make their case if it seems that the community suffers in a zero sum game (Regan 1995; Etzioni 1999; Raab 2005; Rössler 2005, 101; Solove 2008, 89; Nissenbaum 2010, 85–88; O'Hara 2013).

Hence most liberal views temper the benefits to the individual with an account of the fit between individuals' valuations and the flourishing of liberal and/or democratic society. Privacy facilitates personal autonomy, key to the development of individuality (Westin 1967, 35–37). It protects a 'backstage' where individuals can indulge in emotional release, including sexual release, grief and those actions that act like a safety valve, like throwing darts at a picture of the boss (Goffman 1959; Westin 1967, 37–40). Or it may furnish a space for reflection, self-evaluation and selective communication with others (Westin 1967, 40–43). The values that have been most scrutinised in the literature are human dignity, personal identity, intimate relations, and individual autonomy.

Dignity

If privacy enables people to behave in authentic and socially respectable ways, respect for privacy is a kind of respect for persons (Inness 1992, 11). One basic formulation of the idea is respecting them as capable of judging their own interests and making rational choices (Benn 1971). Indeed, it is hard to imagine how rational choice could be possible in the absence of a private space in which to reflect (O'Hara 2021a).

However, that can't be the whole story. For instance, children gradually learn how to become rational choosers and as such are given increasing privacy by their parents as they grow older and make progress. This type of respect explains the parent–child relationship, but it doesn't really explain why even strangers usually (if not always) respect children's privacy. If I see someone else's four-year-old boy, I know that he is not a rational chooser yet, but I don't interfere in his decision-making or feel any responsibility to do so (except in emergencies, when he is about to throttle the hamster). Inness argued that this also misses the point that some rational choices are more important than others, and that privacy is particularly necessary to protect 'distinctive emotions' (1992, 11). Schoeman went further, pointing out that the choices we make – while looming large in liberal theory – don't play an enormous part in our lives, and our actions are more often influenced by factors we don't and cannot choose (1992, 158). In general, rational choice is a lofty, Brahmin view – few people have ever explicitly represented themselves as respecting rational choosers *per se*. If it simply means that we don't interfere in people's decisions, that is as likely to be norm-driven as deriving from respect of others' autonomous choices.

A more successful description of human dignity is the value protected by the right to be let alone: 'inviolate personality' (Warren and Brandeis 1890, 82), which was later posited as the link connecting the Prosser privacy torts, Fourth Amendment constitutional protections and Brandeis' celebrated dissent in *Olmstead* (Bloustein 1964, 166). The roots of inviolate personality are older, dating to the Romantic reaction to the Enlightenment's urban sensibilities (Sennett 2002, 150ff.; Spacks 2003, 55–56; Rosen and Santesso 2013). Whereas the eighteenth century saw the world as ultimately social, with philosophers such as Burke, Smith and Hume arguing that the personality (especially its moral core) developed socially during interactions with others, later thinkers registered the pressures and inauthenticity of urban life. Artists such as William Cowper began to crave withdrawal, because 'wisdom is a pearl with most success/Sought in still water', while later Romantics began to retreat into the self, extolling, with Wordsworth, 'the individual Mind that keeps her own/Inviolate retirement, subject there/To Conscience only, and the law supreme/Of that intelligence which governs all' (Spacks 2003, 201–216).

The individual personality, subject to its own dictates and withdrawn from human contact, evolved in the legal literature into the dignified personality demanding protection. This was glossed as 'the individual's independence, dignity and integrity ... as a unique and self-determining being' (Bloustein 1964, 163), a moral value supported by the law providing 'civil relief against turning a man's private life into a public spectacle as well as against impairing his private intimacies by intruding upon them ... by assuring [him] that his life is not the open and indiscriminate object of all eyes' (Bloustein 1964, 185). This value arises from the individual's mere existence, and Bloustein followed Warren and Brandeis in postulating a spiritual dimension to it. The Fifth Amendment, absolving people from incriminating themselves, was also cast along these lines: 'treatment which probes the conscience and seeks directly to change the internal processes of the personality ... denies [the prisoner] the right to set his own conscience in order' (Gerstein 1970, 253; Wasserstrom 1978, 322), connecting it directly with religious integrity.

There must be a question about whether spiritual argument is persuasive in our secular age, or indeed in a polity less inclined to religiosity than the United States. If not, then it will be essential to rescue somehow the main point that an intrusion into dignity goes beyond contingent psychological harms such as 'distress, anguish, humiliation, despair, anxiety, mental illness, indignity, mental suffering, and psychosis' even if it is their cause. '[A]t issue is not a form of trauma, mental illness or distress, but rather individuality or freedom' (Bloustein 1964, 187).

Identity

A more sophisticated view transcends respect for the individual, to focus on protecting the processes necessary for nurturing or achieving the self. Jeffrey Reiman argued that privacy 'protects the individual's interest in becoming, being, and remaining a person', underlying 'moral ownership' of the individual's body (1976, 314). Privacy provides a space (the Goffmanian backstage) in which people can organise themselves, create the impressions they want to create and be understood as they wish to be understood. There are many mechanisms and resources for this, ranging from improvised private spaces to protecting secrets. It has even been argued that underwear, private to the wearer, can help mould a personality, acting as 'a resource for identity construction', and in particular 'bolstering [women's] cultural capital' (Tsaousi and Brewis 2013, 1, 2; Wood 2016).

Philip Agre defined the right to privacy as 'the freedom from unreasonable constraints on the construction of one's own identity' (1998, 7). Mireille Hildebrandt endorsed this definition as rendering explicit the relationship between privacy and identity, bringing in notions of a mutable and vulnerable self, implying that privacy is emergent, connecting it to liberty, and also making an association with what is reasonable and unreasonable (2015, 80).

It certainly packs a lot in, a whole theory of and outlook on the importance of privacy and the construction of the self, but is this a strength? Like Napoleon's stretched supply lines, it is vulnerable to attack from a number of directions. It explicitly deploys philosophically sophisticated concepts that would be unlikely to feature in any ordinary language account of privacy, or in the justifications that surface in normal social situations and conflicts (outside law courts and university seminar rooms).

Most episodes of reasonable privacy have little or nothing to do with identity, so it may be too particular an account. The Tsarist-era *provocateur* Vasili Rozanov's definition of private life was 'picking your nose and looking at the sunset' (quoted in Huxley 1978, 114–115). If we do these things, are we really constructing our identities? While many episodes (such as intimate sexual moments) do give us freedom to express ourselves without interference and explore possible selves, others screen us off without giving much leeway to experiment or to vary the normal order of things (Schoeman 1992, 15). Identity construction is surely a minority sport, while quotidian activities which leave identity unchanged still require privacy (Spacks 2003, 172), and shouldn't we have rights to (some of) these as well?

The inclusion of reasonableness brings a hint of circularity. No one is in favour of unreasonable constraints upon themselves, while everyone accepts constraints that they believe reasonable. So it follows automatically from the definition that everyone is in favour of privacy. So why do so many people willingly sacrifice their data to social networks, for example? It is a consequence of the definition that no one whose data is being processed, shared and sold with consent suffers a breach of their privacy rights, because in their view *nothing unreasonable can be happening to them.* The privacy paradox may tell us that users behave inconsistently with some of their core beliefs, but if they willingly use the site, they seem to endorse the view that it is acting reasonably, and therefore their rights to privacy cannot be violated in this respect.

Furthermore, it doesn't seem unlikely that many important identity-forming moments involve interaction, and unwelcome interaction at that, with others, family members, strangers and those in authority. Identity has a social aspect, and it may well require unwilling sociability, observance (even surveillance) and loss of autonomy. 'I form the consciousness of being the author of my acts in the world ... principally on the occasion of my contacts with an other, in a social context' (Ricoeur 1966, 56–57); 'the more privatised the psyche, the less it is stimulated' (Sennett 2002, 4). Socialisation may be inevitable to give language, and even experiences and mental states, coherence (Wittgenstein 1953, §§243ff.); 'the form of the self is one which is conventional' (Mead 1934, 209). While many think that the subject must remain in control, so that 'this dialogical dimension must not eclipse the *monological* component that must be provided by the subject if he truly wants to see himself as autonomous' (Rössler 2005, 133, her emphasis, and again Mead 1934), others go so far as to say that social definition of the self requires conflict (MacIntyre 2007, 31).

Knowing oneself depends on knowing and being known by others (Hegel 1977; Mead 1934; Sartre 1958; Benn 1971, 227). I must recognise (i) a world out there distinct from me, in which (ii) some things are also knowing, perceiving subjects, who (iii) reciprocally perceive me as a knowing, perceiving subject, from which it follows that *I must be aware* that I am perceived as such. This requires exposure to others. 'A person, perhaps, is best seen as one who was long enough dependent upon other persons to acquire the essential arts of personhood. Persons essentially are *second* persons' (Baier 1985, 94, her emphasis).

In early years, such dependence must involve intimate interaction, usually within a family, where privacy of the small nurturing group will be valuable (see Part V, Level 1). Attentional and decisional privacy of the family enables the selection of good or bad influences by primary carers. Beyond that, interactions become less and less censored (and censorable), and the focus shifts to the decisional privacy of the individual adult, able to choose, to an extent, the people they interact with.

Sartre was troubled by how 'the look of the other' would circumscribe the possibilities for the subject, precipitating 'the solidification and alienation of my own possibilities' (Sartre 1958, 263). The opinion of the other as to the subject's identity is influential. This is one reason why privacy is important for theories of autonomy and identity, because greater privacy means less influence from others. While the look of the other isn't a physical constraint impacting on liberty, it is a restriction on decisional privacy (Rössler 2005,

151–152). Whether Sartre's complaints were merely routine existentialist *angst*, kicking against the pricks of sociability ('hell is other people', as he also wrote), is beyond the scope of this book, but without interaction, the individual is virtually powerless to achieve anything, even if that interaction closes down possibilities – constraint within a cooperative relationship need not be alienating.

The weight of the look of the other may depend on a number of factors. In level 3, I cited the male gaze as a constraint on women's autonomy. Social emotions such as guilt and disappointment can support or undermine our self-image, while suggesting the bounds of our selves to us (Albahari 2006, 141). Our social and moral responsibilities depend on the actions that are ours, help define us, and are negotiated with others (Schechtman 1996, 17), so that 'we are never more (and sometimes less) than the co-authors of our narratives. Only in fantasy do we live what story we please' (MacIntyre 2007, 213). On this view, the look of the other inhibits the subject's agency, while also making a palette of actions available to them (i.e. the subject). To get the balance between potential and inhibition correct, different types of privacy may need to be pursued and balanced against each other. Meanwhile, of course, others do not passively accept the subject's own decisions, but themselves pursue their own strategies. Our dissonant identities and distinct social roles are part of this dialectic, and may need to be kept private in a *cordon sanitaire* (Schoeman 1992, 133–135; Rössler 2005, 185–192), but as they cannot be the only salient factors, they cannot be the sole justification of the right to privacy. External influences are so important and pervasive that it must prove a Sisyphean task to separate the reasonable from the unreasonable constraints, as Agre required.

Agre's characterisation may be more salient in a technological context. Hildebrandt noted that surveillance by online data infrastructure has the partial sense of the look of the other, but without the reciprocity that even Sartre had to concede. The subject of surveillance is unable to understand the perceptive capacities of the surveillant architecture (even if the subject is aware of the use of online data, they are highly unlikely to know the full extent and purpose of the surveillance). Part of the solution, for Hildebrandt, is the counter-profiling of the surveillant systems to restore (some) reciprocity (2015, 222–224), although my intuition is that this still leaves too much on the individual's shoulders, who would often prefer to be let alone than to be empowered in this way.

Intimacy

Identity as the locus of value for privacy looks unlikely to succeed to general satisfaction, as the ideas are so complex and open-ended that they complicate rather than clarify. A potentially simpler route is to find its value in its contribution to *intimacy*, not for the close relationships it actually produces but social respect for the autonomy of an individual to develop intimate relationships (Arendt 1998, 38; Fried 1968; Gerstein 1978; Inness 1992, 95–112; Schoeman 1992, 20–22). Clearly intimacy is important, and privacy important for it.

However, we will struggle to make a *conceptual* link between the two, for example using the language of human rights (cf. Schoeman 1992, 1). Privacy is conceived as an individual right (Inness 1992, 45–46) and often involves the solitude of an individual (Silber 2002, 77), while the state of intimacy involves more than one person. We would also have to deal with the paradox that, if privacy for the intimates is increased relative to outsiders, it is diminished relative to each other (Altman 1975, 22). These issues could no doubt be hedged around with caveats and epicycles, but it would make for a messy theory.

A more basic problem in demanding a strong link between the two is that intimacy itself, though a more familiar idea than identity or dignity, is not easy to define. Inness defined it in terms of care, liking and love, and intimate relationships as 'characterized by considerations such as consent, fairness, and mutuality' (1992, 79), which seems to problematise, for example, the relationship between a mother and her baby. Solitary and lonely individuals have claims to privacy as well (Reiman 1976, 307–308), so we need to be shown how to transcend paradigm cases. Inness' view was that privacy shows our respect for others' capacity to *form* intimate relationships (1992, 95), although her claim that someone who had led a life devoid of caring and love 'lacked a dimension of person-hood' (1992, 106) seems strong.

Her account is nevertheless more plausible than Gerstein's alternative, in which intimacy is a kind of ecstatic inner state which requires privacy to be sustainable. Such a state may, if shared, be classed as a type of intimacy, but it is hardly characteristic of common intimate relationships, such as mother/baby, or the loving routine of a long-term marriage. Gerstein himself discussed sex and mystical religious experience, which hardly exhaust the sphere of intimate behaviour, and surely can't determine the limits of privacy rights (1978, 265–267).

Fried (1968) argued that privacy was necessary for intimacy, which again appears too strong (cf. Part III, Level 3). The ability to secure privacy fairly easily may simply be one of the privileges of living in a wealthy and secure society, becoming connected with intimacy thanks to social conditioning. 'Sexual intercourse could be just as pleasurable in public (if we grew up unashamed) as is eating a good dinner in a good restaurant' (Wasserstrom 1978, 331). In Huxley's *Brave New World*, different kinds of friendship have become valued – ones that appear superficial from the reader's perspective, based on liking, mutual hearty activities, and promiscuous sex. Deep friendship and committed relationships are seen as detrimental to the social order, and so privacy, and the demand for it, are frowned upon. Only anti-hero Bernard Marx has a positive preference for privacy and intimacy in his search for meaningful relationships, the result of which being that he never has any relationships at all, so strange and 'other' does he seem to his fellows. Huxley described a detailed and convincing, though fictional, world in which privacy has lost its gloss because of its inability to deliver valuable consequences.

Huxley was satirising the jazz age, but might have been skewering our own society mediated by social networks, in which algorithms propose social (Facebook), professional (LinkedIn) and sexual (Tinder, Grindr) relationships for us. The choices that we exercise are no longer substantive and constitutive of identity, demanding privacy and space to reflect on them (Benn 1971), but rather a process of selection from a recommendation list, which is more likely to provide satisfactory choices the more transparent we are to the algorithm (O'Hara 2021a). As a result of gradual social and technological change, the contribution privacy makes to the development and maintenance of our intimate relationships has morphed, even diminished, if not disappeared entirely.

If we leave the wealthier democracies, overcrowded and inadequate housing is a day-to-day problem and a way of life in many parts of the world (Altman 1975, 38), and don't necessarily impact as powerfully on those who have practised means of negotiating their privacy (Biswas-Diener and Diener 2009). Where there are serious and demonstrable constraints on the autonomy of individuals (particularly girls), several factors are usually in play, including poverty, insecurity of various kinds, patriarchy and lack of education, and whatever privacy the household has managed to secure may be part of the problem for intimacy of its members rather than the solution (MacKinnon 1987; Rössler 2005, 20; Rashid 2006). 'Within restricted physical environments, norms of family privacy and intimacy are laid bare.' Such environments can be 'physically constraining ... morally challenging ... and ... structurally violent' but 'Intimacy in this context is both a negotiation of personal space and a space for sustaining intimate relationships' (Datta 2016, 328). Development may not help immediately; slum clearance schemes in Victorian England, it has been argued, *reduced* privacy because they 'were designed to bring the poor out into the open, where they could be observed, reproved, and instructed by their superiors' (Olsen 1974, 276). These are complex and difficult issues, but we need to transcend a Western framework if we are going to talk about the *essential* contribution of privacy, as opposed to a more limited and relative claim (Bolotta 2019). If we relativise Fried's argument to the social strata in which he moved, however, then we must delete the assertion of necessity.

In certain areas, privacy is *detrimental* to the formation of successful close relationships. Parents only gradually allow their children privacy, letting them make mistakes that are not too devastating, slowly learning about relationships and what is and is not appropriate. With privacy, they would make more, and more problematic, mistakes. Online, young people's privacy from their parents is relatively easy to achieve, and sometimes puts them in danger, for instance from grooming (Williams et al. 2012; Wood and Wheatcroft 2020).

Privacy-as-intimacy also struggles to account for abusive relationships. Because she defined intimacy in terms of care, Inness felt she could safely ignore abusers' claims to privacy (1992, 89–90). Yet this is doubly mistaken. First, despite all that one might hope, both perpetrators and victims have been known to cling strongly to the belief that abuse is driven by (and evidence of) love. Those studying the area have felt the need to acknowledge this at least sometimes to represent the complexities in such relationships accurately (Power et al. 2006; Pocock et al. 2019). It is suggestive, if not decisive, that this area is labelled Intimate Partner Violence (IPV) in healthcare. Inness cited social norms of intimacy to try to get round this problem (1992, 87), but whether this is sufficient is moot, particularly if a patriarchal society with few rights for women is under consideration.

Even if we grant its sufficiency, a second problem is that, by ruling abusive relationships out of scope, she negated the force of the powerful argument that privacy in the home can be a means for abusers to ration outsider access to their victims (MacKinnon 1987). Given the prevalence of support for justifications of spousal abuse, and beliefs that women even benefit from such ill-treatment (Haj-Yahia 2002; Khawaja et al. 2008; Linos et al. 2010), this uncomfortable point about the dangers of private space should not be lost in a technical argument about whether or not the spaces are *really* private.

What about non-abusive transactional relationships? Inness suggested that paid sex is not intimate, because it is not motivated by love or care, and therefore not private (1992, 76). Gerstein, leaning on Scheler's phenomenology of shame (Scheler 1987; Emad 1972), argued that 'one of the functions of sexual shame [is] to distract the lovers' attention from the sexual organs so that the way will be open for the experience of genuine intimacy' (Gerstein 1978, 269), i.e. a rapturous feeling transcending the merely physical. But this too is surely mistaken.

First of all, it seems a stretch to say that sex is not an intimate matter even when totally transactional. Physical intimacy will often be prominent, with a direct and pleasant focus on the sexual organs. This focus, incidentally, is not necessarily 'an indulgence of selfish satisfactions' (Gerstein 1978, 269), as it also applies to sex between emotionally intimate partners. Second, commodified encounters need not be devoid of emotional aspects (Sanders 2008; Jones and Hannem 2018). Conversely, expectations of the psychological benefits of close intimacy are increasingly associated with a wider range of social experiences (Sennett 2002, 5). Inness' attempt to dissociate unemotional fornication from intimacy appears to be influenced by her correlation of justified privacy claims with the privacy protections supported by the US Supreme Court. Of course, the Court is not likely to find sex work deserving of constitutional protection, but how indicative is this?

Clearly this is a whole industry that lives in the shadows. Even if there is no reasonable expectation of either privacy, favourable treatment from the law, or a sympathetic moral hearing, it creates undeniably strong demand for privacy. Sex workers have strong privacy preferences for obvious reasons, and construct separate identities and compartmentalise their lives in order to achieve them (Raguparan 2017, 71–72). Architectures for prostitution, both physical and online, trade privacy affordances off against the industry's requirement for marketing (Ashworth et al. 1988, 209). Research into sex work walks straight into complex demands for privacy, security and ethics (Dewey and Zheng 2013). It would seem impossible to describe the situation of workers or clients without some reference to privacy, even if the industry is unprotected in law.

Inness triangulated the exclusively emotional aspects of intimacy with the practice of the US legal system, hoping thereby to get an account of the value of privacy in terms of intimacy. The upshot was the exclusion of areas of life which are commonly labelled 'intimate', and in which the demand for privacy features strongly. Paradigm cases of intimacy, where fragrant people do fragrant things for fragrant reasons, are well worth protecting, but provide little guidance as to how we should extrapolate to imperfect people, sleazy things or self-indulgent reasons – the harder cases to judge.

We observe the notion of intimacy changing almost before our eyes. Fried, and Gerstein especially, described a rarefied vision of intense, sexual, ecstatic, spiritual love, but by 1992 Inness was including practical, unromantic decisions focused on the body, such as abortion and contraception, while widening the field to encompass everyday relationships of love and care, including

Platonic ones. Today's mores might demand a wider focus still further to include consensual relations, with protection against unwelcome and non-consensual encounters. Inness suggested that touching a woman's shoulder would not count as an invasion of her privacy (1992, 9), but three decades later, following #MeToo, I have witnessed women criticise men strongly for attracting their attention by doing precisely that. Meanwhile, our age is probably too cynical to entertain an idealistic account of intimacy like Gerstein's any more. Discussions of intimacy veer easily into the realm of sexual intimacy, although this is only one type of intimate relationship. Given these dramatic changes over a relatively short period of time, it seems highly unlikely that they will suddenly cease to evolve. Intimate relationships are undoubtedly valuable, but for those who want to ground privacy rights on them, they may prove to be shifting sands.

Autonomy

Arguments about privacy-as-intimacy stress the autonomy of individuals to choose their relationships. This suggests that the net might be cast more widely to value privacy for its support for autonomy in all spheres of life. Indeed, on the implausible privacy-as-control model, privacy *is* a type of autonomy, the ability to determine how one appears to others, especially informationally.

If the *value* of privacy was its support for autonomy, we could locate its advantages in, for example, enabling a Goffmanian backstage, allowing roles to be challenged, adapted and disrupted (Schoeman 1992, 20–22, 156; Sennett 2002, 35–36), and removing chilling effects and self-censorship to avoid negative feedback. It could help us avoid coercion (Nissenbaum 2010, 81–84), including the gathering of data to amend the choices open to us (Zuboff 2019; Hildebrandt and O'Hara 2020), and intensive surveillance leading to compliance through fear (Gilliom 2001, 129–130). Schoeman summarised the resulting social freedom as 'having opportunities to pursue with others significant ends without enduring unfair and unreasonable social sacrifices' (1992, 193).

Beate Rössler's account of privacy's support for autonomy is the most complete and general, and raises important issues for level 7.

Her overarching goal was the protection of liberal democracy, and she argued that the ability to live a self-determined, autonomous and authentic life relies on principles of civil liberties being expressed concretely in the practices and norms of privacy (2005, 10, 81). From a different direction, Gerstein came to a similar conclusion, arguing that protecting criminals' rights (against self-incrimination) would be 'fraudulent' if based merely on their civil liberties, because that would indefensibly undermine victims' liberties for the benefit of the guilty. Defences of criminals' rights had to be firmly rooted in respect for the privacy and dignity of all (1970, 260). Hence civil liberties demand the protection of the practice of privacy in society as an essential precondition.

Rössler was most interested in decisional privacy, supporting individuals in social relations, informational privacy, securing their expectations about others' views of them, and spatial privacy, for withdrawal and reflection (2005, 17–18). Some of her other remarks implied attentional privacy and psychological privacy from the reference list are also important. Autonomous individuals must have all these to decide authentically what kind of life they wish to live, and to take steps to achieving it. Informational privacy is the most important; if this is breached without their knowledge, they act on the basis of a false model of their social contexts (2005, 117). Cervantes' *Don Quixote* illustrates this brilliantly; in Part 2 of the novel, virtually all of the characters have read Part 1, published ten years earlier, and are fully aware of Quixote's delusions, enabling them to exploit him for their own entertainment.

For Rössler, autonomy is the prior and more important notion – privacy's value is contingent on its success in securing autonomy (2005, 26). Resting the value of privacy on adventitious grounds opens up the possibility of its being downgraded when it fails. With Rössler's account, the risk is evident, because she holds autonomy to very high standards.

While she resisted feminist arguments that autonomy is an individualistic, self-interested, power-fixated idea inimical to relations of care and commitment (2005, 102–106), she was unable to accept standard liberal accounts of the private space as a refuge from scrutiny and the foundation of the public realm, which cannot 'bring to fruition the proposal of equal liberties for all' (2005, 31–33). She required autonomy to be equally distributed, but argued that it is not. Women in particular have always been denied freedom in the home (Rössler 2005, 24–25, 40; Stetson 1898): (i) women are typically assigned roles as keepers of the household; (ii) this impacts on their ability to take opportunities outside the home; (iii) they do an unfair share of housework and maintenance of the household; (iv) this impacts negatively on their social status; (v) children are socialised within households, influencing their own gender identities and keeping the cycle going (2005, 158). A truce between feminism and Rössler's austere liberal democracy was anchored on the propositions that privacy is crucial for reproducing the gender order, that autonomy is not achieved even in the private household, and therefore privacy in the home, on current social norms, is of low value. It is contradictory for the liberal to defend household privacy for that reason (2005, 20), which led her to reject arguments, such as Arendt's and Shils', that the private space should be free from scrutiny (2005, 106–110).

She appeared to respect an ideal private sphere, arguing for instance that 'everything (legitimately)' done within the home should be protected (2005, 124). On almost all understandings of the status of social norms, norm-following is a heuristic route to being an ethical person, turning virtue into a habit (Burke 1968, 183), and is therefore arguably legitimate. But Rössler stayed firm on the lack of freedom for women in the household, so that norm-following there *betrays* the freedom of the individual and is therefore *not* legitimate (cf. her critique of communitarianism – 2005, 98–102). Since most of humanity since the year dot, even now, adheres voluntarily and even enthusiastically to highly gendered household norms, it seems to follow that there has been little or no autonomy throughout human history (cf. Habermas 1989, 46–48), and that therefore the value of privacy and the private sphere, which consists in its support for autonomy, has been vastly overrated.

But the difficulties of this as a defence of privacy should now be clear. If the private space is problematic, then it is arguably legitimate for the state, or moral authorities (even social networks), to interfere in home life to adjust it in the 'right' direction (Rössler 2005, 155). This raises a series of conflicts, between the freedom of the individual and the liberal insistence on equal autonomy, between the public realm of justice and the private realm of intimacy, and in what Habermas called 'the colonization of the lifeworld', where rule-based administrative systems impinge on the humane inner rationality of an intimate group (1987, 367–373; Rössler 2005, 157). Insisting on public standards of justice in the home means that conventional modes of conduct cannot be morally permissible or socially countenanced even in what is traditionally understood as the private sphere (2005, 166).

Where is the backstage now? Although Rössler quoted Goffman with approval (2005, 149), it is not obvious how it will survive this scrutiny. Her response was that sanctioned social interference must address types rather than tokens, drawing attention to *structures* of domination. 'It was evident that [lack of autonomy in the household] had just as much to do with *individual* relations, families and persons, yet these were not necessarily of interest as individual cases, but at most as paradigms' (2005, 178, her emphasis). So interference may take the form of proselytising and agitprop, rather than intrusion.

Yet this hardly solves the problem. In the first place, it is still a breach of decisional privacy if members of the household are shamed into altering their practices. If 'privacy ... prevents interference, pressures to conform, ridicule, punishment, unfavourable decisions, and other forms of hostile reaction' (Gavison 1980, 363; and indeed Rössler 2005, 85), how could such proselytising have a positive effect on degendering the household without breaches of decisional privacy? Second, some sort of measurement or accounting of the norms in the individual (token) household is required if it is to be established that the people within it are properly autonomous, and therefore that their privacy is valuable enough to defend.

Rössler argued that 'the liberal concept of privacy is ... fundamentally contradictory' (2005, 20). The contradiction she detected was one between moral and social norms, levels 7 and 5. The contradiction only appears when we try to cash out the value of privacy in terms of autonomy, because the moral norms in question are only tangentially to do with privacy. If we suspend the connection of privacy and autonomy, we may take advantage of three potential responses. First, Rössler's own, is to use the moral norms to critique the social norms, and demand equal autonomy in the home. Second, a conservative response, is to critique the moral norms with the social norms, holding the existing standards of the home to outweigh autonomy. The third response is to deny there is even a clash, by denying that liberalism's moral norms reach down into the household. This is in effect the position of John Locke, John Stuart Mill and John Rawls (Rössler 2005, 27–33). One reading of Mill's harm principle 'that the sole end for which mankind are warranted, individually or collectively, in interfering with the liberty of action of any of their number, is self-protection' (Mill 1991, 14), is that 'self' includes 'household', and so 'mankind' should cede the moral regulation of the household to its members. Hence it would be illegitimate to interfere on the basis of moral principles held, however sincerely, by outsiders.

Hence the commitment to privacy as a means of delivering equal autonomy ends up, upon collision with the reality of imperfect social norms, *undermining* the privacy of the household, bearing out an oft-repeated criticism of liberals' attitude to those it hopes to free:

> in the liberal tradition, communities – such as family and nation – were not believed to have independent existence [from their individual members] and therefore have always been looked at with suspicion ... a natural object of ... critique, and ... attack, because they were seen as power structures of an alien and nondemocratic nature. (Legutko 2016, 92, 94)

Reductionism

Functional accounts of privacy such as those in the last two sections may ultimately be reductionist (Rössler 2005, 69–71). If privacy has a function, then rights to it can be glossed as rights to that function, and then what additional role does the right to privacy have?

Rössler's own account is illustrative. She envisaged a substantive role for privacy in securing autonomy (2005, 72–73), but its disappointing expression in the real world meant that its function became a stick to beat it with. We ended up in a reductionist position even while trying to avoid it, as privacy has a role to play but does not play it. It thus needs to be *sacrificed* to ensure its *function* is implemented (we need to put private space under surveillance to prove that everyone in it has autonomy). 'Man can become his own creator, completely self-determining only in a completely trans-parent society' (Shils 1997, 166), which turns out to be also true of Woman.

Whether reductionism is a stable position is doubtful. Thomson's classic argument claimed that privacy rights can be reduced to a cluster of other rights, especially to property and personhood (1975). Yet that does not entail priority of one kind over the other (Inness 1992, 29). Even if privacy rights were examples of another kind of right, they could still be a special case, deserving of different and more rigorous moral treatment (Inness 1992, 120–121).

Inness certainly had a point that Thomson didn't try very hard to detect commonalities in the privacy rights she discerned (Inness 1992, 30). Thomson focused on the examples of possessing a pic-ture (a property issue) and eavesdropping on an argument (a person-hood issue, attentional privacy in the reference list). For Thomson, the question of deciding what is a privacy *right* – i.e. when privacy has normative force – is a two-stage process, although this was only implicit in her account. Some event E happens or is anticipated. Stage one is to determine whether or not E is a privacy breach. If it is, stage two is to determine whether I have a right to be protected against it or whether I just have to lump it. Thomson did not dis-cuss stage one, because she took it as uncontroversial that we can recognise a breach when we see one.

On the other hand, Inness problematised stage one, and ignored stage two, expecting that identifying privacy would, via her kitchen sink definition, also deliver an account of what privacy rights were appropriate. This is the anticipated advantage of a common con-ceptual and normative core of privacy (Inness 1992, 32) but can't be realised because it mixes up the conceptual (level 1) and the moral (level 7).

Does it make sense to talk of privacy in the absence of rights to it? Of course. Suppose I am at a football match with a large crowd. I need to make a sensitive phone call, and so I need some privacy, but I am surrounded by fans. There is nowhere private. But surely, despite *having* no privacy, I have no *right* to privacy in the football ground for this purpose. The owners are not responsible for finding me a private space to make my phone call, and I cannot find them in the wrong for failing. A stage one analysis tells us that my privacy is breached: wherever I stand, my call cannot be made without risk of being overheard. The stage two analysis is that I have no right to privacy there, and I will have to wait until the game is over, or alternatively leave the ground, to make my call. Conversely, if I do find privacy (in the café, say), that is a lucky happenstance, but nothing I had a right to.

Thomson's argument can be rephrased like this. At stage one, we need to decide whether or not E is a privacy breach, putting our native speaker *nous* to work. Then stage two requires a normative argument. However, only some types of what we recognise as privacy deserve normative protection. But because neither native speaker competence, nor a use-based enumeration such as the reference list, is a good guide to privacy *rights*, as opposed to privacy *tout court*, any argument for a positive normative valuation of privacy needs to come from elsewhere. Where better, concluded Thomson, than related but better-understood rights such as property (Westin 1967, 362–363) and personhood?

Having said that, she hardly established her case. With respect to property rights, the affective pre-legal relationship of ownership, and its treatment by law are philosophically complex (Austin 2013; Ripstein 2013). Do we have property rights because property is private or privacy rights over it because it is property? Inness argued that they must be separable since privacy claims often extend beyond property claims (1992, 33). It's a nice question beyond the scope of this book; Inness' examples of love letters and diaries, which she characterised as property, aren't decisive because they might also be seen as related to personhood because of their content (1992, 37).

Thomson's personhood example was when 'my husband and I are having a quiet fight behind closed windows and cannot be heard by the normal person who passes by'. Someone who points an amplifier at the window 'violates our right not to be listened to, which is one of the rights included in the right over the person' (1975, 280). One problem here is that the right not to be listened to is a relatively blunt instrument compared to any privacy rights we may have. If someone trains an amplifier on an argument, then he can listen to the conversation. This finds its place in the reference list as a subtype of attentional privacy. However, there is a subtle difference between the violation of personhood rights not to be listened to, and many conceptions of privacy in this respect. Specifically, on a standard conception of attentional privacy, if Mr and Mrs Thomson are having a firm and frank exchange of views (they did in fact divorce in 1980), someone breaches their privacy only if they actually understand what is said. If the eavesdropper pays little attention, or is a non-English speaker, then, whether or not what they have done is reprehensible and an affront to personhood, they haven't actually breached the Thomsons' *privacy*, at least as they intended, despite their attempt to.

To make that clear, we can distinguish three obviously related but separate conceptions of attentional privacy relevant to this example, breached in the following (different) ways: (i) pointing an amplifier at the argument and hearing it; (ii) pointing an amplifier at the argument, hearing it and understanding/remembering/noting what is said; and (iii) pointing an amplifier at the argument, and recording it, allowing it to be deciphered at leisure. Someone who only managed breach (i) clearly has more access than the Thomsons desire but still doesn't know much – he probably guesses that they had a row via tone of voice, but he doesn't know what about. While we are being completist, we might note a fourth type of privacy breach (inspired by Inness 1992, 34). In (i) to (iii), the intruder is not noticed, but (iv) if the battling Thomsons see the intruder across the street, they might quite naturally cease their argument, so here their *decisional* privacy has been breached and their freedom of action duly curtailed. It is not clear that the richness of the range of possibilities here can be captured by the personhood account *without* resort to the different conceptions of privacy subtended by the technology of remote amplification. That would seem to rule out the reduction of privacy rights to personhood rights.

One potential reply from Thomson would be that the personhood rights appear coarser-grained because we waive our privacy-as-personhood rights in trivial circumstances. Inness demurred, by considering twin examples of someone looking through my window (a) with a momentary glance while passing, and (b) staring for the whole day. On the reductionist privacy-as-personhood account, each of these would have to be seen as a violation of a right, but they are clearly not equal (Nissenbaum 2010, 73). (A) is trivial, (b) serious, but Inness found it implausible that the difference in our responses could be explained by a waiver of rights.

But how have I waived my privacy in those instances but not in the other ones? My behavior has remained the same, while the other's changes, but it is *I* who have waived my Thomsonian right. She could also argue that a nonwaived right to privacy exists in both cases, the difference being that I hold the right to privacy as less stringent in certain situations. (Inness 1992, 35, her emphasis)

This latter option once more requires explication in terms of different conceptions of privacy, and won't work as a reductionist account.

Inness' argument doesn't do the trick, however. When privacy and privacy rights are elided in a kitchen sink definition, then inevitably one has to deal with trivial breaches with the heavy artillery of rights discourse, and of course this appears odd. Inness wrote of 'privacy violation claims', but without a clear separation this is ambiguous between claims that *privacy* was breached and claims that *rights* were violated. Inness misrepresented Thomson in her reconstruction of the argument – one does not 'waive one's privacy', as she put it, but rather one waives one's *rights*. One can *surrender* one's privacy (for example, by standing in the window open to scrutiny), but if privacy is breached it is breached full stop, whether or not one is complicit and whether or not any rights have been waived or claimed.

Plural privacy conceptions connected by family resemblance enable us to put some distance between Inness' two examples, and so complete the case against Thomsonian reductionism. While they are both breaches of attentional privacy (b) is, as Inness pointed out, in a different league to (a), because (a) is accidental and (b) deliberate. It is hard to argue that exactly the same thing is going on in the two examples; the conceptions of privacy subtended are different (for example [b] would allow note-taking and the observation of significant pieces of behaviour).

When it comes to rights, it is hard to say how they can have been breached in (a); since the glance was accidental, the unwitting passer-by certainly bears no responsibility. In (b), my *privacy* is clearly breached by someone staring in. I have not in this case waived my rights – my privacy is breached, and the waiver question concerns only what I want to do about it. If I do have privacy rights here, I can waive them either by tacitly consenting to the staring (e.g. continuing to behave normally and disregarding the snooper), or by taking no action afterwards. Or I can pursue them by holding the intruder to account as best I can.

Hence the rights situation varies across the different conceptions of privacy breached, and so whatever story we tell about privacy rights, it cannot simply be reduced to an account of personhood – the conception of privacy breached is a first-order input to the deliberation. So socially embedded is privacy that it 'is seldom protected in the absence of some other interest' (Gavison 1980, 348), so we must expect it to correlate with other rights. Thomson's argument fails, but reductionist contentions only open up because of pressure to ascribe a particular function to privacy. If we resist that temptation, then privacy can stand on its own.

Values do not define privacy

If functional accounts tend to collapse into reductionism, this supports the contention that level 7 accounts can't *define* privacy, for two reasons. First, the level 7 functional accounts that we have seen describe the valued outcomes of privacy. But privacy has a number of disvalued outcomes too, which aren't covered, and hence 'privacy' only has a definition by this means when it is positively valued. Second, when privacy is seen solely in this light, it is not obvious that it has any role other than as a means to functional ends.

To conclude our discussion of level 7, and of the levels taken individually, it is arguable that here is where the disarray is. The value of privacy can mean several different things – the value to a functioning society, to an idealised individual, to particular individuals, to ideological views of the world. It can be implicated in harms to individuals, groups or societies. The picture is complicated further if we try to define it as all and only the normatively positive instances of what a less sophisticated audience calls 'privacy', and even further if we try to triangulate that definition with the output of law courts (even if we arbitrarily restrict the scope of that to US law). The hardest case to make is that privacy has intrinsic value – commentators are largely agreed that that is a non-starter – but it does seem to be valuable for its own sake at least some of the time.

I have made the case that we should detach the conceptual and legal discussions from the moral and political ones (following Gavison, but she complicates the picture unnecessarily by allowing 'privacy' to be ambiguous between a state and a value – 1980, 348). My best hypothesis for the disarray at level 7 is that the literature has fallen victim to blind-men-describing-elephant syndrome. Each has focused on a particular quality of privacy which enables something good to happen, and extrapolated from that to a stronger statement about what privacy *is* or *does*. It is certainly important for democracy, autonomy, intimacy and so on, and we should indeed value it if we value any of those things. Thus far no disarray and no dispute, simply parallel appraisals. Privacy aids all the values above, and more, and few would dissent from that (Gavison 1980, 361–362).

Unfortunately, where an overarching principle is desired (cf. Part I, Disarray 1) and one politico-moral account is privileged, they can't all be right. The moment we start to talk of *the* value of privacy, we invite dispute – even if we explicitly restrict ourselves to the rich capitalist democracies of the twenty-first century. If our claim is meant to be culturally neutral, then it has even less validity. By narrowing down, coherence is achieved, if at all, at the cost of parochialism, anachronism, cultural imperialism, and many other isms and solecisms, describing one aspect well but missing the insights of others. 'The shortcoming of ... this approach, is not that it gets things wrong, generally speaking, but that it leaves a gap' (Nissenbaum 2010, 9).

Worse, privacy, like any means to an end, can cut both ways. A hammer can be used to build a house or knock it down. Similarly, privacy can undermine values as often as it promotes them (Part V, Level 7 will discuss some of these).

Hence the individual functional value account of privacy will always be inadequate. Either we focus on one or two values the support of which is privacy's most important role, in which case we are in danger of essentialism, and may even slide into reductionism in case of privacy's failure to deliver. Or we take the eclectic view (my preference), in which case privacy's contribution will diverge across the experience of individuals and groups, and we can conclude nothing in general about it. The claim that privacy had intrinsic value initially led us to functionalism, but it may be that eclectic functionalism lands us back with a quasi-intrinsic account, in which privacy is a jolly useful thing with many benefits realised differently for different people and groups. Each person or group may be able to give reasons for their privacy preferences, but they will not converge. Hence if, emulating Glaucon in the *Republic*, we ask whether privacy's value is provided by itself (intrinsically), by the benefits it brings (functionally), or both (Plato 1997b, 990, 357), the answer is 'both'.

Privacy is not a moral claim, but an object of one. It is often deeply desired, if variably across individuals, groups, generations, genders, classes and nationalities. It works for and against us. It is hard to imagine simple pleasures, psychic well-being, role adoption, authentic choices, intimate relations, human freedom, nose-picking or democracy without a modicum of privacy. Breaches of it, even trivial ones, are a source of irritation, indications that we are not being treated 'properly' or respectfully.

It tends to be valued when it is perceived to be in need of defence. This perception might be that of an intellectual elite, a social group under threat or a wider population. The nature of the threat will dictate the nature of the positive account, as we saw in the disproportionate focus on informational privacy in the long twentieth century from Warren and Brandeis through to the GDPR.

Privacy plays many a moral and political role, but ethical and legal arguments are often a sideshow. My own level 7 view, for what it is worth, is that norms carry most of the weight of social privacy management and coordination, and respect for existing social norms is in and of itself a good, all things being equal. They emerge and solidify (sometimes ossify) to make their functional contribution to durable, legible, resilient societies.

The law obviously contributes to the expectations and regularities norms provide, but the common law has the extra advantage of being bottom up, based to a large extent on the actual complaints real people are prepared to make to a court with the power to identify relevant precedent, on the principle of *stare decisis*. Unlike legislation or executive regulation generated by often remote elites, common law respects its jurisdiction as a complex society with a deep history, in which claims to privacy have been negotiated equitably and pragmatically between free people, with occasional judicial intervention for particularly knotty disputes. In this context, Woodrow Hartzog's argument that criticism of 'relatively weak, indirect, or incomplete protections is often misguided' resonates. Modest, fallible and porous privacy protections have a pragmatic role to play because:

> It is often worth providing some sort of protection to information even if it is shared with other people. These protections do not always need to be vigorous or direct. ... In an age of hyper socialization, courts and lawmakers should embrace the modest protection of semi-public information and recognize that the wide diversity of privacy harms require equally diverse solutions. (Hartzog 2014, 351)

Hence I believe that that the discernible outputs of level 5 norms and level 6 common law have extra politico-moral weight. They change organically, unwilled by central authorities, and in many cases at the pace of social change, alongside language change via evolving level 1 privacy conceptions (which similarly emerge organically from description, debate and complaint from wider populations).

As can be seen from the preceding discussion, that is a minority view. One obvious problem with it is that our conceptions and understanding of privacy evolve most rapidly and radically when there are disputes, where technocratic bureaucracies are imposing their own rationalised logic or where new conceptions are emerging thanks to new technology. Another is that social norms can have abhorrent outcomes, such as when norms about the private sphere, family and honour result in honour killings (Bond 2014). In such cases, social norms and common law may lag behind the need for action or resistance. Hence, even if my position is defensible, there will still be occasions where other principles need to be brought to bear because norms and common law are inadequate, and so as stated it is not complete.

However, my aim is not to expound my own position, but to sketch the landscape of all the levels of discourse about privacy. The seven-level framework makes it clear that neither values, social norms nor the law can simply *define* privacy, even relative to a single society. Definition is a level 1 issue, and if we elide the levels we will find ourselves confused again by pluralism of viewpoints and apparent conceptual disarray.

Part IV

Commentary on the framework

Part III has suggested one way of putting a little structure on the immense complexity of privacy discourse. I have focused on the experience of the Western democracies, particularly in the last 50 years, because that is where most of the literature is generated (and where I have spent the last half-century), but the framework is intended to be valid further afield.

To summarise, at level 1 are the privacy claims that one *could* make, if one wished to. At level 4 are the claims one *does* make. At level 5 are the claims that are conventional. At level 6 are those defended by regulation. At level 7 are those that *ought* to be defended. At level 3 is one's conscious awareness of privacy or its lack, and at level 2 are the affordances of the environment (architecture, clothes, systems, including digital systems, etc.) for supporting or undermining privacy claims. I emphasised their separation in Part III, but there are clearly links between them.

In Part IV I will briefly engage with some of the wider issues raised by the framework, first, looking at how the levels interact, and second how they might be applied in non-Western contexts. A third chapter will speculatively reconsider Solove's question of whether there might be an overarching privacy concept standing at level 0 which would be the common denominator of most or all of the conceptions of level 1.

Commentary 1: the interplay of the levels

These discourses of Part III, linked though they are, should remain distinct; we should be clear when we are operating at the different levels, and we should not draw too many conclusions across the levels. For instance, just because my preferences are unreasonable, that does not mean that they can't be my preferences. EU law is meant to support social norms, but that does not mean that we can read off the norms from the legal texts. Just because the social norms are thus-and-so, we shouldn't assume that everyone prefers to be treated in that way. And if a practice is not against the law, that does not mean that it does not breach privacy. When studying or focusing on a level, we need to be aware of other discourses, while resisting the temptation to draw unwarranted conclusions from them.

When we fail to mark these distinctions, definitions of privacy can become overloaded with extraneous material. We can now see that Solove's several criticisms of privacy theories (Part II, Explanation 3) were justified, not because those being criticised were incorrect in what they said, but rather because their 'definitions' straddled the levels. Statements about when privacy is reasonable are properly level 5; those about consent and control are level 4; issues about perception belong at level 3. None of these belongs at the definitional level of particular conceptions; once we have a conception, we can perceive it, consent to breaches, think about what is reasonable and so on. On the other hand, in the three classic papers of Part I, Warren and Brandeis and Prosser retained coherence because they focused exclusively on level 6. Thomson was similarly focused on level 7, and indeed her argument could be rephrased in our terms as saying that level 1 issues are not particularly relevant for the moral rights we may wish to exercise.

Vertical links: separate discourses on the same topic

Is this separation realistic, though? Many level 1 privacy conceptions involve psychological, social or even moral phenomena at other levels. Clearly it is neither possible nor desirable to keep the levels hermetically sealed from each other. They will often overlap, and intrude upon other discourses. A privacy breach feels bad (level 3) because a norm has been broken (level 5). My preferences (level 4) may be unreasonable (level 5). I want to share information (level 4) because my social network makes it feel good to do so (level 3). Data protection law (level 6) gives me some control over the use of my personal data (level 4). Contextual integrity (level 5) is ethically important (level 7). I find it hard to be motivated (level 4) by the possibility of manipulation of my data (level 1). Face recognition technology (level 2) makes my laptop seem much more secure (level 3), justifying the increased price. A new conception of privacy (level 1) will often emerge because of new harms (level 4), perceptions of harm (level 3), or changes to privacy technology (level 2). When Prosser (1960) discussed the 'mores test' for privacy torts, he explained that social norms and expectations (level 5) inform the law (level 6), while the law cannot protect the individual preferences (level 4) of a 'hypersensitive individual' or 'eremite'.

We need to be careful when we look at privacy from the perspective of different levels. To take one example in detail, Goffman defined personal space as 'the space surrounding an individual where within which an entering other causes the individual to feel encroached upon, leading him to show displeasure and sometimes to withdraw' (1971, 30). This subtends a privacy conception – obviously, that one's personal space is not invaded or threatened, that no person is literally too close for comfort – defined with reference to psychosocial phenomena which themselves depend importantly on psychological and social inputs.

The concept of personal space may not seem to make very much sense at all in the absence of a notion of privacy, in which case it might be argued that it is impossible to separate the definitional/ conceptual level 1 from the phenomenological level 3 (and possibly others). This is mistaken in two ways. First of all, Goffman's definition is not a definition of privacy, but of *personal space*. The corresponding *privacy* conception is that of *keeping personal space clear of intruders*. The definition of personal space is *prior* to the privacy conception it subtends.

Second, it is not exclusively a human trait (Stricklin et al. 1979; Hemelrijk 1999; Graziano and Cooke 2006; Lorimer et al. 2019), and indeed was first theorised by zoologists, before being noticed 'to have relevance for the study of human behavior' (Sommer 1959, 247). We can talk of animals having/desiring privacy, but even if there are continuities with humans it is a stretch to say that the common ethological observation of personal space maps easily onto the complex human notion of privacy (though cf. Westin 1967, 7–10 for an alternative view). Hall in particular, using considerations from a range of psychosocial factors, conceptualised it not as a straightforward distance measure that could be seen as a proxy for privacy but rather a function of what communication cues were possible at different distances and how the space was utilised for communication (1966). He also suggested the idea of *social distance*, an analogous and connected distance beyond which someone feels anxious because of a *lack* of contact.

Given the prior notion of personal space, we can easily describe the privacy conception of its breach or invasion (level 1), and the environmental settings that permit or prevent breaches, such as instances of extreme overcrowding, like a rush hour metro train, a lift or an inhumane prison (level 2), The phenomenological level 3 will be implicated strongly, as a breach will almost certainly reach individual awareness given the feelings described by Goffman. Most people's preferences (level 4) will take their lead from their feelings, unless there are other factors deemed more important, but their management of their space will also depend on their expectations of others' likely behaviour, so social norms (level 5) enter the equation too. Different understandings of norms – particularly across gender, and with respect to gender roles (Uzzell and Horne 2006; Iachini et al. 2016), or with certain psychological states (Gessaroli et al. 2013) – may have to be negotiated, or lead to conflict (Altman 1975, 67–79).

Similarly, the issues relevant to a discussion may be associated with different levels. For instance, Inness defined privacy as 'the state of possessing control over a realm of intimate decisions, which includes decisions about intimate access, intimate information, and intimate actions' (1992, 140), thereby involving control (level 4) and the value of intimacy (level 7). Many of her arguments were intended to correspond with legal decisions and 'the discussion of intimacy found in tort and constitutional privacy law' (1992, 92n.2) to 'provide a foundation for laws and legal rulings' (level 6). That means the definition of intimacy needed to be tractable for that purpose. Intimacy could not be connected with the agent's motivations (1992, 86), which made it unsuitably individualistic (as well as failing to exclude self-deluded abusers); 'the personal point of view is a social construct, and, hence, will usually reflect the dominant social understanding of intimacy' (level 5 – 1992, 87).

As an account of the US Supreme Court's protection of the intimate sphere, and the range of inputs to its thinking, Inness' work is cogent, but the kitchen sink definition straddling the levels raises as many questions as it answers. (How) does it apply to non-Americans, or to those outside the realm of intimacy (solitary or lonely people)? And if the US Supreme Court is in a privileged position in the definition of privacy-as-intimacy, what happens when it changes its mind? Did *Roe v Wade* and its repeal change the nature of intimacy? How far can the actual decisions of the Court (level 6) be used as evidence for the normative thesis (level 7) Inness wanted to push (1992, 84–86)?

Different levels of discourse bring in different methods of influence. Legal scholar Lawrence Lessig (1999, 86–99) noted that architecture (level 2), economic incentives (level 4), norms (level 5) and regulation (level 6) may be combined or interact to restrain behaviour. Many governments and private actors try to regulate covertly, with a utilitarian mix of these constraints. Yet they have varying levels of legitimacy, as we might expect by their being generated by different types of discourse. We need to ensure that the discourses of one level do not get suborned inappropriately to justify constraints at another, as Hildebrandt warned:

> replacing legal regulation with technical regulation may be more effi-
> cient and effective, and as long as the default settings are a part of

the hidden complexity people simply lack the means to contest their manipulation. ... Why not use nudging to influence your constituency, if it 'works' better than law? (2015, 165)

Most rich contexts provoke questions straddling the levels. Jennifer Ringley's Jennicam was discussed in Part III to make a point at level 4, but provides material for discourses from all the levels. Different conceptions (level 1) of privacy relevant to Jennicam include that one's private space is inviolate, one's behaviour is not open to scrutiny, access to (images of) one's body is restricted, and one's person is not the subject of attention. Ringley was clearly complicit in breaches of these conceptions, despite (or because of) protective social norms (level 5), and laws (level 6). Most people's preferences (level 4) are to have privacy in these senses, and they feel violated or ashamed when they do not (level 3). Ringley had control, and achieved her (unusual) preference to eschew privacy in these senses (level 4). Despite having control through the early cam technology (level 2), she had no privacy. In terms of value (level 7), she was accused of various crimes including narcissism, but she seems to have felt that her actions enhanced her autonomy, and facilitated curation of her identity at the time; the experience seems to have been affirming for her. She also cited feminist reasons for her experiment. Now, she is apparently hard to find online, and has adopted a more conventional lifestyle. Or has she? Since her life is no longer the subject of surveillance, it is impossible for the outsider to know. Herein we see a level 5 paradox about privacy norms – by allowing us to verify that she led an utterly conventional, not to say dull, life, she became unconventional, interesting and, to many, somewhat unsettling. No discussion of the Jennicam can restrict itself to just one of the levels.

As another example, South Korean *molka* videos are films of unsuspecting women in toilets or changing rooms, taken with hidden cameras (*molkas*) and posted on the Internet (there is surprisingly little literature on this disturbingly prevalent activity, but see Armesto-Larson 2020, 205–206). The conceptions of privacy involved are relatively clear (Wood 2004), and the level 2 affordances consist of the capabilities of the technology and the data infrastructure, together with the physical environment (which is usually a concealed space including places to hide cameras, such as toilet roll holders and hand dryers). There is virtual unanimity that *molka* are morally wrong, showing no respect for the dignity of the victim (level 7), and we might expect that very few ladies welcome such attentions (level 4); the practice is associated with some suicides, including of celebrities.

However, we can't use these strong assertions to avoid unpleasant truths. While all pornography, consensual and non-consensual, is illegal in South Korea, *molka*'s legal status is blurred, with many activists arguing that the system itself is skewed and proportionate punishments rarely handed out (level 6). Others may say that, despite high profile cases of severe harm, victims are rarely psychologically damaged by an attack, if only because they remain unaware (level 3), although one result of the practice being widespread is that women have been increasingly nervous and anxious in public facilities. We might also suspect sexist social norms, while the disguised cameras sell openly and well, meaning that norms against them have relatively weak force (level 5). Finally, of course, the perpetrators and consumers of *molka* videos also have their own preferences, opposite to those of the victims (level 4). Even if we don't feel inclined to respect them, we cannot wish away strong demand. Just because the rights and wrongs of this practice are pretty clear and unequivocal, that does not mean that across the levels the complexity typical of the privacy space will not emerge.

Influence across the discourses

In all this complexity, influence certainly passes between the levels. Law sits at the nexus of personal preferences, social norms and moral principles, and has to negotiate them (Dworkin 1986). However, it doesn't accept inputs uncritically. A civil case usually means individual preferences have clashed, so the law must be a tiebreak between them. Legislation can be crafted to support social norms, or to change or suppress them. The relationship between law and norms was described, not that long ago, in pretty much the same terms as our understanding of privacy, as being in 'terminological disarray' (Scott 2000, 1607). Richard Posner tried to understand law and norms in terms of economics (1978, 1981), while his son Eric used game theory (2009) – both intriguing but in the end schematic and hardly convincing attempts to reduce levels 5 and 6 to level 4.

The actual content of the law will depend on the norms and habits of the community it regulates; why would we make behaviour illegal that would never be contemplated? The phenomenology of privacy will depend on one's ideas of respect, and how one is, and should be, treated by others. The morality of a particular exposure will depend on all sorts of social and psychological variables – publishing a photo of an unveiled woman in the company of a man may be innocuous in some societies, and a serious threat to the woman in others. Hence the appropriateness and form of privacy experience, expectation or regulation will depend on a range of evidence taken from across the discourses.

To take a detailed example, architecture is designed with specific privacy conceptions in mind, and its affordances depend in particular on the characteristics of the society in which it is built. For example, the garden of a private suburban house may be simply marked out by the extent of the lawn, or a small fence a foot high or less, or even just a sign. The affordances of this latter environment are hardly protective of the private space at all; an intruder could simply step over the fence, or ignore the sign. However, the design is appropriate for those contexts where, as a matter of fact, individuals simply don't barge into others' gardens. Social norms about trespass do the work, not the environment, which affords access trivially (and is therefore more convenient for the owner and legitimate visitors). Where the owner is a celebrity, norms against intrusion have less force, and so more of the privacy protection would be built into the environment directly, for example, by an imposing brick wall with broken glass set in the top. Phenomenology is also important in a successful design – the owner must feel secure and private, even if the garden is completely exposed.

In monasteries, monks sometimes were allowed private cells for study, but they were organised so that chair, desk and bed (if there was one) would be visible from the doorway, which itself might only be curtained off (Webb 2007, 159–160). Architecture clearly affects behaviour, which can lead to changes in norms (Hartzog 2018, 42). However, we can't always assume this process will be effective or straightforward, as with a recent cretinous trend for open plan bathrooms in hotels – a toilet visible to one's *amour* being the perfect backdrop for that romantic weekend (Saner 2013).

An encrypted cybersecure system may be brilliantly designed to keep hackers away from private information, but if level 5 norms of authority, expertise and management in the organisation make it simple to deceive an employee into handing over the password over the phone to someone posing as 'the IT guy', or if post-COVID norms of home-working mean that people use the system on their own insecure devices at home, what price its level 2 brilliance (Krombholz et al. 2015)?

Fundamentally, we cannot understand what makes a privacy architecture work, what privacy it will afford, without being aware of social norms and other levels, and how they will contribute to the ways in which such architectures are perceived and used. Equally, if we fail to respect the distinctions between architecture and other fields, then we will impute to the architecture powers it does not have. The suburban architect only gives the householder control of access to the garden, with its tiny fence, in a world where norms deter others from stepping over it. The fence – necessary as a signal – physically stops nobody.

People are generally extremely able at negotiating these inter-weaving influences, in a 'personal adjustment process' (Westin 1967, 5–6). Their means of controlling access to themselves exploit resources from all levels, including the environmental conditions, social norms, preferences of others to either mix or avoid, surveillance systems and so on, integrating them 'like the instruments of an orchestra' (Altman 1975, 32). Yet no account at a given level of discourse can be derived from, or reduced to, accounts at other levels, just as the clarinet's contribution is not dictated by that of the bassoon, or violins, or even the total combination of all the other instruments. Orchestration is a separate compositional art.

Commentary 2: privacy across space and time

Following his survey of radically different privacy preservation mechanisms, Altman asked rhetorically: 'is it proper to say that some societies are highly private and others are nonprivate?' His answer was negative: 'if one examines carefully a culture with seemingly little privacy, privacy mechanisms will eventually be uncovered. ... mechanisms for separating the self and non-self – that is, for regulating interpersonal boundaries to achieve a desired level of privacy – are universal and present in all societies' (Altman 1975, 42).

This is a strong claim, as he admitted. I don't doubt its empirical truth, although an unconcerned society isn't an impossibility (cf. Schoeman 1984b, 6–8). We should beware that privacy 'is the kind of thing that almost asks to be treated as a universal human phenomenon, and thus often is' (Saltzman 2019, 10).

Let's consider two slightly weaker statements. First, the application of privacy conceptions to any society is possible, even one that is carefree about privacy. We could, for example, distinguish between a society where privacy is barely salient, and a society (like *Brave New World*) in which privacy is understood and discouraged. We could judge of the former how a privacy-respecting visitor might function within it, and work out of the latter how to protect ourselves against intrusion. It might be possible to make generalisations, such as that only complex societies with a high degree of economic and social specialisation uphold conceptions of privacy that support self-expression (Schoeman 1992, 115), but we should do this only tentatively.

Second, while cultural divergence does not necessarily entail conceptual difference (Solove 2008, 185), it seems very likely that any two societies remote from each other will struggle to understand each other's privacy ideas because a different set of conceptions is significant within them. A radically foreign society may appear dramatically different from the perspective of another, but it is quite likely to have a rich set of salient conceptions of its own, subtended by its different practices and technologies that may not be evident from the external perspective (e.g. Westin 1967, 31–33; Altman 1975, 12–14; Ess 2005; Solove 2008, 183ff.). The idea of fine-grained privacy conceptions should help; we can ask not only what conceptions relevant to *us* might be detectable in a remote culture, but also what (different) conceptions *they themselves* might consider, or have considered, salient, as well as describing context-relative architectures, norms, ethics etc. This will hardly be an exact science. 'The historian's perennial challenge is to describe the past using and while constrained by the language of the present; the latter rarely fits the former and inevitably risks contorting it' (Saltzman 2019, 10).

We see it even in similar countries. In Britain it is usual to draw curtains in the evening to prevent passers-by gawping in when the lights go on. In the Netherlands, culturally similar, it is standard to carry on non-intimate night-time activities, eating, chatting or watching the telly, with the blinds open and the room well-illuminated. No such wonders as leylandii bushes, net curtains or dim lighting for the Dutch. There are compensatory social norms; whereas the British find it unavoidably tempting to look into people's homes at the slightest possibility, the Dutch are scrupulous at not peering in from the pavement, so the net effect in terms of observation from outside is probably about the same. This is reflected culturally; the TV quiz *Through the Keyhole*, where contestants were shown round a celebrity's house and had to guess their identity, was a hit in nosy Britain, running for twenty-four series, whereas the Dutch equivalent, *Met de Deur in Huis*, was cancelled after a mere fifteen programmes because of disappointing ratings.

This is not merely a phenomenon of spatial remoteness. The passage of time also reveals diversity. No attitude toward privacy is unchanging (Solove 2008, 65). For instance, the nuclear family was not an intimate environment in medieval times, and privacy was not an actively positive norm (Schoeman 1992, 121). The early medieval monastic codes of seclusion and communal living became ever harder to sustain as preferences changed, particularly after the Black Death, and monks and nuns wanted more contact with the outside world, less community life with their fellows and more opportunity for what we might call privacy – 'a room of one's own or at least some comfortable retreat in which to converse, play chess or music with one's special friends, religious or secular' (Webb 2007, 193–214, quote from 213). Privacy always had its defenders (Westin 1967, 369ff.; Etzioni 1999, 189; Nissenbaum 2010, 92), but at the end of the nineteenth century the desire of the bourgeois householder for independence and concealment from the curious eyes of the masses surfaced in a number of ways in Western culture, including in the home (Hepworth 1999), law (Warren and Brandeis 1890) and art, as with the novels of Henry James (Schoeman 1992, 165–191). Were they kicking against the new mass society (Solove 2008, 82) or establishing a necessary condition of the modern age (O'Hara 2021a)? Complexity increased, and privacy for the servants threatened the privacy of the masters, now gossip could be traded in the new media market for tittle-tattle (Olsen 1974). Privacy has always been a status symbol (Altman 1975, 38), but now it is easier than ever for the individual to reject – or be rejected by – society, leading both to greater demand for privacy, and greater concern about loneliness (Webb 2007, 221).

Given a set of salient conceptions, a society will contain environmental affordances, people will have their own phenomenology and preferences, against a background of norms, perhaps regulations, and perhaps ethical or theological claims. It should not be impossible to explain privacy conceptions across cultures, even to people who are neither interested in them nor motivated to entertain them. Western men can appreciate the notion of hiding the face behind a veil even though they tend not to do it themselves, while those with no digital presence can understand a search for their name, even if they may struggle to appreciate the implications fully. Lack of deep cultural immersion will naturally put limits on how types of privacy are appreciated by outsiders, so empathy may be hard to achieve. But fathoming the discourses from levels 1 to 7 is not out of the question for someone prepared to listen sympathetically without imposing their own preconceptions.

Translating between cultures

It is not unknown to have to understand a culture from afar. Historians, translators and anthropologists do it all the time in the face of indeterminacies of meaning. Richard Rorty discussed two especially pertinent genres of historiography: rational and historical reconstructions (1984, 49–56). In the former, our own interests are foremost, and in the latter we try to reconstruct the other as they saw themselves. The cross-cultural study of privacy is no different, and needs an artful combination of the two. L. P. Hartley's declaration that 'The past is a foreign country; they do things differently there' is frustratingly unspecific. Do they do *the same things differently*, or *different things*? The answer is to an extent in the eye of the beholder.

Theories of privacy tend to begin with the term 'privacy'. One way of demonstrating our common understanding, as we have seen, is by observing agreement in its use. However, that ceases to be helpful in cross-cultural investigations because not everyone will use the term 'privacy' in the same way. Non-English speakers obviously won't, and the term 'privacy' was only used in a recognisably modern way from about 1700 on (Sennett 2002, 16–17). When we encounter cultures remote from our own, we require the resources of translation, hermeneutics and ethnography. Earlier, I made the point that Peeping Tom was understood to have breached Lady Godiva's privacy a thousand years ago. To determine this, it is not enough to see whether the locals of Coventry described his prying in those terms, because they would not have – the word did not exist. We have to consider the evolution of the story, what was found significant to record and emphasise, what morals were drawn, etc. Three centuries later, the word 'pryvetee' had appeared to cover personal or secret business (Hanks 1984), handing Chaucer a pun in the *Miller's Tale*: the miller sees Nicholas the student in contemplation, and assumes he is pondering 'Goddes pryvetee', God's concealed plans for His creation, but Nicholas is really contemplating pryvetee of a different kind, the miller's wife's 'private parts', with which he is planning to get acquainted asap. Even then the literate minority had a relatively small and unspecialised vocabulary to describe privacy-related ideas or architectures (Webb 2007, 50).

The resulting split between a hermeneutic insider's account and an interpretative outsider's account is a perennial issue in any investigation of a community of which one is not a member (Quine 1960; Benton and Craib 2001, 93–106; Skinner 2002, 1–7). Words are not everything; they are tools to get things, including privacy-related things, done. Privacy is also a tool to get other things done, as well as an end in its own right. 'Our social practices help to bestow meaning on our social vocabulary … [and] our social vocabulary helps to constitute the character of those practices' (Skinner 2002, 174). But if we describe privacy practice in a remote culture, it has to make sense as something *they would do and understand*, whose description is in terms available to them.

Nevertheless, a reader of this book is probably interested in that which is denoted by the term 'privacy' here and now, so our own parochial understanding is not irrelevant. When we look beyond our own culture, it is from our own culture that we get the ideas that guide our explorations. We are not devoid of evidence; the issue is interpreting it, and success and failure are neither binary nor determinate. The seven discourses outlined in Part III are not separate from each other, by virtue of the holism described in Commentary 1, but can be teased apart heuristically, and this in many circumstances will aid the deconstruction of the holistic presentation of other cultures into bite-sized chunks. We look for evidence of practice that would make sense to these others, while simultaneously seeking family resemblances to our own discourses of privacy. It is easy to over-interpret, but equally we shouldn't be frozen into paralysed bewilderment.

As an example, in her study of privacy in the eighteenth-century Chinese novel *Dream of the Red Chamber*, Cathy Silber was alert to the danger of 'the imposition of my own culture-bound notions of privacy by simply looking for what I already understand the content of privacy to be' (2002, 55–56) and formulated a method for avoiding it. Inness' definition of privacy-as-control suggested the invocation of power and Foucault's idea that where there is power, we find resistance. Silber inverted Foucault's principle to 'where there is resistance, there is power', which indicated the methodology of looking for resistance, and therefore breaches, in the text she was analysing.

All very well – but resistance to what? And breaches of what? While still aware that 'the breach diagnostic can easily end up associating every cough with pneumonia' (2002, 56), Silber did not describe how she came up with the examples she did, which included such behaviours as eavesdropping and spying, which are pretty obviously connected with privacy on the Western model. There are lots of episodes of resistance and breaches of etiquette and morality in *Dream of the Red Chamber*, but only some are related to privacy. For instance, it is hard to see how the undoing of Xifeng's loan-sharking has anything to do with privacy, and Silber did not suggest that it did. Those events classified as privacy breaches in Western terms usually involve covert scrutiny by eye or ear, and Silber's choices reflected that cultural bias (2002, 57). In fact, it looks suspiciously like she 'solved' the problem of looking for privacy in a culture-bound way by looking for privacy *breaches* in a culture-bound way.

Some examples

However, this is not a failing from my perspective: I am interested in privacy, which is what Silber looked for, even if she failed to live up to her own standards. Her use of imaginative literature gave her access to the phenomenological level, and to the hypothesis that some incidents in *Dream of the Red Chamber* might be informative about social norms, architecture and so on. For instance, she highlighted a couple of incidents in which ladies eavesdropped on their maids and were embarrassed to be discovered, an interesting wrinkle about how the norms around their very unequal status played out. The descriptions of various eavesdropping incidents tell us how the physical architecture of the period facilitated secret observation. Particular conceptions of privacy which we might not have anticipated seem to concern being caught crying, and also to do with sleep (expected to be private, a mechanism for achieving privacy, and surprisingly a state in which privacy can be threatened, for example where characters share dreams). Other conceptions are more familiar, concerning sex, washing, dressing, going to the toilet and family discord.

Observing norms in operation, anthropologist Robert Murphy (1964) described the veiling of male Tuaregs from North Africa as a highly fluid practice that preserved the generalised and adjustable distance between men in marriage, kin and wider groupings. The eyes and mouth, considered as indications of mood, thoughts and mental states, were particularly sensitive because they may inadvertently breach the man's psychological privacy, and hence were veiled to varying degrees depending on the status of the observer. Low-status boys did not veil, and if they did it would be an attempt to assert status; servants and slaves (this being some decades ago), though veiled, would not be assiduous in covering the face and mouth. Despite Tuaregs being a Muslim people, the women were unveiled at this time, perhaps because, although they often played prominent roles within family groups, they had little public role. Meanwhile, those whose status was sacred and secure, such as *hajjis* who had made the pilgrimage to Mecca, could also dispense with the veil.

Murphy's account focused on the norms of concealment and revelation, particularly in the manipulation of the veil. To get a grip of the complexity of what might be, to the casual observer, a slightly fussy set of behaviours with men constantly fiddling with their veils depending on mood and audience, clearly a more than superficial investigation was needed, including conversation and observation, as well as discussion with Tuaregs who had moved away from the tribe to modern cities.

From these norms, Murphy was able to work outward to describe points of interest at other levels. The veil itself was part of what I would classify as the architecture of the situation, whose design provided affordances for concealment, revelation and other signals. Lower status males may have level 4 preferences to veil themselves, but, at least on Murphy's telling, they were usually subsumed by level 5 norms. The level 7 value for the Tuaregs clearly had to do with the maintenance and signalling of the male's status, and no doubt allowed male Tuaregs a good deal of latitude in their dealings with others, particularly negotiations and conflict. A 'long, cold look through a slit of cloth' (Murphy 1964, 45) sounds undoubtedly intimidating to the outsider. Hence power, dignity, autonomy, self-esteem and status were all enhanced by the practice – a fairly conservative preservation of the *status quo*. As well as the obvious facial privacy afforded, the practice also subtended an aspect of psychological privacy, concealment of expression in order to suppress evidence of moods and thoughts, a type of social distancing.

A number of concealment practices share this function of turbocharging an actor's autonomy by creating information asymmetries with observers.

> Price negotiations in the livestock marketplaces in Somaliland are not carried out openly. An exclusive circle of initiated and highly skilled market insiders, the brokers, representing sellers and buyers, use a tactile sign language to bargain. And, additionally, these negotiators cover their signing hands with a shawl (*cumaamad* in Somali) in order to hide the haggling from the curious glances of the bystanders. (Musa and Schwere 2018, 50)

Technology and changing mores are undermining this practice. Mobile phones allow friends and kin to compare prices instantly, while the increasing number of women trading is also a problem; as men and women cannot touch, women have to negotiate verbally (and audibly). Evolving norms are diminishing the affordances of the costume/architecture. Nevertheless, Simmel argued that, in general, fungibility of people and objects allows greater anonymity and thus privacy; he traced the evolution of such generalised interchangeability to the abstractions enabled by the money economy's emergence from barter and exchange (Simmel 2004).

Historically, archaeology and literature may provide a starting point. For instance, thanks in particular to hagiographical writing, we know a fair bit about the religious anchorite movement in medieval Europe. Anchorites, or more usually anchoresses, withdrew from secular society, not by going into a convent or the wilderness but by confining themselves in cells built onto the sides of churches. These give architectural evidence, while some of their uses can be deduced from manuals of anchorite behaviour such as the *Ancrene Wisse* (Millett 2009).

Their attitudes to privacy were inconsistent in modern terms. The ritual for sealing someone in was akin to a funeral rite, as the person was 'dead' to society (Maddocks 2013, 28–29). Christina of Markyate was secluded in a cell so small that she was unable to wear warm clothes in winter, and its entrance was only removed once a day to allow her to relieve herself (Talbot 2009, 100–107). On the other hand, many anchorites had servants and followers, and provided advice or cures for laypeople, as the *Ancrene Wisse* complains with heavy irony:

> It is said of anchoresses that almost every one of them has some old woman to feed her ears, a gossip who tells her all the local tid-bits, a magpie who cackles about all that she sees and hears, so that the saying now runs, 'You can hear the news from a mill or a market, from a smithy or an anchorhouse'. Christ knows this is a sorry saying! – that an anchorhouse, which should be the loneliest place of all, can be compared to these three places that are most full of gossip.
> (quoted in Webb 2007, 87)

Anchorites had rather more decisional privacy than those in religious communities – monks had little freedom of action within the monastery, whereas the anchorite was only under the authority of the local bishop. The life was intended to be solitary, and terms such as 'privite' (an Old French forerunner of Chaucer's 'pryvetee') appeared often in *Ancrene Wisse*. The ideal anchorhold, described in that work, contained two small chambers, an inner room with bed and altar, and a parlour, where the anchoress would meet her maidservant. Much was written about the windows, as the point of contact with the world outside, and even the style of curtain (Webb 2007, 88–89).

The literature and surviving examples of anchorholds allow some reconstruction of the norms and values in play. There are also documents giving the judgements of ecclesiastical regulation (level 6), and problems or difficulties reported to officials, which may give insight into the intentions and preferences of anchorites and anchoresses, including those who had failed or moved on from their vocation (level 4). The individual psychology of anchoresses, even at the level of phenomenology, can perhaps be dimly discerned from their written lives, sometimes from their own writings (Hildegard of Bingen, for example, wrote much about her own experiences, although these were often her visions rather than her quotidian life). In the end, a level 1 conception of privacy subtended by the practice can be reconstructed tentatively from all this evidence, which has to do partly with being alone with God, but partly with detachment from social obligations, freedom from the authority of abbots, mothers superior or parents, freedom from pride ('Hear now, my dear sisters, how evil it is to be vain and boast of good deeds, and how good it is to conceal our good works, and to fly by night, like the night fowl, and to gather in the darkness, that is, privately and secretly, food for the soul', from the *Ancrene Wisse*), and perhaps freedom from worldly distractions or temptations to sin (Webb 2007, 90).

As a final example, sometimes cross-cultural dialogue can be fostered with direct conversation, for example between academics or diplomats, to think about level 6 or 7 issues in scholarly detail. Those at ease across two cultures can usually effect a translation, however imperfect in detail. An external perspective, such as business, can help provide a focal point. For example, Japan worked to negotiate with the EU as to the adequacy of its data protection regime despite cultural differences in 2018 with the vital help of the Japanese business community (Bradford 2020, 150).

More generally, academic discussion of value is likely to uncover fault lines through critical engagement. Individualistic Western notions that have underlain much of the privacy literature appear to lack relevance in Asia, because many cultures in that region have a lesser ontological commitment to the individual (indeed, Buddhist philosophy regards many aspects of the self as illusory, as we will see in the next chapter), and lay greater emphasis on collective and social groups, especially families. Social identity, authority and relations with others are conceived very differently, and sometimes given a historical dimension that plays off the often difficult relations with the proselytising Western powers of the colonial era. Privacy is often connected in Asia with covering up shameful behaviour and is sometimes seen as directly threatening social harmony and stability (Ess 2005). Different practices, traditions, institutions and contexts subtend a (possibly radically) different set of privacy conceptions, which are then encoded, valorised or renounced through architecture, preferences, law, etc. in diverse ways.

Nevertheless, informed, critical engagement is possible given deep links between global research communities. I don't see any reason why Western notions of privacy can't be used to describe practices and behaviour in other cultures (and *vice versa*) – as long as we don't thereby think that *this is what is thought in those cultures*. If we are to use alien notions of privacy, we need to describe the unfamiliar context in detail, and draw and defend parallels. The observer's cultural understanding cannot be assumed to be shared with the observed; it is ethnocentric to assimilate the observed's thinking with one's own, suppressing their distinctive identity and cultural inheritance. It will handicap any dialogue from the beginning.

In particular, to assume that privacy is a human right (which applies to individuals), that informational privacy is the most pressing and salient problem (because it currently looms large in digital economies), or that privacy is a normative good, is an ethnocentric privileging of Western ideology. Of course, in the twenty-first-century West, it is proper that this is done, but no philosophy of privacy intended to have wider scope can meaningfully hold these level 7 propositions axiomatically or as definitive of privacy itself.

Commentary 3: is there a level 0?

The framework covers levels 1–7. I left it open, and will continue so to do, as to whether there is benefit in considering the existence of other levels. In this chapter, I will briefly canvas the possibility of a level 0, below the conception level 1. Whereas level 1 is a fine-grained congeries of relatively context-bound conceptions of privacy, level 0 would include common threads, possibly even the common denominator concept that many have tried to find, and the existence of which Solove denied.

I don't think very much hangs on there being a coherent level 0, and I am sceptical that a perfect account will be found. Indeed, arguments over its nature would parallel the arguments that caused the apparent conceptual disarray in the first place. However, it may be that some broad patterns can be discerned that would allow tentative generalisation across the privacy space. In this chapter, I will put forward some of my own views, with the vital caveat that the discussions of the levels in Part III are untouched by these more speculative remarks.

The approach would be to discuss privacy as neutrally as possible, eschewing conceptual richness for broad characterisation, consistent with its plural nature and the family resemblances between different uses of the term (as a dictionary definition actively courts neutrality). There is no reason why we should not be able to talk about privacy in the abstract, as well as in context-specific ways, but that kind of discussion would do less philosophical work than we might like. We certainly should not be expecting relations such as logical entailment, or necessary and sufficient conditions, between levels 0 and 1 for all the reasons canvassed in Part II. A smooth, convincing level 0 account is likely to fail to cover interesting and unusual privacy conceptions subtended at level 1. On the other hand, we have the resources of the reference list, which has withstood the close work of Parts II and III reasonably well (not, I hasten to add, that I have spent much effort trying to falsify it). Level 0 could contain some generalisations that might be of interest across contexts. I put it no more strongly than that.

The reference list, and the discussion since, vindicated ideas of privacy-as-withdrawal, as opposed to control, secrecy, or personhood. This implies privacy is best represented as a state, relative to others who may be specified or implied, which may need constant negotiation or action to maintain. I have implicitly assumed that that state can apply to both individuals and groups, and will argue directly for that assumption in Part V, Level 1 below. I have also hinted elsewhere that some conceptions of privacy might apply to non-humans or the dead. I will not try to cover these cases here. I will focus on living individuals, in accordance with most of the privacy literature, and leave open the question of whether the account will generalise any further. Hence, the level 0 jottings I present here are clearly and admittedly incomplete.

Linguistic markers of privacy conceptions

If our uses of 'privacy' have a family resemblance, then we would expect 'a complicated network of similarities overlapping and criss-crossing' (Wittgenstein 1953, §66). I suggest that there are important, if defeasible, linguistic markers of such a network where privacy interests might be salient, beginning with a key phrase in English that usually stakes a claim to privacy: *that's my business* or *that's our business* (Hollander 2001; cf. e.g. Rachels 1975, 292, 296; Schoeman 1992, 162; Gilliom 2001, 75, 76, 78, 79; Rössler 2005, 1). Our socialisation includes the internalisation of the idea that many aspects of others' lives aren't our business (Schoeman 1992, 125). On the other hand, cults and totalitarians maintain that everything is everyone's business, and privacy has no place at all (Marshall 1993, 151–152; Arendt 2017).

The phrase is usually intended to warn people away or register outrage at an intrusion (as in Lil Armstrong's splendidly self-explanatory composition for Louis Jordan, 'You Run Your Mouth, and I'll Run My Business, Brother'). Part of its beauty is that it allows expression of the intrinsic value of privacy as well as more prudent reasons for wanting it. More generally, important linguistic markers of privacy interests are the first person (singular and plural) possessive adjectives, in English 'my' and 'our': my information, my body, my personal space, our property, my image, my family, my thoughts, our intimate secret, my friends, my history, our income, my person, our ambitions, my shame, my decision, our meeting, my bodily functions and the skeleton in my closet are all suggestive of private matters and privacy interests.

For example, Solove argued that Prosser's analysis of one of his four torts, unauthorised appropriation of someone's identity, in terms of property (1960, 115–117), was inadequate; he preferred an analysis in terms of the dignity of the victim (2008, 156ff.). Agreed, we shouldn't talk of a *legal* property right here, but possessive feelings do seem to come into it. It's *my* name/identity, or, as Iago put it, 'Who steals my purse steals trash; 'tis something, nothing; 'twas mine, 'tis his, and has been slave to thousands: but he that filches from me my good name robs me of that which not enriches him and makes me poor indeed.'

Possessive adjectives don't necessarily imply actual possession, so much as an important relationship between the essentially indexical referent of the adjective (the 'me' or the 'us') and the object, which would normally take a definite article. I don't own my reputation, my mother, my nationality, my mistakes or my enemies. My enemies? Can they be implicated in a privacy claim? I don't see why not, even if it is unusual. The (Irish?) catchphrase 'is this a private fight, or may anyone join in?' is well-known. More seriously, enemies may have private significance via the inherited obligations of the vendetta, rationalised in medieval Italy as 'private justice', *our business* independent of the jurisdiction of public authorities (Dean 1997). The management of enemies may be an important private interest, as in the advice from *The Godfather Part II*, 'keep your friends close, and your enemies closer', and they have a particularly damaging perspective that may, for example, affect a subject's reputation. Antisthenes counselled 'pay attention to your enemies, for they are the first to discover your mistakes', while one of La Rochefoucauld's *Maxims* states, disconcertingly, that 'Our enemies approach nearer to truth in their judgements of us than we do ourselves.'

The self does not define privacy

What kind of thing is the *subject* of a privacy claim? Theories that focus on withdrawal of an individual often look to the *self* as the thing withdrawn, or to which access is refused (Van Den Haag 1971; Gavison 1980). This is fine in its way, except that the self is the subject of a major literature in philosophy, psychology and elsewhere, and – as always in our inquiry – I am reluctant to rest an account of privacy on major engagement with controversial philosophical issues, still less taking a position on them. Privacy is something anyone can talk about; it should not depend on complex hypotheses about the self, and the terms of debate should be democratically open. The self's pre-reflective phenomenological and social presentation will surely be more influential on privacy (and other) discourses that any underlying philosophical theory.

Coincidentally or not, as privacy became more salient in the long twentieth century, so the self as a concept got unpicked by philosophers, psychologists and psychoanalysts. The transcendent ego shattered into hyphenated splinters such as self-esteem, self-control, self-interest, self-deception and so on (Schoeman 1984b, 30; Martin and Barresi 2006, 255–264), and many deny that there is anything there to be described at all.

Postmodernists argue that the self is at best fragmented and decentred, and more perniciously that it is neither bounded, nor ontologically distinct from others' selves. That would lead pretty quickly to scepticism about privacy (Raab 2005, 287), since there would be no difference in principle between subject and other. Thoroughgoing unconstructive dogmatic scepticism is characteristic of postmodernism, so we shouldn't expect privacy to be spared its philosophical scorched Earth policy. At the wilder shores of postmodern nihilism, or social constructionism (Kenneth Gergen described the self as a type of abuse – 2009, 5–13) as well as loopier positions in other traditions such as panpsychism (Freeman 2006), it will be tough to save privacy in any form. So much the worse for postmodern nihilism and panpsychism, it seems to me, as I am far more certain of privacy than of them, but those who prefer to philosophise wearing berets and smoking Gauloises may think differently.

However, where postmodernists restrict themselves to noting the undoubted difficulties with a neat and unified self, it should be possible to reach an accommodation. Lyotard kicked off postmodernism by arguing that 'A *self* does not amount to much, but no self is an island; each exists in a fabric of relations that is now more complex and mobile than ever before' (1984, 15, his emphasis), which doesn't seem unreasonable. Not being an island doesn't preclude a boundary; certainly if the self is embodied, which would seem to imply some sort of bodily bound. Several theories along such lines have sprung up, such as the paradoxical self (Schneider 1999; Hoffman et al. 2009) and the dialogical self (Hermans and Gieser 2012), where the self is distinct enough to support ideas of privacy and withdrawal, as well as allowing strong social and ontological links with the environment and other selves.

Buddhism treats the self as illusory, which doesn't mean it can't be discussed seriously (Albahari 2006). The various discourses outlined in Part III remain valid despite this scepticism; though an illusion, the self undoubtedly has real effects, including preferences (cravings and desires), norms, private property and so on, all of which stand in the way of ultimate release from karmic suffering. Architectures still have privacy affordances – Buddhist monasteries have walls, while if a Buddhist builder omitted to put a door on the toilet because the self is an illusion, they would quite properly be open to chastisement. There could easily be a Buddhist discussion of the value of privacy, although it would be rather low. It has been argued that the ends of personal enlightenment can still be served by privacy, while Buddhism's rejection of the ontological distinctiveness of the self combined with the association of privacy in many Buddhist countries with shame and secrecy, implies that intimate group privacy has more positive value (Kitiyadisai 2005; Hongladarom 2016).

In any case, privacy cannot require the existence of the self, or be exclusively about its relations, and not only because of the philosophical sophistication and Western bias of the notion. There are disorders of the self – for example, related to schizophrenia (Parnas et al. 2005) or autism (Hobson 2002) – yet those with anomalous or even dysfunctional self-experience can surely have, need and value privacy. The self has also been seen by many as a not-so-desirable social by-product that emerges from a *lack* of privacy; anchoresses, for instance, sought privacy in order to mortify and even eliminate the self (Maddocks 2013, 25).

Hence it is better to think of the self, for our purposes, as a marker of interpersonal bounds, and locus of intentionality and agency, rather than something of philosophical substance to which we owe ontological commitment. It might be multiple, in terms either of centres of agency within it (Hermans and Gieser 2012), or of its components, as in the composite soul of Ancient Egypt (David 2002, 116–118), which included such intriguing and suggestive self-constituents as the body, the name, the shadow, a supernatural avatar, and various life-forces and powers. We might add to the Egyptians' list such modern additions as the digital footprint (Parkinson et al. 2017).

In particular, if we revisit the reference list, we can see that the subject needs to take various forms in order to relate to the other in appropriate ways. I don't claim the reference list is complete, but this does give a sense of the range of forms the subject will have to take.

- Informational privacy: the subject must be *the referent of a linguistic term in the information* (bringing to mind Quine's slogan that 'to be is to be the value of a bound variable' – 1980, 6–7). This also includes the referent of a term in the interpretation of computer data.
- Decisional privacy: *an agent.*
- Private property: *an owner.* In a legal sense, this means it is a legal person. In less formal senses, the subject must have sufficient agency to claim the property and to be embedded in an appropriate social setting supporting the norms of ownership. Ownership is characterised by cognitive (e.g. taking responsibility for maintenance or protection) and affective (e.g. pride, jealousy) components, and may be individual or collective.
- Psychological privacy: *a thinking subject with a first person perspective.*
- Ideological privacy: *a thinking subject with first person perspective, an appropriately socially embedded agent,* and in all likelihood *a rational agent.*
- Spatial privacy: *an embodied subject.*
- Attentional privacy: *an object of external perception.* That could mean an embodied subject (for behavioural observation), a communicating agent (for eavesdropping), presence

in a social setting (for gossip, publicity), an online avatar (for online surveillance) or a rational communicating agent (for interrogation).

- Extrinsic privacy: *a thinking subject with a first person perspective* with a lifeworld to be invaded in the event of a breach.

Hence the subject of a privacy claim may call upon a number of modes of presentation. The subject cannot be monolithic because it is involved with privacy conceptions subtended by different practices and contexts. We are flexible. Arnold Simmel wrote:

> we become what we are not only by establishing boundaries around ourselves but also by a periodic opening of these boundaries to nourishment, to learning, and to intimacy. But the opening of a boundary of the self may require a boundary farther out, a boundary around the group to which we are opening ourselves. (Simmel 1971, 81)

but even this may be too hierarchical a view (Marx 2001, 158, constructed a not entirely convincing taxonomy of self-boundaries). Freda and Picione described the boundary as an 'organic membrane', regulating two-way passage between the subject and the world in 'a relational system which produces, re-produces itself through the plasticity of the boundaries between the person, others and the world, in the becoming time' (2014, 181), gesturing toward the sort of flexibility we need when thinking of privacy.

The variety in the reference list neatly straddles two different approaches to defining the subject: the analytic/liberal tradition which focuses on the self, associated with notions of ownership and rights, and the continental tradition focusing on the subject, bringing in thought, action and reason (Johnson 1993, 3). Within the former, it covers William James' three types of self-as-experienced: a material self (including the body, signifiers such as clothes, and even money), a social self and a spiritual self (1890). It also implicates the three major dimensions that Martin and Barresi posited as necessary for an integrated theory of the self: the experiential dimension of first-person experience, the ontological dimension of what kind of organism constitutes it, and the social dimension (2006, 290–306).

A third connection between pre-reflective ideas of privacy and the self is the magnetic pull of possessive adjectives, those that work as linguistic markers of privacy interests. In cognitive science, self-ownership, the basic sense that these experiences and actions are *mine*, 'can be explained in terms of ecological self-awareness built into movement and perception' (Gallagher 2000, 16). Some claim that this feeling of ownership is an important and separate part of the self (Gallagher 2005, 173–174; Zahavi 2005, 99–146), while others that it is just a way of speaking (Anscombe 1962; Bermúdez 1998; Slors and Jongepier 2014). It is strong, though, so that in experiments such as the 'rubber hand illusion' (where participants watch a rubber hand being stroked while their own hand is being stroked identically out of sight), participants sometimes report that a dummy hand feels as if it is their own (Botvinick and Cohen 1998), while neurocognitive models describe correlates in the brain of feelings of body-ownership (Tsakiris 2010). Property may be included in one's assessment of one's self (Weiss and Johar 2018), as well as traces such as personal data (Parkinson et al. 2017; Kamleitner and Mitchell 2018). Even Buddhist accounts perceive the illusory self as fostering ideas of perspectival owner-ship (of things such as pains that appear to me in ways that those of others do not appear to me – Albahari 2006, 53) and personal ownership (of experiences or attributes as part of me – Albahari 2006, 56).

Ownership of the self doesn't entail identity with it or even the uniqueness of the owner, but now we are getting into deep waters. The philosophy of identity is strewn with complicated and some-times absurd thought experiments about what happens if a body or brain splits/disappears/is duplicated (Shoemaker 2007), which cannot be relevant to our use of the term 'privacy'.

The best-known view of the self along lines sympathetic to this account of privacy, that of William James, used the possessive adjective to describe a person's self, comprising 'not only his body and his psychic powers, but his clothes and his house, his wife and his children, his ancestors and friends, his reputation and works, his lands and horses, and yacht and bank account' (1890, 291). Whether or not one buys James' description of the extended self, it is certainly a decent checklist of the well-dressed pragmatist-about-town's privacy concerns in the *fin de siècle*. Coincidentally or not, he lived in Boston at the same time as Warren and Brandeis, and his *Principles of Psychology* from which this is quoted was published in the same year as their seminal article.

Well, is there a level 0 or not?

None of this is conclusive evidence that a level 0 account of privacy is there to be had, although it is suggestive of where one might go; it is meant to show the characteristics of level 0 discourse. The argument here is limited to privacy as applying to an individual, and so is admittedly incomplete. If Solove (2008) is correct, and I think he is, then there would be no direct logical, reductive, supervenient or semantic link between levels 0 and 1: any level 0 account would be incomplete, and perpetually vulnerable to unanticipated privacy conceptions emerging from novel practices and technologies. We might draw some conditional level 0 conclusions, such as that if something like the Jamesian self is in operation, it could suffice as the subject of individualistic privacy claims.

This is not the only possible level 0 account; others could be developed, such as that of Andrew McStay, who, leaning on the philosophy of Heidegger and Latour, described privacy as an actant (with causal powers) and a black box (an assemblage of different things at various scales that appear to act as durable wholes, and are accepted as such) producing affects (experiences and sensations). Rather than distinguishing the seven levels, McStay recognised the multiplicity, heterogeneity, co-existence and mutual influence of black boxes within a larger black box 'privacy', taking:

> the form of laws, regulations, people's behavior, the design of technology, the scripts that inform and regulate behavior of actants within a system, management structures and processes of how data is collected and used. Privacy as an actant mingles with human and technical systems so to contribute to multi-scalar assemblances, among jostling sites and struggles of association comprised of scripts, affordances, wills and multiple hybrid actors. (2014, 98)

This account shares many of my own convictions about the complexity and lack of systematicity of privacy, although my aim is to reduce rather than revel in it. Its use of the technical term 'actant' means it applies more widely than the privacy of individuals. However, with its foundation in continental philosophy, it may, like the Jamesian account, be too Western-centric to support a general theory of privacy. Furthermore, both the Jamesian account and McStay's provoke high-level debates involving major thinkers, but surely we shouldn't have to wrestle with the charismatic mega-fauna of philosophy and psychology to talk about privacy, if only because people without training can and do have perfectly reasonable conversations about it.

Consequently, I am prepared to go no further than the exercise above describing the heterogenous subject in terms of the forms dictated by the reference list, with any overarching theory tentative and hypothetical. The strong hint that the linguistic markers of possession give about potential privacy interests is also useful and (although based on English) can be exported to alternative cultures (most languages have possessive adjectives, or some variation such as a possessive case or possessive word-modifications).

To close, I re-emphasise that any putative level 0 account of privacy is philosophical in nature, makes no essential reference to matters properly concerning levels 1–7, and has no special status relative to the hierarchy of levels described in Part III. It is a discourse like any other.

Part V

Topics in privacy studies

The main task of this book is now complete, and the framework set out and defended, as best I can and admittedly tentatively. In this concluding section, I would like to illustrate the framework by looking at a few important topics relating to privacy which have either not been covered or not had justice done to them. Fairly arbitrarily, to span the range, I have chosen one topic for each level, and attempt to redescribe them in terms of their proper level. The aim is to show the value of the framework, by using it to focus on the specific issues involved in each particular topic, to isolate the key problems, and to prevent, as far as possible, the discussions from being soiled by extraneous and irrelevant considerations.

The topics are: group privacy, to illustrate ways we conceptualise privacy; cybersecurity, as a means of managing affordances; design of environments, especially online, in such a way as to manage the perceptions of individual users; consent, as a means of getting one's preferences; the private sphere, as grounded in social norms; data protection as a privacy-related legal construct; and the moral question of the conflict between individual privacy and community interests. In some of these topics, I will also discuss, and hopefully dismiss, the reasons for which they have been taken as definitive of privacy.

Level 1 topic: group privacy

If we insist on conceptualising privacy as a desire for solitude by individuals only, this appears paradoxical: 'he says he wants solitude, but then at the same time he wants this other individual to occupy his space. How odd; doesn't he know what privacy is?' Yes he does, and it's not (always) individual solitude. It is a mistake to see the right to be let alone as necessarily a plea for seclusion or solitude (Schoeman 1992, 8; McStay 2014, 40); the subject of the privacy claim may be plural.

Several times, I have touched on the issue of whether privacy is a matter for individuals only, or groups. Modern Western debates over privacy tend to frame it as a battle of the individual against surveillant forces, which, legally, it is. However, conceptions of privacy are *not* legal rights, and furnish a vocabulary much more attuned to vernacular feelings, needs and irritations. Historians and anthropologists demonstrate over and again how it features diversely in different societies, and that simple narratives of privacy's 'emergence' or 'decline' cannot capture the variety of ways in which distance from others is managed. In Europe, even those conflicts that are relatively visible because they come to court 'were for the most part between two social groups' (Vincent 2016, 4), rather than individuals, although it was often the head of a household who litigated on behalf of those under his, occasionally her, authority. The individual seeking seclusion 'is hard to locate amid the crowded households and thin walls of urban or rural communities anywhere in fourteenth-century Europe' (Vincent 2016, 2), and this remained the case (Thomas 1973, 629, for the sixteenth and seventeenth centuries; Sennett 2002, 47–122 for the eighteenth).

It has been suggested that 'the mistaken assertion that the notion of physical privacy was absent in medieval society perhaps derives from the modern assumption that privacy is individual and absolute, rather than communal and relative' (Shaw 1996, 450).

My lack of expertise in Asian views of privacy means I shan't discuss them in detail, but many scholars have argued that:

> as more collective and social in their orientation, [East Asian] countries and cultures … lay comparatively less emphasis on the individual – and so we find there no immediate counterpart to the Western *ontological* understanding of the atomistic individual that funds Western concepts of privacy as first of all *individual* privacy (by contrast, for example, the earlier concepts of privacy operating in Thailand were *collective* concepts – such as the concept of family privacy vis-à-vis the larger community and state). (Ess 2005, 4–5, his emphasis)

If an account of privacy is to avoid being Western-centric, the subject cannot only be an individual.

The family as a paradigm

The paradigm case of a group privacy subject is the family. It is arguable that the privacy of a family transcends that of the individual members, and cannot meaningfully be distributed across them. Representing mothers 'embedded in the care and nurturance of young families' as independent, atomistic individuals 'is, quite simply, nonsensical' (Gilliom 2001, 123), while the requirements of the infant render a discussion of *its* individual privacy even less plausible. It is quite possible that close family relationships are among the strongest drivers of privacy as something actively sought, even in our individualistic times.

The family itself needs to transmit what Sartre described as 'family truth', its unique transgenerational perspective, across its vectors including care for infants. This, while it might be influenced by outsiders, depends where possible on the subjective experience of the parents, *rapport* with the child, and reinforcement by other relatives, so that the infant becomes a family member as well as a person: 'by this love and through it, by that person, skilful or unskilful, rough or tender, the way her history made her, the child is manifested to himself' (Sartre 1981, 57).

This conception of privacy subtended by the family unit is operative enough, but not universal. It has been decried by many opponents, both fictional, from the guardians of Plato's *Republic* (who wanted to make the whole of society a single family – Arendt 1998, 223), to the controllers of *Brave New World*, and real, from eco-communards (Erärantä et al. 2009) to eighteenth-century aristocrats (Sennett 2002, 94) to critical theorists (Deleuze and Guattari 1983) to totalitarians (Arendt 2017). In the modern era, the state has taken an increasing interest in these functions (Habermas 1989, 155). Indeed, the nuclear family seems to be a relatively recent development, in tandem with the valorisation of childhood (Sennett 2002, 91–94; Solove 2008, 51). Nevertheless, that does not mean that in earlier times the 'family truth' wasn't a private matter for wider kin groups, ancestors, clans and tribes, to whom parents of children had their own responsibilities.

Hence, it does violence to normal privacy discourse to 'read' the claim that 'my wife and I want privacy' to mean 'I want privacy relative to everyone, with the exception that I do not want privacy relative to my wife, and my wife *mutatis mutandis*.' Although that is not nonsense, surely it is more congruent with standard usage to say 'my wife and I, together, as a couple, want *our* privacy'. It is no coincidence that it is *my wife* with whom I wish privacy, as opposed to the postman, or Silvio Berlusconi, or the board of Unilever. There is a special connection with intimates, which means that we conceptualise privacy as applying to them together as a unit, not distributed across the individuals separately.

The group privacy of the family has often been an obstacle to the individual privacy of women within it (Stetson 1898, 258; Allen 1988, 69; Solove 2008, 52) – and also of men too, though they have usually had more power to achieve their preferences. While the family sets up a barrier to the outside world, the result is more intense interaction within. This has historically applied not only to family members, but also servants *qua* members of the household. Until recently, people behaved with remarkable indiscretion in front of their servants who 'really didn't count' (Sennett 2002, 76; Spacks 2003, 196–198). As G. K. Chesterton put it, a wealthy lady, asked if anyone is with her, 'doesn't answer, "Yes: the butler, the three footmen, the parlour-maid, and so on", though the parlour-maid may be in the room or the butler behind her chair'. The proverb that 'no man is a hero to his valet' means that the valet is privy to most of his master's behaviour, honourable and dishonourable alike. This may also be a characteristic of other societies, such as imperial China (Silber 2002, 59, 68).

Group privacy

Many present-day evocations of privacy apply to groups, and the 'private lives' of groups are important to us (Schoeman 1992, 113). Individuals are often willing to trade or sacrifice their privacy for the privacy of the group (Westin 1967, 12–18; Altman 1975, 22; Vincent 2016). It is quite possible that many privacy conceptions in everyday use emerged in group rather than individual contexts, and that a significant minority, if not a majority, of calls for privacy demand it for groups (Schoeman 1992, 193). The discussion in Warren and Brandeis of the 'right to be let alone', which has some-times been taken to refer to the solitude of an individual, is clearly focused largely on intimate groups such as families.

Claims that privacy, as a type of withdrawal, can only apply to individuals (Inness 1992, 45–46) miss the subtlety that it is sought 'in large part not to isolate people but to enable them to relate intim-ately or in looser associations that serve personal and group goals ... to enshroud with respect an association of people that is meaningful in its own terms' (Schoeman 1992, 21). Gavison's assertion that per-fect privacy is complete inaccessibility to others (1980, 350) there-fore misrepresents the plurality of privacy in two directions (albeit she agrees it is an impossible state). First, multiple conceptions of privacy may be in play at any one time, some of which may be breached and others not. Second, withdrawal from *some* people may be the means to closer or undisturbed communion with *others*.

Given that a group subtends a privacy conception, we have to ask whether the conception applies to each of the individuals within it or to the group as a whole. If we take a group with some officers (treasurer, administrator, secretary, etc.), and a privacy conception that who fills those positions remains secret to outsiders, is this is a conception that applies to each individual – so that *Jane Smith's* privacy is breached if it is revealed that she is the treasurer – or to the group as an entity separate from the set of its members?

The former is really privacy of association, a kind of attentional privacy for individuals, and many suggested examples of group privacy are of this kind. Bloustein emphasised those relationships where testimony in a court of law may not be compelled, such as husband–wife, priest–penitent, lawyer–client, physician–patient, contractual relations and journalistic privilege (1977, 226–234). These seem to be cases where the conceptions subtended apply *to* individuals *within* groups, not to groups themselves. His aim was to secure 'the right to associate with others in confidence' in order to ensure healthy civil society (1977, 278; Schoeman 1992; Allen 2011, 4).

Group privacy of the latter type has been eclipsed thanks to two unfortunate sources of occlusion. First, legal privacy rights apply solely to individuals. Even when this is phrased as a right to family life, it's an *individual's* right to a family life. The second pressure is the dominant liberal, individualistic ideology of wealthy democracies. Rössler's liberal account, for example, explicitly contrasted individual privacy with the privacy of very large institutions (2005, 1–2) but ignored the borderline cases of small voluntary or intimate groups. Liberalism's individualistic point of view (Fawcett 2018, 120–125) makes it hard to do justice to group interests within the paradigm. Thus it appears paradoxical that people should claim privacy in order to open themselves up to attention from others within groups and associations. One common rationalisation prompted by this liberal paradox is to redefine privacy as control over access, as we have seen (Rössler 2005, 71–76), but this flawed strategy can be dispensed with once the individualist mindset is transcended.

Types of group

Westin was clear that organisations have privacy interests (1967, 46–56), and 'it is a vital lubricant of the organizational system in free societies' (1967, 56). What kind of groups can we reasonably describe as having privacy interests? That requires thought about what groups there are.

We can characterise groups by their members (extensionally) or by the principle of their formation (intensionally). Given n people, there will be $(2^n - (n+1))$ possible groups extensionally speaking with more than one member (so 10 people between them can form 1,013 groups). However, it is more informative to define groups with a predicate describing membership – 'the group of people that X'. In that case, there are even more potential groups because we might find that two groups defined by different predicates had coincidentally the same members. The group of Real Madrid fans in the class might happen to be exactly the same people as the group of deaf people in the class, but clearly the two groups, though identical in extension, will have different agendas, and will be liable to grow apart as new members join and founder members lose interest. Their extensional equivalence is accidental.

Groups come in a number of types. First, there are groups that we consciously form and join – associations, teams, regiments, companies – sometimes called face-to-face collectivities (Altman 1975, 22). Some we are automatically conscripted into, such as families, which demand a level of commitment that we do not volunteer for. Other associations are formed for leisure, to solve problems or to further our interests. Associations can be large but formal (such as companies), or informal but small (little platoons – Burke 1968), and with the advent of ubiquitous networked devices, quite large informal geographically distributed groups can emerge (sometimes called *social machines* – O'Hara and Robertson 2017; Shadbolt et al. 2019). With that technology, the notion of a face-to-face collectivity looks dated. Let's call these conscious groups *associations*.

Group privacy in the full sense is likely to be especially salient for associations. Companies and other organisations that are legal persons can own private property. Some examples of their decisional privacy have been discussed (Westin 1967, 47–49). An association can have spatial privacy in a corporate capacity, for instance in the hire of a meeting room – the privacy is of the meeting, not of the individuals within it. The identity of the finance minister is not a private matter, but the Cabinet meeting is. A convent might be surrounded by a wall, not only to protect the privacy of the nuns, but of the order itself. However, revealing the confidential minutes of a company's strategy awayday isn't often regarded as a breach of the company's *privacy* rather than of *confidentiality*. Other types from the reference list, such as psychological privacy, ideological privacy and extrinsic privacy are rarely invoked for associations.

Groups that aren't associations are less convincing as subjects for group privacy. There are transient groups that happen to become significant at a point in time, although we may not have joined them deliberately, such as the passengers on a bus, the sufferers from a disease or the children in a class. There are groups that we are not part of, but we create in order to conceptualise and order the world, such as do-gooders, the lads who vandalise the village, or 'foreigners'. Quite often, this kind of group-making is described using a neologistic boo-word, *othering*: pronouncing someone as alien and different, excluded from the in-group (Bernasconi 2012). Othering is frowned upon, although it is hard to see how society could function if we didn't manage exclusion somehow. There are also wider groups characteristic of the major ideologies of modernity, whose existence is generally made manifest intellectually to their members via narratives, reports and a framing of common interests – for instance, the *proletariat*, the *gay community* or the population of a *nation*.

It seems counterintuitive to consider larger or more abstract groups in privacy terms. It may be that, for example, a group of people of the same nationality may in some circumstances have a common interest in keeping their nationality private (say, during wartime), but it is hard to see how a *nation* might have a similar privacy interest. The interest in that particular case devolves to the individuals, or to small associations within the group, not the larger group as a totality.

The situation is not completely straightforward, because there are exceptions where 'private' is contrasted with 'public', so the workings of a trade union, political party or multinational company might be referred to as private matters, and they may own private property as legal persons. Functionaries of organisations, even including the state itself, need the ability to develop ideas, negotiate and resolve conflicts 'in private', 'behind the scenes', being creative while not fully accountable (Bloustein 1977, 280–283). The privacy in question consists in deflecting attention from individuals, but (i) they act within a role, in the organisation's interests, and

(ii) a breach leads to scrutiny of the organisation itself. A mandated breach of this kind for a public corporation is often referred to as 'transparency' (Fung et al. 2007). It may make sense to say (with Westin 1967) that transparency in this sense is a breach of the privacy of the organisation, although I tend to the view (without defending it here) that these are matters of secrecy or confidentiality for the organisation that in this case are not subtypes of privacy.

Algorithmic clusters

The reason group privacy has become a hot topic in recent years is yet another technological advance, in which people are clustered using machine learning algorithms to find hidden similarities in their behaviour from their data trails, a practice essential to e-commerce, targeted advertising and policymaking. Groups are formed automatically as a target for scrutiny, and one might be a member of many groups (e.g. the class of women, 35–45, with university education, living in the suburbs, with one to three children, whose Amazon purchases exceeded $1,000 last year) without actually being aware of it at all.

The aim of clustering is to access the group, not the individual (Eubanks 2019, 6–7). A company wants to make a sale, it doesn't care to whom, while many political conflicts are attacks on groups, not individuals, as in the immortal lines from Joseph Heller's World War II novel *Catch-22*:

> 'They're [the German army and air force] trying to kill me,' Yossarian told him calmly.
>
> 'No one's trying to kill you,' Clevinger cried.
>
> 'Then why are they shooting at me?' Yossarian asked.
>
> 'They're shooting at everyone,' Clevinger answered. 'They're trying to kill everyone.'
>
> 'What difference does that make?'

Action on a non-evident group defined exogenously creates important ethical issues, which are difficult to address by laws that focus on the rights of individuals. For instance, in 2014, an experiment was carried out on nearly 700,000 unaware Facebook users.

News feeds to these people were manipulated so that expressions of sentiment were filtered, with the result that those who received more negative news were more likely to write negative stories themselves, and *mutatis mutandis* for the positive group. The authors proudly announced, 'the results show emotional contagion' (Kramer et al. 2014). There was an immediate outcry, which caused a dip in Facebook's share price, but within a few weeks of the news breaking it had actually risen. One wonders if the outcry was confected in order to perpetuate the myth of Facebook's omniscience (O'Hara 2015a). However that may be, the research was arguably unethical, consistent with the tradition of that wretched company (even though the researchers were unable to identify any of their experimental subjects). However, whether the privacy breach covers the totality, rather than applying separately to each individual user within the group, is debatable.

Given such considerations, and although some have argued otherwise (Taylor 2017), I would suggest that while algorithmic clustering is a novel epistemological problem that subtends privacy conceptions for clustered individuals (e.g. decisional privacy about the choices one may be allowed to make, such as whether a credit rating prevents or allows one to take out a mortgage), they do not apply to the group as a whole. Its members do not conceive themselves as having common interests (typically not being aware of the group's existence at all), and such groups have little internal structure whose workings might be exposed.

Level 2 topic: security algorithms do not define privacy

In a digital environment, the privacy conception in play typically concerns either the processing of information about a person, or the inference of new information about them. Particularly thanks to the current urgent need to protect informational privacy, there has been an increased focus on architectural and structural affordances for security. That a system is secure may not mean that privacy is protected. A welfare system may breach its clients' privacy by collecting information about them and their financial circumstances. Of course it holds this information, most of which was donated by the clients or generated by their interactions with it, in confidence and with consent, and it will be stored safely with this in mind. But the prioritised security vector is with respect not to outside hackers but to the clients themselves, to prevent them gaining access to funds to which they are not entitled, or to prevent them from amending or falsifying their information (Gilliom 2001; Coles-Kemp et al. 2018; Eubanks 2019). The protection of *clients'* security may be a secondary purpose. A secure commercial environment may be stronger in its protection of valuable inferred data, profiles and predictive models than of the 'raw' data, which may be of less value, but more revealing of private details such as names and credit card numbers.

Data anonymisation

An umbrella term for ways of suppressing such revelation of private details is *anonymisation*, which consists of measures applied to sensitive datasets to reduce the risk of disclosing information about individuals to a sufficiently low or negligible level. The risk can't be reduced to zero, without removing all detail and making the dataset completely useless (Ohm 2010; Duncan et al. 2011; Barocas and Nissenbaum 2014, 50; Rubinstein and Hartzog 2016; Elliot et al. 2018). Anonymisation measures include removing information that might help identify people (*identifiers*, e.g. names, social security numbers and birthdates), making it harder to link information (e.g. showing a series of purchases but removing the bank details that connect them), making information less precise (e.g. turning an age, '42', into a range '36–45'), and injecting random values here and there. The affordances of the data to protect privacy are boosted but at the cost of making it harder for legitimate researchers as well as hackers to interrogate.

Many data controllers (i.e. those who determine when and how data will be processed) have believed that data can be made non-disclosive simply by applying a few such basic rules to the dataset, thereby allowing the transformed data to be shared safely with others or sold on (Ohm 2010 calls this practice *release-and-forget*). The transformation makes the data less useful but still not useless. While such measures leave a risk of reidentification, it is often hoped that it is acceptably small.

This complacency has led to some disastrous decisions to share anonymised data or even to place it online for free download. The most notorious was in 2006 when AOL released data about searches on their platform, intending it to be used by scientists to discover interesting patterns that could be used to improve search algorithms (Arrington 2006). They removed obvious identifiers from the data, but crucially it was possible to link searches (i.e. to know two searches were done by the same household). But our searches are remarkably disclosive. For example, someone searching quite often for addresses in a particular town is likely to live there, and searching more than once for a non-famous name usually means the searcher is that person. If they also search for particular topics, such as medical conditions or odd sexual interests, that allows revealing inferences about their problems and peccadillos. In the AOL dataset were some quite creepy searches; Person #927 searched for 'skin mold', 'mange', 'corpse bride', 'dog sex' (five times) and 'square dancing steps', clearly someone of eclectic interests. Not everyone in the data could be identified, but one was, and quite detailed profiles of others could be assembled (possibly allowing identification in future). It was a privacy disaster, exposed by data journalists and criticised by academics (Ohm 2010), and executives' heads rightly rolled. For other egregious examples, see (Narayanan and Shmatikov 2008; Trotter 2014).

AOL's mistake was to assume that data can be rendered safe to share by the affordances of manipulative techniques alone, ignoring the wider environment. Imagine an anonymised medical dataset, minus whatever might be irrelevant for medical purposes (for medical data, a person's name is rarely needed, nor their precise age, but it is usually important to know their sex, approximate age, and perhaps occupation type). If a snooper knows a few details about the person they are searching for, they can match them against whatever remains in the data. If, for instance, they knew gender, date of admission to hospital, age and an approximate postcode or zip code (perhaps by following them), that would probably be sufficient to identify them (i.e. the person searched for) in the database. Now the snooper has found their quarry, they will learn more about them and may be able to use the new information to identify them in other anonymised datasets. Note that no perfect anonymisation algorithm is possible because we can never know in advance what auxiliary information the snooper can access.

In any case, the ability to find someone's identity may be irrelevant. If someone wants to send people targeted adverts as spam, all they really need to know is what type of person they are and where to send the ads, not the identity of the recipient (Barocas and Nissenbaum 2014, 54), and anonymised data may still be revealing in such respects.

Some have drawn negative conclusions about anonymisation as a result (Ohm 2010), but all this proves is that anonymisation done badly, using techniques restricted to transforming the data, creates vulnerabilities. Yet it can be done well and effectively with a wider understanding of the level 2 affordances of the data's context (Cavoukian and El Emam 2011; Elliot et al. 2018). Anonymity of the data (i.e. the extent to which it is resistant to giving up details about individuals within it) is a property not of the dataset itself, but the data *in its context*. This depends not only on the data but also on what extra knowledge and skills those looking at the data have, the tools they have to apply to the data, the ease of getting hold of it and so on. In short, it also depends on the level 2 affordances of the data's context in the round or what has been called the *data environment* (Elliot et al. 2018). This includes the dataset, the people who have access to it, any other data that can be used to help decode it, and the security and governance measures in place. It should also take account of the risks involved – how sensitive is the data? How valuable is the information it holds? Can the information be found from other sources? Is it out of date?

Hence, anonymisation, properly done, can be valuable, but managing the data environment is relatively expensive compared to release-and-forget. It might involve ensuring that researchers have access to the data only under strict conditions, which may be governed by contract, or by sterner measures such as only allowing physical access on a particular computer unconnected to the Internet. At the limit, the data controller can refuse to let others get their hands on the data, instead working out the answers to their queries for them (and not passing them on if they are too revealing). The availability of relevant auxiliary data should be monitored constantly, so that if sharing the anonymised data became more risky through time, measures would need to be tightened. Anonymisation certainly has a part to play in a safe data economy, but only done conscientiously with an understanding of the level 2 affordances of the data environment as a whole. Applying technical measures to the data is not enough.

Cybersecurity

Cybersecurity is the use of technical mechanisms to prevent access to data on computer networks, to protect privacy, secure intellectual property or copyright material, protect national security against foreign governments or prevent ransomware attacks that render data useless. The Internet and the World Wide Web were designed to allow data to flow easily (O'Hara and Hall 2021), and so the privacy affordances of the 'raw' architecture are relatively minimal, while search engines like Google only make information easier to get hold of. The cybersecurity business has grown rapidly around securing this information environment. Firewalls, passwords, encryption and cryptography, multi-factor authentication, biometrics and extensions to protocols are means by which experts improve the affordances of the online environment (Brooks et al. 2018). There is a cottage industry devoted to scanning systems for vulnerabilities (Perlroth 2021), which most major companies fix automatically and periodically (with patches that may increase the complexity of the system, creating new vulnerabilities). There is an arms race between cybersecurity experts protecting data, and hackers who want to get at it, especially financial data, passwords and personal details, and with a number of states backing the hackers, it is not obvious that the good guys are winning (Hubback 2020). As the abilities (and resources) of hackers grow, the privacy affordances of the information architecture correspondingly decline (which does not necessarily mean that users' privacy declines overall, because, for instance, regulation might make up the gap).

Cybersecurity, like law, is a discipline that gets hegemonic about privacy, tending to assume it is guaranteed by crypto-graphic techniques that can be proven mathematically to conceal information to the desired degree. Unfortunately, as with anonymisation, this can't be the case; the affordances of the technological environment are certainly an important part of the picture, but this level 2 discourse leaves many other factors at other levels unaffected.

To take one example, an increasingly influential cybersecurity tool is *differential privacy* (Dwork 2014), a quantifiable method of protecting data by changing some of the values in a database randomly. This is highly sophisticated, and some have argued that differential privacy is what privacy *is*, or at least that it can serve as a standard metric for privacy violations (Dwork 2014, 317). This won't do.

In the first place, as a measure to protect *informational* privacy, it leaves most of the reference list untouched. More importantly, it is focused on a single highly specific privacy conception that has not emerged from ordinary language discourse, but one that computer scientists have formalised and are able to reason about. It is none the worse for that, but while it is undoubtedly an important technical standard, it is highly artificial. The conception is this: (i) if two databases are identical except that one contains a single row of data about an individual A and the other does not, (ii) the databases remain in the custody of an honest curator who is prepared to answer queries about them, and (iii) the algorithm for retrieving information from the databases injects random noise, then (iv) the setup is differentially private if it is hard, simply by putting queries to the curator, to find out any more about A from one database than the other. In other words, it is hard for the outsider to tell whether A is in the database or not. What does 'hard' mean? A parameter ε can be defined such that the probability that the outsider can find A in the databases is less than ε; the closer ε is to 0, the more private the retrieval algorithm, but all things being equal the less useful the data. Differential privacy works for groups as well as for individuals.

This is a complicated and brilliant idea, and will inevitably be part of the future suite of cyber protections. However, it is pretty obvious that it is not a privacy conception that feels very intuitive. It is also massively dependent on the affordances of the system in which it is embedded. For instance, it depends on the integrity of the database curator, and on the data not falling into the hands of the adversary. The whole thing could be side-stepped if the adversary simply paid the curator $1,000 to hand over a USB stick with the database on it. Given that the right environment is in place, then the affordances of differential privacy will deliver the desired result. Even then, privacy needs to be balanced against the utility of the data, so that if we need to know something very much, ε might have to be adjusted upwards, and there will always be querents prepared to put their own information needs above the privacy needs of those represented in the data. Some have even complained that differential privacy reveals how much information about identifiable individuals might be available from similar datasets (Barocas and Nissenbaum 2014, 56).

Even if the entire environment can be technically designed, it will still have to fit into a social context. At that point, the system has to be usable or users will become a point of vulnerability (Krombholz et al. 2015). The cybersecurity perspective often sees the human as the weakness in a carefully designed cryptographic system – which from one point of view it is (Adams and Sasse 1999). But the human is the *sine qua non* of the whole thing. It is rather like designing a highly secure house without windows or doors, and then complaining that the owner has drilled a hole in the roof to get in.

Beyond that, digital privacy is always threatened by what is called the *analogue hole*, the fact that, be they ever so encrypted and cybersecure, signals have to be converted into readable messages or information for their receivers to read and understand, and when they are unencrypted, they can be captured by someone simply leaning over the receiver's shoulder. The analogue hole did for digital rights management techniques for protecting copyrights of music or film – people simply recorded the content on their smartphones and distributed it themselves (Sicker et al. 2007, 574).

Cybersecurity is essential in digital modernity, and brilliant work is being done in the sector. But it cannot live by its own crypto-graphic standards exclusively. Whatever affordances it provides had better meet up with the purposes of the system and the needs and wants of the users, as Charles Raab pithily explained:

> [I]t is no comfort to a privacy-aware individual to be told that inaccurate, outdated, excessive and irrelevant data about her are encrypted and stored behind hacker-proof firewalls until put to use by (say) a credit-granting organization in making decisions about her. (Raab 2005, 285)

Level 3 topic: design for apparency

Most populated environments are wholly or partly human-constructed, so privacy can be designed in or out. In particular, the online environment is an entirely artificial confection, and legal scholar Woodrow Hartzog has drawn attention to the role of design in its function and business models (Hartzog 2018, 197–229). Social media design focuses on increasing user engagement and modifying behaviour, often below the level of awareness (Zuboff 2019; Saura et al. 2021), so these characteristics of the design do not feature as first-order phenomenological objects but have phenomenological effects. Hartzog gave the example of the shift of the menu bar for the mobile Facebook app to the bottom of the screen, closer to the user's thumbs, reducing perceived effort for posting and sharing, to maximise the amount of information that users donate.

Phenomenology isn't the only aspect of design, even of interface design, but certain aspects of the user's understanding can be steered by misleading experiences, for instance making users feel private even when their data is haemorrhaging in the general direction of Facebook. Manipulative interfaces have been called *dark patterns*, making it hard for users to express or achieve preferences, concealing rather than revealing function (Luguri and Strahilevitz 2021).

Offline, we have a strong sense of context, and are able to move between them and adjust attitudes reasonably smoothly. Online, contexts are neither signalled nor distinguished, provoking *context collapse* when audiences that ought to be discrete (and discreet?) merge and access a wider range of information than they should – employers access social media, family members access content intended for friends, and so on (Marwick and boyd 2011).

This problem was not invented by social media, but offline it is unusual. Goffman found that mental patients in an asylum had no ability to compartmentalise, being constantly under surveillance by an unchanging group and fully accountable for their actions at all times (1961a), while the tragic case of Oliver Sipple, whose heroism led to widespread publicity, which resulted in the public revelation of his homosexuality, estrangement from his family and eventually a lonely death, was purely a mass media phenomenon (Lever 2012, 31–33).

The immediate experience of being on Twitter is of a conversation between a small number of participants, while the presence of a large potential audience is far less evident. This prompts letting off steam, relieving tensions and even rehearsing offensive or damaging ideas. Throughout history, people have ranted ungenerously and offensively about what irritates them. The rants used to disappear into the ether and did not usually have terrible consequences, Henry II's denunciation of Thomas Becket being a counterexample. Not anymore. @TheRealKingHenry's tweets about @TomCantuar would probably have got the king excommunicated years before the assassination, as well as countless death threats from trolls for Becket.

Context collapse impacts on privacy (Vitak 2012). Although privacy is under pressure from social network companies and their users (Hartzog 2018, 198–205), in phenomenological terms threats from the latter are easier to represent and understand. Users tend to develop strategies to conceal information from other individuals, rather than from the companies which are by far the bigger hazard (Young and Quan-Haase 2013). Online privacy is a relatively abstract conception, and making its erosion apparent and available to a user's conscious experience isn't easy. There is a tradition of academic research into the presentation and visualisation of privacy-related information for lay users (Reeder et al. 2008; Ghazinour et al. 2009; Van Kleek et al. 2018), but it has not been integrated into any major systems (unsurprisingly, given social networking companies' incentives) and hasn't caught on.

Human–computer interaction (HCI) has a repertoire of phenomenological presentational techniques, ranging from the blue underlined text of hyperlinks, the shadows that signal a drop-down menu, the motion of the cursor over a computer screen, the way one's cursor turns into a watch when a service is delayed, the pad-lock that appears in a browser's address bar to signify the encrypted transfer of data, and the red light that shows one's webcam is oper-ating. Design principles such as *seamfulness* (Chalmers and Galani 2004), the opposite of seamlessness, and *apparency* (schraefel et al. 2020) have been introduced into the psychological/design argot of HCI to denote a design goal for artefacts and apps: that their form, function and demands are not only transparent to the user, but *apparent* too. To appreciate the difference, a design that made the use of personal data transparent might allow the user to navi-gate a series of questions asking who was getting the data, on what terms, and so on. Though open and honest, it might be too boring and unengaging to be used very often. A design that made the use of data apparent might be, say, a scrolling bar at the bottom of the screen informing the reader each time data was passed onto a third party. Of course it would whizz past way too quickly to read, but that in itself would convey an important message about the scale of the practice.

In much design, sadly, misdirection is more common than apparency. Sensors in objects such as sex toys (Carman 2017), mattresses (Song 2018) and, God help us, even toilets (Grego et al. 2021) gathering and disseminating usage data surprise users, because their presence is not necessary for function, obvious to the observer or signalled. This will be a growing problem with the Internet of Things, where 'smart' objects are connected to the Internet, often for no particularly good reason. Design focuses on the 'thing' situated in a human world (mattress, fridge, car), but regulation treats them inappropriately as computers (Hartzog 2018, 260–275; schraefel et al. 2020). A child plays with a smart doll (i.e. a play-thing), but it is regulated as a computer, whose privacy-breaching data practices are deemed to be already agreed via acceptance of the privacy policy, despite not being evident (present to users' con-sciousness) because concealed by design (Keymolen and Van der Hof 2019).

The phenomenology of online privacy for most users is uninformative without a connection to real-world things. For instance, voice assistants are privacy-threatening, alongside the useful services they offer. They are constantly listening, in order to fulfil their voice activation function, yet this is not always made apparent (for example, by lighting up when it is listening). Experience is subliminally mediated through expectations, for example by giving voice assistants feminine names and voices to exploit gendered expectations of caring and nurturing instead (Woods 2018). Smart things' software has to be upgraded with regular security patches and new versions, so that, for example, a smart doll may be reprogrammed after purchase with attitudes differing from the parents' – for instance, about gender roles, which may be too traditional for some parents or too 'woke' for others. Why not make this apparent?

Even the privacy policy, a contract that sets out how the company will use the data it gathers, can be made more apparent through design. It is a cliché that no one reads privacy policies (McDonald and Cranor 2008), but as our online experiences get richer and more nuanced, why not devolve some of the tedious contract boilerplate directly into the user interface? Courts are not (yet) interested in experiential augmentations of the privacy policy/contract, but perhaps they should be (Hartzog 2018, 212). Furthermore, acquiescence to the policy is demanded at the least convenient time, interrupting access to the service at the point of demand. A far better moment would be when the user was (i) more able to reflect about future needs, and (ii) more aware of how, and how often, the app would use and leak personal data (schraefel et al. 2020, 103).

Level 4 topic: consent does not define privacy

One of the most important mechanisms for facilitating subjects in achieving a measure of control over their privacy is *consent*, especially salient now as a chief pillar of data protection law (Manson and O'Neill 2012; Lowrance 2012, 67–86; Barocas and Nissenbaum 2014). In the EU's GDPR, consent to have one's personal data processed is a legitimate ground for data processing, as long as it was valid, freely given, specific, informed and active. It also features in other types of law. For instance, publication of a piece of work is, in common law, communication with the consent of the author to a wide public (Warren and Brandeis 1890, 79–82).

It has been argued that consent is or ought to be referenced in a definition of privacy, because it negates a privacy violation (i.e. intrusion with consent is not a breach of privacy – e.g. Solove 2008, 102). However, this is another example of a kitchen sink privacy definition; consent is a *means of control*, but does not fundamentally alter the nature of privacy itself. It enables individuals to make the world more to their liking, either by directly achieving their privacy preferences or at least preventing those breaches that bother them. It removes many objections to privacy breaches (Benn 1971, 226) but does not stop them being breaches. One may accept breaches that one 'puts up with', that aren't welcomed, but are the price for some other service (Rössler 2005, 113).

Consent must have an object, and so the consenter must have consented *to something*. That something is *the proposed breach of privacy*. To consent to a breach of privacy is to anticipate and allow the breach to take place, not to magic it away, just as when I consent to a medical procedure, that procedure still happens. It would be odd to say that what had been consented to disappeared after consent was given.

When someone requests consent, they typically provide explanation and justification of those actions that would breach normal standards, not of the proposed action as a whole, so those standards can be conditionally waived (Manson and O'Neill 2012, 75). The request highlights the transgressive or potentially harmful aspects of the breach of privacy required for the proposed action to be performed. As Westin put it, 'there is no violation of the right to privacy when persons give general consent to be recorded or watched' (1967, 419). It is the *right* that is not violated (it is waived), *despite* the breach of privacy itself.

Consent does not change the ontological status of an event; it legitimises it within a legal or moral framework, and leads to reclassification *within that framework*. It cannot change a privacy breach into something else, although it can, and does, change an illegal or immoral privacy breach into a legal or moral one. 'Obligations and expectations are presupposed by informed consent practices. ... Informed consent ... offers a standard and controllable way of setting aside obligations and prohibitions for limited and specific purposes' (Manson and O'Neill 2012, 73). The emphasis is on control, given a standard framework understood by all parties that works as a mechanism for the individual's personal preferences to be respected and privileged.

Consent changes the way we describe an event. Sex with consent is still sex, but it is not an assault; a medical operation with consent is still an operation, but not paternalistic or negligent. A privacy breach with consent still exposes the subject, and so is still a privacy breach, but not a violation of rights or autonomy. Someone who consents to appear on *Big Brother* loses their privacy in the relevant respect, and it cannot be restored or protected by their consent. Consent shifts the responsibility for the breach onto the subject.

The conditions for valid consent

It is an idealisation to say that consent is a mechanism for us to get our preferences. We give or withhold consent to the options available, which, although it allows us to optimise our choice from what is on offer, may be a long way from what we prefer. The choice is usually agree/disagree, rather than a negotiation to find a win-win. Furthermore, our preferences are apt to change over time, whereas consent may not be easy to withdraw once given. Still, none of this is in itself bad – it may be the simplest means of finding a course of action acceptable to everyone, and limiting deception and coercion (O'Neill 2003).

However, consent can only pull even this lesser trick under certain circumstances. It needs to be *informed* – that is, the subject must be properly aware of what is being proposed, and how it breaches privacy. Typically, the subject is presented with *notice*, a description of what is proposed. There will also be limits – the consent is not usually open-ended but restricted to a particular day, time, person or set of people, and will expire once the event is over (Manson and O'Neill 2012, 73).

Note, in passing, that the subject will require decisional privacy to consider the proposal without undue pressure. It has to be *voluntary*. If, for example, an employer includes an intrusive personality test as a compulsory part of its recruitment procedure, consent is not fully voluntary (Westin 1967, 420). Meaningful consent requires alternative options, but these may not be feasible choices for someone in need. Here, for instance, is a statement from a government welfare agency.

> The human services department will use your social security number when contacting people or agencies to obtain information needed to determine your eligibility and verify information you have given. For example your social security number may be used to check your income and/or employment information with past or present employers, financial resources through IRS, unemployment compensation, disability benefits received from state or federal resources and any other appropriate local, state, or federal agency to verify information you have given. ... [a long and open-ended series of further examples follows] ...
>
> I give my consent to the agency to make whatever contacts are necessary to determine my eligibility for assistance and to verify information I have given in this application. (quoted in Gilliom 2001, 18)

Protection against fraud is important of course. But how can one withhold one's consent in grave financial hardship? Could a poor, stressed, possibly poorly educated person really juggle their rights and needs in an appropriately dispassionate way? And how do phrases like 'any other appropriate ... agency' and 'whatever contacts are necessary' limit the actions of the department? Consent can legitimise breaches of privacy only when it is not coerced, but, as the revealing phrase has it, beggars cannot be choosers (Westin 1967, 264–265).

I have focused on consent as an explicit, semi-formal response to notice of a desired or required breach of privacy. Consent can also be informal and *implied* by someone's voluntarily entering a situation where privacy will inevitably be breached. Someone entering a supermarket should expect all the inconveniences of being in public, and if they later complain that people were looking at them, or observing what they carried in their basket, then we would say not that privacy had been breached without consent, but rather that they didn't understand supermarket shopping. Exactly where consent is implied by a subject's acquiescence is a fuzzy boundary, particularly in employment (Summers 2000), intimate relationships (Higgins et al. 2010), religious practice (Helfand 2018) and medical practice (Aveyard 2002). Young people who need to learn the boundaries can be particularly vulnerable to misunderstandings (Fantasia 2011).

Cognitive limitation

There are well-known problems with consent for complex actions at scale. First, a complex breach may be hard to describe properly. Even with a sincere intention to be transparent, simplicity and clarity of message may mean that important detail is missed, the so-called *transparency paradox* (Barocas and Nissenbaum 2014, 58–59). The explanation of the intended breach, even in good faith, may be meaningless to the subject (Etzioni 1999, 155–160). Apparency may be more valuable than the transparency demanded by the notice-and-consent regime (schraefel et al. 2020).

Where there is immense complexity, as when data is harvested at scale and auctioned off to third parties, transparency may be futile. So much data is used, so frequently, that controlling it by fine-grained consent has been likened to a distributed denial of service attack on our brains (Hartzog 2018, 65). With apps and websites, notice takes the form of a privacy policy, long, legalistic and tedious to read, quite possibly by design (McDonald and Cranor 2008) – it might justly be said that the privacy policy is the last refuge of the scoundrel. So pervasive is the world of social networking and smartphone apps that it has been argued that to opt out of these is to opt out of social life altogether and so cannot be truly voluntary (Hartzog and Selinger 2013; Angwin 2014). Can consent under such conditions be informed and uncoerced?

Consent requires a tricky cognitive task, necessitating a difficult trade-off between an immediate gain (perhaps access to a service), and a longer-term, less tangible risk. Some harms, such as spam, are minimal but common, while others have a smaller probability but greater seriousness, such as identity theft, and balancing these is hard (Acquisti 2014, 84). Can the risk be estimated at all? Objectivity is made harder when we are asked for consent at the point when the *quid pro quo* is about to be delivered, when the subject is maximally focused on the immediate benefit (schraefel et al. 2020), as noted in the previous topic.

Furthermore, a series of individually low-risk events may become cumulatively high-risk. The data gathered by each use of each app on a phone might not amount to much, but if it were aggregated the resulting dossier would be quite revealing, just as personality tests given annually to employees create a detailed picture of a person's adaptation and evolution through time.

We should also note that consent does not scale well at the request side. If an organisation asks for consent for privacy breaches from a large number of subjects frequently, then it cannot treat them as individuals or respect their idiosyncratic preferences. It will have to automate, or at least standardise, marginalising individual concerns. 'Consent' will be take-it-or-leave-it. Even if this does not result in coercion through sheer force of numbers (Westin 1967, 265), it is hardly likely to help subjects achieve their own preferences, or indeed produce optimal results across society (Baruh and Popescu 2017).

In sum, consent works well enough for the unusual event, and when we have time to make a considered decision, but if it is to cover routine and frequent events we can't spare the cognitive resources to renew it periodically. Choice becomes overwhelming if there is too much of it (B. Schwartz 2004; Schwartz and Ward 2004; Barocas and Nissenbaum 2009; Hartzog 2018), and if consent's main purpose is to cover the backs of those who wish to breach our privacy, it is only marginally working to our benefit.

However, no one has thought up a good alternative to keep the wheels of a privacy-invasive knowledge economy turning. Consent does at least have the virtue of respecting the autonomy of the subject, however inadequately. In contrast, if the breach is constrained by some other means (for example, regulation), then *that* determines what privacy people should have *without* consulting them and *independently* of their preferences (Solove 2013). They may find choice hard, but they may prefer to have it, even so. Consent is a mechanism for achieving preferences; if privacy is to be imposed or removed independently of what people want (say, for moral reasons), then consent is redundant.

Level 5 topic: the private sphere does not define privacy

An important determinant of our reasonable expectations is the conventional division of social life into public and private spheres (Sennett 2002). Philosopher Stanley Benn drew a distinction between (i) attempts to do something in private, requiring withdrawal or concealment, and (ii) private affairs, areas classified as private, into which it would be impertinent to snoop, which remain private even when snooped upon (1971, 223). The latter are defined by norms that can be invoked simply by pointing them out. 'Please keep your distance. This is a private conversation.' 'Mind your own business.' The same conception of privacy may be invoked by (i) and (ii), but (i) concerns the question of whether it is breached in fact, while (ii) concerns the legitimacy of any breach that may occur.

A rich set of social norms is required to define the private sphere, which will also help protect it. Someone who wished to intrude should have a reason strong enough to override the norms (Benn 1971, 234). Hence the statement 'This is a private matter' may be open to debate, but, while assertive in form, is a disguised imperative, 'go away, this is none of your business', staking a claim to legitimate privacy before the interloper can establish a counterclaim to intrusion.

The private sphere is complemented by a public sphere, where one engages with strangers or acquaintances with whom one has functional relationships. In the public sphere, relationships with others are different – everyone has a right to occupy the public arena, and one has to sacrifice some privacy to take part. Some types of information about the subject are matters of public record (such as unspent criminal convictions), and so others are entitled to know them. The relations between the two spheres are fluid, along with the norms that define them, and those societies that have them value them differently.

Traditionally, following Aristotle, the public sphere was the arena in which people (usually men) excelled (Arendt 1998, 22–78; Schoeman 1992, 117). Dame Rebecca West, tongue in cheek, noting that the Greek root of the word 'idiot' meant a private person, suggested that:

> Idiocy is the female defect: intent on their private lives, women follow their fate through a darkness deep as that cast by malformed cells in the brain. It is no worse than the male defect, which is lunacy: they are so obsessed by public affairs that they see the world as by moon-light, which shows the outlines of every object but not the details indicative of their nature. (West 2020, 3)

The pre-modern virtue of honour required the achievement of a public reputation for honesty, chivalry and bravery influenced by and reflected in social standing; privacy would only obstruct this quest (and had an association with honour's opposite, shame – Arendt 1998, 73). When Don Quixote deludes himself into thinking he is a knight, he immediately leaves the private space of his home for an extensive series of travels and public deeds. In the eighteenth century, the public life of the coffeehouses, where anyone could talk to anyone, was seen as stimulating (Habermas 1989), whereas private clubs, 'akin to the company of the family' (contemporary quote in Sennett 2002, 92), were often seen as dull – the 'same old faces' (Sennett 2002, 83–84). In Enlightenment society, a set of rights emerged that defined and guaranteed the public sphere, of freedom of speech, press, assembly and association (Habermas 1989, 83).

Nissenbaum's fine-grained emphasis on context led her to argue that the public/private distinction was a crude attempt to shoehorn a multiplicity of distinctive norms into a binary division (2010, 141), and indeed most cultures have a variable, and probably contested, distinction between the two. Many areas are hybrid. In the Western world, work has gradually shifted from being an aspect of home life, with crafts and sales being carried on from the home and supported by the family, to a public arena of offices, factories and productive 'office hours' (Habermas 1989, 151–159), yet the connections between the intimate sphere and the market, in which the individual is distinguished as a property owner, were always tight (Habermas 1989, 55–56). From the nineteenth century on the private sphere has been idealised, not always unproblematically, as a refuge from a challenging outside world, where one can be 'oneself', rather than inauthentically adopting public roles to interact with strangers (Sennett 2002, 16–24, 177–183). When new practices or technologies subtend new conceptions of privacy, will they be private matters in Benn's second sense (for instance, is participation in an online multiplayer game a private matter?)? It won't always be simple to 'read off' norms about the legitimacy or otherwise of breaches, and we may have to wait until norms develop, or try to steer their development by campaigning and proselytising (Hetcher 2004).

It is possible to define the public sphere as what remains following the demarcation of the private (Rössler 2005) or alternatively the private sphere as the *residuum* (Aristotle 1995, 8, 1252a24ff.; Sennett 2002), or to define both separately, risking overlaps or gaps between the two. However, they are not direct opposites. In modern times, the distinction goes three ways: the household or intimate space (private sphere); a common sphere in which all participants are theoretically equal, wherein evolve public opinion and the public interest independent of the state (public sphere); and the legitimate domain of the state itself (Arendt 1998, 38–73; Habermas 1987; Rössler 2005, 5–6). This tripartite distinction has become more salient with the emergence of ideologies that privilege state action and justify government appropriation of private property. In the rest of this chapter, for ease, I will restrict myself to the private sphere and the public, non-state sphere, and I will argue that we cannot use these normative distinctions to define privacy itself. The norms follow conceptions of privacy and its breach, and do not constitute them.

The norms defining these spheres single out the private sphere as an area of life where outside interference is not generally legitimate, a characterisation famously articulated in the seventeenth century by Sir Edward Coke as one's home being one's castle. Again, the Enlightenment helped create and protect the sphere with new rights supporting the conjugal patriarchal family and the transactions of property owners (Habermas 1989, 83). In contrast, authoritarian or paternal views of the world tend to manipulate or suppress such norms to shrink the private sphere, accepting greater scope for legitimate state interference; meanwhile democracy and liberalism should work in theory (if not always in practice – see below) to protect them. Boundaries may change rapidly – the lockdown rules imposed widely during the COVID-19 pandemic had the effect of shrinking the private space by preventing socialising or travel, while at the same time increasing attentional privacy by forcing citizens to withdraw from each other. Decisions to travel became a public matter, because a legitimate public interest had emerged.

The norms for the private sphere can be characterised in a number of ways. They are a special realm of non-governmental activities (Rössler 2005, 6), but this may not produce a clear demarcation (2005, 20). Indeed, the current polarisation in US politics is partially down to disputes about where federal interference is legitimate (e.g. gun ownership). The private sphere may also be described in terms of the types of information generated within it (Nissenbaum 2010, 89–102) or via enumerations of matters generally considered private (privacy universals, perhaps), such as grief, suffering, trauma, injury, nudity, sex, urination and defecation (Solove 2008, 147). However, the universality of even those has its limits; defecation was a recognised public event for French royalty in the seventeenth century (Spacks 2003, 7). Mill's principle that interference (by either the state or members of the public) is justified only when someone's activities harm others (Mill 1991, 14) draws the boundary using the individual's interests. Doubtless the relevant norms defining the private sphere as a social construct will be drawn from all of the above eclectically.

The household is often taken as the private space *par excellence*, the 'sacred precincts of private and domestic life' (Warren and Brandeis 1890, 76). In antiquity, the head of the household enjoyed total dominion (Arendt 1998, 27–28), and post-war human rights treaties bundled together privacy, family and household in a job lot. Many accounts of the household draw attention to its highly idiosyncratic nature and the difficulty of applying moral codes. From 1873:

> To try to regulate the internal affairs of a family, the relations of love
> or friendship, or many other things of the same sort, by law or by
> the coercion of public opinion is like trying to pull an eyelash out of

a man's eye with a pair of tongs. They may put out the eye, but they will never get hold of the eyelash. (Stephen 1993, 107–108)

Nevertheless, norms based around the household have been under pressure in recent decades, as for example with the slogan 'the personal is the political'. Where liberalism is equated with individualism, then the demands of individuals within a household may reduce the private space it holds. In modern times, the head was expected to consider the well-being of the whole household, and for example Mill never considered the possibility that privacy within the home may systematically lead to intrusion for, or even harm to, some of its members, especially women (Rössler 2005, 30–31). If we allow for that, then liberalism, far from protecting the household, may deliver the conclusion that the private sphere should be open to scrutiny and held to account after all (Rössler 2005, 23). Free expression in social media commentary and reality TV have intruded further, enabling the occupants of private spaces to revert to the Aristotelian ideal of 'being' in public: 'We seem to experience no joy in having secrets, unless these are the secrets meant to enhance our egos through being displayed on the Internet, on TV, on the first pages of tabloids and inside glossy magazines' (Bauman 2010, 11). Part III, Level 7 has already drawn attention to this dilemma.

Many definitions that restrict privacy to sensitive matters can be understood as saying that privacy requires prevention of access to whatever is understood as being in the private sphere. On that view, for example, being followed in public is not a breach of privacy, whereas Peeping Tom does breach privacy in our homes (Wacks 2010, 42–43). But we see that one can be 'in private' without having privacy (in some respect). Individuals lead distinct lives; the household is not equivalent to the Goffmanian 'backstage', because one may still need a backstage relative to one's cohabitees, even if they are intimate members of one's own family (Rössler 2005, 149). Even religious hermits had petitioners and admirers in their solitude. St James of Cyrrhestica, a hermit of the fifth century, was described, almost in *Monty Python* terms, as having an attack of acute diarrhoea in front of his followers (Webb 2007, 21–22).

Similarly, while we can't restrict privacy to the private sphere, neither can we say that nothing that happens in public is a private matter. The public sphere is defined by norms, some of which are norms of privacy. One can be 'private in public' (Nissenbaum 2010, 113–125; Oswald 2017). A lecture in a university is a public event but remains private in the sense that most people are not allowed in. The lecture therefore has public and private aspects. The complex norms governing sensibility in the eighteenth century were designed to present a morally upright inner life for public consumption, thereby shrinking psychological privacy. But not eliminating it: certain thoughts, especially involving women's desires, had to be concealed in order to avoid disgrace (Spacks 2003, 55–86). Many feel that CCTV cameras in public spaces infringe their privacy in ways that the mere presence of other people does not; others have got used to them, factoring technological surveillance into their general experience of the public arena (O'Hara and Shadbolt 2008, 212, 215; Sousa and Madensen 2016; Gurinskaya 2020; Birnhack and Perry-Hazan 2020). Signage around CCTV, for example, may support people's ability to preserve their privacy in public spaces, while also improving security by deterring crime (Lippert 2009). In the Netherlands, the stadium of the football team ADO Den Haag is equipped with security cameras that photograph every member of the crowd both as they arrive and during play, with iris scanning to keep out banned supporters. This, with splendid *chutzpah*, is called the 'Happy Crowd Control' system (Spaaij 2013, 170).

Hence we can't use ideas of the private and public sphere as means to define privacy, as the conversation still seems to be about what *breaches of privacy* are more or less likely to be legitimate in them. As I have already argued extensively, it is conceptually smoother to accept that breaches happen all the time, sometimes in the private sphere, sometimes in the public, sometimes they matter, sometimes they don't. They are perhaps more likely to matter in the private sphere than the public. But trying to use the two spheres to define what privacy is will throw up anomalies – for example, a stalker is different from a curious bystander. Even if the stalker only ever stands in public places where they are perfectly entitled to be, they are surely breaching privacy even if we discount the intimidating threat such behaviour carries. Far simpler to identify breaches of privacy across the two spheres (as well as in the actions of the state) and to treat them on their merits (which will certainly depend on which sphere they take place in).

Level 6 topic: data protection does not define privacy

Since the 1960s, the centre of legal gravity has shifted to the niche area of informational privacy. One likely reason for this is concern about all-powerful databases (Westin 1967), while another is that informational privacy may be more tractable to address than other types on our reference list. The legal output has been the development of a hybrid area called *data protection*, which, although privacyish in places, stands to privacy rather as salad cream stands to mayonnaise. Because of its prominence, 'there is a great risk of equating privacy and data protection' (Wright and Raab 2014, 279), a warning we need to heed.

C'est magnifique, mais ce n'est pas la privacité

Note that, *unlike* privacy, data protection is defined by law. It is a legal concept, and we understand it by reading legislation and case law. It may be that the increasing prominence of data protection in all walks of life will lead to the development of norms and preferences about it but not yet. Data protection is proclaimed a legal, not a moral, right, for example in Article 8 of the Charter of Fundamental Rights of the European Union (2000/2009).

Different jurisdictions treat information differently. The US tends to treat privacy as a means to liberty (Whitman 2004), which has had the side effect of creating a sector-based system in which some types of information, such as financial or healthcare information, are protected, and certain other types of privacy, such as attentional privacy, are especially well-regulated in areas where the state has a special interest, for instance in searches and surveillance. In EU law, privacy is treated as an aspect of dignity, and so there are few distinctions between types of information in principle (some particularly sensitive information types, such as genetic and biometric information, are singled out for stronger protection). Hence information-sharing practices that Americans would think fairly normal are either outlawed or regulated in the EU. Opinion is split as to where privacy is better protected (Bamberger and Mulligan 2015). Most new attempts to legislate for informational privacy tend to follow a European template, in form if not in spirit, as in China (Weber et al. 2020; O'Hara and Hall 2021, 134–135).

Data protection arose in the 1970s, when it was realised that information was an economic resource and technical progress was outstripping legislation (Westin 1967, 414; Ware 1973). This created two analogous dilemmas. First, easy information flow enables business opportunities, but threatens privacy: where should we draw the line? Second, should we allow information to cross borders, potentially allowing it to be processed beyond the reach of local law, or should we restrict it, thereby threatening international trade? Data protection was a compromise between free trade and privacy brokered by the OECD in a set of guidelines published in 1980 (OECD 2013), to create a more level playing field on which the interests of the individual were balanced against those of the data controller. The strategy was to make information processing fair, limited and transparent, ensuring it was collected and processed only for stated purposes, held securely, with rights for individuals identifiable from it (data subjects) to amend it, query the processing, and in many cases give or withhold consent. In the absence of data subjects' consent, there are a limited number of alternative grounds for legal processing. In the US, the Fair Information Practice Principles (FIPPs) cover similar ground.

The OECD principles (bolstered by the Council of Europe's 1981 convention 108 to implement Article 8 of the European Convention on Human Rights for data processing) were implemented most effectively in the EU, via the Data Protection Directive of 1995, and later the GDPR of 2018. The GDPR strengthened the Directive in four specific and powerful ways. First, the Directive was implemented indirectly; each member state had to draft and pass its own legislation, leading to inconsistency. The GDPR is far less democratic, imposed directly on all member states from the centre. Second, the GDPR tightens up many of the Directive's provisions, and expands its reach, including updating it to try to address issues created by the World Wide Web and e-commerce. Third, the small penalties of the Directive become swingeing fines in the GDPR. Fourth, the GDPR is designed to apply to measures affecting EU citizens anywhere in the world, so has global scope (Bradford 2020), following on from the Court of Justice of the European Union's aggressive interpretation of the Directive to increase the EU's global profile in data protection. For instance, its decision against Google Spain establishing the right to be forgotten was a landmark in the pushback against global tech companies (O'Hara 2015b). The progression from the Directive to the GDPR, and its geopolitical implications, is described in (O'Hara and Hall 2021, 83–91).

Data protection is focused on *personal data*, defined as information from which the identity of a living individual, the *data subject*, can be directly or indirectly inferred, or which can be used to facilitate decisions concerning that individual (the US equivalent, PII, is defined inconsistently across American legislation, often via an enumeration of identifying information, such as social security numbers, bank account numbers and so on). Hence 'Kieron O'Hara is 5′11‴' is personal data, and 'X is 5′11‴' may be, depending on how easily it can be deduced that X is the author of this book. 'The average height of men aged 55–65 in Hampshire is 5′11‴' is not personal data, as it is not about anyone in particular, and tells you very little about any individual, even a man in Hampshire *unless* there are very few men of that age in Hampshire, in which case we can make some probabilistic deductions.

Data protection is the subject of a colossal literature, to which I have made a minuscule contribution (e.g. O'Hara and Shadbolt 2008, 2015; O'Hara 2015b; O'Hara and Hall 2021), but this brief section can hardly do justice to all that. Its modest aim is to set out the relationship between data protection and privacy. Data protection tries to balance the privacy interests of the data subject and the economic or other interests of the data controller. This makes ineliminable reference to prior privacy interests, which cannot therefore be changed (although they can be protected) by data protection.

The practice of data processing subtends a conception of privacy – i.e. that one's personal data is *not* being processed – but so narrow and abstract is it that it is hard to see its intuitive appeal. If, for example, someone took a spreadsheet of data about a million people and computed some average statistics, this would technically be a breach of this conception of privacy, but in itself would hardly impinge upon the million.

Indeed, it is hard to see the computer processing of data *per se* as a *privacy* breach at all, since all the computer is dealing with is uninterpreted bits, 0s and 1s. The privacy breach arrives when the wider system interprets the output of the program as information about individuals (O'Hara and Hall 2021, 12–18). Even when commentators attack the misuse of data, they focus on its misuse in the service of far more serious breaches of different, more salient privacy conceptions (such as identity theft, targeted misinformation or surveillance), for which data processing is only the means (e.g. Véliz 2020, 7–26). In practice, problematic data processing is legal more often than not (e.g. once you have clicked acceptance of the privacy policy). The challenge for privacy campaigners concerned about data protection is often to motivate the gap between egregious privacy breaches that concern people, and the data processing that enables them.

What is processing? It is defined as:

> any operation or set of operations which is performed on personal data or on sets of personal data, whether or not by automated means, such as collection, recording, organisation, structuring, storage, adaptation or alteration, retrieval, consultation, use, disclosure by transmission, dissemination or otherwise making available, alignment or combination, restriction, erasure or destruction. (GDPR, article 4(2))

As can be seen, some of these will tend to *increase* privacy – notably destroying or erasing the data, but also altering it, for example by anonymising it. Some, such as storage, will have marginal direct effects – if I copy a spreadsheet onto a USB stick I am processing the data in it, but the file may never be opened in that operation (of course, it may be disseminated by this route).

Furthermore, data protection does not protect privacy as its main purpose, even on this unintuitive conception. Personal data is processed, and privacy therefore breached, all the time. If the data controller breaches one's privacy fairly and lawfully, then they have a defence in law, and thereby can extract whatever value or advantage they anticipate from the analysis. Exceptions built into data protection, for the purposes of scientific research, national security, defence, public safety or archiving, reduce grounds of complaint still further – the Google Spain 'right to be forgotten' case was triggered by a legitimate archive that years after its creation had become searchable from the Web (O'Hara 2015b). Although the case was won by the data subject and the link removed from the search page, the archive itself was unaffected by the judgement.

Data protection deals only with personal data, yet privacy can be breached by processing other kinds of data too. A generalised profile of a person can be built using data about similar people to them to model their likes, dislikes and interests, and used for example to target advertising. These can critically alter their choices (cf. e.g. Allam et al. 2014). The individual is typically not identifiable from the profile, because it is *applied to them*, not *created about them*.

Data legally gathered and held (for example, from one's smartphone, or the 'like' buttons one has clicked) can also be used as the basis for privacy-breaching inferences beyond the immediate information provided. These are more revealing than many might guess. Smartphone data can be used to work out health-related metrics (Kelly et al. 2020), how sloshed you are (Arnold et al. 2015), your mood (LiKamWa et al. 2013), your level of engagement with the task at hand (Urh and Pejović 2016), your context (Sadhu et al. 2019) or maps of your home (Luo et al. 2015). Data from its camera, or even its accelerometer, can be used to guess your passwords (Owusu et al. 2012; Wang et al. 2020). Social media data might be interrogated to find where you live (Yamaguchi et al. 2013; Xu et al. 2014), why you are going where you are going (Meng et al. 2017), your mental health (Ford et al. 2019), whether you are a suicide risk (De Choudhury et al. 2016), whether you are about to take part in a riot (Charitonidis et al. 2017) or whether you are a troll (Alvari et al. 2019). These inferences are valuable: Facebook is thinking about how to get your device to do its smart machine learning for it, rather than going to the bother of harvesting the data itself and dealing directly with it, thereby avoiding the GDPR (Wu et al. 2019). These inferences don't need to be 100 per cent accurate; improvements of a few percentage points in predictions, if monetised over a very large number of interactions, translate into pretty handsome returns on the investment.

Data protection also protects against things that are only tangentially related to privacy. For instance many issues to do with the safety of children are wrapped up in a spurious narrative of protecting their privacy by controlling access to their data (Edwards 2013, 316). As a more challenging example, Apple cites data protection law, and the design of their systems to *promote* privacy, to deny users of the Siri voice assistant access to the data held about them, which should be theirs by right. Because the system is so privacy-protective, Apple itself holds no identifiers and so can't find a user directly. However, it has been pointed out that:

> They do save many kinds of information of similar or even greater use in re-identification alongside your identifier. Indeed, Apple note that because it is onerous to send details such as relationships with family members, reminders, and playlists to the server each time a Siri session is started ... they send those initially, and store them there. Even if we were to accept that a device specific identifier was not personal data ... a list of their contacts and their relations to you is relatively trivial even for non-experts to use to re-identify individuals by using easily accessible data sources, like social media. (Veale et al. 2018, 112)

The value of data protection

That is not to say that data protection is a bad, or badly executed, idea; only that as privacy protection it is no less partial and discrete than Prosser's torts. Its importance stems from its positioning to regulate 'data surveillance' (Westin 1967, 173–178; Zuboff 2019). Three types of privacy breach are relevant to the surveillance economy. The first is an *attentional* concern about datafication – so many things that one does are captured and held as data, that one is permanently exposed to scrutiny (Véliz 2020). The second is a worry about *psychological* privacy or even ideological privacy in dictatorial regimes – conclusions are drawn from one's behaviour, preferences and thoughts (accurately or otherwise), and people held to account (Crawford and Schultz 2014). The third is a *decisional* issue – via the collection of data (which may not be about oneself), the environment may be amended in order to reduce one's autonomy and to nudge or pre-empt one's decisions (Hildebrandt and O'Hara 2020), by capitalists to make money, and governments for policymaking or policing.

These three breaches don't preclude other types of harm from the data economy – for instance, Twitterstorms undermine the rule of law by short-circuiting due process and making a mockery of the presumption of innocence (Ronson 2015). Targeted advertising can subvert the democratic process (Borgesius et al. 2018). Misinformation, trolling and hate speech are socially harmful, e.g. during the COVID-19 pandemic (Howard 2020). The tech giants create network effects that favour monopoly and exaggerate their political sway (Fukuyama et al. 2021). Those additional harms no doubt have privacy aspects, though not as their principal feature.

Data protection law is one of a relatively small set of clubs in the bag for dealing with these complex problems (competition law is another – O'Hara and Hall 2021, 117–124). From the point of view of the data controller, it sets out those grounds for data processing that are defensible in the event of a dispute, and so is helpful for managing data consumers' business risk. Its main effect from the point of view of the data subject is to scope their consent, providing some protection against both minor inconveniences and major injustices that can follow from the use of outdated, inaccurate, irrelevant, excessive or randomly gathered information, especially in the absence of public interest. But it is a blunt tool for a complex job that requires precision. The risk of a breach of privacy in this more tangible sense is pretty small per piece of data, but potentially very large across an unknown dossier of accumulated digital information.

Data protection is built on the assumption of the importance of control. Hence it is a means of achieving a preference about whether data is processed, either by consenting or in the event of illegality by exposing unfair processing. Nevertheless, this is a source of weakness (Raab 2005, 283–289, 309–310). Many have drawn attention to the asymmetries of power between giant companies and individuals, and between companies and the under-resourced and hard-pressed regulators (Ceross 2018; Hörnle 2019). Control doesn't scale – as more information about us is used, shared, transferred and sold, we have correspondingly less cognitive space to give informed consent (Barocas and Nissenbaum 2009; Hartzog 2018, 62–67). Data protection and the FIPPs focus on individuals' rights to object but less on companies' obligations, when one might argue that systems that respect their users need to be designed as such, not kept in line *post hoc* by the flawed consent mechanism (Cavoukian 2011; Barocas and Nissenbaum 2014, 57, 66; Hartzog 2018, 61–62).

As a result of the weight of expectations on data protection, it has grown to fill the space available to it, so much so that many commentators write as if it is the major part of privacy. Solove's own positive proposal, an interesting taxonomy of actual privacy harms that require legal remedy, was intended to provide an expansionary account of privacy to counter Prosser's narrow approach and to cover privacy in the round. However, he in effect developed a data protection taxonomy. His whole model is structured around a data subject, a category of person created by data protection law (2008, 103). Of his four groups of harmful activities – information collection (2008, 106–117), information processing (2008, 117–136), information dissemination (2008, 136–161) and invasion (2008, 161–170) – the first three are wholly to do with information, so the remaining category is therefore a much smaller catch-all for all non-informational privacy, but even this is discussed in largely informational terms.

How practical is data protection?

As a hybrid, data protection resembles the proverbial horse designed by committee. It has two motivating premises for the protection of individuals – the neoliberal idea that people are the best judges of their own interests and should be given the tools to defend themselves because no one else, including the state, can be trusted to do it properly; and the liberal idea that everyone is entitled to protection of their human rights because they are perpetually under threat. Neither premise is well-chosen to foster trust in digital modernity.

To act, data subjects need a suspicion that there is an excessive or inappropriate dataset held about them, demand to see it, and then go through a more or less painful process to get it changed. This is a high-cost and tedious chore, and who has time? Actually, Brian Parkinson (a former PhD student jointly supervised by me), made time. Part of his eye-opening research was to gather as much information as possible about himself by exercising his data protection rights. Quite apart from finding the organisations (not all of which responded, and some of which are legally exempt from the obligation), spotting gaps in responses and trying to decode data-gobbledegook, it took him a full year of work and cost several thousands of pounds (by which time, of course, another year of personal data had built up about him – Parkinson 2018). There were 633 organisations that he managed to trace, and each one erected its own pain barrier.

Attempts to supplement data protection with synergetic measures such as technologies, international agreements and industry self-regulation (Raab 2005, 301–303) have usually disappointed. There has been a steady stream of measures and tools (often called privacy-enhancing technologies, or PETs) to further empower the data subject. For example, the Platform for Privacy Preferences (P3P) was a protocol to allow users and websites to express their preferences to enable negotiation with data controllers (Grimm and Rossnagel 2000; Reay et al. 2009). Do Not Track was an addition to the Web protocol to allow people to express their preference not to be tracked by browsers (Bott 2012). I have trodden this path, advocating Personal Data Stores (PDSs) and Personal Information Management Systems (PIMS) for allowing data subjects to manage (and even store) at least some of the data held about them (Van Kleek and O'Hara 2014; O'Hara and Shadbolt 2015). The inventor of the Web, Tim Berners-Lee, hopes to revive its reputation with his Solid platform, which includes many PDS-style ideas on top of a decentralised architecture (Mansour et al. 2016; Buyle et al. 2020). As well as technical fixes, some have proposed to bring trust law to bear, so that trustees can exercise data subjects' powers for them (Delacroix and Lawrence 2019; O'Hara 2020b). Industry has provided a series of benchmarks or privacy seals to increase confidence in e-commerce and other trust-based transactions (Etzioni 1999, 160–162; Rifon et al. 2006; LaRose and Rifon 2006, 2007; Balboni and Dragan 2018).

The Achilles' heel of these otherwise admirable projects is that, during the quarter-century or so in which they have been tried, it has been hard to find a single person outside the legal-technological complex with sufficient interest in the problem to use them, so they have all died, are dying, or will die through neglect. The attractions of empowerment are often overstated, and if privacy is control, we are in trouble.

Having said that, data protection, if not a superpower, *is* a power, and is something of a brake on law-abiding companies. Even if the threat of legal action is rare, the level of penalties open to regulators with the GDPR is now high enough, like the potential payouts from being successfully sued in the US, to act as a curb on powerful organisations. Furthermore, the 'Brussels effect' of the GDPR's global reach (Bradford 2020) seems to have precipitated a 'race to the top'. Europe's market is too big for multinationals to ignore, and it is expensive to craft different policies for different jurisdictions, so the tendency is to develop privacy policies adequate for the most stringent (although some US companies have reacted to the GDPR by pulling out of their European markets – O'Hara and Hall 2021, 106–107). Some innovations in this area, such as Privacy and Data Protection Impact Assessments, promise to have greater impact than regulatory box-ticking, because of the awareness and risk management insight they bring (Raab 2005, 303–307; Wright and de Hert 2012; Hempel and Lammerant 2015). After investing in the development of data protection – which has even been referred to as the EU's 'First Amendment' (Petkova 2019) – the EU has a world-beating supply of top-level expertise across government, academe and the private sector. It is undoubtedly the leader in the field, and will remain so for the foreseeable future. The GDPR has set a global standard, and few firms with international ambition can ignore it.

Level 7 topic: community values versus privacy

Privacy for groups and individuals often benefits society; it is not a zero sum game. However, not all privacy is beneficial, and its negative aspects can be highlighted in communitarian thinking. In general, if one is an adherent of a goal-driven ideology such as socialism, feminism, environmentalism, etc., privacy may stand in the way of the desired goal. Confucian Chinese and early modern English villagers alike valued social stability, and produced self-policing societies in which privacy was suborned to a crowdsourced surveillance (Thomas 1973, 628–630; Liang et al. 2018; Leibold 2020; O'Hara and Hall 2021, 139–140; Miles 2021). In a British survey of 2021, the number of Labour Party members, socialists concerned about equality, who were seriously concerned about privacy was substantially lower than the already low national figure (CPS 2021).

Privacy can provide cover for deceit, hypocrisy, crime, moral cowardice and ignorance about the lives of others. It impedes public debate on matters of significance, such as sexual abuse, and inhibits individuals from making selective disclosures, increasing their vulnerability and shame (Schoeman 1984b, 1; Wasserstrom 1978, 329–332). Secrecy is potentially an anti-social device, and postmodern theories problematising the self make privacy seem a spurious good (Raab 2005, 287–289). Even supporters of privacy agree that some breaches are good, for example the videos taken of the beating of Rodney King or the murder of George Floyd (Rössler 2005, 128).

Posner argued that the law positively should *not* protect against disclosures of embarrassing or discreditable information, because these aid the public good, whereas informational asymmetries created by suppressing disclosure make it harder for markets to work efficiently (Posner 1978, 1983; Akerlof 1970). On this view, protection should be limited to torts based on misleading utterances and writings (libel, slander, forgery), and law should support the spread of factual information (freedom of speech, freedom of information). If X has a piece of private information about Y, then Y's privacy is bought at the cost of X's free speech. Or put another way, Y's informational self-determination requires others to interact with them (i.e. Y) based on a carefully manicured, false or even misleading profile, and 'a seldom-remarked corollary to a right to misrepresent one's character is that others have a legitimate interest in unmasking the misrepresentation' (Posner 1978, 334–335, and for a milder statement, Post 2001, 2087–2089). This can be a tricky balance – sometimes the public good is genuinely involved, as when X knows something damaging that is legitimately a matter of public concern about Y, such as they lied about their background on their election literature. Sometimes it is only what the public is interested in, such as tittle-tattle about a pop star's sex life. This is a particular issue in the US, where free speech is fetishised, and has powerful constitutional protection.

Posner's reading opens up interesting vistas. For example, the type of blackmail that aims to extort money or favours from people in return for concealing true but embarrassing information looks, on his account, not unlike an antisocial type of privacy protection (Solove 2008, 151–154). The blackmailer only threatens to do what is legal and arguably their duty. What is wrong with blackmail and why does the law side with the victims? Posner's rationalisation was that it did not lead to optimal economic or social outcomes (1993; Miceli 2020), while others have maintained it stifles the discussion and development of norms (McAdams 1996) or supplants the justice system with contractual arrangements (Brown 1993). Some have defended blackmailers as straightforward economic actors, bargaining for the value of the information they hold (Block 2001), putting blackmail in a category with patents (Miceli 2020) and nondisclosure agreements (Miceli 2021).

Under the term *kompromat*, the release of damaging information is even a style of politics (Aydın-Düzgit 2012; Choy 2020; O'Hara and Hall 2021, 157–168) that has affected the US, for example with the release of emails and diplomatic cables to WikiLeaks, and nude photos of a Congresswoman (Grimaldi 2021, 111–112). It is hard to argue that this is good, exactly, even as the public has more information to make its democratic judgements. We might want to split the difference, that privacy has moral value incommensurable with market value (Cohen 2000).

Sometimes, privacy is held up as an enabler of current injustice and power structures. Robert Altman's 1970 film *M*A*S*H*, a pacifist excoriation of war, treats privacy as a bourgeois luxury for the privileged few and a legitimate target for the movie's let-it-all-hang-out counterculture heroes. Two key moments centre on breaches of privacy to humiliate its villains, Majors Burns and Houlihan. Absolutely no sympathy is shown to either character (in a film that certainly has its sentimental moments), and the strong implication is that by their warmongering sins they have sacrificed their claims to privacy or respect.

Even more exaggerated is the view taken by totalitarian regimes, demanding complete commitment, loyalty and identification with the regime. Private life, civil society and confidential relationships are all deliberately undermined to leave no space for the individual to flourish and possibly rebel. Even the Nicodemite option of outwardly conforming and eschewing meaningful opposition, while retaining inner integrity, is closed down. Meanwhile, the regime itself is afforded complete opacity in its decision-making, which can then appear (and often is) capricious and arbitrary, and therefore difficult to predict and counter (Westin 1967, 25; Arendt 2017, 397–629; Blaydes 2018).

Surveillance, anonymity and little platoons

The interests of ghastly regimes are hardly arguments for anything. However, informal breaches of attentional privacy are useful for the collective security of a group or community (Nissenbaum 2010, 188–189). Anonymity is a handy cloak for the sinful and the troll, and cities offer greater affordances for it, noted as early as 1549, when William Thomas observed of Venice that 'no man there marketh another's doings ... which undoubtedly is one principal cause that draweth so many strangers thither' (Thomas 1963, 83). Adam Smith argued:

> A man of low condition ... is far from being a distinguished member of any great society. While he remains in a country village his conduct may be attended to, and he may be obliged to attend to it himself. In this situation, and in this situation only, he may have what is called a character to lose. But as soon as he comes into the great city, he is sunk in obscurity and darkness. His conduct is observed and attended to by nobody, and he is therefore very likely to neglect it himself, and to abandon himself to every sort of profligacy and vice. (Smith 1999, 383)

This reflection led anthropologist Margaret Mead to argue that legitimate personal privacy can morph into illegitimate concealment from the law, and advocated the use of surveillance devices such as the precursors of CCTV 'to ensure the public safety, without which privacy itself becomes a nightmare isolation' (quoted in Westin 1967, 65).

Some pro-privacy pro-autonomy claims are rooted in the over-valuation by some academics of nonconformist behaviour. For instance, Reiman worried about individuals' 'psycho-political metamorphosis', which certainly does sound painful. He was concerned that people constantly under surveillance moderate their behaviour and thoughts, seeking out a 'happy medium' of inoffensive conventionality (Reiman 1995). But is that so wrong? Social life involves riffing and improvising on well-known and familiar themes, whereas utterly unconventional behaviour brings with it a heavy cognitive load and strains on social relationships (Theriault et al. 2021). Extremism is a chosen and constant state of tension with the surrounding society (Stevens and O'Hara 2015). Being within a group or association with its own norms and traditions is an important guarantor of freedom, as Burke (1968), Tocqueville and Arendt (1968) argued. The 'little platoons' of society apply social pressure, but because of their limited reach it can be resisted when excessive (Shils 1981; Schoeman 1992, 113).

Communitarianism

Communitarianism is a political philosophy that valorises social solidarity against decontextualised individualism. Locke, Adam Smith and Mill wrote their classic defences of liberty and rights in an age of relative, if inefficient, oppression (Berkowitz 2021). 'Not surprisingly, social philosophers whose societies experienced these highly restrictive conditions did not concern themselves with the danger of legitimizing individual rights to excess' (Etzioni 1999, 194). Etzioni's communitarian philosophy was intended to counter the individualism of both counterculture and yuppiedom that, while part of the American inheritance, had become excessive pursuit of self-interest in his view (1999, 198).

Etzioni found inspiration in the Fourth Amendment, which balances the rights of the individual with the public good via the notion of reasonable search (1999, 203). He noted that privacy was a matter not only of rights but also of obligations – for example, requirements to remain clothed or not drink alcohol in public spaces. Paradoxically, more privacy from our fellow citizens results in the need for greater government control and intrusion: 'crimes are best prevented when a community abhors the behavior' (1999, 213). Snooping citizens can create informal enforcement mechanisms that are often better at suppressing antisocial behaviour than crude policing or rule-based legislation (Shemtob 2013); lack of such mechanisms 'often necessitates state-imposed limits on private choices' (Etzioni 1999, 214). Etzioni argued that in several areas, including HIV testing of pregnant women, providing government with decryption keys for encrypted messages, and compulsory ID cards, losses of privacy are more than made up for by gains to the common good. Megan's Laws were not disproportionate breaches of sex offenders' privacy either, although Etzioni didn't think they would work for other reasons.

This recontextualisation was a corrective to the positive literature on privacy, but because communitarianism had its own agenda, it produced its own kitchen sink definition, muddling three extraneous discourses with the conceptual: 'the realm in which an actor … can *legitimately* act without disclosure and accountability to others. Privacy is thus a *societal license* that exempts a category of acts ... from communal, public, and governmental scrutiny' (Etzioni 1999, 196, his emphasis). This mixes up the level 7 idea of legitimacy and the level 5 notion of a societal licence, while most of Etzioni's actual discussion is of legal discourse at level 6. He denied that illegitimate states of withdrawal were episodes of privacy at all, but rather 'concealment or secrecy, terms that imply illicit, if not illegal, behavior' (1999, 197).

Kitchen sink definitions produce disarray. As well as finding himself arguing that 'the private lives of public figures' are not private (1999, 197), Etzioni also asserted that decisional and attentional privacy are two completely different things (as opposed to two types of the same thing). He insisted that, if they were not, those acts which must be carried out in private, such as 'nudity, sexual intercourse and toilet functions', must be described as 'acts that are public and private, which, of course, makes no sense' (1999, 212). This is baffling. They are not public in any sense – unless someone did them *in public*, in which case they would indeed be public. But it should be clear by now that we can be comfortable with acts being both public and private, and indeed on the previous page Etzioni had written that acts like voting *are* public and private (1999, 211). He did admit the strong distinction between decisional and attentional privacy led to 'some initial awkwardness' (1999, 212), and these issues are to an extent terminological. But they could be avoided altogether by keeping the normative kitchen sink out of the definition in the first place.

Managing and protecting the natural and built environment

If the stance of pure communitarianism against privacy leads to confusion, there may be a more pragmatic view. The environment will loom larger in future policy. While the main lever for reducing or even reversing climate change is to control the amount of carbon emissions, this is not directly in the gift of governments, so they must somehow control the emissions of their citizens and residents. There are low-intrusion ways of doing this, for example through carbon taxes or trading schemes, but the former are politically difficult and the latter often gamed. It is likely that surveillance (for example via smartphones) will be needed to estimate individuals' carbon footprints, and to nudge appropriately, as human surveillance is already used, to rather dubious effect, to conserve endangered species and ecosystems (Adams 2019). Smartphone data is informative about emissions from transport (Bagheri et al. 2020), and some people have voluntarily taken up apps that measure their footprint (Sagawe et al. 2016). If these early adopters become numerous or influential enough, one could imagine creeping compulsion and social pressure to sacrifice privacy for the greater good of combating climate change.

The communitarian goal has been transformed by technology via the notion of a *smart city* (Townsend 2014; O'Hara and Hall 2021, 221–228). While the smartness of a city is in the eye of the beholder, and as often as not is a branding device for extracting urban development funding, a number of trends are discernible. Smart cities are real places, some designed and built to be smart, like the Songdo International Business District in South Korea, NEOM in Saudi Arabia or a number of places in China (which is also exporting the technology to the developing world, often with a focus on surveillance and branded 'safe cities'). In existing cities, smart functionality is added to legacy infrastructure, often in hip places like Amsterdam or Barcelona. Singapore has marketed itself as a 'smart nation'.

Smart cities rest on three technological developments. The Internet of Things connects physical objects to the Internet, so that, for example, sensors in the environment can gather information and send it to a central processor, while instructions can be sent to actuators to control, say, lighting, heating or ventilation. Mobile technology based on 5G standards allows large volumes of data to pass wirelessly between devices, connecting even mobile objects (such as cars) to the Internet of Things. Most obviously, individuals' smartphones can form part of this network as a result. Third, gains in artificial intelligence and machine learning make it possible to process giant quantities of data in real or near-real time, analysing not only complete datasets but also streams of data that are constantly refreshing and renewing. All of this means that devices simple and complex, personal and publicly owned, mobile and embedded in the built environment, can be connected via a high-bandwidth data infrastructure to gather information about an urban area, and either to take action directly, or to send signals to residents, to alter the environment in response to changing needs.

This means that a smart city can pursue performance targets, for example to reduce its carbon emissions, crime, pollution or transport congestion, or to achieve efficiency in, for instance, water supplies, waste disposal, power supply or health services. Targets could be set centrally, or democratically by citizens themselves. Apps could allow individuals either to take part in the city's governance or to help support their own problem-solving (such as finding cycle-friendly routes, remotely controlling devices in their homes or accessing government services).

The upshot of this is to create an infrastructure designed to deliver various socially approved values to do with the environment, transport, health, e-democracy and so on, powered by a large measure of surveillance. In the case of a safe city on the Chinese model, the technology may be extremely intrusive and used against citizens who protest or form opposition movements in the name of social stability. In the Western world, the aim would be to 'nudge' citizens into behaving in socially responsible ways (Thaler and Sunstein 2008). The cost in both types of place is naturally in terms of attentional, informational and decisional privacy. The alternative values (all perfectly reasonable and sensible) are introduced in opposition to privacy, although of course the data gathering and processing can be more or less intrusive (and in Europe at least governed by the GDPR). However, a survey of the smart city literature showed remarkably little evidence that much attention was paid to privacy (Angelidou 2017). Furthermore, smart city functionality is designed to be measured, unlike privacy, so the work of ensuring that the latter is not the loser in a very quantified paradigm is of necessity hard.

Openness

Finally, the *summa summarum* of these ideas is the optimistic ideology of sharing information and experience by default. Jarvis coined the word 'publicness' to connote an ethic of openness, sharing and collaborating to form a public (2011, 1n.1). Rather than dwelling on the negatives, this perspective accentuates the positives of openness, framing privacy as a *loss* of opportunity for connection.

> We can now find the publics we wish to join based not on the gross labels, generalizations, and borders drawn about us by others – red vs. blue, black vs. white, nation vs. nation – but instead on our ideas, interests, and needs: cancer survivors, libertarians, revolutionaries, Deadheads, vegetarians, single moms, geeks, hunters, birders, and privacy advocates. (2011, 10–11)

The publicness ideology flips the privacy-for-autonomy argument on its head. If one is unduly concerned about what others think, driven by shame, reticence, modesty, humility, delicacy or whatever, then one will micromanage one's public image for different audiences, concealing information and letting it out sparingly and strategically. But this is a limiting and constraining view of the world, not to mention inauthentic, tiring and obsessive. If one sloughs off shame and stops worrying about minuscule risks, then this *in itself* will be liberating (Wasserstrom 1978, 329–332). One still needs to preserve one's *decisional* privacy for this to be truly authentic and empowering, but ceasing to worry about informational and attentional privacy frees one from snoopers, and is a surer route to true autonomy.

Jarvis despaired of a definition of privacy and focused on informational privacy (perhaps because his main interest was the digital realm). His value argument was fundamentally utilitarian, based on the creation of socially valuable resources through revelation and linking, synergetic with his definition of publicness. Privacy and publicness should influence the choices made by anyone seeking information, either from someone or about them. 'Privacy is an ethic of knowing. Publicness is an ethic of sharing' (Jarvis 2011, 110). The slogans betrayed his kitchen sink definition, bringing level 7 concerns into his level 1 conceptions.

The ethic of privacy consisted of nine principles: don't steal information or deceive to get it; be transparent about what you will do with it; protect confidential information; give credit to the source of information you use; give people access to information about them; don't use it against people; give enough context so that it is not misleading; only reveal information about someone for good motives; in disseminating information, add value (Jarvis

2011, 110–112). Similarly, nine principles made up his ethic of openness: be transparent; be open; be collaborative; give respect; give value; share information that might be useful; share only information that might be useful; use common representation standards to facilitate reuse; public knowledge is a public good, so resist efforts to reduce it (2011, 113).

Some of this is motherhood and apple pie, some back-covering pragmatics, but Jarvis sketched a style of engagement with information that constitutes an ideology of public interaction, where the uses to which information is put are the important factor, as opposed to the means of its acquisition, its sensitivity or the technology with which it is disseminated. His basic insights were that (i) privacy and publicness are not pitted against each other in a zero sum contest, and individual interests were reflected in some of his principles, and (ii) the utilitarian foundation demands measurable benefits from sharing.

The touted benefits of publicness made for a long list (Jarvis 2011, 43–62). It allows companies, artists and campaigners to build productive relationships with their publics; enables collaborations, including serendipitous ones, and crowdsourcing; neutralises stigmas, such as that surrounding homosexuality; allows people to get credit for their ideas. As this is a utilitarian philosophy, publicness would have to deliver on these and other benefits, and also not facilitate negative counter-reactions (such as making it easier for hostile elements to infiltrate interest groups).

Jarvis extolled the virtues of Facebook from this perspective. While privacy is selective – one shares different things with different people – fine-grained control within social media is not desirable. Working out which of one's contacts falls into which sharing type – close family member, extended family member, colleague, team member, interest group, boozing companion, church member, sharer of terrible secret, lover, former lover, potential lover, lover's friend – is a thankless and tedious task that no one will ever undertake thoroughly enough. The broad-brush controls and defaults of social networks are OK for most purposes, and a bit of thought and care should do the rest. Social media, on this view, are neutral enablers. Jarvis quoted Zuckerberg as saying 'we're good at building products that hit the desire people have'; 'as time goes on and more people find that it's valuable to share things, they might share more things. ... In the future, things should be tied to your identity, and they'll be more valuable that way' (Jarvis 2011, 18, 23).

Jarvis, like other commentators on social networking and the read/write Web from about this time (e.g. O'Hara and Shadbolt 2008; Nissenbaum 2010), specifically entertained what we might call 'surface' concerns about information posted for one group of people being seen by others. In the intervening time, these worries have been borne out in part, for instance from old tweets containing immature remarks in poor taste, often racist or sexist, that resurface (or are resurfaced) years later, to destroy the career or ruin the livelihood of many a repentant grown-up, whose lachrymose apology is rarely enough to sate the sanctimonious mob.

But the bigger privacy concern about social media is 'deeper' – the data exhaust that one creates simply by *interacting* online, hoovered up by Facebook, Google, WeChat, JioChat and others to build up profiles that can be sold or queried. What one actually says online is less important than the contacts one makes, the like buttons one presses, the links one clicks. Structured data trails beat unstructured, overt information every day of the week (Zuboff 2019). Deep privacy breaches like these enable surface information sharing, but of course the data exhaust is not shared, and therefore doesn't feature in the positive ethic of publicness extolled by Jarvis.

It seems unlikely that this would concern supporters of openness. The critique is rooted in defence of human dignity, which the openness lobby views in utilitarian terms as a value that can be traded off for greater benefits. Jarvis, for instance, found it literally incomprehensible that Germans might object to Google Street View photographing their property without permission, given the public benefits it provides (2011, 25–30). But the desire to avoid desecration is strong and not easy to trade off (Mahoney et al. 2005, 58–62; Pargament et al. 2005; Frimer et al. 2015). At a more visceral level, it may simply be that they don't want to be pushed around by an arrogant American company, even one whose aims may be laudable and public-spirited.

At one stage, Jarvis considered and rejected Berners-Lee's dictum that one should be open only with non-personal information (2011, 52). Many of his exemplar open folk, including himself, shared information about themselves, even if those who guarded their privacy were entitled to keep their counsel if they wished. I confess that I found most of Jarvis' open citizens quite ghastly, but that is personal taste. If we can share information about ourselves if and when we like, we end up reproducing the introvert/extravert distinction online. This seems to be unobjectionable: each group despises the other, but *chacun à son goût*. The nagging questions for the philosophy of publicness concern surveillance and the deep invasions of privacy that capture the lives of introverts and extraverts alike, and while the latter may be sanguine about it, the value of the data captured is hoarded by its originators, not distributed across the public arena, thereby undercutting the utilitarian defence of publicness.

Nothing to hide, nothing to fear?

Communitarianism goes well beyond the Burkean view of little platoons. Etzioni wrote of 'the community' approving and censuring others – a powerful force, whereas Burke, Smith, Tocqueville, Arendt and Schoeman all defended associations and traditions as means *both* of correcting bad behaviour *and* protecting the individual against government and the giant social forces and undifferentiated masses unleashed by individualism. What Etzioni blithely called the 'subtle fostering of prosocial conduct' (1999, 213) might – as Mill warned – become oppressive (citizens' and governments' snooping might complement each other, and not in a good way, Gilliom 2001, 88–89). Communitarianism trades off the individual (and their privacy rights) against society (the common good), with little sense that supporting individual rights might strengthen both individuals and the community via support for associations (Schoeman 1992; Solove 2008, 90–91).

We should not accept the framing of privacy as individual-versus-community. Most disputes are between individuals (Rössler 2005, 101), as Etzioni accepted (1999, 206). However, these are put in the shade when the interests of the community are weighed against those of the individual, because the former must almost always outweigh the latter, and furthermore the individual's interests may be partially subsumed under the community's. If the individual's whereabouts are unknown, then it cannot be determined whether they were the criminal who committed such-and-such a crime (and if they are innocent they cannot prove it). Every time a murderer is caught using intrusive DNA testing, perhaps of relatives rather than the murderer's own (Maguire et al. 2014), privacy is knocked back. If their medical records are not available for research because of their privacy preferences, then the community will benefit that much less by the correspondingly skewed datasets (as will the individual, if they need treatment in the future). This means that, in the absence of an argument that privacy serves 'common, public, and collective purposes' (Regan 1995, 221), even if the individual's preference carries moral weight, their interests will still inevitably be 'balanced against the greater social good, which results in privacy being frequently undervalued in relation to many conflicting interests' (Solove 2008, 78–79). And during crises, decisions are taken without the time (or inclination) to consider them thoroughly, leading to reductions in privacy because of short-term, short-sighted considerations (Véliz 2020, 42–43).

Communitarian views underpin one of the most pernicious arguments against privacy, often summarised as 'nothing to hide, nothing to fear'. In other words, it has most value for wrongdoers and aficionados of shameful pursuits. We have all doubtless reread Camus' *The Plague* in pandemic lockdown, in which Cottard narrates a story

> about a poor devil who's arrested one fine morning all of a sudden. People had been taking an interest in him and he knew nothing about it. They were talking about him in offices, entering his name on card-indexes. Now do you think that is fair? Do you think people have a right to treat a man like that?

Spoiler alert: Cottard has found his vocation in the quarantine as a black marketeer!

Well, privacy also protects us from the wrongdoing of others (Véliz 2020, 59–60, where she helpfully reminded us that Eric Schmidt, formerly of Google, has not only made the nothing-to-hide argument, but also asked Google to hide information about him – make of that what you will!). The eponymous Clarissa asserted in Samuel Richardson's novel of 1748 that 'I believe Mr Lovelace is far from being so good as he ought to be: but if every man's private life were searched into by *prejudiced people*, set on for that purpose, I know not whose reputation would be safe.' Indeed, we don't even need prejudice when the power of government is involved, just the capacity of the state. As I have written elsewhere:

> Attempts to complain about ... intrusion are standardly met by the stunningly false reply that 'if you keep within the law you have nothing to fear'. A response that would be correct, but somewhat less persuasive, would be 'if you keep within the law, and the government keeps within the law, and its employees keep within the law, and the computer holding the database doesn't screw up, and the system is carefully designed according to well-understood software engineering principles and maintained properly, and the government doesn't scrimp on the outlay, and all the data are entered carefully, and the police are adequately trained to use the system, and the system isn't hacked into, and your identity isn't stolen, and the local hardware functions well, you have nothing to fear'. (O'Hara and Stevens 2006a, 251–252)

Negotiating conflicting values

No assurance that a technology will be used only for a certain set of functions and no more can be taken seriously. Wherever any pair of values clash, and a trade-off made, there will be mission creep (Westin 1967, 68; Wacks 2010, 71–77). No government can bind its successor, even if it thinks it can. In particular, technologies that invade privacy will be the thin end of the wedge, because once in place their supplementary uses become evident. Gilliom argued that the 'privacy paradigm' is ineffective against countervailing values and government imperatives (2001, 7–8), partly because it is too abstract to capture what for him is the real point, that surveillance is built on systems of power and domination, and therefore not open to rational debate (2001, 9).

The imbalance need not be as bad as that to be highly detrimental to privacy. There are all sorts of injunctions against secondary use of data, but there are always clauses to permit it as well. Put yourself in the shoes of a civil servant, tasked with doing something useful, such as increasing the amount of recycling or reducing the numbers of wildfires. You find out that there is a sensitive dataset that would help you perform your socially valuable task, but it is hedged around with restrictions and rules – for example, it can only be used to tackle terrorism. Does the person from the ministry therefore give up? No, the rules tell you what key words you need to use, and you write a proposal for access to the data that emphasises how your task might possibly impact on terrorism, however implausibly. If necessary you will enlist superiors to boost your case, which they will be pleased to do. You will get access, nine times out of ten. The gatekeepers of the dataset will respond much more sympathetically to the demands of a well-intentioned colleague whose motives they apprehend, than to the noisy rhetoric surrounding a forgotten promise made by unremembered politicians one or more electoral cycles ago. This will all be done in good faith, contributing to the good of the society everyone hopes to serve. Such public servants 'have often been so sure of their own purposes and ethics that they have been insufficiently sensitive to the issues of privacy created by the uses of [their] processes' (Westin 1967, 411).

A classic example is the British ID card, an emergency wartime measure meant to expire at the end of the war, intended to deal only with (i) the dislocation of the population following mass evacuations in 1939, (ii) the administration of rationing and (iii) the production of statistics following the postponement of the 1941 census. By the time of its tardy abolition in 1952 (after two changes of government), it had gained twenty-nine extra functions, including the tracing of bigamists (Wadham et al. 2006, 6–8).

Many commentators have wrestled with the problem of how to cement privacy's importance in the policymaking process. Gavison suggested adopting a broad principle, but this would be easy to pay lip service to (1980, 377–381). Westin suggested 'measuring the seriousness of the need to conduct surveillance; deciding what degree of reliability will be required of the surveillance instrument; determining whether true consent to surveillance has been given; and measuring the capacity for limitation and control of the surveillance if it is allowed' (1967, 414, similar to Etzioni 1999, 12–14). Contextual integrity provides one possible formalism to make the trade-offs clearer, and give an indication of where privacy may be preserved even while other values are served more effectively (Nissenbaum 2010, 166–178).

However, such (sensible) steps are easy to state in the abstract, but the problem will still return. Someone pursuing a solution to a pressing social problem, tempted to ignore the claims of privacy, will be equally tempted to ignore the measurement of the claims of privacy. We can write whatever circuit-breakers we like into the law, but once precise rules are formulated, they can be gamed. A rule cannot contain the conditions of its own operation (Carroll 1895; Wittgenstein 1953, §§188–201, 219; Goffman 1961b, 35), and creatively interpreting rules will always seem a reasonable course of action for someone pursuing an alternative social good in good faith (Morreim 1991; Warren et al. 2015; Jahn 2016).

Conclusion: privacy in the time of COVID

Privacy is a complex social phenomenon, and the aim of this book was to provide a framework to enable us to negotiate its complexity across contexts, cultures and times. The major point I wanted to establish is that 'privacy' is a clear and meaningful term in common use among competent native speakers of English requiring no expertise to understand, as opposed to a technical construct of expert discourse that is arguably (and often argued to be) incoherent. What we need to understand, when we discuss privacy, is which discourse(s) we are involved in, and recognise the limits of those discourses in drawing conclusions elsewhere. When privacy is being discussed, are we focused on what it is, how it is achieved, how it affects us as individuals, or social creatures, etc.? Are the arguments empirical or normative, descriptive or moral? What someone wants is very different from what they ought to want, or what the state determines they shall have, or what their environment enables them to achieve. Furthermore, careful statement of the detail of a situation even in an unfamiliar culture will enable the application of privacy discourses to that situation, but only if again we are alive to the different levels of discourse at which we are operating. In short: recognise the discourse you are in, and be very careful about exporting its conclusions to other discourses.

To summarise the argument, Part I reviewed the state of affairs with respect to privacy's definition. The opening chapter plotted a change in emphasis in academic writing – until 1975, academics and lawyers would cheerfully write about privacy without feeling obliged to define it, but gradually from the 1960s, increasingly many did produce their own definitions. As organising academics is like herding cats, the result was 'chaos' (Inness 1992) and 'disarray' (Solove 2008). The second chapter, in contrast, reviewed standard uses of the term 'privacy' and discovered a messy but tractable set, set out in the reference list. Is there disarray or not? Can we resolve the tension?

Part II considered three explanations for the disarray. First, we rejected the explanation that privacy is an essentially contested concept. It is not appraisive, because, as several examples showed, we tend to agree on the term's application and disagree about its value, whereas we agree on the value of an ECC such as justice, and disagree on its application. Furthermore, the meaning of 'privacy' hasn't evolved, but rather received additions or accretions when new contexts emerged through social or technological change. Second, we agreed that 'privacy' is a family resemblance term but were forced to reject this as an explanation of the disarray; family resemblance explains *agreement*, not disagreement. Our third attempt at an explanation was that academics tend to include within their definitions extraneous elements designed to swing the argument in their direction, to produce what were termed 'kitchen sink definitions'.

In that context of the third explanation, Part III categorised the extraneous elements in a framework of different discourses where they have their proper places. Seven levels were set out: privacy conceptions, the affordances of architecture, phenomenology, preferences, social norms, regulation and values. Part IV looked at the interplay of these discourses, how the framework might be used to look at historical and cultural variation, and what a level 0 devoted to purely abstract conceptual matters might look like in some respects. Part V then located some specific privacy debates at their proper level of discourse.

In the course of the discussion, we also came across some particular ideas, methods, institutions and technologies that are strongly associated with privacy, that some have claimed actually define privacy. However, while our view of privacy is naturally strongly influenced by these ideas, they cannot determine what privacy is. These ideas are given in various chapter and section titles scattered through the last three parts of the book: 'X does not define privacy'. It may be helpful at this point to list these ten ideas.

- Control does not define privacy (p. 131).
- Contextual integrity does not define privacy (p. 154).
- The law does not define privacy (p. 159).
- US law does not define privacy (p. 162).
- Values do not define privacy (p. 202).
- The self does not define privacy (p. 231).
- Security algorithms do not define privacy (p. 250).
- Consent does not define privacy (p. 261).
- The private sphere does not define privacy (p. 267).
- Data protection does not define privacy (p. 273).

Our ideas about privacy change with context – thinking, for example, of how technologies such as CCTV, social media and smartphones have altered our thinking in unpredictable ways, very differently in different individuals. The COVID-19 pandemic was one of the most, perhaps the most, dramatic global events since World War II, and it has unsurprisingly had its effects. In the remainder of this final chapter, I will use the pandemic as a lens through which to map current trends.

COVID's metamorphoses

A global pandemic focuses minds, and changes them. Patterns of behaviour and powers of government that might have seemed impossible are now accepted following COVID-19. Although articles describing the 'new normal' have become the cliché of the 2020s, it is too early to tell whether norms are changing. However, there is no doubt that managing a pandemic requires juggling privacy at most of the levels.

At level 1, it is not obvious that the situation has subtended any *new* privacy conceptions, especially as the situation, though unprecedented in scale, ushered in few new practices, with several similarities to the quarantined world Camus' *The Plague* described in 1947. Lockdown increases involuntary spatial privacy – one is discouraged or prevented from meeting others physically. At the same time it decreases decisional privacy – one cannot go where one wishes, and a number of ministers and officials around the world, including the Dutch king and the British Prime Minister, were criticised (or fired) because of their associations with others. Most people were denied control over aspects of their lives, including whether to work, travel and associate. Surveillance became a key means of tracing contacts in order to try to suppress the spread of the virus, although how effectively was debatable.

At level 2, the main architectural change was the development of technology for contact tracing, especially smartphone apps. Apple and Google worked together to produce an interface to exchange Bluetooth signals that was interoperable between their ubiquitous iPhones and Android devices, so that whenever two phones with the app were close together for a period, it was logged on the phones. If one of the users tested positive for the virus, then their contacts, including unwitting ones, could be alerted (O'Hara and Hall 2021, 100).

This caused a controversy, especially in Europe. Google and Apple's API produced a peer-to-peer, decentralised, privacy-protecting system, whereby information about contacts was distributed through the phone network. However, epidemiologists wanted to get hold of the anonymised information in a centralised storage area, in order to track the spread of the virus. This proved to be impossible using the Google/Apple system, and attempts by some governments, including the British, to try to produce a centralised app failed, largely because of lack of expertise in the devices concerned (White and van Basshuysen 2021). Furthermore, as more European countries adopted the Google/Apple API, however involuntarily, attempts to centralise became less viable because they weren't interoperable with decentralised systems in other countries – an important factor given the porous borders in Europe (O'Hara and Hall 2021, 100–102). Centralised systems had other problems. It was pointed out that the design of certain apps facilitated data leakage; the Care19 app in North and South Dakota was found, by virtue of the services it incorporated, to be sharing data with Google and location tech firm Foursquare (Cohen et al. 2020).

The Google/Apple API is the example mentioned at the end of the last chapter where privacy unusually trumped the public good. This happened thanks to two unusual dynamics. First, the design of the system was taken out of public hands by private providers. They were of course concerned with the public good, but they also had worries about their own reputational risk from privacy issues down the line, caused by precisely the type of mission creep described in the last chapter, had governments written the rules. This prevented that, while removing democratic oversight from the system altogether. Second, recall a point made in Part IV, Commentary 1, that computer code and regulations can each be seen as means of constraining behaviour (Lessig 1999). The Google/Apple API shifted the burden from regulation to code, which made decentralisation an affordance of the architecture, not something written into law, and therefore something that could not be gamed or routed around without hacking into the systems. Such are the different properties of level 2 and level 6. Note that we should keep three discussions separate: what *are* the affordances of the API (level 2); what *should* they be, and what democratic oversight *should* there be (level 7); what legal constraints *must* the API meet, and what democratic oversight *is* there (level 6)?

Data from a number of unusual sources was used to track the spread of the virus, as part of an emerging discipline of digital epidemiology, harvesting, analysing, and interpreting data not initially collected for healthcare, to enhance traditional surveillance methods. Examples include social media data, frequently used search terms, data from health trackers and other wearable devices, mobile phone location data, e-commerce data, and smart home data (Kostkova et al. 2021). One study established that 'location, Bluetooth, GPS, External API based on track users, DP-3T, ID Network Location, Textual Analysis, Logbook systems, Meta data, Data Logging, Online Tracking, Third-party sources and Mobile Crowd-sending could be used as sources to track COVID-19 and other future diseases symptoms and infections' (Ribeiro-Navarrete et al. 2021, 10). These datasets and streams all provide affordances for breaching privacy to reveal people's health status, movement and associations, which might be of use in managing the spread of the virus. We know from the Google/Apple API that the existence of these datasets, and the desire of epidemiologists to get their hands on them, don't mean that access is always granted.

Finally, the analysis of medical records was facilitated by impressive developments in privacy-preserving machine learning, creating techniques to analyse data without direct access to the records themselves. Centralised medical systems such as the UK's National Health Service were particularly hospitable hosts for such research (Williamson et al. 2020).

At level 3, anecdotally at least, there is some evidence that personal space is evolving so that people feel safer with more distance. Pedestrians veer to the sides of the pavement to avoid each other. The extent of personal space, and the discomfort of being close to people, seem to have increased according to some experimental results – even in areas where the risk of COVID transmission is nil, such as virtual reality spaces (Holt et al. 2022).

One might expect, at level 4, preferences about surveillance to change, to shift in favour (O'Hara and Hall 2021, 97–102). However, some states report reluctance to adopt track and trace systems, and the Google/Apple decentralisation strategy proved far more acceptable in the US than a centralised system (Zhang et al. 2020).

One interesting area concerns the use of cash. The privacy affordances of cash are vast; those of digital payments are minimal, and unfortunately for privacy, cash has been widely seen as on the way to extinction (Arvidsson 2019; Prasad 2021). With the pandemic (i) accelerating the growth of e-commerce, and (ii) revealing cash as an infection vector, one would expect the use of cash to decline further. Indeed, it seems that fewer cash transactions are being made. However, at least in the UK, the pandemic has seen a growth in the amount of cash in circulation. Partly this was caused by people stockpiling it alongside toilet rolls and spaghetti in the early uncertain days, and with the decline in cash transactions, those stockpiles remained intact, holding their value while inflation was low. However, another reason may be the growth of the shadow economy, as furloughed workers topped up their incomes. The privacy affordances of cash give many citizens reason to prefer it (Economist 2021a).

It will take some time to become clear whether social norms at level 5 have been changed by the pandemic. Certainly the norms governing the distinction between the public and private spheres have been diluted. Many preferred, and some were ordered, to work from home, so the clear division between work and free time was smudged (Chung et al. 2020). Whether these preferences turn into norms, or whether firms will gradually insist that workers return to their offices and workplaces, where workers can interact, IT equipment can be easily monitored, and productivity assessed, is a question that won't be resolved for a while. Many commentators have emphasised the household's role as a Goffmanian backstage (Rössler 2005, 149–150), but now it is often the background to our work Zoom calls. The likelihood of children, spouses, pets or parcel-delivery people crashing the conference further blurs the boundaries, to the detriment of privacy (cf. Rössler 2005, 232n.5). Outside those areas with decent digital infrastructure, more problems are likely to emerge, which may hinder the general adoption of remote working however attractive it may appear (Matli 2020).

Privacy norms were a factor in the control of the virus. An early comparison of the Netherlands and Taiwan, both of which initially relied on self-discipline, blamed the higher death rate in the former on the 'Western emphasis on autonomy'. The Taiwanese response 'relies essentially … not on its citizens' anonymous individual responsibility, but on a completely transparent form of supervised self-discipline. And although the Taiwanese measures are considerably more intrusive, paradoxically, they result in a remarkably liberal policy' (Liu and Bos 2020).

At level 6, many governments imposed lockdown rules of greater or lesser strictness, controversially taking away the decisional privacy of citizens, and enforcing their spatial privacy. Some made contact tracing apps semi-compulsory, following policies that had proved valuable in the past with precursors such as SARS (O'Hara and Stevens 2006b). Asian cultures took to these measures more readily, eschewing privacy-protecting solutions such as the Google/Apple API: South Korean contact tracers were able to download the financial transactions of those who tested positive, and obtain the CCTV footage from shops they had visited to find those they had come into contact with (Carr et al. 2021). The Chinese government maintained strict lockdown rules to late 2022. The existence of data about proximity proved to be a strong temptation for law enforcement agencies, as when the German Luca contact tracing app was used illegally by police to track down potential witnesses to a crime (Henry 2022). But while there was a lot of discussion of the data protection aspects of mandated apps, their impact on individual freedoms and the rule of law was less explored (Lintvedt 2021).

While few governments practised compulsion with respect to vaccinations, a number of firms demanded their employees be vaccinated, some sectors (such as healthcare) imposed compulsion (Frati et al. 2021), and many venues required vaccination certificates for entry, so decisional privacy was often breached at the sub-governmental level. Europeans and Americans both had privacy concerns about certificates or coronavirus passes (NL Times, 2021). Even before COVID, there had already been a debate in the US following a measles epidemic amongst unvaccinated Orthodox Jews in Brooklyn in 2019; ultimately their religious exemption prevailed.

Finally, at level 7, the debate between the interests of the individual versus those of the community loomed large through all the political discussion, even though it could be argued that the interests of both are served by vaccination (Giubilini 2020). However, the decisional privacy of anti-vaxxers was deemed more important than the community interest in herd immunity in most places, which translated into slow rollout of vaccines in places such as some of the US and Continental Europe where scepticism was a major force.

There was also concern that though this was an area of public security, governments were too often deferring to private-sector solutions, allowing technology such as the Google/Apple API to determine how the pandemic was addressed. Democratic oversight demanded more, not less, regulation (Cohen et al. 2020; O'Hara and Hall 2021, 101–102), but whether this would lead to more or less privacy was moot (White and van Basshuysen 2021, and for the opposite view, Part V, Level 7 above).

The ethics of data-driven medical research may be ripe for rewriting. At the corporate level, there is some evidence of greater willingness for organisations to relax their own regulations and share at least anonymised medical records, given the important of data-driven diagnostics for the fight against the pandemic (Economist 2021b), maybe using new institutions such as data trusts (O'Hara 2020b).

In 2016, Alphabet's AI subsidiary DeepMind hit the headlines when it struck a deal with London's Royal Free NHS Trust to get over a million patient records without consent in order to develop machine learning algorithms for detecting kidney disease. The deal was deemed illegal by the data protection regulator and has been criticised for a number of perfectly justified reasons: the system ultimately developed had no beneficial impact; the trust secured no guarantees that DeepMind wouldn't use the data for other purposes; they handed the data over, rather than continuing to exercise control over the data environment (Véliz 2020, 162–165). Yet should the illegality and imprudence of the deal incline us against using data to train machine learning algorithms (that is, to fine-tune and test them)? It has relatively little negative impact on individuals in the data, and so is arguably not in itself unethical. Consent may be hard to get obtain, especially for large or historical datasets. The privacy breach, on the conception that personal data is being processed, is pretty abstract, as long as there is no direct connection back to the data subjects. Granted, one should not break the law, and granted, the trust should have done much more to ensure that the deal worked for patients. Granted, it is possible to do machine learning on data without taking possession of the data, and the trust could have ensured it retained control of the data environment (Elliot et al. 2018). The situation could and should have been handled better. But, post-pandemic, some may want to question the negative ethical valuation of using data for training medical algorithms in good faith.

Accelerating trends

COVID illustrates that while some privacy trends happen at the scale of decades, crises can also cause rapid and perhaps unreflective change. The destruction of the World Trade Center on 11 September 2001 led to a major and intrusive ramping up of security, perhaps inevitably, in terms of both intelligence capabilities and ill-considered legislation such as the USA PATRIOT Act (Lyon 2003). The Snowden revelations (Greenwald 2014) of the extent of global Internet surveillance was another crisis that had an effect in Europe. At the time, the GDPR was in the making, bogged down with thousands of tabled amendments and some disagreement between the European Parliament and the Commission, even though all agreed an update of the Data Protection Directive was required. Snowden cleared the logjam, and the resulting regulation was far more privacy-sensitive than would have happened had he not revealed that the US was bugging Angela Merkel's mobile phone (Hillebrand 2013).

COVID was a crisis at least on this scale. Public views of the value of surveillance, and the acceptable limits of government, have at a minimum been challenged and probably shifted in the aggregate. Arguments about the limits of the public sphere have become more virulent (Schradie 2020).

The net result of the pandemic may be the acceleration of long-term anti-privacy trends, of which the spread of digital technology, and its unpredictable offshoots such as social media, is the main driver. Modernity is shifting, from what we might call a classic twentieth-century analogue modernity based around individualism expressed through choice, using mechanisms such as democracy, free markets, freedom of association and so on, to a twenty-first-century digital modernity, populated by people connected as individuals by networked devices (O'Hara 2020a). But in digital modernity, individuality is no longer expressed through choice, partly because the technology confronts us with too many choices to manage, but also partly because technological systems arguably know at least as well as us what choices we might make, based on the rich data held about us and those similar to us (Cremonesi et al. 2012). The result is that rather than constructing our own worlds from menus of options, we are increasingly allowing the world to be moulded around us, based on the profiles that fit us, in a process of *personalisation* (Bauman 2010; Cohn 2019; O'Hara 2021a).

The issue for privacy is clear. Authentic, autonomous choice demands privacy, a space into which the individual can retire and consider options and consequences. Not only does personalisation not require privacy, it actually gets in the way, because the more information systems have about us, the better the services they can offer (Chellappa and Sin 2005; Golbeck 2016).

The negative privacy affordances of the technology are changing preferences and evolving norms. More people are willingly opening themselves up for scrutiny. At level 6, we increasingly see data-driven policymaking, a corollary of which is that citizens benefit from policy only if they are evident and legible in the data. And these trends in the West are supersized in China, with its face recognition expertise, social credit systems and widespread digital payments (O'Hara and Hall 2021, 125–144).

The trend line is not destiny, and I am certainly not a technological determinist. It is possible that moral debate at level 7 will be the saviour of informational privacy. Perhaps in future a Private Lives Matter movement will topple statues of Mark Zuckerberg and Tim Berners-Lee. But don't put your last anonymous dollar bill on it.

References

Acquisti, Alessandro (2014). 'The economics and behavioral economics of privacy', in Julia Lane, Victoria Stodden, Stefan Bender and Helen Nissenbaum (eds), *Privacy, Big Data, and the Public Good: Frameworks for Engagement*, New York: Cambridge University Press, 76–95.

Acquisti, Alessandro, Laura Brandimarte and George Loewenstein (2015). 'Privacy and human behavior in the age of information', *Science*, 347(6221), 509–514, https://doi.org.10.1126/science.aaa1465.

Adams, Anne and Martina Angela Sasse (1999). 'Users are not the enemy', *Communications of the ACM*, 42(12), 41–46, https://doi.org/10.1145/322796.322806.

Adams, William M. (2019). 'Geographies of conservation II: technology, surveillance and conservation by algorithm', *Progress in Human Geography*, 43(2), 337–350, https://doi.org/10.1177/030913251 7740220.

Adorjan, Michael, Tony Christensen, Benjamin Kelly and Dorothy Pawluch (2012). 'Stockholm syndrome as vernacular resource', *Sociological Quarterly*, 53(3), 454–474, https://doi.org/10.1111/j.1533-8525.2012.01241.x.

Agre, Philip E. (1998). 'Introduction', in Philip E. Agre and Marc Rotenberg (eds), *Technology and Privacy: the New Landscape*, Cambridge, MA: MIT Press, 1–28.

Akerlof, George A. (1970). 'The market for "lemons": quality uncertainty and the market mechanism', *Quarterly Journal of Economics*, 84(3), 488–500.

Albahari, Miri (2006). *Analytical Buddhism: The Two-Tiered Illusion of Self*, Basingstoke: Palgrave Macmillan.

Alemany, J., E. del Val, J. Alberola and A. García-Fornes (2019). 'Enhancing the privacy risk awareness of teenagers in online social networks through soft-paternalism mechanisms', *International Journal of Human-Computer Studies*, 129, 27–40, https://doi.org/10.1016/j.ijhcs.2019.03.008.

Allam, Ahmed, Peter Johannes Schulz and Kent Nakamoto (2014). 'The impact of search engine selection and sorting criteria on vaccination beliefs and attitudes: two experiments manipulating Google output', *Journal of Internet Medical Research*, 16(4), e100, https://doi.org/10.2196/jmir.2642.

Allen, Anita L (1988). *Uneasy Access: Privacy for Women in a Free Society*, Totowa, NJ: Rowman & Littlefield.

Allen, Anita L. (2011). *Unpopular Privacy: What Must We Hide?* New York: Oxford University Press.

Altman, Irwin (1975). *The Environment and Social Behavior: Privacy, Personal Space, Territory, Crowding*, Monterey: Brooks/Cole.

Alvari, Hamidreza, Elham Shaabani, Soumajyoti Sarkar, Ghazaleh Beigi and Paulo Shakarian (2019). 'Less is more: semi-supervised causal inference for detecting pathogenic users in social media', in *WWW '19: Companion Proceedings of the 2019 World Wide Web Conference*, New York: ACM, 154–161, https://doi.org/10.1145/3308560.3316500.

Anderson, Ross and Tanya Berger-Wolf (2018). 'Privacy for tigers', presented at the *27th USENIX Security Symposium*, video at www.usenix.org/conference/usenixsecurity18/presentation/anderson, slides at www.usenix.org/sites/default/files/conference/protected-files/securit y18_slides_anderson.pdf.

Angelidou, Margarita (2017). 'The role of smart city characteristics in the plans of fifteen cities', *Journal of Urban Technology*, 24(4), 3–28, https://doi.org/10.1080/10630732.2017.1348880.

Angwin, Julia (2014). *Dragnet Nation: A Quest for Privacy, Security, and Freedom in a World of Relentless Surveillance*, New York: Times Books.

Ansari, Mohd Zeeshan, Areesha Fatima Siddiqui and Mohammad Anas (2020). 'Inferring political preferences from Twitter', in João Manuel R. S. Tavares, Satyajit Chakrabarti, Abhishek Bhattacharya and Sujata Ghatak (eds), *Emerging Technologies in Data Mining and Information Security: Proceedings of IEMIS 2020, Volume 3*, Singapore: Springer, 581–589, https://doi.org/10.1007/978-981-15-9774-9_54.

Anscombe, G. E. M. (1962). 'On sensations of position', *Analysis*, 22(3), 55–58, https://doi.org/10.2307/3326426.

Aplin, Tanya, Lionel Bently, Phillip Johnson and Simon Malynicz (2012). *Gurry on Breach of Confidence: The Protection of Confidential Information*, 2nd edition, Oxford: Oxford University Press.

Are, Carolina (2021). 'The Shadowban Cycle: an autoethnography of pole dancing, nudity and censorship on Instagram', *Feminist Media Studies*, https://doi.org/10.1080/14680777.2021.1928259.

Arendt, Hannah (1968). *Between Past and Future: Eight Exercises in Political Thought*, New York: Viking.

Arendt, Hannah (1978). *The Life of the Mind: Thinking*, New York: Harcourt Brace Jovanovich.

Arendt, Hannah (1998). *The Human Condition*, 2nd edition, Chicago: University of Chicago Press.

Arendt, Hannah (2017). *The Origins of Totalitarianism*, London: Penguin.

Aristotle (1989). 'Poetics', in D. A. Russell and Michael Winterbottom (eds), *Classical Literary Criticism*, Oxford: Oxford University Press, 51–90.

Aristotle (1995). *Politics*, Oxford: Oxford University Press.

Aristotle (2011). *Aristotle's Nicomachean Ethics*, Chicago: University of Chicago Press.

Armesto-Larson, Brooklynn (2020). 'Nonconsensual pornography: criminal law solutions to a worldwide problem', *Oregon Review of International Law*, 21, 177–213.

Arnold, Zachary, Danielle Larose and Emmanuel Agu (2015). 'Smartphone inference of alcohol consumption levels from gait', in *Proceedings of the 2015 International Conference on Healthcare Informatics*, IEEE, https://doi.org/10.1109/ICHI.2015.59.

Arrington, Michael (2006). 'AOL proudly releases massive amounts of private data', *TechCrunch*, 7 August 2006, https://techcrunch.com/2006/08/06/aol-proudly-releases-massive-amounts-of-user-search-data/.

Arvidsson, Niklas (2019). *Building a Cashless Society: The Swedish Route to the Future of Cash Payments*, Cham: Springer.

Ashby, Matthew P. J. (2017). 'The value of CCTV surveillance cameras as an investigative tool: an empirical analysis', *European Journal on Criminal Policy and Research*, 23(3), 441–459, https://doi.org/10.1007/s10610-017-9341-6.

Ashworth, G. J., P. E. White and H. P. M. Winchester (1988). 'The red-light district in the West European city: a neglected aspect of the urban landscape', *Geoforum*, 19(2), 201–212, https://doi.org/10.1016/S0016-7185(88)80029-0.

Aspinall, Julie (2006). *Oh My God! The Biography of Chantelle*, London: John Blake Publishing.

Austin, Lisa M. (2013). 'Possession and the distractions of philosophy', in James Penner and Henry E. Smith (eds), *Philosophical Foundations of Property Law*, Oxford: Oxford University Press, 182–201.

Aveyard, Helen (2002). 'Implied consent prior to nursing care procedures', *Journal of Advanced Nursing*, 39(2), 201–207, https://doi.org/10.1046/j.1365-2648.2002.02260.x.

Aydın-Düzgit, Senem (2012). 'No crisis, no change: the third AKP victory in the June 2011 Parliamentary elections in Turkey', *South European Society and Politics*, 17(2), 329–346, https://doi.org/10.1080/13608746.2011.640426.

Bagheri, Mehrdad, Milos N. Mladenovic, Iisakki Kosonen, Jukka K. Nurminen, Claudio Roncoli and Antti Ylä-Jääski (2020). 'A computational framework for revealing competitive travel times with low-carbon modes based on smartphone data collection', *Journal of Advanced Transportation*, volume 2020, article ID 4693750, https://doi.org/10.1155/2020/4693750.

Baier, Annette (1985). 'Cartesian persons', in Annette Baier, *Postures of the Mind: Essays on Mind and Morals*, Minneapolis: University of Minnesota Press, 74–92.

Baker, Lindsay (2014). 'Mourning glory: two centuries of funeral dress', *BBC Culture*, 3 November, 2014, www.bbc.com/culture/article/20141103-mourning-glory-funeral-style.

Balboni, Paolo and Theodora Dragan (2018). 'Controversies and challenges of trustmarks: lessons for privacy and data protection seals', in Rowena Rodrigues and Vagelis Papakonstantinou (eds), *Privacy and Data Protection Seals*, The Hague: T. M. C. Asser Press, 83–111, https://doi.org/10.1007/978-94-6265-228-6_6.

Baldwin, David A. (1997). 'The concept of security', *Review of International Studies*, 23(1), 5–26.

Bamberger, Kenneth A. and Deirdre K. Mulligan (2015). *Privacy on the Ground: Driving Corporate Behavior in the United States and Europe*, Cambridge, MA: MIT Press.

Bandara, Ruwan, Mario Fernando and Shahriar Akter (2020). 'Privacy concerns in e-commerce: a taxonomy and a future research agenda', *Electronic Markets*, 30(3), 629–647, https://doi.org/10.1007/s12525-019-00375-6.

Banisadr, Masoud (2004). *Masoud: Memoirs of an Iranian Rebel*, London: Saqi Books.

Banta, Natalie M. (2016). 'Death and privacy in the digital age', *North Carolina Law Review*, 94(3), 927–990.

Barocas, Solon and Helen Nissenbaum (2009). 'On notice: the trouble with notice and consent', in *Proceedings of the Engaging Data Forum: The First International Forum on the Application and Management of Personal Electronic Information*, https://papers.ssrn.com/sol3/papers.cfm?abstract_id=2567409.

Barocas, Solon and Helen Nissenbaum (2014). 'Big data's end run around anonymity and consent', in Julia Lane, Victoria Stodden, Stefan Bender and Helen Nissenbaum (eds), *Privacy, Big Data, and the Public Good: Frameworks for Engagement*, New York: Cambridge University Press, 44–75.

Barron, Lee (2010). 'From social experiment to postmodern joke: *Big Brother* and the progressive construction of celebrity', in Julie Anne

Taddeo and Ken Dvorak (eds), *The Tube Has Spoken: Reality TV and History*, Lexington: University Press of Kentucky, 27–46.

Baruh, Lemi (2010). 'Mediated voyeurism and the guilty pleasure of consuming reality television', *Media Psychology*, 13(3), 201–221, https://doi.org/10.1080/15213269.2010.502871.

Baruh, Lemi and Zeynep Cemalcılar (2015). 'Rubbernecking effect of intimate information on Twitter: when getting attention works against interpersonal attraction', *Cyberpsychology, Behavior, and Social Networking*, 18(9), 506–513, http://doi.org/10.1089/cyber.2015.0099.

Baruh, Lemi and Mihaela Popescu (2017). 'Big data analytics and the limits of privacy self-management', *New Media and Society*, 19(4), 579–596, https://doi.org/10.1177/1461444815614001.

Bauman, Zygmunt (2010). 'Privacy, secrecy, intimacy, human bonds, utopia – and other collateral casualties of liquid modernity', in Harry Blatterer, Pauline Johnson and Maria R. Markus (eds), *Modern Privacy: Shifting Boundaries, New Forms*, Basingstoke: Palgrave Macmillan, 7–22.

Baumann, Annika, Johannes Haupt, Fabian Gebert and Stefan Lessmann (2019). 'The price of privacy: an evaluation of the economic value of collecting clickstream data', *Business and Information Systems Engineering*, 61(4), 413–431, https://doi.org/10.1007/s12 599-018-0528-2.

Baumol, William J. (1990). 'Entrepreneurship: productive, unproductive, and destructive', *Journal of Political Economy*, 98(5/1), 893–921, https://doi.org/10.1086/261712.

Becher, Tony (1994). 'The significance of disciplinary differences', *Studies in Higher Education*, 19(2), 151–161, https://doi.org/10.1080/03075 079412331382007.

Benn, Stanley I. (1971). 'Privacy, freedom and respect for persons', in J. Roland Pennock and J. W. Chapman (eds), *Privacy and Personality*, Abingdon: Routledge, 1–26. Page references to (Schoeman 1984a, 223–244).

Bennett, Colin J. (2008). *The Privacy Advocates: Resisting the Spread of Surveillance*, Cambridge, MA: MIT Press.

Bentham, Jeremy (1995). *The Panopticon Writings*, London: Verso.

Benton, Ted and Ian Craib (2001). *Philosophy of Social Science: The Philosophical Foundations of Social Thought*, Basingstoke: Palgrave.

Berg, Chris (2018). *The Classical Liberal Case for Privacy in a World of Surveillance and Technological Change*, Cham: Palgrave Macmillan.

Berkowitz, Eric (2021). *Dangerous Ideas: A Brief History of Censorship in the West From the Ancients to Fake News*, London: Westbourne Press.

Bermúdez, José Luis (1998). *The Paradox of Self-Consciousness*, Cambridge, MA: MIT Press.

Bernasconi, Robert (2012). 'Othering', in Francis Halsall, Julia Jansen and Sinead Murphy (eds), *Critical Communities and Aesthetic Practices: Dialogues with Tony O'Connor on Society, Art, and Friendship*, Dordrecht: Springer, 151–157, https://doi.org/10.1007/978-94-007-1509-7_13.

Betten, F. S. (1925). 'Miscellany', *The Catholic Historical Review*, 11(2), 285–289.

Bicchieri, Cristina (2006). *The Grammar of Society: The Nature and Dynamics of Social Norms*, Cambridge: Cambridge University Press.

Bicchieri, Cristina (2017). *Norms in the Wild: How to Diagnose, Measure, and Change Social Norms*, New York: Oxford University Press.

Bicchieri, Cristina and Erte Xiao (2009). 'Do the right thing: but only if others do so', *Journal of Behavioral Decision Making*, 22(2), 191–208, https://doi.org/10.1002/bdm.621.

Binns, Reuben (2022). 'Tracking on the Web, mobile and the Internet-of-Things', *Foundations and Trends in Web Science* 8(1–2), 1–113, http://dx.doi.org/10.1561/1800000029.

Birnhack, Michael and Lotem Perry-Hazan (2020). 'School surveillance in context: high school students' perspectives on CCTV, privacy, and security', *Youth and Society*, 52(7), 1312–1330, https://doi.org/10.1177/0044118X20916617.

Biswas-Diener, Robert and Ed Diener (2009). 'Making the best of a bad situation: satisfaction in the slums of Calcutta', in Ed Diener (ed.), *Culture and Well-Being: The Collected Works of Ed Diener*, Dordrecht: Springer, 261–278, https://doi.org/10.1007/978-90-481-2352-0_13.

Blanning, Tim (2007). *The Pursuit of Glory: Europe 1648–1815*, London: Allen Lane.

Blaydes, Lisa (2018). *State of Repression: Iraq Under Saddam Hussein*, Princeton: Princeton University Press.

Block, Walter (2001). 'The logic of the argument on behalf of legalising blackmail', *Bracton Law Journal*, 33, 61–80.

Bloustein, Edward J. (1964). 'Privacy as an aspect of human dignity: an answer to Dean Prosser', *New York University Law Review*, 39, 962–1007. Page references to (Schoeman 1984a, 156–202).

Bloustein, Edward J. (1977). 'Group privacy: the right to huddle', *Rutgers Camden Law Journal*, 8(2), 219–283.

Boesen, Julie, Jennifer A. Rode and Clara Mancini (2010). 'The domestic panopticon: location tracking in families', in *UbiComp '10: Proceedings of the 12th ACM International Conference on Ubiquitous Computing*, New York: ACM, 65–74, https://doi.org/10.1145/1864349.1864382.

Bolotta, Giuseppe (2019). 'Making sense of (humanitarian) emotions in an ethnography of vulnerable children: the case of Bangkok slum children', in Thomas Stodulka, Samia Dinkelaker and Ferdiansyah Thajib (eds), *Affective Dimensions of Fieldwork and Ethnography*, Cham: Springer, 29–48, https://doi.org/10.1007/978-3-030-20831-8_4.

Bond, Johanna (2014). 'Honour as familial value', in Aisha K. Gill, Carolyn Strange and Karl Roberts (eds), *'Honour' Killing and Violence: Theory, Policy and Practice*, London: Palgrave Macmillan, 89–107, https://doi.org/10.1057/9781137289568_5.

Borgesius, Frederik J. Zuiderveen, Judith Möller, Sanne Kruikemeier, Ronan Ó Fathaigh, Kristina Irion, Tom Dobber, Balazs Bodo and Claes de Vreese (2018). 'Online political microtargeting: promises and threats for democracy', *Utrecht Law Review*, 14(1), 82–96, https://doi.org/10.18352/ulr.420.

Bott, Ed, 'Why Do Not Track is worse than a miserable failure', *ZDNet*, 21 September 2012, www.zdnet.com/article/why-do-not-track-is-worse-than-a-miserable-failure/.

Botvinick, Matthew and Jonathan Cohen (1998). 'Rubber hands "feel" touch that eyes see', *Nature*, 391, 756, https://doi.org/10.1038/35784.

Boutros, Fadi, Naser Damer, Jan Niklas Kolf, Kiran Raja, Florian Kirchbuchner, Raghavendra Ramachandra, Arjan Kuijper, Pengcheng Fang, Chao Zhang, Fei Wang, David Montero, Naiara Aginako, Basilio Sierra, Marcos Nieto, Mustafa Ekrem Erakin, Uğur Demir, Hazım Kemal Ekenel, Asaki Kataoka, Kohei Ichikawa, Shizuma Kubo, Jie Zhang, Mingjie He, Dan Han, Shiguang Shan, Klemen Grm, Vitomir Štruc, Sachith Seneviratne, Nuran Kasthuriarachchi, Sanka Rasnayaka, Pedro C. Neto, Ana F. Sequeira, Joao Ribeiro Pinto, Mohsen Saffari and Jaime S. Cardoso (2021). 'MFR 2021: Masked Face Recognition Competition', in *Proceedings of the 2021 IEEE International Joint Conference on Biometrics (IJCB)*, https://doi.org/10.1109/IJCB52358.2021.9484337.

Bradford, Anu (2020). *The Brussels Effect: How the European Union Rules the World*, New York: Oxford University Press.

Bradley, John S. and Bradford N. Gover (2010). 'Speech levels in meeting rooms and the probability of speech privacy problems', *The Journal of the Acoustical Society of America*, 127(2), 815–822, https://doi.org/10.1121/1.3277220.

Brailovskaia, Julia, Elke Rohmann, Hans-Werner Bierhoff and Jürgen Margraf (2018). 'The brave blue world: Facebook flow and Facebook Addiction Disorder (FAD)', *PLoS One*, 13(7), e0201484, https://dx.doi.org/10.1371/journal.pone.0201484.

Braude, Stephen E. (1991). *First Person Plural: Multiple Personality and the Philosophy of Mind*, New York: Routledge.

Braude, Stephen E. (2020). 'Does telepathy threaten mental privacy?' *Journal of Scientific Exploration*, 34(2), 199–208, https://doi.org/10.31275/20201829.

Brems, Eva (ed.) (2014). *The Experience of Face Veil Wearers in Europe and the Law*, Cambridge: Cambridge University Press.

Brooks, Charles J., Christopher Grow, Philip Craig and Donald Short (2018). *Cybersecurity Essentials*, Indianapolis: John Wiley & Sons.

Brown, Jennifer Gerarda (1993). 'Blackmail as private justice', *University of Pennsylvania Law Review*, 141(5), 1935–1974, https://doi.org/10.2307/3312579.

Brunton, Finn and Helen Nissenbaum (2015). *Obfuscation: A User's Guide for Privacy and Protest*, Cambridge, MA: MIT Press.

Buck, Ashley E., Kathleene M. Lange, Katey Sackett and John E. Edlund (2019). 'Reactions to homosexual, transgender, and heterosexual public displays of affection', *Journal of Positive Sexuality*, 5(2), 34–47.

Burgess, Matt (2021). 'Why iOS 14.5 is Apple's biggest privacy update yet', *Wired*, 27 April 2021, www.wired.co.uk/article/ios-14-5-update-app-tracking.

Burghartz, Susanna (2015). 'Covered women? Veiling in early modern Europe', *History Workshop Journal*, 80(1), 1–32, https://doi.org/10.1093/hwj/dbv028.

Burke, Edmund (1968). *Reflections on the Revolution in France*, Harmondsworth: Penguin.

Buyle, Raf, Ruben Taelman, Katrien Mostaert, Geroen Joris, Erik Mannens, Ruben Verborgh and Tim Berners-Lee (2020). 'Streamlining governmental processes by putting citizens in control of their personal data', in Andrei Chugunov, Igor Khodachek, Yuri Misnikov and Dmitrii Trutnev (eds), *Electronic Governance and Open Society: Challenges in Eurasia – Proceedings of the 6th International Conference, EGOSE 2019*, Cham: Springer, 346–359, https://doi.org/10.1007/978-3-030-39296-3_26.

Calo, M. Ryan (2011). 'The boundaries of privacy harm', *Indiana Law Journal*, 86(3), 1131–1162.

Carman, Ashley (2017). 'Sex toy company admits to recording users' remote sex sessions, calls it a "minor bug"', *The Verge*, 10 November 2017, www.theverge.com/2017/11/10/16634442/lovense-sex-toy-spy-surveillance.

Carr, Geoffrey, Slavea Chankova, Hal Hodson, Alok Jha and Oliver Morton (2021). 'Testing and tracing could have worked better against covid-19', *The Economist Technology Quarterly*, 27 March 2021,

www.economist.com/technology-quarterly/2021/03/23/testing-and-trac
ing-could-have-worked-better-against-covid-19.

Carroll, Lewis (1895). 'What the tortoise said to Achilles', *Mind*, 4, 278–280.

Carter, Pam, Graeme T. Laurie and Mary Dixon-Woods (2015). 'The social licence for research: why care.data ran into trouble', *Journal of Medical Ethics*, 41(5), 404–409, https://doi.org/10.1136/medethics-2014-102374.

Cavoukian, Ann (2011). *Privacy by Design: The 7 Foundational Principles*, Toronto: Information and Privacy Commissioner of Ontario, https://iapp.org/media/pdf/resource_center/pbd_implement_7found_princip les.pdf.

Cavoukian, Ann and Khaled El Emam (2011). *Dispelling the Myths Surrounding De-identification: Anonymization Remains a Strong Tool for Protecting Privacy*, Toronto: Information and Privacy Commissioner of Ontario, www.ipc.on.ca/wp-content/uploads/2016/11/anonymizat ion.pdf.

Ceross, Aaron (2018). 'Examining data protection enforcement actions through qualitative interviews and data exploration', *International Review of Law, Computers and Technology*, 32(1), 99–117, https://doi.org/10.1080/13600869.2018.1418143.

Chalmers, Matthew and Areti Galani (2004). 'Seamful inter-weaving: heterogeneity in the theory and design of interactive systems', in *DIS '04: Proceedings of the 5th Conference on Designing Interactive Systems: Processes, Practices, Methods, and Techniques*, New York: ACM, 243–252, https://doi.org/10.1145/1013 115.1013149.

Channon, Henry 'Chips' (2021). *The Diaries 1918–38*, London: Hutchinson.

Chao, Bernard, Catherine Durso, Ian Farrell and Christopher Robertson (2018). 'Why courts fail to protect privacy: race, age, bias, and technology', *California Law Review*, 106(2), 263–324.

Charitonidis, Christos, Awais Rashid and Paul J. Taylor (2017). 'Predicting collective action from micro-blog data', in Jalal Kawash, Nitin Agarwal and Tansel Özyer (eds), *Prediction and Inference from Social Networks and Social Media*, Cham: Springer, 141–170, https://doi.org/10.1007/978-3-319-51049-1_7.

Chellappa, Ramnath K. and Raymond G. Sin (2005). 'Personalization versus privacy: an empirical examination of the online consumer's dilemma', *Information Technology and Management*, 6(2–3), 181–202, https://doi.org/10.1007/s10799-005-5879-y.

Choi, Jay Pil, Doh-Shin Jeon and Byung-Cheol Kim (2019). 'Privacy and personal data collection with information externalities', *Journal* of *Public Economics*, 173, 113–124, https://doi.org/10.1016/j.jpub eco.2019.02.001.

Choy, James P. (2020). '*Kompromat*: a theory of blackmail as a system of governance', *Journal of Development Economics*, 147, 102535, https://doi.org/10.1016/j.jdeveco.2020.102535.

Chung, Heejung, Hyojin Seo, Sarah Forbes and Holly Birkett (2020). *Working From Home During the COVID-19 Lockdown: Changing Preferences and the Future of Work*, University of Kent and University of Birmingham, https://kar.kent.ac.uk/83896/1/Working_from_home_ COVID-19_lockdown.pdf.

Chung, Younshik and Wilfred W. Recker (2013). 'Spatiotemporal analysis of traffic congestion caused by rubbernecking at freeway accidents', *IEEE Transactions on Intelligent Transportation Systems*, 14(3), 1416–1422, https://doi.org/10.1109/TITS.2013.2261987.

Clarke, Roger (1988). 'Information technology and dataveillance', *Communications of the ACM*, 31(5), 498–512, https://doi.org/10.1145/ 42411.42413.

Cocking, Dean (2008). 'Plural selves and relational identity: intimacy and privacy online', in Jeroen van den Hoven and John Weckert (eds), *Information Technology and Moral Philosophy*, New York: Cambridge University Press, 123–141.

Cohen, Julie E. (2000). 'Examined lives: informational privacy and the subject and object', *Stanford Law Review*, 52(5), 1373–1438.

Cohen, Julie E. (2013). 'What privacy is for', *Harvard Law Review*, 126(7), 1904–1933.

Cohen, Julie E., Woodrow Hartzog and Laura Moy (2020). 'The dangers of tech-driven solutions to COVID-19', *TechStream*, 17 June 2020, www.brookings.edu/techstream/the-dangers-of-tech-driven-solutions-to-covid-19/.

Cohen, Tammy (2008). *Up the Creek Without a Paddle: The True Story of John and Anne Darwin: The Man Who 'Died' and the Wife Who Lied*, London: John Blake Publishing.

Cohn, Jonathan (2019). *The Burden of Choice: Recommendations, Subversion, and Algorithmic Culture*, London: Rutgers University Press.

Coker, Calvin R. (2017). 'Murder, miscarriage, and women's choice: prudence in the Colorado personhood debate', *Western Journal of Communication*, 81(3), 300–319, https://doi.org/10.1080/10570 314.2016.1245439.

Coles-Kemp, Lizzie, Debi Ashenden and Kieron O'Hara (2018). 'Why should I? Cybersecurity, the security of the state and the insecurity of the citizen', *Politics and Governance*, 6(2), 41–48, https://doi.org/ 10.17645/pag.v6i2.1333.

Collier, David, Fernando Daniel Hidalgo and Andra Olivia Maciuceanu (2006). 'Essentially contested concepts: debates and applications', *Journal of Political Ideologies*, 11(3), 211–246.

Connolly, William E. (1983). *Terms of Political Discourse*, 2nd edition, Princeton: Princeton University Press.

Conrad, Joseph (1912). *A Personal Record: Some Reminiscences*, New York: Doubleday.

Coupe, Timothy and Satverg Kaur (2005). 'The role of alarms and CCTV in detecting non-residential burglary', *Security Journal*, 18(2), 53–72, https://doi.org/10.1057/palgrave.sj.8340198.

CPS (2021). *CPS publishes landmark survey by Dr Frank Luntz on politics, economics and culture wars, Centre for Policy Studies*, press release, Centre for Policy Studies, www.cps.org.uk/media/press-releases/q/date/2021/07/06/cps-publishes-landmark-survey-by-dr-frank-luntz-on-poli/#.

Crabtree, Andy, Peter Tolmie and Will Knight (2017). 'Repacking "privacy" for a networked world', *Computer Supported Cooperative Work*, 26(4–6), 453–488, https://doi.org/10.1007/s10606-017-9276-y.

Crawford, Kate and Jason Schultz (2014). 'Big data and due process: toward a framework to redress predictive privacy harms', *Boston College Law Review*, 55(1), 93–128.

Cremonesi, Paolo, Franca Garzotto and Roberto Turrin (2012). 'Investigating the persuasion potential of recommender systems from a quality perspective: an empirical study', *ACM Transactions on Interactive Intelligent Systems*, 2(2), article 11, https://doi.org/10.1145/2209310.2209314.

Dahl, Norman O. (2011). 'Contemplation and *eudaimonia* in the *Nicomachean Ethics*', in Jon Miller (ed.), *Aristotle's* Nicomachean Ethics: *A Critical Guide*, Cambridge: Cambridge University Press, 66–91.

Datta, Ayona (2016). 'The intimate city: violence, gender and ordinary life in Delhi slums', *Urban Geography*, 37(3), 323–342, https://doi.org/10.1080/02723638.2015.1096073.

David, Rosalie (2002). *Religion and Magic in Ancient Egypt*, London: Penguin.

De Choudhury, Munmun, Emre Kiciman, Mark Dredze, Glen Coppersmith and Mrinal Kumar (2016). 'Discovering shifts to suicidal ideation from mental health content in social media', in *CHI '16: Proceedings of the 2016 CHI Conference on Human Factors in Computing Systems*, New York: ACM, 2098–2110, https://doi.org/10.1145/2858036.2858207.

de Laat, Paul (2008). 'Online diaries: reflections on trust, privacy, and exhibitionism', *Ethics and Information Technology*, 10(1), 57–69, http://dx.doi.org/10.1007/s10676-008-9155-9.

de Vries, Bouke (2019). 'The right to be publicly naked: a defence of nudism', *Res Publica*, 25(3), 407–424, https://doi.org/10.1007/s11 158-018-09406-z.

Dean, Trevor (1997). 'Marriage and mutilation: vendetta in Late Medieval Italy', *Past and Present*, 157, 3–36.

DeGroot, Jocelyn (2014). ' "For whom the bell tolls": emotional rubbernecking in Facebook memorial groups', *Death Studies*, 38(2), 79–84, https://doi.org/10.1080/07481187.2012.725450.

Delacroix, Sylvie and Neil D. Lawrence (2019). 'Bottom-up data trusts: disturbing the "one size fits all" approach to data governance', *International Data Privacy Law*, 9(4), 236–252, https://doi.org/ 10.1093/idpl/ipz014.

Deleuze, Gilles and Felix Guattari (1983). *Anti-Oedipus: Capitalism and Schizophrenia*, Minneapolis: University of Minnesota Press.

Dewey, Susan and Tiantian Zheng (2013). *Ethical Research with Sex Workers: Anthropological Approaches*, New York: Springer.

D'Orlando, Fabio (2011). 'The demand for pornography', *Journal of Happiness Studies*, 12(1), 51–75, http://dx.doi.org/10.1007/s10 902-009-9175-0.

Driessens, Oliver (2013). 'The celebritization of society and culture: understanding the structural dynamics of celebrity culture', *International Journal of Cultural Studies*, 16(6), 641–657, https://doi. org/10.1177/1367877912459140.

Duncan, George T., Mark Elliot and Juan-José Salazar-González (2011). *Statistical Confidentiality: Principles and Practice*, New York: Springer.

Dwork, Cynthia (2014). 'Differential privacy: a cryptographic approach to private data analysis', in Julia Lane, Victoria Stodden, Stefan Bender and Helen Nissenbaum (eds), *Privacy, Big Data, and the Public Good: Frameworks for Engagement*, New York: Cambridge University Press, 296–322.

Dworkin, Ronald (1986). *Law's Empire*, Cambridge, MA: Belknap Press.

Economist, The (2021a). 'The pandemic has seen a surprising surge in cash use', *The Economist*, 29 May 2021, www.economist.com/britain/2021/ 05/29/the-pandemic-has-seen-a-surprising-surge-in-cash-use.

Economist, The (2021b). 'The big-pharma firm that saw the future', *The Economist*, 5 June 2021, www.economist.com/business/2021/06/03/ the-big-pharma-firm-that-saw-the-future.

Edwards, Lilian (2013). 'Privacy, law, code and social networking sites', in Ian Brown (ed.), *Research Handbook on Governance of the Internet*, Cheltenham: Edward Elgar, 309–352.

El Guindi, Fadwa (1999). *Veil: Modesty, Privacy and Resistance*, Oxford: Berg.

Elliot, Mark, Kieron O'Hara, Charles Raab, Christine M. O'Keeffe, Elaine Mackey, Chris Dibben, Heather Gowans, Kingsley Purdam and Karen McCullagh (2018). 'Functional anonymisation: personal data and the data environment', *Computer Law and Security Review*, 34(2), 204–221, https://doi.org/10.1016/j.clsr.2018.02.001.

Emad, Parvis (1972). 'Max Scheler's phenomenology of shame', *Philosophy and Phenomenological Research*, 32(3), 361–370, https://doi.org/10.2307/2105567.

Emberson, Lauren L., Gary Lupyan, Michael H. Goldstein and Michael J. Spivey (2010). 'Overheard cell-phone conversations: when less speech is more distracting', *Psychological Science*, 21(10), 1383–1388, https://doi.org/10.1177/0956797610382126.

Enos, Olivia (2020). *Why the US Should Issue an Atrocity Determination for Uighurs*, The Heritage Foundation Backgrounder no.3529, http://report.heritage.org/bg3529.

Epstein, Robert, Mayuri Pandit and Mansi Thakar (2013). 'How love emerges in arranged marriages: two cross-cultural studies', *Journal of Comparative Family Studies*, 44(3), 341–360, https://doi.org/10.3138/jcfs.44.3.341.

Eräranta, Kirsi, Johanna Moisander and Sinikka Pesonen (2009). 'Narratives of self and relatedness in eco-communes: resistance against normalized individualization and the nuclear family', *European Societies*, 11(3), 347–367, https://doi.org/10.1080/14616690902764757.

Ess, Charles (2005). ' "Lost in translation"?: Intercultural dialogues on privacy and information ethics (Introduction to special issue on Privacy and Data Privacy Protection in Asia)', *Ethics and Information Technology*, 7(1), 1–6, https://doi.org/10.1007/s10676-005-0454-0.

Etzioni, Amitai (1999). *The Limits of Privacy*, New York: Basic Books.

Etzioni, Amitai (2015). *Privacy in a Cyber Age: Policy and Practice*, New York: Palgrave Macmillan.

Eubanks, Virginia (2019). *Automating Inequality: How High-Tech Tools Profile, Police, and Punish the Poor*, paperback edition, New York: Picador.

Fanon, Frantz (1965). 'Algeria unveiled', in Frantz Fanon, *A Dying Colonialism*, New York: Grove Press, 35–68.

Fantasia, Heidi Collins (2011). 'Really not even a decision any more: late adolescent narratives of implied sexual consent', *Journal of Forensic Nursing*, 7(3), 120–129, https://doi.org/10.1111/j.1939-3938.2011.01108.x.

Faust, Gretchen (2017). 'Hair, blood and the nipple: Instagram censorship and the female body', in Urte Undine Frömming, Steffen Köhn, Samantha Fox and Mike Terry (eds), *Digital Environments: Ethnographic Perspectives Across Global Online and Offline Spaces*, Bielefeld: Transcript Verlag, 159–170, https://doi.org/10.25595/493.

Fawcett, Edmund (2018). *Liberalism: The Life of an Idea*, 2nd edition, Princeton: Princeton University Press.

Fifer, Barbara and Martin Kidston (2003). *Wanted! Wanted Posters of the Old West*, Helena MT: Farcountry Press.

Finlay, Joanne Smith (2022). 'Why scholars and activists increasingly fear a Uyghur genocide in Xinjiang', *Journal of Genocide Research*, 23(3), 348–370, https://doi.org/10.1080/14623528.2020.1848109.

Finn, Rachel L., David Wright and Michael Friedewald (2013). 'Seven types of privacy', in Serge Gutwirth, Ronald Leenes, Paul de Hert and Yves Poullet (eds), *European Data Protection: Coming of Age*, Dordrecht: Springer, 3–32, https://doi.org/10.1007/978-94-007-5170-5_1.

Floridi, Luciano (2005). 'The ontological interpretation of information privacy', *Ethics and Information Technology*, 7(4), 185–200, https://doi.org/10.1007/s10676-006-0001-7.

Ford, Elizabeth, Keegan Curlewis, Akkapon Wongkoblap and Vasa Curcin (2019). 'Public opinions on using social media content to identify users with depression and target mental health care advertising: mixed methods survey', *JMIR Mental Health*, 6(11), e12942, https://doi.org/10.2196/12942.

Forst, Rainer (2015). 'Noumenal power', *Journal of Political Philosophy*, 23(2), 111–127, https://doi.org/10.1111/jopp.12046.

Francis, Mary (2021). 'The treatment of privacy in professional codes of ethics: an international survey', *Library Quarterly*, 91(3), 304–321, https://doi.org/10.1086/714320.

Frankfurt, Harry G. (1971). 'Freedom of the will and the concept of a person', *Journal of Philosophy*, 68(1), 5–20.

Fraser, Nancy (1981). 'Foucault on modern power: empirical insights and normative confusions', *Praxis International*, 1(3), 272–287.

Frati, Paola Raffaele La Russa, Nicola Di Fazio, Zoe Del Fante, Giuseppe Delogu and Vittorio Fineschi (2021). 'Compulsory vaccination for healthcare workers in Italy for the prevention of SARS-CoV-2 infection', *Vaccines*, 9(9), 966, https://doi.org/10.3390/vaccines9090966.

Frazer, J. G. (1987). *The Golden Bough: A Study in Magic and Religion*, abridged edition, London: Macmillan.

Freda, Maria Francesca and Raffaele De Luca Picione (2014). 'The identity as a system of translation of the boundary between subject and context', in Sergio Salvatore, Alessandro Gennaro and Jaan Valsiner (eds), *Multicentric Identities in a Globalizing World: Yearbook of Ideographic Science Volume 5*, Charlotte NC: Information Age Publishing, 179–192.

Freeman, Anthony (ed.) (2006). *Consciousness and its Place in Nature: Does Physicalism Entail Panpsychism?* Exeter: Imprint Academic.

Frege, Gottlob (1980). 'On concept and object', in Peter Geach and Max Black (eds), *Translations From the Philosophical Writings of Gottlob Frege*, 3rd edition, Oxford: Blackwell, 42–55.

Fried, Charles (1968). 'Privacy', *Yale Law Journal*, 77, 475–493. Page references to (Schoeman 1984a, 203–222).

Friedman, Ori, Madison L. Pesowski and Brandon W. Goulding (2018). 'Legal ownership is psychological: evidence from young children', in Joann Peck and Suzanne B. Shu (eds), *Psychological Ownership and Consumer Behavior*, Cham: Springer, 19–31, https://doi.org/10.1007/978-3-319-77158-8_2.

Frimer, Jeremy A., Caitlin E. Tell and Jonathan Haidt (2015). 'Liberals condemn sacrilege too: the harmless desecration of Cerro Torre', *Social Psychology and Personality Science*, 6(8), 878–886, https://doi.org/10.1177/1948550615597974.

Frith, H. and K. Gleeson (2004). 'Clothing and embodiment: men managing body image and appearance', *Psychology of Men and Masculinities*, 5(1), 40–48, https://psycnet.apa.org/doi/10.1037/1524-9220.5.1.40.

Fukuyama, Francis, Barak Richman and Ashish Goel (2021). 'How to save democracy from technology: ending big tech's information monopoly', *Foreign Affairs*, 100(1), 98–110.

Fuller, Vincent J. (1982). 'United States vs John W. Hinckley Jr', *Loyola of Los Angeles Law Review*, 33(2), 699–703.

Fung, Archon, Mary Graham and David Weil (2007). *Full Disclosure: The Perils and Promise of Transparency*, New York: Cambridge University Press.

Gallagher, Shaun (2000). 'Philosophical conceptions of the self: implications for cognitive science', *Trends in Cognitive Sciences*, 4(1), 14–21, https://doi.org/10.1016/S1364-6613(99)01417-5.

Gallagher, Shaun (2005). *How the Body Shapes the Mind*, Oxford: Clarendon Press.

Gallie, W. B. (1956a). 'Essentially contested concepts', *Proceedings of the Aristotelian Society*, 56, 167–198.

Gallie, W. B. (1956b). 'Art as an essentially contested concept', *Philosophical Quarterly*, 6(23), 97–114.

Gallois, Cindy, Peta Ashworth, Joan Leach and Kieren Moffat (2017). 'The language of science and social licence to operate', *Journal of Language and Social Psychology*, 36(1), 45–60, https://doi.org/10.1177/02619 27X16663254.

Gamson, Joshua (2011). 'The unwatched life is not worth living: the elevation of the ordinary in celebrity culture', *PMLA*, 126(4), 1061–1069.

Gates, Kelly A. (2011). *Our Biometric Future: Facial Recognition Technology and the Culture of Surveillance*, New York: New York University Press.

Gavison, Ruth (1980). 'Privacy and the limits of law', *Yale Law Journal*, 89(3), 421–471. Page references to (Schoeman 1984a, 346–402).

Gerety, Tom (1977). 'Redefining privacy', *Harvard Civil Rights-Civil Liberties Law Review*, 12(2), 233–296.

Gergen, Edward J. (2009). *Relational Being: Beyond Self and Community*, New York: Oxford University Press.

Gerstein, Robert S. (1970). 'Privacy and self-incrimination', *Ethics*, 80(2), 87–101, https://doi.org/10.1086/291757. Page references to (Schoeman 1984a, 245–264).

Gerstein, Robert S. (1978). 'Intimacy and privacy', *Ethics*, 89(1), 76–81, https://doi.org/10.1086/292105. Page references to (Schoeman 1984a, 265–271).

Gerstein, Robert S. (1982). 'California's constitutional right to privacy: the development of the protection of private life', *Hastings Constitutional Law Quarterly*, 9(2), 385–427.

Gervais, Sarah J., Theresa K. Vescio, Jens Förster, Anne Maass and Caterina Suitner (2012). 'Seeing women as objects: the sexual body part recognition bias', *European Journal of Social Psychology*, 42(6), 743–753, https://doi.org/10.1002/ejsp. 1890.

Gervais, Sarah J., Theresa K. Vescio, Jens Förster, Anne Maass and Caterina Suitner (2013). 'Erratum: seeing women as objects: the sexual body part recognition bias', *European Journal of Social Psychology*, 43(4), 319, https://doi.org/10.1002/ejsp. 1934.

Gessaroli, Erica, Erica Santelli, Giuseppe di Pellegrino and Francesca Frassinetti (2013). 'Personal space regulation in childhood autism spectrum disorders', *PLoS One*, 8(9), e74959, https://doi.org/10.1371/jour nal.pone.0074959.

Ghazinour, Kambiz, Maryam Majedi and Ken Barker (2009). 'A model for privacy policy visualization', in *33rd Annual IEEE International Computer Software and Applications Conference*, https://doi.org/ 10.1109/COMPSAC.2009.156.

Gilles, Susan M. (1995). 'Promises betrayed: breach of confidence as a remedy for invasions of privacy', *Buffalo Law Review*, 43(1), 1–84.

Gilliom, John (2001). *Overseers of the Poor: Surveillance, Resistance, and the Limits of Privacy*, Chicago: University of Chicago Press.

Giubilini, Alberto (2020). 'An argument for compulsory vaccination: the taxation analogy', *Journal of Applied Philosophy*, 37(3), 446–466, https://doi.org/10.1111/japp.12400.

Glapka, Ewa (2018). ' "If you look at me like at a piece of meat, then that's a problem" – women in the center of the male gaze: Feminist Poststructuralist Discourse Analysis as a tool of critique', *Critical Discourse Studies*, 15(1), 87–103, https://doi.org/10.1080/17405 904.2017.1390480.

Godin, Gaston, Mark Conner and Paschal Sheeran (2005). 'Bridging the intention-behaviour gap: the role of moral norm', *British Journal of Social Psychology*, 44(4), 497–512, https://doi.org/10.1348/01446660 4X17452.

Goffman, Erving (1959). *The Presentation of Self in Everyday Life*, New York: Doubleday.

Goffman, Erving (1961a). *Asylums*, New York: Doubleday.

Goffman, Erving (1961b). *Encounters: Two Studies in the Sociology of Interaction*, Indianapolis: Bobbs-Merrill.

Goffman, Erving (1971). *Relations in Public*, New York: Basic Books.

Golbeck, Jennifer (2016). 'User privacy concerns with common data used in recommender systems', in Emma Spiro and Yong-Yeol Ahn (eds), *Social Informatics: Proceedings of the 8th International Conference, SocInfo 2016*, Cham: Springer, 468–480, https://doi.org/10.1007/978-3-319-47880-7_29.

Goold, Benjamin, Ian Loader and Angélica Thumala (2013). 'The banality of security: the curious case of surveillance cameras', *British Journal of Criminology*, 53(6), 977–996, https://doi.org/10.1093/bjc/azt044.

Gover, Bradford N. and John S. Bradley (2004). 'Measures for assessing architectural speech security (privacy) of closed offices and meeting rooms', *The Journal of the Acoustical Society of America*, 116(6), 3480–3490, https://doi.org/10.1121/1.1810300.

Grant, Aimee (2016). ' "I … don't want to see you flashing your bits around": exhibitionism, othering and good motherhood in perceptions of public breastfeeding', *Geoforum*, 71, 52–61, https://doi.org/10.1016/j.geoforum.2016.03.004.

Graziano, Michael S. A. and Dylan F. Cooke (2006). 'Parieto-frontal interactions, personal space, and defensive behavior', *Neuropsychologia*, 44(6), 845–859, https://doi.org/10.1016/j.neuropsychologia.2005.09.009.

Greenwald, Glenn (2014). *No Place to Hide: Edward Snowden, the NSA and the Surveillance State*, London: Hamish Hamilton.

Grego, Sonia, Jin Zhou, Krishnendu Chakrabarty, Brian Stoner, Jose R. Ruiz and Deborah A. Fisher (2021). 'Automated stool image analysis by artificial intelligence in a smart toilet', *Gastroenterology: AGA Abstracts*, 160(6) supplement, S-582–S-583, https://doi.org/10.1016/S0016-5085(21)02090-4.

Grimaldi, Cecilia (2021). 'A post for change: social media and the unethical dissemination of nonconsensual pornography', *Hastings Entertainment and Communication Law Journal*, 43(1), 109–133.

Grimm, Rüdiger and Alexander Rossnagel (2000). 'Can P3P help to protect privacy worldwide?', in *MULTIMEDIA '00: Proceedings of the 2000 ACM Workshops on Multimedia*, New York: ACM, 157–160, https://doi.org/10.1145/357744.357917.

Guffey, Elizabeth E. (2015). *Posters: A Global History*, London: Reakton.

Gurinskaya, Anna (2020). 'Predicting citizens' support for surveillance cameras: does police legitimacy matter?' *International Journal of Comparative and Applied Criminal Justice*, 44(1–2), 63–83, https://doi.org/10.1080/01924036.2020.1744027.

Habermas, Jürgen (1987). *The Theory of Communicative Action Volume 2: Lifeworld and System: A Critique of Functionalist Reason*, Cambridge: Polity Press.

Habermas, Jürgen (1989). *The Structural Transformation of the Public Sphere: An Inquiry Into a Category of Bourgeois Society*, Cambridge: Polity Press.

Hacking, Ian (1995). *Rewriting the Soul: Multiple Personality and the Sciences of Memory*, Princeton: Princeton University Press.

Haj-Yahia, Muhammad M. (2002). 'Beliefs of Jordanian women about wife-beating', *Psychology of Women Quarterly*, 26(4), 282–291, https://doi.org/10.1111/1471-6402.t01-1-00067.

Hall, Edward T. (1966). *The Hidden Dimension*, New York: Doubleday.

Hall, Jeremy and Philip Rosson (2006). 'The impact of technological turbulence on entrepreneurial behavior, social norms and ethics: three Internet-based cases', *Journal of Business Ethics*, 64(3), 231–248, https://doi.org/10.1007/s10551-005-5354-z.

Halley, M. Martin and William F. Harvey (1968). 'Medical vs legal definitions of death', *JAMA*, 204(6), 423–425, https://doi.org/10.1001/jama.1968.03140190005002.

Hancock, Claire (2017). 'Feminism from the margin: challenging the Paris/ *banlieues* divide', *Antipode*, 49(3), 636–656, https://doi.org/10.1111/anti.12303.

Hancock, Holly (2016). '*Weller & Ors v Associated Newspapers Ltd* [2015] EWCA Civ 1176: Weller case highlights need for guidance on photography, privacy and the press', *Journal of Media Law*, 8(1), 17–31, https://doi.org/10.1080/17577632.2016.1188504.

Hanks Jr., D. Thomas (1984). ' "Goddes pryvetee" and Chaucer's Miller's Tale', *Christianity and Literature*, 33(2), 7–12.

Hart, H. L. A. (1955). 'Are there any natural rights?' *The Philosophical Review*, 64(2), 175–191, https://doi.org/10.2307/2182586.

Hart, H. L. A. (1983). 'Definition and theory in jurisprudence', in H. L. A. Hart, *Essays in Jurisprudence and Philosophy*, Oxford: Clarendon Press, 21–47.

Hartley, Jenny (ed.) (2012). *The Selected Letters of Charles Dickens*, Oxford: Oxford University Press.

Hartzog, Woodrow (2014). 'The value of modest privacy protections in a hyper social world', *Colorado Technology Law Journal*, 12(2), 333–351.

Hartzog, Woodrow (2018). *Privacy's Blueprint: The Battle to Control the Design of New Technologies*, Cambridge, MA: Harvard University Press.

Hartzog, Woodrow and Evan Selinger (2013). 'Quitters never win: the costs of leaving social media', *The Atlantic*, 15 February 2013, www.theatlantic.com/technology/archive/2013/02/quitters-never-win-the-costs-of-leaving-social-media/273139/.

Hasinoff, Amy Adele (2014). 'Blaming sexualization for sexting', *Girlhood Studies*, 7(1), 102–120, https://doi.org/10.3167/ghs.2014.070108.

Hassan, Louise M., Edward Shiu and Deirdre Shaw (2016). 'Who says there is an intention-behaviour gap? Assessing the empirical evidence of an intention-behaviour gap in ethical consumption', *Journal of Business Ethics*, 136(2), 219–236, https://doi.org/10.1007/s10551-014-2440-0.

Hayek, F. A. (2001). *The Road to Serfdom*, Abingdon: Routledge.

Hayes, Catherine, John Fulton, Andrew Livingstone, Claire Todd, Stephen Capper and Peter Smith (2021). *Beyond Disciplinarity: Historical Evolutions of Research Epistemology*, Abingdon: Routledge.

Hayes, Rebecca M. and Molly Dragiewicz (2018). 'Unsolicited dick pics: erotica, exhibitionism or entitlement?' *Women's Studies International Forum*, 71, 114–120, https://doi.org/10.1016/j.wsif.2018.07.001.

Heckel, Robert V. (1976). 'Grin and bare it: locus of control in streakers', *Journal of Community Psychology*, 4(2), 145–148, https://doi.org/10.1002/1520-6629(197604)4:2<145::AID-JCOP2290040207>3.0.CO;2-L.

Hegel, G. W. F. (1977). *Hegel's Phenomenology of Spirit*, Oxford: Oxford University Press.

Helfand, Michael A. (2018). 'Implied consent to religious institutions: a primer and a defense', *Connecticut Law Review*, 50(4), 877–926.

Hemelrijk, Charlotte (1999). 'An individual-orientated model of the emergence of despotic and egalitarian societies', *Proceedings of the Royal Society B: Biological Sciences*, 266(1417), 361–369, https://doi.org/10.1098/rspb.1999.0646.

Hempel, Leon and Hans Lammerant (2015). 'Impact assessments as negotiated knowledge', in Serge Gutwirth, Ronald Leenes and Paul de Hert (eds), *Reforming European Data Protection Law*, Dordrecht: Springer, 125–145.

Henry, Joseph (2022). 'German police reportedly misused Luca COVID tracing app data to find witnesses for a man's death', *Tech Times*, 13 January 2022, www.techtimes.com/articles/270485/20220113/german-police-reportedly-misused-luca-covid-tracing-app-data-find.htm.

Hepworth, Mike (1999). 'Privacy, security and respectability: the ideal Victorian home', in Tony Chapman and Jenny Hockey (eds), *Ideal Homes? Social Change and Domestic Life*, London: Routledge, 17–29.

Herley, Kent R. and Heith Copes (2009). ' "Keepin' my mind right": identity maintenance and religious social support in the prison context', *International Journal of Offender Therapy and Comparative Criminology*, 53(2), 228–244, https://doi.org/10.1177/0306624X08315019.

Hermans, Hubert J. M. and Thorsten Gieser (eds) (2012). *Handbook of Dialogical Self Theory*, Cambridge: Cambridge University Press.

Hetcher, Steven A. (2004). *Norms in a Wired World*, Cambridge: Cambridge University Press.

Higgins, Jenny A., James Trussell, Nelwyn B. Moore and Kenneth J. Davidson Sr. (2010). 'The language of love? Verbal versus implied consent at first heterosexual intercourse: implications for contraceptive use', *American Journal of Health Education*, 41(4), 218–230, https://doi.org/10.1080/19325037.2010.10599148.

Hildebrandt, Mireille (2015). *Smart Technologies and the End(s) of Law*, Cheltenham: Edward Elgar.

Hildebrandt, Mireille and Kieron O'Hara (eds) (2020). *Life and the Law in the Era of Data-Driven Agency*, Cheltenham: Edward Elgar.

Hillebrand, Claudia (2013). 'Merkelphone scandal shocks Europe but spies are unmoved', *The Conversation*, 26 October 2013, https://theconversation.com/merkelphone-scandal-shocks-europe-but-spies-are-unmoved-19567.

Hobson, Peter (2002). *The Cradle of Thought: Exploring the Origins of Thinking*, London: Macmillan.

Hoffman, Louis, Sharon Stewart, Denise Warren and Lisa Meek (2009). 'Toward a sustainable myth of self: an existential response to the postmodern condition', *Journal of Humanistic Psychology*, 49(2), 135–173, https://doi.org/10.1177/0022167808324880.

Hollander, John (2001). 'The language of privacy', *Social Research*, 68(1), 5–28.

Holt, Daphne J., Sarah Zapetis, Baktash Babadi, Jordan Zimmerman and Roger B. H. Tootell (2021). 'Personal space increases during the COVID-19 pandemic in response to real and virtual humans', *Frontiers in Psychology*, 13, https://doi.org/10.3389/fpsyg.2022.952998.

Holt, Samantha and Nicola Yuill (2014). 'Facilitating other-awareness in low-functioning children with autism and typically-developing preschoolers using dual-control technology', *Journal of Autism and Developmental Disorders*, 44(1), 236–248, https://doi.org/10.1007/s10 803-013-1868-x.

Hongladarom, Soraj (2016). *A Buddhist Theory of Privacy*, Singapore: Springer.

Hopkins, Tiffany A., Bradley A. Green, Patrick J. Carnes and Susan Campling (2016). 'Varieties of intrusion: exhibitionism and voyeurism', *Sexual Addiction and Compulsivity*, 23(1), 4–33, https://doi.org/ 10.1080/10720162.2015.1095138.

Hörnle, Julia (2019). 'Juggling more than three balls at once: multilevel jurisdictional challenges in EU Data Protection Regulation', *International Journal of Law and Information Technology*, 27(2), 142–170, https:// doi.org/10.1093/ijlit/eaz002.

Howard, Philip N. (2020). *Lie Machines: How to Save Democracy From Troll Armies, Deceitful Robots, Junk News Operations, and Political Operatives*, Yale: Yale University Press.

Hubback, Joseph (2020). *Cybersecurity Technology Efficacy: Is Cybersecurity the New "Market for Lemons"?* Debate Security, www. debatesecurity.com/cybersecurity-technology-efficacy-is-cybersecurity-the-new-market-for-lemons/.

Hubbard, Phil (2013). 'Kissing is not a universal right: sexuality, law and the scales of citizenship', *Geoforum*, 49, 224–232, https://doi.org/ 10.1016/j.geoforum.2012.08.002.

Hughes, Everett Cherrington (1958). 'License and mandate' in *Men and Their Work*, Glencoe, IL: Free Press, 78–88.

Huxley, Aldous (1978). *The Human Situation: Lectures at Santa Barbara 1959*, London: Chatto & Windus.

Iachini, Tina, Yann Coello, Francesca Frassinetti, Vincenzo Paolo Senese, Francesco Galante and Gennaro Ruggiero (2016). 'Peripersonal and interpersonal space in virtual and real environments: effects of gender and age', *Journal of Environmental Psychology*, 45, 154–164, https:// doi.org/10.1016/j.jenvp. 2016.01.004.

Ibarra, Eugenio Velasco (2020). '*Lee v Ashers Baking Company Ltd and Others*: the inapplicability of discrimination law to an illusory conflict of rights', *Modern Law Review*, 83(1), 190–201, https://doi.org/10.1111/1468-2230.12482.

Inness, Julie (1992). *Privacy, Intimacy and Isolation*, New York: Oxford University Press.

Jahn, Jody L. S. (2016). 'Adapting safety rules in a high reliability context: how wildland firefighting workgroups ventriloquize safety rules to understand hazards', *Management Communication Quarterly*, 30(3), 362–389, https://doi.org/10.1177/0893318915623638.

James, William (1890). *The Principles of Psychology*, Volume i, London: Macmillan.

Jarvis, Jeff (2011). *Public Parts: How Sharing in the Digital Age Improves the Way We Work and Live*, New York: Simon & Schuster.

Jeffrey, Richard (1974). 'Preferences among preferences', *Journal of Philosophy*, 71(13), 377–391, https://doi.org/10.2307/2025160.

Jiang, Li, Aimee Drolet and Carol A. Scott (2018). 'Countering embarrassment-avoidance by taking an observer's perspective', *Motivation and Emotion*, 42(5), 748–762, https://doi.org/10.1007/s11031-018-9673-7.

Jimroglou, Krissi M. (1999). 'A camera with a view: JenniCAM, visual representation, and cyborg subjectivity', *Information, Communication and Society*, 2(4), 439–453, https://doi.org/10.1080/136911899359493.

Johnson, Barbara (1993). 'Introduction', in Barbara Johnson (ed.), *Freedom and Interpretation: Oxford Amnesty Lectures of 1992*, New York: Basic Books, 1–16.

Jones, D. Gareth and Maja I. Whitaker (2013). 'The contested realm of displaying dead bodies', *Journal of Medical Ethics*, 39(10), 652–653, http://dx.doi.org/10.1136/medethics-2012-100983.

Jones, Stephen P. (1997). 'Reasonable expectations of privacy: searches, seizures, and the concept of Fourth Amendment standing', *University of Memphis Law Review*, 27(4), 907–985.

Jones, Zoey and Stacey Hannem (2018). 'Escort clients' sexual scripts and constructions of intimacy in commodified sexual relationships', *Symbolic Interaction*, 41(4), 488–512, https://doi.org/10.1002/symb.379.

Jourard, Sidney M. (1966). 'Some psychological aspects of privacy', *Law and Contemporary Problems*, 31(2), 307–318.

Julie, Richard S. (2000). 'High-tech surveillance tools and the Fourth Amendment: reasonable expectations of privacy in the technological age', *American Criminal Law Review*, 37(1), 127–143.

Kalven Jr, Harry (1966). 'Privacy in tort law: were Warren and Brandeis wrong?' *Law and Contemporary Problems*, 31(2), 326–341.

Kamleitner, Bernadette and Vincent-Wayne Mitchell (2018). 'Can consumers experience ownership for their personal data? From issues of scope and invisibility to agents handling our digital blueprints', in Joann Peck and Suzanne B. Shu (eds), *Psychological Ownership and Consumer Behavior*, Cham: Springer, 91–118, https://doi.org/10.1007/978-3-319-77158-8_6.

Kelley, J. F. and Alphonse Chapanis (1982). 'How professional persons keep their calendars: implications for computerization', *Journal of Occupational Psychology*, 55(4), 241–256, https://doi.org/10.1111/j.2044-8325.1982.tb00098.x.

Kelly, Daniel, Joan Condell, Kevin Curran and Brian Caulfield (2020). 'A multimodal smartphone sensor system for behaviour measurement and health status inference', *Information Fusion*, 53, 43–54, https://doi.org/10.1016/j.inffus.2019.06.008.

Keymolen, Esther and Simone Van der Hof (2019). 'Can I still trust you, my dear doll? A philosophical and legal exploration of smart toys and trust', *Journal of Cyber Policy*, 4(2), 143–159, https://doi.org/10.1080/23738871.2019.1586970.

Khawaja, Marwan, Natalia Linos and Zeina El-Roueiheb (2008). 'Attitudes of men and women towards wife beating: findings from Palestinian refugee camps in Jordan', *Journal of Family Violence*, 23, 211–218, https://doi.org/10.1007/s10896-007-9146-3.

Kitiyadisai, Krisana (2005). 'Privacy rights and protection: foreign values in modern Thai context', *Ethics and Information Technology*, 7(1), 17–26, https://doi.org/10.1007/s10676-005-0455-z.

Knowles, Megan L. and Kristy K. Dean (2018). 'Present but invisible: physical obscurity fosters social disconnection', *European Journal of Social Psychology*, 48(1), 86–92, https://doi.org/10.1002/ejsp. 2274.

Kokolakis, Spyros (2017). 'Privacy attitudes and privacy behaviour: a review of current research on the privacy paradox phenomenon', *Computers and Security*, 64, 122–134, https://doi.org/10.1016/j.cose.2015.07.002.

Koops, Bert-Jaap, Bryce Clayton Newell, Tjerk Timan, Ivan Škorvánek, Tomislav Chokrevski and Maša Galič (2017). 'A typology of privacy', *University of Pennsylvania Journal of International Law*, 38(2), 483–575.

Kosinski, Michal (2021). 'Facial recognition technology can expose political orientation from naturalistic facial images', *Scientific Reports*, 11, article 100, https://doi.org/10.1038/s41598-020-79310-1.

Kosinski, Michal, David Stillwell and Thore Graepel (2013). 'Private traits and attributes are predictable from digital records of human behavior', *Proceedings of the National Academy of Sciences*, 110(15), 5802–5805, https://doi.org/10.1073/pnas.1218772110.

Koskela, Hille (2004). 'Webcams, TV shows and mobile phones: empowering exhibitionism', *Surveillance and Society*, 2(2/3), 199–215, https://doi.org/10.24908/ss.v2i2/3.3374.

Kostkova, Patty, Francesc Saigí-Rubió, Hans Eguia, Damian Borbolla, Marieke Verschuuren, Clayton Hamilton, Natasha Azzopardi-Muscat and David Novillo-Ortiz (2021). 'Data and digital solutions to support surveillance strategies in the context of the COVID-19 pandemic', *Frontiers in Digital Health*, 3, 707902, https://doi.org/10.3389/fdgth.2021.707902.

Krach, Sören, Jan Christopher Cohrs, Nicole Cruz de Echeverría Loebell, Tilo Kircher, Jens Sommer, Andreas Jansen and Frieder Michel Paulus (2011). 'Your flaws are my pain: linking empathy to vicarious embarrassment', *PLoS One*, 6(4), e18675, https://doi.org/10.1371/journal.pone.0018675.

Kramer, Adam D. I., Jamie E. Guillory and Jeffrey T. Hancock (2014). 'Experimental evidence of massive-scale emotional contagion through social networks', *Proceedings of the National Academy of Sciences*, 111(24), 8788–8790, https://doi.org/10.1073/pnas.1320040111.

Krombholz, Katharina, Heidelinde Hobel, Markus Huber and Edgar Weippl (2015). 'Advanced social engineering attacks', *Journal of Information Security and Applications*, 22, 113–122, https://doi.org/10.1016/j.jisa.2014.09.005.

Kumaraguru, Ponnurangam and Lorrie Faith Cranor (2005). *Privacy Indexes: A Survey of Westin's Studies*, Institute for Software Research International, report CMU-ISRI-5-138, http://repository.cmu.edu/cgi/viewcontent.cgi?article=1857&context=isr.

Lackey, Douglas P. (1985). 'Divine omniscience and human privacy', *Philosophy Research Archives*, 10, 383–391, https://doi.org/10.5840/pra19841011.

Langer, Markus and Cornelius J. König (2018). 'Introducing and testing the Creepiness of Situation Scale (CRoSS)', *Frontiers of Psychology*, 9:2220, https://doi.org/10.3389/fpsyg.2018.02220.

Lankford, Adam and James Silver (2020). 'Why have public mass shootings become more deadly? Assessing how perpetrators' motives and methods have changed over time', *Criminology and Public Policy*, 19(1), 37–60, https://doi.org/10.1111/1745-9133.12472.

LaRose, Robert and Nora J. Rifon (2006). 'Your privacy is assured – of being disturbed: websites with and without privacy seals', *New Media and Society*, 8(6), 1009–1029, https://doi.org/10.1177/1461444806069652.

LaRose, Robert and Nora J. Rifon (2007). 'Promoting *i*-safety: effects of privacy warnings and privacy seals on risk assessment and online privacy behavior', *Journal of Consumer Affairs*, 41(1), 127–149, https://doi.org/10.1111/j.1745-6606.2006.00071.x.

Laurence, Stephen and Eric Margolis (1999). 'Concepts and cognitive science', in Eric Margolis and Stephen Laurence (eds), *Concepts: Core Readings*, Cambridge, MA: MIT Press, 3–81.

Leary, Mary Graw (2011). 'Reasonable expectations of privacy for youth in a digital age', *Mississippi Law Journal*, 80(3), 1035–1094.

Lee, Hwansoo (2020). 'Home IoT resistance: extended privacy and vulnerability perspective', *Telematics and Informatics*, 49, article 101377, https://doi.org/10.1016/j.tele.2020.101377.

Lees, Emma (2021). '*Fearn v Tate Galleries*: privacy and the law of nuisance', *Environmental Law Review*, 23(1), 49–55, https://doi.org/10.1177/1461452921998452.

Legutko, Ryszard (2016). *The Demon in Democracy: Totalitarian Temptations in Free Societies*, New York: Encounter.

Leibold, James (2020). 'Surveillance in China's Xinjiang region: ethnic sorting, coercion, and inducement', *Journal of Contemporary China*, 29(121), 46–60, https://doi.org/10.1080/10670564.2019.1621529.

Lessig, Lawrence (1999). *Code: and Other Laws of Cyberspace*, New York: Basic Books.

Lever, Annabelle (2012). *On Privacy*, New York: Routledge.

Liang, Fan, Vishnupriya Das, Nadiya Kostyuk and Muzammil M. Hussain (2018). 'Constructing a data-driven society: China's social credit system as a state surveillance infrastructure', *Policy and Internet*, 10(4), 415–453, https://doi.org/10.1002/poi3.183.

LiKamWa, Robert, Yunxin Liu, Nicholas D. Lane and Lin Zhong (2013). 'MoodScope: building a mood sensor from smartphone usage patterns', in *MobiSys '13: Proceedings of the 11th Annual International Conference on Mobile Systems, Applications, and Services*, New York: ACM, 389–402, https://doi.org/10.1145/2462456.2464449.

Lindsay, William R., Imelda Marshall, Clare Neilson, Kathleen Quinn and Anne H. W. Smith (1998). 'The treatment of men with a learning disability convicted of exhibitionism', *Research in Developmental Disabilities*, 19(4), 295–316, https://doi.org/10.1016/S0891-4222(98)00010-9.

Link, Perry (2002). 'China: the anaconda in the chandelier', *New York Review of Books*, 11 April 2002, www.nybooks.com/articles/2002/04/11/china-the-anaconda-in-the-chandelier/.

Linos, Natalia, Marwan Khawaja and Mohannad al-Nsour (2010). 'Women's autonomy and support for wife beating: findings from a population-based survey in Jordan', *Violence and Victims*, 25(3), 409–419, https://doi.org/10.1891/0886-6708.25.3.409.

Lintvedt, Mona Naomi (2021). 'COVID-19 tracing apps as a legal problem: an investigation of the Norwegian "Smittestopp" app', *Oslo Law Review*, 8(2), 69–87, https://doi.org/10.18261/issn.2387-3299-2021-02-01.

Lippert, Randy (2009). 'Signs of the surveillant assemblage: privacy regulation, urban CCTV, and governmentality', *Social and Legal Studies*, 18(4), 505–522, https://doi.org/10.1177/0964663909345096.

Lisle, Debbie (2004). 'Gazing at Ground Zero: tourism, voyeurism and spectacle', *Journal for Cultural Research*, 8(1), 3–21, https://doi.org/10.1080/1479758042000797015.

Liu, Cha-Hsuan and Jaap Bos (2020). 'Could the "liberal" Dutch have learned from Taiwan's approach to coronavirus?' *The Guardian*, 19 May, 2020, www.theguardian.com/commentisfree/2020/may/19/libe ral-dutch-taiwan-coronavirus-covid-19-netherlands.

Liversage, Anika (2014). 'Secrets and lies: when ethnic minority youth have a *nikah*', in Prakash Shah, Marie-Claire Foblets and Mathias Rohe (eds), *Family, Religion and Law: Cultural Encounters in Europe*, London: Ashgate, 165–180.

Lockwood, Thornton (2014). 'Competing ways of life and ring composition [*NE* x 6–8]', in Ronald Polansky (ed.), *The Cambridge Companion to Aristotle's Nicomachean Ethics*, New York: Cambridge University Press, 350–369.

Lodi, Hafsa (2020). *Modesty: A Fashion Paradox: Uncovering the Causes, Controversies and Key Players Behind the Global Trend to Conceal, Rather Than Reveal*, London: Neem Tree Press.

Logan, Wayne A. and J. J. Prescott (eds) (2021). *Sex Offender Registration and Community Notification Laws: An Empirical Evaluation*, New York: Cambridge University Press.

Lorimer, Jamie, Timothy Hodgetts and Maan Barua (2019). 'Animals' atmospheres', *Progress in Human Geography*, 43(1), 26–45, https://doi.org/10.1177/0309132517731254.

Lowrance, William W. (2012). *Privacy, Confidentiality, and Health Research*, Cambridge: Cambridge University Press.

Luguri, Jamie and Lior Jacob Strahilevitz (2021). 'Shining a light on dark patterns', *Journal of Legal Analysis*, 13(1), 43–109, https://doi.org/10.1093/jla/laaa006.

Luo, Chengwen, Hande Hong, Long Cheng, Kartik Sankaran and Mun Choon Chan (2015). 'iMap: automatic inference of indoor semantics exploiting opportunistic smartphone sensing', in *Proceedings of the 12th Annual IEEE International Conference on Sensing, Communication, and Networking (SECON)*, IEEE, https://doi.org/10.1109/SAHCN.2015.7338350.

Lwin, May O., Andrea J. S. Stanaland and Anthony D. Miyazaki (2008). 'Protecting children's privacy online: how parental mediation strategies affect website safeguard effectiveness', *Journal of Retailing*, 84(2), 205–217, https://doi.org/10.1016/j.jretai.2008.04.004.

Lykke, Lucia C. and Philip N. Cohen (2015). 'The widening gender gap in opposition to pornography, 1975–2012', *Social Currents*, 2(4), 307–323, https://doi.org/10.1177/2329496515604170.

Lyon, David (2003). *Surveillance After September 11th*, Cambridge: Polity Press.

Lyotard, Jean-François (1984). *The Postmodern Condition: A Report on Knowledge*, Manchester: Manchester University Press.

Machery, Edouard (2009). *Doing Without Concepts*, New York: Oxford University Press.

MacIntyre, Alasdair (2007). *After Virtue*, 3rd edition, Notre Dame: University of Notre Dame Press.

MacKinnon, Catherine A. (1987). 'Privacy v. equality: beyond Roe v. Wade', in Catherine A. MacKinnon, *Feminism Unmodified: Discourses on Life and Law*, Cambridge, MA: Harvard University Press, 93–102.

Macmanus, Susan A., Kiki Caruson and Brian D. Mcphee (2013). 'Cybersecurity at the local government level: balancing demands for transparency and privacy rights', *Journal of Urban Affairs*, 35(4), 451–470, https://doi.org/10.1111/j.1467-9906.2012.00640.x.

Maddocks, Fiona (2013). *Hildegard of Bingen: The Woman of Her Age*, London: Faber & Faber.

Maguire, C. N., L. A. McCallum, C. Storey and J. P. Whitaker (2014). 'Familial searching: a specialist forensic DNA profiling service utilising the National DNA Database® to identify unknown offenders via their relatives – the UK experience', *Forensic Science International: Genetics*, 8(1), 1–9, https://doi.org/10.1016/j.fsigen.2013.07.004.

Mahoney, Annette, Mark S. Rye and Kenneth I. Pargament (2005). 'When the sacred is violated: desecration as a unique challenge to forgiveness' in Everett L. Worthington Jr (ed.), *Handbook of Forgiveness*, New York: Routledge, 57–71.

Mancini, Susanna (2012). 'Patriarchy as the exclusive domain of the other: the veil controversy, false projection and cultural racism', *International Journal of Constitutional Law*, 10(2), 411–428, https://doi.org/10.1093/icon/mor061.

Manson, Neil C. and Onora O'Neill (2012). *Rethinking Informed Consent in Bioethics*, Cambridge: Cambridge University Press.

Mansour, Essam, Andrei Vlad Sambra, Sandro Hawke, Maged Zereba, Sarven Capadisli, Abdurrahman Ghanem, Ashraf Aboulnaga and Tim Berners-Lee (2016). 'A demonstration of the Solid platform for Social

Web applications', in *Proceedings of the 25th International Conference Companion on World Wide Web*, New York: ACM, 223–226, https://doi.org/10.1145/2872518.2890529.

Markey, Maureen E. (1995). 'The price of landlord's "free" exercise of religion: tenant's right to discrimination-free housing and privacy', *Fordham Urban Law Journal*, 22(3), 699–831.

Marková, Ivana (1987). *Human Awareness: Its Social Development*, London: Hutchinson Education.

Marshall, Peter (1993). *Demanding the Impossible: A History of Anarchism*, London: Fontana.

Martin, Raymond and John Barresi (2006). *The Rise and Fall of Soul and Self: An Intellectual History of Personal Identity*, New York: Columbia University Press.

Marwick, Alice E. and danah boyd (2011). 'I tweet honestly, I tweet passionately: Twitter users, context collapse, and the imagined audience', *New Media and Society*, 13(1), 114–133, https://doi.org/10.1177/1461444810365313.

Marx, Gary T. (2001). 'Murky conceptual waters: the public and the private', *Ethics and Information Technology*, 3(3), 157–169, https://doi.org/10.1023/A:1012456832336.

Matich, Margaret, Rachel Ashman and Elizabeth Parsons (2019). '#freethenipple – digital activism and embodiment in the contemporary feminist movement', *Consumption Markets and Culture*, 22(4), 337–362, https://doi.org/10.1080/10253866.2018.1512240.

Matli, Walter (2020). 'The changing work landscape as a result of the Covid-19 pandemic: insights from remote workers life situations in South Africa', *International Journal of Sociology and Social Policy*, 40(9–10), 1237–1256, https://doi.org/10.1108/IJSSP-08-2020-0386.

McAdams, Richard H. (1996). 'Group norms, gossip, and blackmail', *University of Pennsylvania Law Review*, 144(5), 2237–2292, https://doi.org/10.2307/3312653.

McArthur, Robert L. (2001). 'Reasonable expectations of privacy', *Ethics and Information Technology*, 3(2), 123–128, https://doi.org/10.1023/A:1011898010298.

McClain, Linda C. (1995). 'Inviolability and privacy: the castle, the sanctuary, and the body', *Yale Journal of Law and the Humanities*, 7(1), 195–241.

McDonald, Aleecia M. and Lorrie Faith Cranor (2008). 'The cost of reading privacy policies', *I/S: A Journal of Law and Policy for the Information Society*, 4(3), 543–568.

McKenzie, Pamela J. (2020). 'Informational boundary work in everyday life', in Anneli Sundqvist, Gerd Berget, Jan Nolin and Kjell Ivar Skjerdingstad (eds), *Sustainable Digital Communities: 15th International Conference, iConference 2020*, Cham: Springer, 96–103, https://doi.org/10.1007/978-3-030-43687-2_8.

McLellan, Josie (2011). *Love in the Time of Communism: Intimacy and Sexuality in the GDR*, Cambridge: Cambridge University Press.

McPherson, David (2020). *Virtue and Meaning: A Neo-Aristotelian Perspective*, Cambridge: Cambridge University Press.

McStay Andrew (2014). *Privacy and Philosophy: New Media and Affective Protocol*, New York: Peter Lang.

Mead, George Herbert (1934). *Mind, Self and Society*, Chicago: University of Chicago Press.

Meindl, James N. and Jonathan W. Ivy (2017). 'Mass shootings: the role of the media in promoting generalized imitation', *American Journal of Public Health*, 107(3), 368–370, https://doi.org/10.2105/AJPH.2016.303611.

Meng, Chuishi, Yu Cui, Qing He, Lu Su and Jing Gao (2017). 'Travel purpose inference with GPS trajectories, POIs, and geo-tagged social media data', in *Proceedings of the 2017 IEEE International Conference on Big Data*, IEEE, https://doi.org/10.1109/BigData.2017.8258062.

Messer-Davidow, Ellen, David R. Shumway and David J. Sylvan (eds) (1993). *Knowledges: Historical and Critical Studies in Disciplinarity*, Charlottesville: University Press of Virginia.

Miceli, Thomas J. (2020). 'Trading in information: on the unlikely correspondence between patents and blackmail law', *Review of Industrial Organization*, 56(4), 637–650, https://doi.org/10.1007/s11151-020-09749-z.

Miceli, Thomas J. (2021). 'Reconciling blackmail and nondisclosure agreements: an economic approach', *Managerial and Decision Economics*, 42(2), 268–274, https://doi.org/10.1002/mde.3232.

Miles, James (2021). 'Busybodies, backed by AI, are restoring the party's visibility', *The Economist*, 26 June 2021, www.economist.com/special-report/2021/06/23/busybodies-backed-by-ai-are-restoring-the-partys-visibility.

Mill, John Stuart (1991). 'On liberty', in John Stuart Mill, *On Liberty and Other Essays*, Oxford: Oxford University Press, 5–128.

Miller, Arthur R. (1971). *Assault on Privacy: Computers, Data Banks and Dossiers*, Ann Arbor: University of Michigan Press.

Millett, Bella (2009). *Ancrene Wisse: Guide for Anchoresses: A Translation*, Liverpool: Liverpool University Press.

Monk, Andrew, Jenni Carroll, Sarah Parker and Mark Blythe (2004a). 'Why are mobile phones annoying?' *Behaviour and Information Technology*, 23(1), 33–41, https://doi.org/10.1080/01449290310001638496.

Monk, Andrew, Evi Fellas and Eleanor Ley (2004b). 'Hearing only one side of normal and mobile phone conversations', *Behaviour and Information Technology*, 23(5), 301–305, https://doi.org/10.1080/0144929041000 1712744.

Moors, Annelies (2009). 'The Dutch and the face-veil: the politics of discomfort', *Social Anthropology*, 17(4), 393–408, https://doi.org/ 10.1111/j.1469-8676.2009.00084.x.

Morgan, Anthony and Christopher Dowling (2019). 'Does CCTV help police solve crime?' *Trends and Issues in Crime and Criminal Justice*, 576, 1–16, https://search.informit.org/doi/abs/10.3316/agispt.2019050 2009784.

Morreim, E. Haavi (1991). 'Gaming the system: dodging the rules, ruling the dodgers', *Archives of Internal Medicine*, 151(3), 443–447, https:// doi.org/10.1001/archinte.1991.00400030013003.

Moscati, Ivan (2019). *Measuring Utility: From the Marginal Revolution to Behavioral Economics*, New York: Oxford University Press.

Mulgan, Richard (2007). 'Truth in government and the politicization of public service advice', *Public Administration*, 85(3), 569–586, https:// doi.org/10.1111/j.1467-9299.2007.00663.x.

Mullen, Alexandra (2003). 'Heroes, humbugs and hypocrites', *The Hudson Review*, 56(3), 549–556, https://doi.org/10.2307/3852705.

Mulligan, Deirdre K., Colin Koopman and Nick Doty (2016). 'Privacy is an essentially contested concept: a multi-dimensional analytic for mapping privacy', *Philosophical Transactions of the Royal Society A*, 374:20160118.

Mulvey, Laura (2009). 'Visual pleasure and narrative cinema', in Laura Mulvey, *Visual and Other Pleasures*, 2nd edition, Basingstoke: Palgrave Macmillan, 14–29.

Munar, Ana María (2010). 'Digital exhibitionism: the age of exposure', *Culture Unbound*, 2(3), 401–422, https://doi.org/10.3384/ cu.2000.1525.10223401.

Murphy, Richard S. (1996). 'Property rights in personal information: an economic defense of privacy', *Georgetown Law Journal*, 84(7), 2381–2417.

Murphy, Robert F. (1964). 'Social distance and the veil', *American Anthropologist*, 66(6 pt.1), 1257–1274. Page references to (Schoeman 1984a, 34–55).

Musa, Ahmed M. and Raphael Schwere (2018). 'The hidden tactile negotiation sign language in Somaliland's livestock markets', *Bildhaan: An International Journal of Somali Studies*, 18, 50–69, https://doi.org/ 10.5167/uzh-171294.

Nagenborg, Michael (2017). 'Hidden in plain sight', in Tjerk Timan, Bryce C. Newell and Bert-Jaap Koops (eds), *Privacy in Public Space: Conceptual and Regulatory Challenges*, Cheltenham: Edward Elgar, 47–63, https://doi.org/10.4337/9781786435408.00008.

Najdowski, Cynthia J. (2017). 'Legal responses to nonconsensual pornography: current policy in the United States and future directions for research', *Psychology, Public Policy, and Law*, 23(2), 154–165, https://psycnet.apa.org/doi/10.1037/law0000123.

Najib, Kawtar and Peter Hopkins (2019). 'Veiled Muslim women's strategies in response to Islamophobia in Paris', *Political Geography*, 73, 103–111, https://doi.org/10.1016/j.polgeo.2019.05.005.

Narayanan, Arvind and Vitaly Shmatikov (2008). 'Robust de-anonymization of large sparse datasets', in *2008 IEEE Symposium on Security and Privacy*, https://doi.org/10.1109/SP.2008.33.

Nash, Susie (2008). *Northern Renaissance Art*, Oxford: Oxford University Press.

Nellis, Mike (2012). ' "Cold intimacies": community notification, satellite tracking, and the ruined privacy of sex offenders', in Daniel Guagnin, Leon Hempel, Carla Ilten, Inga Kroeger, Daniel Neyland and Hector Postigo (eds), *Managing Privacy Through Accountability*, New York: Palgrave Macmillan, 165–187.

Newell, Bryce Clayton (2011). 'Rethinking reasonable expectations of privacy in online social networks', *Richmond Journal of Law and Technology*, 17(4).

Nielson, Samuel P. (2020). 'Beaches and Muslim belonging in France: liberty, equality, but not the burkini!' *Cultural Geographies*, 27(4), 631–646, https://doi.org/10.1177/1474474020918907.

Nissenbaum, Helen (2010). *Privacy in Context: Technology, Policy and the Integrity of Social Life*, Stanford: Stanford University Press.

NL Times (2021). 'Netherlands concerned about privacy in future EU Covid travel pass', *NL Times*, 24 May 2021, https://nltimes.nl/2021/05/24/netherlands-concerned-privacy-future-eu-covid-travel-pass.

Norberg, Patricia A., Daniel R. Horne and David A. Horne (2007). 'The privacy paradox: personal information disclosure intentions versus behaviors', *Journal of Consumer Affairs*, 41(1), 100–126, https://doi.org/10.1111/j.1745-6606.2006.00070.x.

O'Brien, David (1979). *Privacy, Law and Public Policy*, New York: Praeger.

Oceja, Luis V., Marc W. Heerdink, Eric L. Stocks, Tamara Ambrona, Belén López-Pérez and Sergio Salgado (2014). 'Empathy, awareness of others, and action: how feeling empathy for one-among-others motivates helping the others', *Basic and Applied Social Psychology*, 36(2), 111–124, https://doi.org/10.1080/01973533.2013.856787.

OECD (2013). *The OECD Privacy Framework*, www.oecd.org/digital/ieconomy/privacy-guidelines.htm.

O'Hara, Kieron (2011). *Conservatism*, London: Reaktion.

O'Hara, Kieron (2012). *Huxley: A Beginner's Guide*, Oxford: Oneworld.

O'Hara, Kieron (2013). 'Are we getting privacy the wrong way round? *IEEE Internet Computing*, 17(4), 89–92, https://doi.org/10.1109/MIC.2013.62.

O'Hara, Kieron (2015a). 'Data, legibility, creativity … and power', *IEEE Internet Computing*, 19(4), 73–79, https://doi.org/10.1109/MIC.2015.88.

O'Hara, Kieron (2015b). 'The right to be forgotten: the good, the bad, and the ugly', *IEEE Internet Computing*, 19(4), 73–79, https://doi.org/10.1109/MIC.2015.88.

O'Hara, Kieron (2016). 'The seven veils of privacy', *IEEE Internet Computing*, 20(2), 86–91, https://doi.org/10.1109/MIC.2016.34.

O'Hara, Kieron (2020a). 'The contradictions of digital modernity', *AI and Society*, 35(1), 197–208, https://doi.org/10.1007/s00146-018-0843-7.

O'Hara, Kieron (2020b). 'Data trusts', *European Data Protection Law Review*, 6(4), 484–491, https://doi.org/10.21552/edpl/2020/4/4.

O'Hara, Kieron (2021a). 'Personalisation and digital modernity: deconstructing the myths of the subjunctive world', in Uta Kohl and Jacob Eisler (eds), *Data-Driven Personalisation and the Law*, Cambridge: Cambridge University Press, 55–73.

O'Hara, Kieron (2021b). 'Burkean conservatism, legibility and populism', *Journal of Political Ideologies*, 26(1), 81–100, https://doi.org/10.1080/13569317.2020.1844371.

O'Hara, Kieron and Wendy Hall (2021). *Four Internets: Data, Geopolitics and the Governance of Cyberspace*, New York: Oxford University Press.

O'Hara, Kieron and Dave Robertson (2017). 'Social machines as an approach to group privacy', in Linnet Taylor, Luciano Floridi and Bart van der Sloot (eds), *Group Privacy: New Challenges of Data Technologies*, Cham: Springer, 101–122, https://doi.org/10.1007/978-3-319-46608-8_6.

O'Hara, Kieron and Nigel Shadbolt (2008). *The Spy in the Coffee Machine: the End of Privacy As We Know It*, Oxford: Oneworld.

O'Hara, Kieron and Nigel Shadbolt (2015). 'The right to be forgotten: its potential role in a coherent privacy regime', *European Data Protection Law Review*, 1(3), 178–189, https://doi.org/10.21552/EDPL/2015/3/5.

O'Hara, Kieron and David Stevens (2006a). *inequality.com: Power, Poverty and the Digital Divide*, Oxford: Oneworld.

O'Hara, Kieron and David Stevens (2006b). 'Democracy, ideology and process re-engineering: realising the benefits of e-government in

Singapore' in Jinpeng Huai, Vincent Shen C. J. Tan (eds), *Workshop on e-Government: Barriers and Opportunities, World Wide Web Conference (WWW '06)*, wwwconference.org/proceedings/www2006/ www.w3c.org.hk/www2006/papers/re-eng_sg.pdf.

Ohm, Paul (2010). 'Broken promises of privacy: responding to the surprising failure of anonymization', *UCLA Law Review*, 57, 1701–1777.

Oliver, Kelly (2017). 'The male gaze is more relevant, and more dangerous, than ever', *New Review of Film and Television Studies*, 15(4), 451–455, https://doi.org/10.1080/17400309.2017.1377937.

Olsen, Donald J. (1974). 'Victorian London: specialization, segregation, and privacy', *Victorian Studies*, 17(3), 265–278.

Omand, David (2013). 'NSA leaks: how to make surveillance both ethical and effective', *The Guardian*, 11 June 2013, www.theguardian.com/ commentisfree/2013/jun/11/make-surveillance-ethical-and-effective.

O'Neill, Onora (2003). 'Some limits of informed consent', *Journal of Medical Ethics*, 29(1), 4–7, http://dx.doi.org/10.1136/jme.29.1.4.

Oppenheim, Felix E. (1975). 'The language of political inquiry: problems of clarification', in Fred I. Greenstein and Nelson W. Polsby (eds), *Handbook of Political Science Volume I: Political Science: Scope and Theory*, Reading MA: Addison-Wesley, 283–335.

Ortega y Gasset, José (1961). *Meditations on Quixote*, New York: W. W. Norton.

Oswald, Flora, Alex Lopes, Kaylee Skoda, Cassandra L. Hesse and Cory L. Pedersen (2020). 'I'll show you mine so you'll show me yours: motivations and personality variables in photographic exhibitionism', *Journal of Sex Research*, 57(5), 597–609, https://doi.org/10.1080/00224 499.2019.1639036.

Oswald, Marion (2017). 'Jordan's dilemma: can large parties still be intimate? Redefining public, private and the misuse of the digital person', *Information & Communications Technology Law*, 26(1), 6–31, https://doi.org/10.1080/13600834.2017.1269870.

Owusu, Emmanuel, Jun Han, Sauvik Das, Adrian Perrig and Joy Zhang (2012). 'ACCessory: password inference using accelerometers on smartphones', in *HotMobile '12: Proceedings of the 12th Workshop on Mobile Computing Systems and Applications*, New York: ACM, article 9, https://doi.org/10.1145/2162081.2162095.

Palfrey, John and Urs Gasser (2008). *Born Digital: Understanding the First Generation of Digital Natives*, New York: Basic Books.

Pardailhé-Galabrun, Annik (1991). *The Birth of Intimacy*, Cambridge: Polity Press.

Pargament, Kenneth I., Gina M. Magyar, Ethan Benore and Annette Mahoney (2005). 'Sacrilege: a study of sacred loss and desecration and their implications for health and well-being in a community sample', *Journal for the Scientific Study of Religion*, 44(1), 59–78, https://doi.org/10.1111/j.1468-5906.2005.00265.x.

Park, Yong Jin (2015). 'Do men and women differ in privacy? Gendered privacy and (in)equality in the Internet', *Computers in Human Behavior*, 50, 252–258, https://doi.org/10.1016/j.chb.2015.04.011.

Parker, Richard B. (1974). 'A definition of privacy', *Rutgers Law Review*, 27, 275–296.

Parkinson, Brian (2018). *Personal Data: Definition and Access*, University of Southampton PhD thesis, https://eprints.soton.ac.uk/427140/.

Parkinson, Brian, David E. Millard, Kieron O'Hara and Richard Giordano (2017). 'The digitally extended self: a lexicological analysis of personal data', *Journal of Information Science*, 44(4), 552–565, https://doi.org/10.1177/0165551517706233.

Parnas, Josef, Paul Møller, Tilo Kircher, Jørgen Thalbitzer, Lennart Jansson, Peter Handest and Dan Zahavi (2005). 'EASE: Examination of Anomalous Self-Experience', *Psychopathology*, 38(5), 236–258, https://doi.org/10.1159/000088441.

Patel, David S. (2012). 'Concealing to reveal: the informational role of Islamic dress', *Rationality and Society*, 24(3), 295–323, https://doi.org/10.1177/1043463112440683.

Pedersen, Darhl M. (1997). 'Psychological functions of privacy', *Journal of Environmental Psychology*, 17(2), 147–156, https://doi.org/10.1006/jevp.1997.0049.

Penney, Steven (2007). 'Reasonable expectations of privacy and novel search technologies: an economic approach', *Journal of Criminal Law and Criminology*, 97(2), 477–529.

Pentland, Alex (2008). *Honest Signals: How They Shape the World*, Cambridge, MA: MIT Press.

Perlroth, Nicole (2021). *This Is How They Tell Me The World Ends: The Cyber-Weapons Arms Race*, New York: Bloomsbury.

Peters, Kim, Jolanda Jetten, Dagmar Radova and Kacie Austin (2017). 'Gossiping about deviance: evidence that deviance spurs the gossip that builds bonds', *Psychological Science*, 28(11), 1610–1619, https://doi.org/10.1177/0956797617716918.

Petkova, Bilyana (2019). 'Privacy as Europe's First Amendment', *European Law Journal*, 25(2), 140–154, https://doi.org/10.1111/eulj.12316.

Phillipson, Gavin (2003). 'Transforming breach of confidence? Towards a common law right of privacy under the Human Rights Act', *Modern Law Review*, 66(5), 726–758, https://doi.org/10.1111/1468-2230.6605003.

Pierce, James (2019). 'Smart home security cameras and shifting lines of creepiness: a design-led inquiry', in *CHI '19: Proceedings of the 2019 CHI*

Conference on Human Factors in Computing Systems, New York: ACM, paper no.45, https://doi.org/10.1145/3290605.3300275.

Plato (1997a). 'Phaedrus', in John M. Cooper (ed.), *Plato: Complete Works*, Indianapolis: Hackett, 506–556.

Plato (1997b). 'Republic', in John M. Cooper (ed.), *Plato: Complete Works*, Indianapolis: Hackett, 971–1223.

Plotnik, Joshua M. and Nicola S. Clayton (2015). 'Convergent cognitive evolution across animal taxa: comparison of chimpanzees, corvids and elephants', in Eric Margolis and Stephen Laurence (eds), *The Conceptual Mind: New Directions in the Study of Concepts*, Cambridge, MA: MIT Press, 29–56.

Pocock, Mary, Debra Jackson and Caroline Bradbury-Jones (2019). 'Intimate partner violence and the power of love: a qualitative systematic review', *Health Care for Women International*, 41(6), 621–646, https://doi.org/10.1080/07399332.2019.1621318.

Posner, Eric A. (2009). *Law and Social Norms*, Cambridge, MA: Harvard University Press.

Posner, Richard A. (1978). 'An economic theory of privacy', *Regulation*, 2(3), 19–26. Page references to (Schoeman 1984a, 333–345).

Posner, Richard A. (1981). 'The economics of privacy', *The American Economic Review*, 71(2), 405–409.

Posner, Richard A. (1983). *The Economics of Justice*, Cambridge, MA: Harvard University Press.

Posner, Richard A. (1993). 'Blackmail, privacy, and freedom of contract', *University of Pennsylvania Law Review*, 141(5), 1817–1847, https://doi.org/10.2307/3312575.

Posner, Richard A. (2005). 'Our domestic intelligence crisis', *Washington Post*, 21 December 2005, www.washingtonpost.com/archive/opinions/2005/12/21/our-domestic-intelligence-crisis/a2b4234d-ba78-4ba1-a350-90e7fbb4e5bb/.

Post, Robert C. (1989). 'The social foundations of privacy: community and self in the common law tort', *California Law Review*, 77(5), 957–1010.

Post, Robert C. (2001). 'Three concepts of privacy', *Georgetown Law Journal*, 89, 2087–2098.

Power, Charmaine, Tina Koch, Debbie Kralik and Debra Jackson (2006). 'Lovestruck: women, romantic love and intimate partner violence', *Contemporary Nurse*, 21(2), 174–185, https://doi.org/10.5172/conu.2006.21.2.174.

Prasad, Eswar S. (2021). *The Future of Money: How the Digital Revolution is Transforming Currencies and Finance*, Cambridge, MA: Belknap Press.

Prosser, William L. (1960). 'Privacy', *California Law Review*, 48, 383–423. Page references to (Schoeman 1984a, 104–155).

Quine, Willard Van Orman (1960). *Word and Object*, Cambridge, MA: MIT Press.

Quine, Willard Van Orman (1980). 'On what there is', in Willard Van Orman Quine, *From a Logical Point of View*, 2nd revised edition, Cambridge, MA: Harvard University Press, 1–19.

Raab, Charles (2005). 'The future of privacy protection', in Robin Mansell and Brian S. Collins (eds), *Trust and Crime in Information Societies*, Cheltenham: Edward Elgar, 282–318.

Raab, Charles (2012). 'The meaning of "accountability" in the information privacy context', in Daniel Guagnin, Leon Hempel, Carla Ilten, Inga Kroeger, Daniel Neyland and Hector Postigo (eds), *Managing Privacy Through Accountability*, New York: Palgrave Macmillan, 15–32.

Rabelo, Verónica Caridad and Ramaswami Mahalingam (2019). ' "They really don't want to see us": How cleaners experience invisible "dirty" work', *Journal of Vocational Behaviour*, 113, 103–114, https://doi.org/ 10.1016/j.jvb.2018.10.010.

Rachels, James (1975). 'Why privacy is important', *Philosophy and Public Affairs*, 4(4), 323–333. Page references to (Schoeman 1984a, 290–299).

Radden, Jennifer (1996). *Divided Minds and Successive Selves: Ethical Issues in Disorders of Identity and Personality*, Cambridge, MA: MIT Press.

Raguparan, Menaka (2017). ' "If I'm gonna hack capitalism": racialized and indigenous Canadian sexworkers' experiences within the neoliberal market economy', *Women's Studies International Forum*, 60, 69–76, http://dx.doi.org/10.1016/j.wsif.2016.12.003.

Raitanen, Jenni and Atte Oksanen (2018). 'Global online subculture surrounding school shootings', *American Behavioral Scientist*, 62(2), 195–209, https://doi.org/10.1177/0002764218755835.

Rashid, Sabina Faiz (2006). 'Emerging changes in reproductive behaviour among married adolescent girls in an urban slum in Dhaka, Bangladesh', *Reproductive Health Matters*, 14(27), 151–159, https:// doi.org/10.1016/S0968-8080(06)27221-5.

Rauhofer, Judith (2008). 'Privacy is dead, get over it! Information privacy and the dream of a risk-free society', *Information and Communications Technology Law*, 17(3), 185–197, https://doi.org/10.1080/1360083080 2472990.

Rawls, John (1971). *A Theory of Justice*, Oxford: Oxford University Press.

Rawls, John (2005). *Political Liberalism*, expanded edition, New York: Columbia University Press.

Reay, Ian, Scott Dick and James Miller (2009). 'A large-scale empirical study of P3P privacy policies: stated actions vs. legal obligations', *ACM Transactions on the Web*, article 6, https://doi.org/10.1145/1513 876.1513878.

Reeder, Robert W., Patrick Gage Kelley, Aleecia M. McDonald and Lorrie Faith Cranor (2008). 'A user study of the expandable grid applied to P3P privacy policy visualization', in *WPES '08: Proceedings of the 7th ACM Workshop on Privacy in the Electronic Society*, New York: ACM, 45–54, https://doi.org/10.1145/1456403.1456413.

Regan, Priscilla M. (1995). *Legislating Privacy: Technology, Social Values, and Public Policy*, Chapel Hill: University of North Carolina Press.

Rehnquist, William H. (1974). 'Is an expanded right to privacy consistent with fair and effective law enforcement? Or: privacy, you've come a long way, baby', *University of Kansas Law Review*, 23(1), 1–22.

Reiheld, Alison (2015). ' "The event that was nothing": miscarriage as a liminal event', *Journal of Social Philosophy*, 46(1), 9–26, https://doi.org/10.1111/josp.12084.

Reiman, Jeffrey H. (1976). 'Privacy, intimacy, and personhood', *Philosophy and Public Affairs*, 6(1), 26–44. Page references to (Schoeman 1984a, 300–316).

Reiman, Jeffrey H. (1995). 'Driving to the panopticon: a philosophical exploration of the risks to privacy posed by the highway technology of the future', *Santa Clara High Technology Law Journal*, 11(1), 27–44.

Rhodes, Lorna A. (2005). 'Pathological effects of the supermaximum prison', *American Journal of Public Health*, 95(10), 1692–1695, https://doi.org/10.2105/AJPH.2005.070045.

Ribeiro-Navarrete, Samuel, José Ramón Saura and Daniel Palacios-Marqués (2021). 'Towards a new era of mass data collection: assessing pandemic surveillance technologies to preserve user privacy', *Technological Forecasting and Social Change*, 167, 120681, https://doi.org/10.1016/j.techfore.2021.120681.

Richards, Neil M. and Daniel J. Solove (2010). 'Prosser's privacy law: a mixed legacy', *California Law Review*, 98(6), 1887–1924.

Richmond, Hugh (1986). 'The Dark Lady as Reformation mistress', *Kenyon Review*, new series, 8(2), 91–105.

Ricoeur, Paul (1966). *Freedom and Nature: the Voluntary and the Involuntary*, Chicago: Northwestern University Press.

Ricoeur, Paul (1977). *The Rule of Metaphor*, Toronto: University of Toronto Press.

Rifon, Nora J., Robert LaRose and Sejung Marina Choi (2006). 'Your privacy is sealed: effects of Web privacy seals on trust and personal disclosures', *Journal of Consumer Affairs*, 39(2), 339–362, https://doi.org/10.1111/j.1745-6606.2005.00018.x.

Ripstein, Arthur (2013). 'Possession and use', in James Penner and Henry E. Smith (eds), *Philosophical Foundations of Property Law*, Oxford: Oxford University Press, 156–181.

Robinson, Roxana (2013). 'Burn your letters?' *New Yorker*, 22 May 2013, www.newyorker.com/books/page-turner/burn-your-letters.

Romanosky Sasha, and Alessandro Acquisti (2009). 'Privacy costs and personal data protection: economic and legal perspectives', *Berkeley Technology Law Journal*, 24(3), 1060–1100.

Ronson, Jon (2015). *So You've Been Publicly Shamed*, London: Pan Macmillan.

Roquet, Paul (2013). 'The domestication of the cool cat', in Ulla Haselstein, Irmela Hijiya-Kirschnereit, Catrin Gersdorf and Elena Giannoulis (eds), *The Cultural Career of Coolness: Discourses and Practices of Affect Control in European Antiquity, the United States, and Japan*, Lanham MD: Lexington, 237–250.

Rorty, Richard (1984). 'The historiography of philosophy: four genres', in Richard Rorty, J. B. Schneewind and Quentin Skinner (eds), *Philosophy in History*, Cambridge: Cambridge University Press, 49–75.

Rosen, David and Aaron Santesso (2013). 'Inviolate personality and the literary roots of the right to privacy', *Law and Literature*, 23(1), 1–25, https://doi.org/10.1525/lal.2011.23.1.1.

Rössler, Beate (2005). *The Value of Privacy*, Cambridge: Polity Press.

Rovane, Carol (1998). *The Bounds of Agency: An Essay in Revisionary Metaphysics*, Princeton: Princeton University Press.

Roy, J. (1999). '*Polis* and *oikos* in Classical Athens', *Greece and Rome*, 46(1), 1–18.

Rubenfeld, Jed (1989). 'The right of privacy', *Harvard Law Review*, 102(4), 737–807.

Rubinstein, Ira S. and Woodrow Hartzog (2016). 'Anonymization and risk', *Washington Law Review*, 91(2), 703–760.

Russell, Bertrand (1950). 'An outline of intellectual rubbish', in Bertrand Russell, *Unpopular Essays*, New York: Simon & Schuster, 71–111.

Russell, Bertrand (1956). 'The philosophy of logical atomism', in R. C. Marsh (ed.), *Logic and Knowledge: Essays 1901–1950*, London: Allen & Unwin, 175–281.

Sadhu, Vidyasagar, Saman Zonouz, Vincent Sritapan and Dario Pompili (2019). 'HCFContext: smartphone context inference via sequential history-based collaborative filtering', in *2019 IEEE International Conference on Pervasive Computing and Communications (PerCom)*, IEEE, https://doi.org/10.1109/PERCOM.2019.8767396.

Sagawe, Arno, Burkhardt Funk and Peter Niemeyer (2016). 'Modeling the intention to use carbon footprint apps', in Jorge Marx Gómez and Brenda Scholtz (eds), *Information Technology in Environmental Engineering: Proceedings of the 7th International Conference on Information Technologies in Environmental Engineering (ITEE*

2015), Cham: Springer, 139–150, https://doi.org/10.1007/978-3-319-25153-0_12.

Saint, Nick (2010). 'Eric Schmidt: Google's policy is to "get right up to the creepy line and not cross it" ', *Business Insider*, 1 October 2010, www.businessinsider.com/eric-schmidt-googles-policy-is-to-get-right-up-to-the-creepy-line-and-not-cross-it-2010-10.

Saltzman, Benjamin A. (2019). *Bonds of Secrecy: Law, Spirituality, and the Literature of Concealment in Early Medieval England*, Philadelphia: University of Pennsylvania Press.

Samuelson, P. A. (1938). 'A note on the pure theory of consumer's behaviour', *Economica*, new series, 5(17), 61–71, https://doi.org/10.2307/2548836.

Sandel, Michael (2020). *The Tyranny of Merit: What's Become of the Common Good?* London: Allen Lane.

Sanders, Teela (2008). 'Male sexual scripts: intimacy, sexuality and pleasure in the purchase of commercial sex', *Sociology*, 42(3), 400–417, https://doi.org/10.1177/0038038508088833.

Saner, Emine (2013). 'Open-plan bathrooms: the ultimate hotel horror?' *The Guardian*, 26 September 2013, www.theguardian.com/travel/shortcuts/2013/sep/26/open-plan-bathroom-hotel-toilet.

Sartre, Jean-Paul (1958). *Being and Nothingness: An Essay in Phenomenological Ontology*, London: Methuen.

Sartre, Jean-Paul (1981). *The Family Idiot: Gustave Flaubert 1821–1857*, volume 1, Chicago: University of Chicago Press.

Saura, José Ramón, Daniel Palacios-Marqués and Agustín Iturricha-Fernández (2021). 'Ethical design in social media: assessing the main performance measurements of user online behavior modification', *Journal of Business Research*, 129, 271–281, https://doi.org/10.1016/j.jbusres.2021.03.001.

Scanlon, Thomas (1975). 'Thomson on privacy', *Philosophy and Public Affairs*, 4(4), 315–322.

Scarre, Geoffrey F. (2012). 'Privacy and the dead', *Philosophy in the Contemporary World*, 19(1), 1–16, https://doi.org/10.5840/pcw201219112.

Schechtman, Marya (1996). *The Constitution of Selves*, Ithaca: Cornell University Press.

Scheler, Max (1987). 'Shame and feelings of modesty', in Max Scheler, *Person and Self-Value: Three Essays*, Dordrecht: Martinus Nijhoff, 1–85.

Schildkraut, Jaclyn (2019). 'A call to the media to change reporting practices for the coverage of mass shootings', *Washington University Journal of Law and Policy*, 60, 273–292.

Schneider, K. G., R. J. Hempel and T. R. Lynch (2013). 'That "poker face" just might lose you the game! The impact of expressive suppression and mimicry on sensitivity to facial expressions of emotion', *Emotion*, 13(5), 852–866, https://psycnet.apa.org/doi/10.1037/a0032847.

Schneider, Kirk J. (1999). *The Paradoxical Self: Toward an Understanding of Our Contradictory Nature*, 2nd edition, Amherst: Humanities Press.

Schoeman, Ferdinand David (ed.) (1984a). *Philosophical Dimensions of Privacy: An Anthology*, Cambridge: Cambridge University Press.

Schoeman, Ferdinand David (1984b). 'Privacy: philosophical dimensions of the literature', in Ferdinand D. Schoeman (ed.), *Philosophical Dimensions of Privacy: An Anthology*, Cambridge: Cambridge University Press, 1–33.

Schoeman, Ferdinand David (1992). *Privacy and Social Freedom*, Cambridge: Cambridge University Press.

Schradie, Jen (2020). ' "Give me Liberty or Give me Covid-19": Anti-lockdown protesters were never Trump puppets', *Communication and the Public*, 5(3–4), 126–128, https://doi.org/10.1177/2057047320969433.

schraefel, m. c., Richard Gomer, Enrico Gerding and Carsten Maple (2020). 'Rethinking transparency for the Internet of Things', in Mireille Hildebrandt and Kieron O'Hara (eds), *Life and the Law in the Era of Data-Driven Agency*, Cheltenham: Edward Elgar, 100–116.

Schueler, G. F. (1995). 'Why "oughts" are not facts (or what the tortoise and Achilles taught Mrs. Ganderhoot and me about practical reason)', *Mind*, 104(416), 713–723.

Schwartz, Barry (2004). *The Paradox of Choice*, New York: HarperCollins.

Schwartz, Barry and Andrew Ward (2004). 'Doing better but feeling worse: the paradox of choice', in P. Alex Linley and Stephen Joseph (eds), *Positive Psychology in Practice*, Hoboken NJ: John Wiley & Sons, 86–104.

Schwartz, Paul M. (2004). 'Property, privacy, and personal data', *Harvard Law Review*, 117(7), 2056–2128.

Scott, James C. (1998). *Seeing Like a State: How Certain Schemes to Improve the Human Condition Have Failed*, New Haven: Yale University Press.

Scott, Robert E. (2000). 'The limits of behavioral theories of law and social norms', *Virginia Law Review*, 86(8), 1603–1647, https://doi.org/10.2307/1073826.

Scott-Hayward, Christine S., Henry F. Fradella and Ryan G. Fischer (2015). 'Does privacy require secrecy? Societal expectations of privacy in the digital age', *American Journal of Criminal Law*, 43(1), 19–59.

Sedley, David (2017). 'Becoming Godlike', in Christopher Bobonich (ed.), *The Cambridge Companion to Ancient Ethics*, Cambridge: Cambridge University Press, 319–337.

Selinger, Evan and Kevin Outterson (2010). 'The ethics of poverty tourism', *Environmental Philosophy*, 7(2), 93–114, https://doi.org/10.5840/env irophil20107217.

Sennett, Richard (2002). *The Fall of Public Man*, London: Penguin.

Shadbolt, Nigel, Kieron O'Hara, David De Roure and Wendy Hall (2019). *The Theory and Practice of Social Machines*, Cham: Springer.

Shaw, Diane (1996). 'The construction of the private in medieval London', *Journal of Medieval and Early Modern Studies*, 26(3), 447–466.

Sheehan, Kim Bartel (1999). 'An investigation of gender differences in on-line privacy concerns and resultant behaviors', *Journal of Interactive Marketing*, 13(4), 24–38, https://doi.org/10.1002/(SICI)1520-6653(199 923)13:4<24::AID-DIR3>3.0.CO;2-O.

Shemtob, Zachary Baron (2013). 'Democracy on display: a case for public sanctions', *Howard Journal of Criminal Justice*, 52(4), 399–413, https://doi.org/10.1111/hojo.12025.

Shils, Edward (1956). *The Torment of Secrecy: The Background and Consequences of American Security Policy*, Glencoe IL: Free Press.

Shils, Edward (1981). *Tradition*, Chicago: University of Chicago Press.

Shils, Edward (1997). *The Virtue of Civility: Selected Essays on Liberalism, Tradition, and Civil Society*, Indianapolis: Liberty Fund.

Shklovski, Irina, Scott D. Mainwaring, Halla Hrund Skúladóttir and Höskuldur Borgthorsson (2014). 'Leakiness and creepiness in app space: perceptions of privacy and mobile app use', in *Proceedings of the SIGCHI Conference on Human Factors in Computing Systems (CHI '14)*, New York: ACM, 2347–2356, https://doi.org/10.1145/2556 288.2557421.

Shoemaker, David W. (2007). 'Personal identity and practical concerns', *Mind*, 116(462), 317–357.

Shryock, Andrew (2004). 'The new Jordanian hospitality: house, host, and guest in the culture of public display', *Comparative Studies in Society and History*, 46(1), 35–62.

Sicker, Douglas C., Paul Ohm and Shannon Gunaji (2007). 'The analog hole and the price of music: an empirical study', *Journal on Telecommunications and High Tech Law*, 5, 573–587.

Silber, Cathy (2002). 'Privacy in *Dream of the Red Chamber*', in Bonnie S. McDougall and Anders Hansson (eds), *Chinese Concepts of Privacy*, Leiden: Brill, 55–78.

Silverstein, Judith L. (1996). 'Exhibitionism as countershame', *Sexual Addiction and Compulsivity*, 3(1), 33–42, https://doi.org/10.1080/10720169608400098.

Simmel, Arnold (1971). 'Privacy is not an isolated freedom', in J. Roland Pennock and J. W. Chapman (eds), *Privacy and Personality*, Abingdon: Routledge, 71–87.

Simmel, Georg (1950). 'Knowledge, truth, and falsehood in human relations' in Kurt H. Wolff (ed.), *The Sociology of Georg Simmel*, New York: Free Press, 307–316.

Simmel, Georg (2004). *The Philosophy of Money*, 3rd enlarged edition, Abingdon: Routledge.

Skinner, Quentin (2002). *Visions of Politics: Volume 1: Regarding Method*, Cambridge: Cambridge University Press.

Slobogin, Christopher and Joseph E. Schumacher (1993). 'Reasonable expectations of privacy and autonomy in Fourth Amendment cases: an empirical look at "understandings recognized and permitted by society"', *Duke Law Journal*, 42(4), 727–775.

Slors, Marc and Fleur Jongepier (2014). 'Mineness without minimal selves', *Journal of Consciousness Studies*, 21(7–8), 193–219.

Smith, Adam (1999). *The Wealth of Nations Books IV–V*, London: Penguin.

Smith, Ailsa, Sean Madden and Robert P. Barton (2016). 'An empirical examination of societal expectations of privacy in the digital age of GPS, cell phone towers, & drones', *Albany Law Journal of Science and Technology*, 26(1), 111–142.

Smith, Barry (2005). '*Jennicam*, or the telematic theatre of a real life', *International Journal of Performance Arts and Digital Media*, 1(2), 91–100.

Solove, Daniel J. (2008). *Understanding Privacy*, Cambridge, MA: Harvard University Press.

Solove, Daniel J. (2013). 'Privacy self-management and the consent dilemma', *Harvard Law Review*, 126(7), 1880–1903.

Solove, Daniel J. (n.d.). 'The legacy of *Privacy and Freedom*', in Alan Westin, *Privacy and Freedom*, new edition, New York: Ig Publishing, vii–ix.

Sommer, Robert (1959). 'Studies in personal space', *Sociometry*, 22(3), 247–260.

Song, Victoria (2018). 'Sleep number denies recording users in their beds, calls creepy privacy policy "an error"', *Gizmodo*, 20 November 2018, https://gizmodo.com/sleep-number-denies-recording-users-in-their-beds-call-1830775153.

Sorokowska, Agnieszka, Piotr Sorokowski, Peter Hilpert, Katarzyna Cantarero, Tomasz Frackowiak, Khodabakhsh Ahmadi, Ahmad M.

Alghraibeh, Richmond Aryeetey, Anna Bertoni, Karim Bettache, Sheyla Blumen, Marta Błażejewska, Tiago Bortolini, Marina Butovskaya, Felipe Nalon Castro, Hakan Cetinkaya, Diana Cunha, Daniel David, Oana A. David, Fahd A. Dileym, Alejandra del Carmen Domínguez Espinosa, Silvia Donato, Daria Dronova, Seda Dural, Jitka Fialová, Maryanne Fisher, Evrim Gulbetekin, Aslıhan Hamamcıoğlu Akkaya, Ivana Hromatko, Raffaella Iafrate, Mariana Iesyp, Bawo James, Jelena Jaranovic, Feng Jiang, Charles Obadiah Kimamo, Grete Kjelvik, Fırat Koç, Amos Laar, Fívia de Araújo Lopes, Guillermo Macbeth, Nicole M. Marcano, Rocio Martinez, Norbert Mesko, Natalya Molodovskaya, Khadijeh Moradi, Zahrasadat Motahari, Alexandra Mühlhauser, Jean Carlos Natividade, Joseph Ntayi, Elisabeth Oberzaucher, Oluyinka Ojedokun, Mohd Sofian Bin Omar-Fauzee, Ike E. Onyishi, Anna Paluszak, Alda Portugal, Eugenia Razumiejczyk, Anu Realo, Ana Paula Relvas, Maria Rivas, Muhammad Rizwan, Svjetlana Salkičević, Ivan Sarmány-Schuller, Susanne Schmehl, Oksana Senyk, Charlotte Sinding, Eftychia Stamkou, Stanislava Stoyanova, Denisa Šukolová, Nina Sutresna, Meri Tadinac, Andero Teras, Edna Lúcia Tinoco Ponciano, Ritu Tripathi, Nachiketa Tripathi, Mamta Tripathi, Olja Uhryn, Maria Emília Yamamoto, Gyesook Yoo and John D. Pierce, Jr (2017). 'Preferred interpersonal distances: a global comparison', *Journal of Cross-Cultural Psychology*, 48(4), 577–592, https://doi.org/10.1177/0022022117698039.

Sousa, William H. and Tamara D. Madensen (2016). 'Citizen acceptance of police interventions: an example of CCTV surveillance in Las Vegas, Nevada', *Criminal Justice Studies*, 29(1), 40–56, https://doi.org/10.1080/1478601X.2015.1088230.

Spaaij, Ramón (2013). 'Risk, security and technology: governing football supporters in the twenty-first century', *Sport in Society*, 16(2), 167–183, https://doi.org/10.1080/17430437.2013.776249.

Spacks, Patricia Meyer (2003). *Privacy: Concealing the Eighteenth-Century Self*, Chicago: University of Chicago Press.

Sparkes, A. W. (1988). 'Idiots, ancient and modern', *Politics*, 23(1), 101–102, https://doi.org/10.1080/00323268808402051.

Spiekermann, Sarah, Jens Grossklags and Bettina Berendt (2001). 'E-privacy in 2nd generation e-commerce: privacy preferences versus actual behavior', in *EC '01: Proceedings of the 3rd ACM Conference on Electronic Commerce*, New York: ACM, 38–47, https://doi.org/10.1145/501158.501163.

Stasavage, David (2020). *The Decline and Rise of Democracy: A Global History From Antiquity to Today*, Princeton: Princeton University Press.

Stashower, Daniel M. (1983). 'On first looking into Chapman's Holden: speculations on a murder', *American Scholar*, 52(3), 373–377.

Steijn, Wouter M. P. and Anton Vedder (2015). 'Privacy concerns, dead or misunderstood? The perceptions of privacy amongst the young and old', *Information Polity*, 20(4), 299–311, https://doi.org/10.3233/ip-150374.

Stein, Alexandra (2021). *Terror, Love and Brainwashing: Attachment in Cults and Totalitarian Systems*, 2nd edition, Abingdon: Routledge.

Stephen, James Fitzjames (1993). *Liberty, Equality, Fraternity*, Indianapolis: Liberty Fund.

Stetson, Charlotte Perkins (1898). *Women and Economics: A Study of the Economic Relation Between Men and Women As a Factor in Social Evolution*, Boston: Small, Maynard.

Stevens, David and Kieron O'Hara (2015). *The Devil's Long Tail: Religious and Other Radicals in the Internet Marketplace*, London: Hurst.

Stigler, George J. (1980). 'An introduction to privacy in economics and politics', *Journal of Legal Studies*, 9(4), 623–644, https://doi.org/10.1086/467657.

Stricklin, W. R., H. B. Graves and L. L. Wilson (1979). 'Some theoretical and observed relationships of fixed and portable spacing behavior of animals', *Applied Animal Ethology*, 5(3), 201–214, https://doi.org/10.1016/0304-3762(79)90056-7.

Summers, Clyde W. (2000). 'Employment at will in the United States: the divine right of employers', *University of Pennsylvania Journal of Labor and Employment*, 3(1), 65–86.

Sumption, Jonathan (2019). *Trials of the State: Law and the Decline of Politics*, London: Profile.

Sundby, Christopher and Suzanna Sherry (2019). 'Term limits and turmoil: *Roe v Wade*'s whiplash', *Texas Law Review*, 98(1), 121–161.

Sunder, Madhavi (2003). 'Piercing the veil', *Yale Law Journal*, 112(6), 1399–1472.

Sutter, Nate and Thomas Holtgraves (2013). 'Perceptions of public mobile phone conversations and conversationalists', *Telematics and Informatics*, 30(2), 158–164, https://doi.org/10.1016/j.tele.2012.09.001.

Swafford, Jan (1996). *Charles Ives: A Life With Music*, New York: W. W. Norton.

Swan, Richelle S., Linda L. Shaw, Sharon Cullity, Mary Roche, Joni Halpern, Wendy M. Limbert and Juliana Humphrey (2008). 'The untold story of welfare reform', *Journal of Sociology and Social Welfare*, 35(3), 133–151.

Talbot, C. H. (2009). *The Life of Christina of Markyate*, Oxford: Oxford University Press.

Tankard, Margaret E. and Elizabeth Levy Paluck (2017). 'The effect of a Supreme Court decision regarding gay marriage on social norms and personal attitudes', *Psychological Science*, 28(9), 1334–1344, https://doi.org/10.1177/0956797617709594.

Taylor, John R. (2003). *Linguistic Categorization: Prototypes in Linguistic Theory*, 3rd edition, Oxford: Oxford University Press.

Taylor, Linnet (2017). 'Safety in numbers? Group privacy and big data analytics in the developing world', in Linnet Taylor, Luciano Floridi and Bart van der Sloot (eds), *Group Privacy: New Challenges of Data Technologies*, Cham: Springer, 13–36, https://doi.org/10.1007/978-3-319-46608-8_2.

Tene, Omar and Jules Polonetsky (2013). 'A theory of creepy: technology, privacy and shifting social norms', *Yale Journal of Law and Technology*, 16, 59–102.

Thaler, Richard H. and Cass R. Sunstein (2008). *Nudge: Improving Decisions About Health, Wealth and Happiness*, New Haven: Yale University Press.

Theriault, Jordan E., Liane Young and Lisa Feldman Barrett (2021). 'The sense of should: a biologically-based framework for modeling social pressure', *Physics of Life Reviews*, 36, 100–136, https://doi.org/10.1016/j.plrev.2020.01.004.

Thomas, Keith (1973). *Religion and the Decline of Magic*, London: Penguin.

Thomas, Keith (2018). *In Pursuit of Civility: Manners and Civilization in Early Modern England*, New Haven: Yale University Press.

Thomas, William (1963). *The History of Italy*, Ithaca: Cornell University Press.

Thomson, Judith Jarvis (1975). 'The right to privacy', *Philosophy and Public Affairs*, 4(4), 295–314. Page references to (Schoeman 1984a, 272–289).

Titchener, E. B. (1898). 'The "feeling of being stared at"', *Science*, new series, 8(208), 895–897.

Torkamann, Helma, Catalin-Mihai Barbu and Jürgen Ziegler (2019). 'How can they know that? A study of factors affecting the creepiness of recommendations', in *RecSys '19: Proceedings of the 13th ACM Conference on Recommender Systems*, New York: ACM, 423–427, https://doi.org/10.1145/3298689.3346982.

Townsend, Anthony M. (2014). *Smart Cities: Big Data, Civic Hackers, and the Quest For a New Utopia*, New York: W. W. Norton.

Travaglino, Giovanni A. and Dominic Abrams (2019). 'How criminal organisations exert secret power over communities: an intracultural appropriation theory of cultural values and norms', *European Review of Social Psychology*, 30(1), 74–122, https://doi.org/10.1080/10463 283.2019.1621128.

Trotter, J. K. (2014). 'Public NYC taxicab database lets you see how celebrities tip', *Gawker*, 23 October 2014, www.gawker.com/the-public-nyc-taxicab-database-that-accidentally-track-1646724546.

Tsakiris, Manos (2010). '*My* body in the brain: a neurocognitive model of body-ownership', *Neuropsychologia*, 48(3), 703–712, https://doi.org/10.1016/j.neuropsychologia.2009.09.034.

Tsaousi, Christiana and Joanna Brewis (2013). 'Are you feeling special today? Underwear and the "fashioning" of female identity', *Culture and Organization*, 19(1), 1–21, https://doi.org/10.1080/14759 551.2011.634196.

Turner, Mark, Steve Love and Mark Howell (2008). 'Understanding emotions experienced when using a mobile phone in public: the social usability of mobile (cellular) telephones', *Telematics and Informatics*, 25(3), 201–215, https://doi.org/10.1016/j.tele.2007.03.001.

Turney, Joanne (2019). 'The horror of the hoodie: clothing the criminal', in Joanne Turney (ed.), *Fashion Crimes: Dressing For Deviance*, London: Bloomsbury, 23–31.

Urh, Gašper and Veljko Pejović (2016). 'TaskyApp: inferring task engagement via smartphone sensing', in *UbiComp '16: Proceedings of the 2016 ACM International Joint Conference on Pervasive and Ubiquitous Computing: Adjunct*, New York: ACM, 1548–1553, https://doi.org/10.1145/2968219.2968547.

Uzzell, David and Nathalie Horne (2006). 'The influence of biological sex, sexuality and gender role on interpersonal distance', *British Journal of Social Psychology*, 45(3), 579–597, https://doi.org/10.1348/01446660 5X58384.

Van den Broeck, Evert, Karolien Poels and Michel Walrave (2015). 'Older and wiser? Facebook use, privacy concern, and privacy protection in the life stages of emerging, young, and middle adulthood', *Social Media and Society*, 1(2), https://doi.org/10.1177/2056305115616149.

Van Den Haag, Ernest (1971). 'On privacy', in J. Roland Pennock and J. W. Chapman (eds), *Privacy and Personality*, Abingdon: Routledge, 149–168.

van der Sloot, Bart (2017a). *Privacy As Virtue: Moving Beyond the Individual in the Age of Big Data*, Cambridge: Intersentia.

van der Sloot, Bart (2017b). 'Where is the harm in a privacy violation? Calculating the damages afforded in privacy cases by the European Court of Human Rights', *Journal of Intellectual Property, Information Technology and E-Commerce Law*, 8(4), 322–351, www.jipitec.eu/iss ues/jipitec-8-4-2017/4641.

Van Kleek, Max, Reuben Binns, Jun Zhao, Adam Slack, Sauyon Lee, Dean Ottewell and Nigel Shadbolt (2018). 'X-Ray Refine: supporting the exploration and refinement of information exposure resulting from smartphone apps', in *CHI '18: Proceedings of the 2018 CHI Conference on Human Factors in Computing Systems*, New York: ACM, paper no.393, https://doi.org/10.1145/3173574.3173967.

Van Kleek, Max and Kieron O'Hara (2014). 'The future of social is personal: the potential of the Personal Data Store', in Daniele Miorandi, Vincenzo Maltese, Michael Rovatsos, Anton Nijholt and James Stewart (eds), *Social Collective Intelligence: Combining the Powers of Humans and Machines to Build a Smarter Society*, Cham: Springer, 125–158, https://doi.org/10.1007/978-3-319-08681-1_7.

Vaux-Montagny, Nicolas (2021). 'Ikea fined $1.3 million over spying campaign in France', *AP News*, 15 June 2021, https://apnews.com/article/europe-france-business-c859fb0f2be4165aa9bd790d78a762cb.

Veale, Michael, Reuben Binns and Jef Ausloos (2018). 'When data protection by design and data subject rights clash', *International Data Privacy Law*, 8(2), 105–123, https://doi.org/10.1093/idpl/ipy002.

Véliz, Carissa (2020). *Privacy Is Power: Why and How You Should Take Back Control of Your Data*, Transworld: London.

Vincent, David (2016). *Privacy: A Short History*, Cambridge: Polity Press.

Vitak, Jessica (2012). 'The impact of context collapse and privacy on social network site disclosures', *Journal of Broadcasting and Electronic Media*, 56(4), 451–470, https://doi.org/10.1080/08838151.2012.732140.

Volkova, Svitlana, Glen Coppersmith and Benjamin Van Durme (2014). 'Inferring user political preferences from streaming communications', in *Proceedings of the 52nd Annual Meeting of the Association for Computational Linguistics*, 186–196, http://acl2014.org/acl2014/P14-1/pdf/P14-1018.pdf.

von Staden, Heinrich (1996). ' "In a pure and holy way": personal and professional conduct in the Hippocratic Oath?' *Journal of the History of Medicine and Allied Sciences*, 51(4), 404–437, https://doi.org/10.1093/jhmas/51.4.404.

Vveinhardt, Jolita, Vilija Bite Fominiene and Regina Andriukaitiene (2019). ' "Omerta" in organized sport: bullying and harassment as determinants of threats of social sustainability at the individual level', *Sustainability*, 11(9), 2474, https://doi.org/10.3390/su11092474.

Wacks, Raymond (2010). *Privacy: A Very Short Introduction*, Oxford: Oxford University Press.

Wadham, John, Caoilfhionn Gallagher and Nicole Chrolavicius (2006). *Blackstone's Guide to The Identity Cards Act 2006*, Oxford: Oxford University Press.

Waldron, Jeremy (1985). 'What is private property?' *Oxford Journal of Legal Studies*, 5(3), 313–349.

Walters, Lori J. (2011). 'The *vieil solitaire* and the *seulette*: contemplative solitude as political theology in Philippe de Mézières, Christine de Pizan, and Jean Gerson', in Renate Blumenfeld-Kosinski and Kiril Petkov (eds), *Philippe de Mézières and His Age: Piety and Politics in the Fourteenth Century*, Leiden: Brill, 119–144, https://doi.org/10.1163/9789004211 445_007.

Walzer, Michael (1983). *Spheres of Justice: A Defense of Pluralism and Equality*, New York: Basic Books.

Wang, Yao, Wandong Cai, Tao Gu and Wei Shao (2020). 'Your eyes reveal your secrets: an eye movement based password inference on smartphone', *IEEE Transactions on Mobile Computing*, 19(11), 2714–2730, https://doi.org/10.1109/TMC.2019.2934690.

Ware, Willis H. (1973). *Records, Computers, and the Rights of Citizens: Report of the Secretary's Advisory Committee on Automated Personal Data Systems*, US Department of Health, Education and Welfare Publication no.(OS)73–94, www.justice.gov/opcl/docs/rec-com-rights.pdf.

Warren, Danielle E., Marietta Peytcheva and Joseph P. Gaspar (2015). 'When ethical tones at the top conflict: adapting priority rules to reconcile conflicting tones', *Business Ethics Quarterly*, 25(4), 559–582, https://doi.org/10.1017/beq.2015.40.

Warren, Samuel D. and Louis D. Brandeis (1890). 'The right to privacy', *Harvard Law Review*, 4, 193–220. Page references to (Schoeman 1984a, 75–103).

Wasserstrom, Richard A. (1978). 'Privacy: some arguments and assumptions', in Richard Bronaugh (ed.), *Philosophical Law: Authority, Equality, Adjudication, Privacy*, Westport: Greenwood Press, 147–162. Page references to (Schoeman 1984a, 317–332).

Webb, Diana (2007). *Privacy and Solitude*, London: Hambledon Continuum.

Weber, Philip Andreas, Nan Zhang and Haiming Wu (2020). 'A comparative analysis of personal data protection regulations between the EU and China', *Electronic Commerce Research*, 20(3), 565–587, https://doi.org/10.1007/s10660-020-09422-3.

Weiskopf, Daniel Aaron (2009). 'The plurality of concepts', *Synthese*, 169, article 145, https://doi.org/10.1007/s11229-008-9340-8.

Weiss, Liad and Gita Venkataramani Johar (2018). 'Psychological ownership in Egocentric Categorization Theory', in Joann Peck and Suzanne B. Shu (eds), *Psychological Ownership and Consumer Behavior*, Cham: Springer, 33–51, https://doi.org/10.1007/978-3-319-77158-8_3.

West, Rebecca (2020). *Black Lamb and Grey Falcon: A Journey Through Yugoslavia*, Edinburgh: Canongate.

Westin, Alan (1967). *Privacy and Freedom*, New York: Ig Publishing.

White, Lucie and Philippe van Basshuysen (2021). 'Privacy versus public health? a reassessment of centralised and decentralised digital contact tracing', *Science and Engineering Ethics*, 27(2), article 23, https://doi.org/10.1007/s11948-021-00301-0.

Whitman, James Q. (2004). 'The two Western cultures of privacy: dignity versus liberty', *Yale Law Journal*, 113, 1151–1221.

Williams, Bernard (1978). *Descartes: The Project of Pure Enquiry*, Harmondsworth: Pelican.

Williams, Rebecca, Ian A. Elliott and Anthony R. Beech (2012). 'Identifying sexual grooming themes used by internet sex offenders', *Deviant Behavior*, 34(2), 135–152, https://doi.org/10.1080/01639625.2012.707550.

Williamson, Elizabeth, Alex J. Walker, Krishnan J. Bhaskaran, Seb Bacon, Chris Bates, Caroline E. Morton, Helen J. Curtis, Amir Mehrkar, David Evans, Peter Inglesby, Jonathan Cockburn, Helen I. Mcdonald, Brian MacKenna, Laurie Tomlinson, Ian J. Douglas, Christopher T. Rentsch, Rohini Mathur, Angel Wong, Richard Grieve, David Harrison, Harriet Forbes, Anna Schultze, Richard T. Croker, John Parry, Frank Hester, Sam Harper, Rafael Perera, Stephen Evans, Liam Smeeth and Ben Goldacre (2020). 'OpenSAFELY: factors associated with COVID-19-related hospital death in the linked electronic health records of 17 million adult NHS patients', *medRxiv*, https://doi.org/10.1101/2020.05.06.20092999.

Wimpory, Dawn C., R. Peter Hobson, J. Mark G. Williams and Susan Nash (2000). 'Are infants with autism socially engaged? A study of recent retrospective parental reports', *Journal of Autism and Developmental Disorders*, 30(6), 525–536, https://doi.org/10.1023/A:1005683209438.

Wittgenstein, Ludwig (1953). *Philosophical Investigations*, Oxford: Blackwell.

Wittgenstein, Ludwig (1961). *Tractatus Logico-Philosophicus*, London: Routledge & Kegan Paul.

Wittgenstein, Ludwig (1969). *On Certainty*, Oxford: Basil Blackwell.

Wittgenstein, Ludwig (1981). *Zettel*, 2nd edition, Oxford: Basil Blackwell.

Witzleb, Normann (2007). 'Monetary remedies for breach of confidence in privacy cases', *Legal Studies*, 27(3), 430–464, https://doi.org/10.1111/j.1748-121X.2007.00058.x.

Wood, Amy C. and Jacqueline M. Wheatcroft (2020). 'Young adult perceptions of Internet communications and the grooming concept', *SAGE Open*, 10(1), https://doi.org/10.1177/2158244020914573.

Wood, David (2004). 'People watching people', *Surveillance and Society*, 2(4), 474–478, https://doi.org/10.24908/ss.v2i4.3358.

Wood, Rachel (2016). ' "You do act differently when you're in it": lingerie and femininity', *Journal of Gender Studies*, 25(1), 10–23, https://doi.org/10.1080/09589236.2013.874942.

Woodhead, Charlotte C. (2002). ' "A debate which crosses all borders": the repatriation of human remains: more than just a legal question', *Art Antiquity and Law*, 7(4), 317–347.

Woods, Heather Suzanne (2018). 'Asking more of Siri and Alexa: feminine persona in service of surveillance capitalism', *Critical Studies in Media Communication*, 35(4), 334–349, https://doi.org/10.1080/15295036.2018.1488082.

Wright, David and Paul de Hert (eds) (2012). *Privacy Impact Assessment*, Dordrecht: Springer.

Wright, David and Charles Raab (2014). 'Privacy principles, risks and harms', *International Review of Law, Computers and Technology*, 28(3), 277–298, https://doi.org/10.1080/13600869.2014.913874.

Wu, Carole-Jean, David Brooks, Kevin Chen, Douglas Chen, Sy Choudhury, Marat Dukhan, Kim Hazelwood, Eldad Isaac, Yangqing Jia, Bill Jia, Tommer Leyvand, Hao Lu, Yang Lu, Lin Qiao, Brandon Reagen, Joe Spisak, Fei Sun, Andrew Tulloch, Peter Vajda, Xiaodong Wang, Yanghan Wang, Bram Wasti, Yiming Wu, Ran Xian, Sungjoo Yoo and Peizhao Zhang (2019). 'Machine learning at Facebook: understanding inference at the edge', in *2019 IEEE International Symposium on High Performance Computer Architecture (HPCA)*, IEEE, https://doi.org/10.1109/HPCA.2019.00048.

Xu, Dan, Peng Cui, Wenwu Zhu and Shiqiang Yang (2014). 'Graph-based residence location inference for social media users', *IEEE MultiMedia*, 21(4), 76–83, https://doi.org/10.1109/MMUL.2014.62.

Yamaguchi, Yuto, Toshiyuki Amagasa and Hiroyuki Kitagawa (2013). 'Landmark-based user location inference in social media', in *COSN '13: Proceedings of the 1st ACM Conference on Online Social Networks*, New York: ACM, 223–234, https://doi.org/10.1145/2512938.2512941.

Young, Alyson Leigh and Anabel Quan-Haase (2013). 'Privacy protection strategies on Facebook: the Internet privacy paradox revisited', *Information, Communication and Society*, 16(4), 479–500, https://doi.org/10.1080/1369118X.2013.777757.

Young, William C. (2007). 'Arab hospitality as a rite of incorporation: the case of the Rashaayda Bedouin of Eastern Sudan', *Anthropos*, 102(1), 47–69.

Zahavi, Dan (2005). *Subjectivity and Selfhood: Investigating the First-Person Perspective*, Cambridge, MA: MIT Press.

Zhang, Baobao, Sarah Kreps, Nina McMurry and R. Miles McCain (2020). 'Americans' perceptions of privacy and surveillance in the COVID-19 pandemic', *PLoS One*, 15(12), e0242652, https://doi.org/10.1371/journal.pone.0242652.

Zhang, Bo and Heng Xu (2016). 'Privacy nudges for mobile applications: effects on the creepiness emotion and privacy attitudes', in *CSCW '16: Proceedings of the 19th ACM Conference on Computer-Supported Cooperative Work & Social Computing*, New York: ACM, 1676–1690, https://doi.org/10.1145/2818048.2820073.

Zuboff, Shoshana (2019). *The Age of Surveillance Capitalism: the Fight for a Human Future at the New Frontier of Power*, London: Profile.

Index

abortion 1, 29, 50–51, 52, 59, 163, 164–165, 167, 192
abuse 21, 49, 70, 170, 191, 212, 231, 283
accountability 33, 157, 196, 202, 247, 258, 271, 278–279, 287–288
ADO Den Haag 272
advertising 10, 51, 107, 114, 120, 121, 127, 154–155, 248, 252, 277, 279
Agre, Philip 184–187
Al-Assad, Bashar 52
Algeria 155
Allen, Anita 37–38, 132
Altman, Irwin 87–88, 105, 138, 141, 217
Amsterdam 289
analogue hole, the 256
anchorites, anchoresses 224–226, 232–233
Ancrene Wisse 224–226
animals 86, 98–99, 211, 229, 305
anonymisation 250–253, 254, 276, 302, 306
anonymity 16, 18, 34, 36, 37, 68, 69, 144, 181, 224, 252–253, 285–286, 305, 309
Antisthenes 230
anti-vaccination *see* vaccination
AOL 251–252
apparency 259–260, 264
Apple 154–155, 278, 302–306
appraisiveness (criterion of an ECC) 48–53, 59, 300
appropriation of name or likeness (tort) 11, 230
architecture *see* privacy, affordances for
Arendt, Hannah 30, 33, 49, 112, 195, 286, 294
Aristotle 56, 135, 151, 180, 268, 271
Armenian massacre/genocide 50–51
Armored Car Robbery 149
Armstrong, Lil 229–230
Asia 125, 174, 226, 242, 305
Asphalt Jungle, The 149
associations 34, 245–247, 286, 294
authenticity 127, 135–136, 182, 183, 194, 204, 269, 291, 308

authority 10, 32, 39, 107, 125, 150, 157, 185, 216, 225–226, 241
autism 232
autonomy 72, 116–119, 137, 170, 171, 173, 178, 181–182, 183, 185–187, 188, 190, 193–197, 203, 213, 224, 262, 266, 279, 286, 291, 305, 308

backstage (Goffman) 112, 182, 184, 193, 196, 271, 305
Baldwin, David A. 53
Barcelona 289
Barresi, John 234
Becket, Thomas 258
Benn, Stanley 267, 269
Bentham, Jeremy 105–106
Bernard of Clairvaux 36
Berners-Lee, Tim 281, 293, 309
big data *see* data analytics
biometrics 253, 274
blackmail 74–75, 284
Bloustein, Edward 163, 183, 245
body, the 32, 33, 82, 87, 98, 100–101, 106, 150, 184, 192, 213, 233, 234–235
Bork, Robert 53, 162
Bowers v Hardwick 163
Brandeis, Louis D. 7–11, 12, 13, 15, 16, 20, 22, 33, 41, 43, 52, 54, 67, 74, 81, 91, 134, 160, 165–166, 168, 183, 204, 209, 235, 244
breach of confidence 8, 11, 27, 146, 168, 246–247
    see also confidentiality
Britain *see* United Kingdom
Brussels Effect, the 162, 275, 282
Buddhism 226, 232, 235
bugging 10, 21, 103, 146, 161, 199–200, 308
Bunker, Chang and Eng 143
Burke, Edmund 178, 183, 286, 294
business (commercial activity) 1, 28, 72, 180, 226, 246–248, 253–254, 257, 268, 274, 279, 282, 292

business, my/mind your own 12, 38–39, 164, 177, 220, 229–230, 267

cameras 54, 56, 89, 91–92, 103, 104, 114, 120, 123, 213–214, 272, 277
see also photography, photographs; webcams
Camus, Albert 295, 301
care 117, 172, 186, 188, 191, 192, 194, 242, 260
Care19 (app) 302
Cartesian philosophy 30–31
cash 304, 309
CCTV *see* closed circuit television
celebrities *see* public figures
cellphone *see* mobile phone
Cervantes, Miguel de 194, 268
Channon, Henry 'Chips' 36
Charter of Fundamental Rights of the European Union 273
Chaucer, Geoffrey 220–221, 225
Miller's Tale, The 220–221
Chesterton, G. K. 243–244
children 29, 35, 82, 104, 109, 117, 121, 127, 133, 163, 167, 173, 182, 186, 188, 190, 195, 235, 242–243, 259–260, 264, 278, 305
chilling effects 120, 128, 193
China 51, 106, 164, 221–223, 244, 274, 283, 289, 290, 308–309
choice 28, 67–68, 124–125, 128, 130, 132, 136, 138, 145, 158, 182–183, 189, 193, 204, 249, 262–263, 265–266, 277, 287, 291, 308
Christina of Markyate 225
civility, civil society 31, 176, 194, 245, 285
Clarke, Roger 17
closed circuit television 100, 106, 114, 272, 286, 301, 305
clothing 90, 106, 113–114, 207, 234, 235
Cocking, Dean 118
cognitive linguistics 55
coherence thesis 2, 3
Coke, Sir Edward 269
Collier, David, et al. 50–51, 53
common law 8, 13, 40, 157, 166, 167, 204–205, 261
communications *see* correspondence
communitarianism 195, 283, 287–288, 289, 294–295
community 1, 20, 56, 109, 127, 177, 181, 215, 219, 221, 239, 241–242, 283–298, 306
competition law 169, 279
concepts 60–62, 85–86
confidentiality 27–28, 74–75, 105, 146, 180, 245, 248, 250, 285, 291
see also breach of confidence
Connolly, William E. 53
Conrad, Joseph 179

consent 12, 21, 82–83, 95, 101, 122, 161, 188, 193, 201–202, 209, 214, 239, 250, 261–266, 274, 279–280, 297, 301, 306–307
conservatism 150–152, 177–179, 196–197, 204, 223–224
contact tracing *see* track and trace
contemplation *see* reflection
context collapse 257–258
contextual integrity 78, 147–156, 178–179, 210, 297–298, 301
contraception 61, 163, 164, 192
contract 8, 29, 56, 92, 149, 245, 253, 260, 284
control *see* privacy, types of, privacy-as-control
correspondence 14, 17, 18, 33–34, 90, 92–94, 98, 154–155, 233
Council of Europe 274
Court of Justice of the European Union 275
COVID-19 216, 270, 279, 301–308
Cowper, William 183
creepiness 121–122, 251
crime, criminal records 25, 27–28, 68, 74–75, 109–110, 118, 119–120, 135, 148–149, 152, 153, 194, 267, 272, 283, 287, 290, 295, 305
Croce, Benedetto 128
cybersecurity 216, 239, 253–256, 301

Dad's Army 144–145, 152
Dakota, North and South 302
'Dark Lady', the 100
dark patterns 257
data analytics 21, 31, 32, 48, 72, 93–94, 98, 167, 248–249, 250, 251, 277, 289, 303, 306
data anonymisation *see* anonymisation
data controllers 251, 253, 274, 275, 276–277, 279, 281
data environment 252–253, 255, 307
data exhaust 293
data processing 21, 54, 56, 114, 121, 126, 185, 236, 250, 261, 274, 276–277, 280, 290
data protection 17, 21, 27, 54, 57, 83, 132, 162, 210, 226, 239, 261, 273–282, 301, 305, 306–307
Data Protection Directive 274–275, 307
Data Protection Impact Assessments 282
data sharing 42, 251, 259, 264–265, 291, 293, 302, 306–307
data subject 83, 274, 275, 277, 279, 280, 281
databases 21, 89, 93, 98, 100, 252, 254–255, 273
DeepMind 306–307
democracy 5, 20, 30, 34, 41, 47, 50, 55–56, 59, 77, 170, 176–177, 182, 190, 194, 195, 197, 203, 204, 207, 231, 245, 270, 275, 279, 285, 290, 303, 306, 308

Descartes, René *see* Cartesian philosophy
design 16, 103–106, 108, 109, 111, 126, 157, 215–216, 223, 236, 239, 253, 255, 257–260, 278, 280, 289, 290, 302
Devil, the 31, 116
diaries 104, 128–129, 199
Dickens, Charles 92, 98, 110
    Bleak House 110–111
digital currency/payments 304, 309
digital modernity 40, 52, 147, 168–169, 256, 281, 308
digital rights management 256
digital technology 17, 21, 52, 54, 56, 72, 106–107, 109–110, 111, 118–119, 121–122, 147, 219, 246, 291, 305, 308
dignity 13, 73, 142, 163, 165, 167, 182–184, 188, 194, 214, 224, 230, 274, 285, 293
discourse 77–79, 84
discrimination 25, 149–150, 153, 176
Do Not Track 281
Dream of the Red Chamber (Cao Xueqin) 221–223
duty 47, 50, 75, 175, 284
Dwork, Cynthia 99

eavesdropping 33–34, 36, 105, 108, 119, 159, 198, 199–200, 222, 233
ECCs *see* essentially contested concepts
e-commerce 67, 107, 127, 172, 248, 275, 282, 303, 304
Egypt, Ancient 98, 233
Eisenstadt v Baird 163
Elliot, Mark 36
email 92–94, 146, 285
embarrassment 98, 112, 114, 123, 124, 172, 222, 284
emotion 17, 31, 123, 125, 168, 181, 182, 187, 192, 249
empirical accounts of privacy *see* privacy, descriptive accounts of
empowering exhibitionism 135
empowerment 3, 18, 21, 25, 48, 132–134, 188, 281–282, 291
encryption 82, 104, 107, 216, 253–254, 255–256, 259, 287
Enlightenment, the 183, 268, 269
environment 288–289, 290
essentially contested concepts (ECCs) 45, 47–59, 65, 73, 77, 87, 300
etiquette 31, 148, 222
Etzioni, Amitai 109–110, 162, 164, 287–288, 294–295
European Convention on Human Rights 14, 167, 270, 274
    Article 8 14, 167, 274
    Article 12 167
European Court of Human Rights 20, 41
European Union 57, 158, 226, 275, 282, 307

European Union law 158, 162, 209, 274, 307–308
exhibitionism 35, 135–136, 149
exposure 2, 31, 82, 83, 91, 99–101, 112, 113–114, 115, 121, 122, 124, 132, 135, 138, 186, 215, 262, 278
extremism 177, 229, 286

face *see* privacy, types of, facial
face recognition technology 55, 100, 106, 210, 308–309
Facebook 25, 116, 189, 248–249, 257, 277, 292–293
Fair Information Practice Principles 274, 280
false light (tort) 11, 38
family, the 14, 17, 36–37, 70, 82, 125, 127, 148, 167, 173, 186, 188–189, 190, 196, 197, 205, 218–219, 223, 226, 235, 242–245, 246, 257, 260, 268, 269, 270–271, 278, 292, 305
family resemblance theory of meaning 45, 57, 59, 60–66, 71, 77, 79, 80, 86, 89–91, 101–102, 159, 173, 201, 221, 228, 229, 300
feminism 49, 194–195, 213, 283
financial contexts 24, 27, 91, 101, 124, 130, 143–144, 180, 234, 235, 250, 251, 254, 263, 273, 275, 304, 305, 309
Finn, Rachel, et al. 17, 18
FIPPs *see* Fair Information Practice Principles
Floridi, Luciano 70
Floyd, George 283
Foucault, Michel 78, 221
Fourier, Charles 177
Foursquare 302
France 155, 270
Freda, Maria Francesca 234
freedom of association *see* privacy, types of, associational
freedom of information 110, 284
freedom of speech 40–41, 56, 83, 166, 176, 268, 284
Frege, Gottlob 61, 62–63
Freud, Sigmund 31
Fried, Charles 116–118, 189, 190, 192
friendship 37, 39, 116, 118, 143, 181, 189, 219, 235, 257, 270

Gallie, W. B. 45, 47–48, 50, 53, 54–56, 59
games 60, 62, 63–64
Gavison, Ruth 35, 68, 81, 99, 168–169, 203, 244, 297
GDPR *see* General Data Protection Regulation
gender 20, 55, 82–83, 95, 114, 115, 122, 126, 127, 132, 142, 149–150, 153, 161, 176, 177, 187, 190, 191, 195–196, 211, 214, 223–224, 243, 252, 260, 268, 271, 272
General Data Protection Regulation 168, 204, 261, 274–277, 282, 290, 307

genetic information 70, 274, 295
genocide 50–51, 59
Georgia (US) 163
Gergen, Kenneth 231
Germany 167, 293, 305
    East Germany 117
Gerstein, Robert 118, 189, 191–193, 194
Get Smart 103
Gilliom, John 22, 134, 296
Glaucon 96, 204
God 80, 116, 172, 220, 226
Godfather Part II, The 230
Godiva, Lady 56, 88, 122, 220
Goffman, Erving 35, 196, 210–211, 258
    see also backstage
Google 111, 122, 253, 295, 302–306
    Alphabet 306
    Google Spain 275, 277
    Google Street View 293
gossip 34, 38, 39, 52, 145, 173, 219, 225,
    234, 284
Great Escape, The 97
Greece, Ancient 30, 33, 49, 55–56, 268, 270
Grindr 189
Griswold v Connecticut 163, 164
guilt 112, 121, 173, 187

Habermas, Jürgen 177, 196
hair 33, 39, 95, 150
Hall, Edward 211
Happy Crowd Control system 272
Hart, H.L.A. 158
Hartley, L.P. 220
Hartzog, Woodrow 205, 257
Hayek, F.A. 30
HCI *see* Human-Computer Interaction
healthcare 24, 28, 51, 121–122, 124, 135,
    143, 145, 180, 191, 245, 251–252,
    262, 264, 273, 277, 287, 290, 295,
    303–304, 306–307
Heidegger, Martin 236
Heller, Joseph 248
Henry II, King of England 258
hermeneutics 148, 151, 158, 220–221
hermits 24, 91, 210, 271
Hildebrandt, Mireille 184, 187–188, 212–213
Hildegard of Bingen 225
Hippocratic Oath, the 180
honour 14, 82, 205, 244, 268
Hopper, Edward 132
horoscopes 95
household 14, 37, 56, 95, 105, 106, 108, 117,
    153, 163, 190, 195–197, 216, 219,
    235, 241, 243–244, 251, 268–271,
    277, 304–305
human rights 21, 72, 188, 227, 268, 270,
    280–281, 287
    see also privacy, right(s) to
Human-Computer Interaction 258–259
Hume, David 171, 183
Huxley, Aldous 126, 173, 189

Brave New World 126, 136, 173, 189,
    217, 243
Brave New World Revisited 126
Island 173

ID *see* identity
ID cards *see* identity cards
identification 27, 34, 82, 83, 99, 100, 101, 107,
    154–155, 249, 250–256, 274–278
identity (ID) 11, 21, 34, 69, 70, 73, 82,
    100–101, 182, 184–188, 189, 192,
    213, 226, 227, 230, 235, 252,
    275, 293
identity cards (ID cards) 158, 287, 297
identity theft 21, 152, 265, 276
idiot/*idiotes* (Greek) 49, 268
Illinois, Supreme Court of 160
Index Librorum Prohibitorum 107
indigenous people 98
individualism, individuality 20, 70, 173, 182,
    184, 194, 212, 226, 236, 242, 245,
    271, 287, 294, 308
information processing *see* data processing
Inness, Julie 1–2, 4, 15, 38, 39, 53, 99, 108,
    128–129, 133, 137–138, 159–160,
    163, 172, 182, 188, 191–193,
    198–201, 212, 221
intellectual property 70, 98, 253, 256, 284
intelligence (spying) 93–94, 120, 307
Internet 109, 122, 136–137, 138, 147, 213,
    253, 259, 271, 289, 307
    Internet of Things 147, 259, 289–290
    see also World Wide Web
interrogation 26, 33, 234
intimacy 17, 18, 21, 32, 33, 35, 37, 38–39,
    66–67, 69, 73, 82, 97, 98, 116–119,
    143, 154, 163, 164, 171, 172, 174,
    182, 183, 185, 186, 188–193, 196,
    203, 204, 212, 232, 234, 243–245,
    264, 268–269, 271
Intimate Partner Violence (IPV) 191
intrusion 8, 10–11, 12, 26, 32–33, 35–36, 58,
    67, 88, 96, 98, 105, 111, 113, 118,
    121–123, 132, 138, 161, 172,
    183–184, 196, 200–202, 211, 215,
    217, 229–230, 261, 263, 267, 271,
    280, 287, 288, 290, 295, 296,
    305, 307
intrusion upon seclusion (tort) 10–11
inviolate personality 8, 183
IPV *see* Intimate Partner Violence
isolation 16, 37, 96, 138, 171–172, 181,
    244, 286
Italy 230
Ives, Charles 144

James, Henry 219
James, William 234, 235, 236–237
James IV, King of Scotland 36
Japan 226
Jarvis, Jeff 42, 47, 52, 290–294

Jennicam *see* Ringley, Jennifer
Jesus 31, 174
JioChat 293
Johnson, Boris 301
Jourard, Sidney 68
justice 47, 49–50, 52, 53, 59, 74, 87, 96, 149,
    150, 176, 188, 196, 230, 279,
    284–285, 300

Kalven, Harry 166
Katz v United States 163
King, Rodney 283
kompromat 285
Koops, Bert-Jaap, et al. 17–19, 26, 78, 159
Kraemer, Martin 155, 174
Kyllo v United States 58, 146

La Rochefoucauld, François de 230
Latour, Bruno 236
Lawrence v Texas 163
Lennon, John 135
Lessig, Lawrence 212
level 0 discourse 80, 207, 228–237, 300
level 1 discourse *see* privacy, conceptions of
level 2 discourse *see* privacy, affordances for
level 3 discourse *see* privacy,
    phenomenology of
level 4 discourse *see* privacy, preferences for
level 5 discourse *see* privacy, norms of
level 6 discourse *see* privacy, regulation
level 7 discourse *see* privacy, ethics of
Lever, Annabelle 37
liberalism 30, 128, 133, 153, 165, 171,
    173–174, 178, 181–182, 184,
    194–197, 234, 245, 270, 271, 273,
    280, 305
libertarianism 181
lie detector 21, 31
liking (social media) 277, 293
limited access to the self *see* withdrawal
LinkedIn 189
litter 25, 32, 142
Locke, John 30, 197, 287
Lombroso, Cesare 31
loneliness 131–132, 188, 212, 219
love 11, 33, 35, 39, 95, 98, 117–118, 127,
    132, 172, 188, 191–193, 199,
    242–243, 270
Loving v Virginia 163
Luca (app) 305
Lucan, 7th Earl of 160
Lyotard, Jean-François 232

M*A*S*H 285
machine learning 93–94, 248–249, 277, 289,
    303–304, 306–307
McConnell, Mitch 165
McNealy, Scott 52
McQueen, Steve 97
McStay, Andrew 33, 112, 133, 236–237

Maduro, Nicolás 52
male gaze 122, 187
Marcus Aurelius 36
markets 83, 128, 130, 219, 268–269, 282,
    284–285, 308
Martin, Raymond 234
Marx, Gary 78–79, 234
Mary, Duchess of Burgundy 36
mass society 149, 219, 294
Maugham, Somerset 98
Mead, Margaret 286
media, mass media 17, 72, 106–107, 122, 135,
    161, 171, 219, 258, 271
medical information *see* healthcare
Megan's laws 109–110, 287
mental/emotional distress 10, 13, 97, 168, 184
meritocracy 133–134
Merkel, Angela 308
Met de Deur in Huis 218
metadata 93, 303
Mill, John Stuart 197, 270–271, 287, 294
Milton, John 96
misinformation 276, 279
mission creep 296–298, 303
mobile phone 35, 38, 100, 132, 146, 224,
    303, 308
modernity 174, 176, 247, 308
    see also digital modernity
modesty 106, 291
molka videos 213–214
monasteries, monks 24, 36, 104, 215, 219,
    225, 232, 246
Moore, Henry 108
mouth 33, 223
Mulligan, Deirdre, et al. 45, 47–48, 53–59
multiple personalities 95
murder(s) 51, 135, 160, 167, 283, 295
Murphy, Robert 223

National Health Service (United Kingdom)
    304, 306–307
Neo-Bankside 130–131
Netherlands, the 218, 272, 301, 305
Nietzsche, Friedrich 31
Nissenbaum, Helen 1–2, 16, 74, 78, 79–80,
    126, 143, 147–156, 175,
    178–179, 268
notoriety 135
nudging 213, 279, 289, 290
nudity 56, 82–83, 88, 90, 100–101, 108,
    113–114, 155, 270, 285, 288

Obergefell v Hodges 163, 165
obscurity 21, 110–111, 286
obtrusion *see* privacy, types of, extrinsic
OECD *see* Organisation for Economic Co-
    operation and Development
Olmstead v United States 163, 164, 183
Omand, Sir David 93–94
openness 42, 155, 290–294
    as criterion of an ECC 48, 54–58

Oppenheim, Felix 86, 87
Oregon 161
Organisation for Economic Co-operation and
 Development (OECD) 57, 274
organisations 32, 34, 80, 110, 163, 216,
 245–248, 265, 282, 306
Orwell, George 105–106, 108, 120
othering 247
Ottoman government 50–51
ownership *see* privacy, types of, private property

P3P *see* Platform for Privacy Preferences
panopticon 105–106, 120
panpsychism 231
Parker, Richard 114
Parkinson, Brian 281
paternalism 37, 132, 262, 269
PDS *see* Personal Data Stores
Pedersen, Dahrl 18, 37, 39, 181
Peeping Tom 56, 88, 101, 108, 113, 122–123,
 220, 271
penance 31, 157
People v Kohrig 160
personal data 17, 27, 30, 51–52, 67, 69–70,
 104, 114, 162, 210, 235, 259, 260,
 261, 275–278, 281, 293–294, 307
Personal Data Stores (PDS) 281
Personal Information Management Systems
 (PIMS) 281
personal space 32–33, 100, 137, 190,
 210–211, 304
personalisation 120, 130, 308
personality 31, 70–71, 95, 163, 183–184
 see also inviolate personality
personality test 21, 31, 263, 265
personally identifying information (PII) *see*
 personal data
personhood 16, 70–71, 73, 167, 176,
 184–188, 198–202, 229
Petrarch 24
PETs *see* privacy-enhancing technologies
Photografter, The 92
photography, photographs 8, 11, 34, 81–83,
 92, 100, 109, 122, 146, 161, 215,
 272, 285, 293
 see also cameras; webcams
phronesis 151, 178, 179
Picione, Raffaele De Luca 234
PII *see* personal data
PIMS *see* Personal Information Management
 Systems
Pinkertons 92
Platform for Privacy Preferences 281
Plato 56, 92–93, 96, 162, 204, 243
 Phaedrus 92–93
 Republic, The 96, 204, 243
policymaking 15, 45, 169, 248, 279, 297, 308
Pompeo, Mike 51
pornography 56, 82–83, 108, 122, 127, 214
Porridge 97

Porter, Cole 118
positivist view of language 61–62
Posner, Eric 215
Posner, Richard 93, 134, 214–215, 284
possessive adjectives 229, 234, 235, 237
Post, Robert 158
postmodernism 231–232, 283
power 30, 48, 70, 80, 134, 143, 164, 169,
 175, 177, 180, 194, 197, 221, 224,
 243, 279–282, 285, 296
practical wisdom *see phronesis*
preferences, first- and second-order 126–127,
 129, 132, 140, 141
Prisoner, The 121
privacy
 accretions to meaning 54–57, 300
 as an actant 133, 236
 affordances for (level 2) 70, 79, 82, 83,
 103–111, 130, 133, 139, 143, 192,
 207, 210–213, 215–216, 218, 219,
 222, 223, 224–225, 226, 232, 236,
 250–256, 300, 302–304
 boundary/edge cases 96–99
 breaches of (definitions/abstract
 discussions) 8–9, 11–12, 13, 14, 19,
 23, 24, 43, 55–56, 57, 68, 73, 79, 83,
 88, 89, 93, 95, 99–101, 103–104, 108,
 112–116, 128–129, 145–146, 153,
 157, 161, 198–201, 204, 209–211,
 213, 221–222, 246–247, 254,
 261–264, 269, 271, 272, 276,
 278–279, 283, 285, 307
 cognitive psychology of 85–86, 175,
 124–125, 233, 234–235, 264–266,
 280, 286
 conceptions of (level 1) 59, 79, 80, 82,
 83, 87–102, 139, 159, 198, 201–203,
 205–206, 207, 209–211, 213, 215,
 218, 219, 222, 225–226, 228–229,
 236, 241–249, 254–255, 269, 276,
 291, 300, 301–302
 costs of 24, 109–110, 111, 120, 130, 170
 cultural variation of 2, 17, 20–21, 23, 32,
 39, 49, 71, 79, 82, 89, 90, 96, 99,
 158, 161, 170–171, 172–173, 174,
 190, 203, 204, 207, 215, 217–227,
 237, 241, 268, 273–274, 299
 dead, for the 98–99, 133, 229
 defining privacy 7–21, 22, 23, 40–43,
 62–65, 66–75, 77–78, 89, 160, 171,
 202–203, 205–206, 209, 269, 272,
 291, 299–301
 descriptive accounts of 37, 48, 51–53, 78,
 80, 130, 133, 139, 142–145,
 150–154, 178
 economics of 30, 124–125, 130, 175, 212,
 214–215, 284
 ethics of (level 7) 41, 42, 74, 75, 77, 80,
 83, 84, 140, 141, 150–154, 155–156,
 158, 164, 166, 170–206, 207,
 209–210, 212–215, 218, 219,

223–224, 226, 227, 248–249, 262,
283–298, 300, 303, 306–307, 309
fictional cases 94–96
functional value of 116, 170, 174,
176–204, 221, 223–224, 225
game theoretical aspects of 97, 181, 215,
283, 292, 298, 303
harms 8, 18–19, 24, 42, 57, 83, 88, 94,
104, 128–129, 143, 161, 164, 167,
168, 171, 184, 197, 202, 205, 210,
214, 262, 265, 270, 271, 279–280
Impact Assessments 282
intrinsic value of 3, 116–117, 173–175,
202–203, 204, 230
kitchen sink definitions of 72–75, 81,
86–88, 115, 132–133, 154, 171,
198, 201, 209, 212, 261, 287–288,
291, 300
law of 7–12, 17–18, 29, 40–41, 42, 53,
57–58, 59, 68, 70–71, 72, 75, 83, 89,
104, 111, 134, 145–146, 148–149,
151, 157–169, 171, 175, 183–184,
192, 199, 202–203, 204–206,
209–210, 212–215, 219, 226, 236,
241, 245, 260, 261–262, 273–282,
284, 286, 288, 301
linguistic markers of 89, 229–230,
234, 237
management 78, 87–88, 117, 204,
211, 253
negotiating limits of 48, 67–68, 87–88,
120, 187, 190, 205, 211, 214, 216,
217, 229, 247, 263, 281, 296–299
normative accounts of 37, 48, 67, 77–78,
80, 133, 139, 142–145, 150–154,
198, 212
normative good, as a 3, 24, 48–53, 59, 67,
70, 96–97, 171–173, 185, 202–203,
227, 300
norms of (level 5) 4, 39, 42, 54, 57, 69,
75, 79, 82, 83, 84, 89, 104, 140, 141,
142–156, 157, 158, 164, 166, 171,
177–178, 183, 191, 194, 195,
196–197, 204, 205–206, 207,
209–216, 218, 219, 222, 223, 224,
225, 232, 239, 267–272, 273, 284,
288, 300, 301, 304–305, 308
paradigm cases of 16, 47, 63, 85, 96–97,
123, 188, 192, 196, 242–244
phenomenology of (level 3) 35, 68, 79,
82, 83, 101, 104, 112–123, 124, 125,
191, 207, 209–211, 214–216, 219,
222, 225, 231, 234, 239, 257–260,
300, 304
pluralism of 2, 40–41, 45, 60–61, 64–66,
71, 80, 85–86, 99–102, 168, 179, 201,
206, 228, 244
politics of 72, 77, 80, 83, 111, 120, 150,
155–156, 162, 164–166, 170, 171,
175, 176, 203, 285

potential breaches of 23, 108
preferences for (level 4) 3, 18, 24, 68, 75,
79, 82, 83, 88, 89, 97, 98–99,
124–141, 146, 147, 149, 155, 157,
158, 166, 171, 173, 174–175, 176,
181, 188, 207, 209–216, 217, 219,
223, 225, 226, 232, 261–266, 273,
279, 281, 295, 300, 304, 308
process, as a 87–88, 141
in public 99–100, 272
reasonable expectations of 68, 145–147,
158, 163, 168, 184–185, 192, 267
regulation (level 6) 70, 80, 83, 93, 104,
140, 141, 157–169, 204, 207, 210,
212–215, 219, 225, 226, 236, 254,
266, 273–282, 300, 303, 305–306,
307, 308
relative nature of 23, 24, 69, 79, 99–100,
103, 125–126, 188, 229, 243
remedies for breaches/harms 15, 24, 49,
51, 79, 88, 164, 168, 280
right(s) to 3, 8, 9–10, 11, 13–15, 17, 18,
41–42, 57, 59, 74, 80, 104, 133,
157–158, 159, 166–169, 170,
172–173, 175, 178–179, 181,
184–185, 187–188, 189, 193,
197–202, 227, 241, 245, 262, 269,
273, 274, 278, 280, 294
role-based 23, 27, 28, 34, 35, 58,
143–145, 148, 187, 193, 195, 204,
211, 223, 247, 260, 269
seals 282
state, as a 3, 48, 67–68, 87–88, 96, 103,
108, 138, 141, 188–189, 203, 212,
229, 288
taxonomies of 17–19, 26, 41, 168, 175,
234, 280
threats to 18, 21, 55, 153, 204, 222,
259–260
typologies of 17–19, 26
use of term 22–39, 44, 60–66, 89, 220,
299, 300
value of 41, 42, 44, 48–53, 67, 70, 72, 74,
77, 80, 136, 160, 170–206, 226, 232,
291, 293, 295, 300, 301
privacy paradox 2, 129–131, 155, 185
privacy policies 149, 259–260, 265, 276, 282
privacy torts, tort law 10–12, 13, 14, 38,
40–41, 162–164, 165–166, 167–168,
183, 210, 212, 230, 278, 284
privacy, types of
associational 18, 38, 56, 166, 176,
244–245, 268, 302, 303, 308
attentional 16, 23, 26, 29, 33–34, 36, 38,
39, 65, 88–89, 91, 95, 97, 99, 101,
108, 113, 115, 118, 121, 126, 135,
137, 162, 186, 194, 198, 199–201,
213, 233–234, 245, 270, 273, 278,
285, 288, 290, 291
behavioural 18

privacy, types of (*continued*)
    bodily 18, 19, 33, 113
    decisional 18, 24, 25, 28–29, 32, 38, 39,
        95, 97, 101, 108, 113, 136, 137,
        154, 162, 165, 167, 186–187, 193,
        194, 196, 200, 225, 233, 246, 249,
        263, 277, 279, 288, 290, 291, 301,
        305–306
    deliberative 36
    differential 254–255
    economic 29, 39, 101
    extrinsic 26, 35–36, 38, 69, 95, 97, 118,
        234, 247
    facial 25, 31, 33, 39, 82, 90, 91, 92, 100,
        115–116, 143, 219, 223–224
    financial 91, 101, 124. 250, 254, 263,
        273, 305
    group 3, 34, 36–37, 38–39, 77, 87, 99,
        131, 163, 167, 204, 229, 232, 239,
        241–249, 255
    ideological 25, 32, 36, 38, 97, 233,
        247, 278
    informational 3, 18, 21, 23, 24, 25,
        27–28, 36, 37, 38, 39, 43, 69, 97, 99,
        108, 111, 116–117, 121, 123, 124,
        125–126, 135, 137, 147–148, 153,
        162, 176, 193, 194, 204, 227, 233,
        250, 254, 273–274, 280, 284, 290,
        291, 309
    intellectual 18, 38
    intrinsic 36
    privacy-as-control 3, 16, 21, 61, 67,
        69–70, 72, 73, 96, 114, 117–119,
        131–141, 154, 162–163, 181, 193,
        209, 210, 212, 213, 216, 221,
        229, 245, 261–266, 279–280, 282,
        301, 302
    privacy-as-intimacy *see* intimacy
    privacy-as-secrecy *see* secrecy
    privacy-as-withdrawal *see* withdrawal
    private property 8, 13, 18, 25, 29–30, 33,
        49, 69, 72, 82, 90, 91, 97, 104, 108,
        143, 154, 198–199, 230, 232, 233,
        235, 246, 247, 269, 293
    proprietary 18, 38
    psychological 25, 30–31, 32, 36, 38, 39,
        90, 91, 92, 97, 101, 113, 163, 194,
        223–224, 233, 247, 272, 278
    spatial 18, 23, 25, 32–33, 35, 36, 37, 39,
        88, 91, 97, 99, 101, 105, 108, 113,
        137, 148, 162, 194, 215, 233, 246,
        301, 305
    see also anonymity; intimacy; isolation;
        reserve; seclusion; secrecy; solitude;
        withdrawal
privacy-enhancing technologies (PETs) 130,
    281–282
private meetings 32, 34, 37, 161, 246, 272
private parts 33, 82, 220–221

private sphere 2, 17, 20, 39, 72, 99, 135,
    176, 194–196, 205, 239, 267–272,
    301, 304
'privite' (Old French) 225
profiles, profiling 21, 187–188, 250–252, 277,
    284, 293, 308
property *see* privacy, types of, private property
Prosser, William 10–12, 13–14, 15, 20, 21, 22,
    38, 40–41, 43, 52, 165, 166, 167–168,
    183, 209, 210, 230, 278, 280
'pryvetee' (Middle English) 220–221, 225
public disclosure of private facts (tort) 11, 16,
    69, 134, 284
public figures 9, 12, 28, 67, 122, 135, 146,
    214, 215, 218, 284, 288
public good 284, 287, 294, 302–303, 306
public interest 12, 83, 89, 269–270, 279
public sphere 11, 20, 39, 55, 70–71, 99, 135,
    176–177, 194, 267–272, 304, 308
publication 9, 10–12, 23, 25, 34, 49–50, 70,
    82–83, 92, 98, 139, 162, 215, 261
publicity 9, 11, 34, 48, 91, 138, 157, 234, 258
publicness 290–294
Pulitzer, Joseph 74
Purcell, Henry 34

Quine, Willard van Orman 66, 233

Raab, Charles 177, 256
rationality, rational choice theory 117, 125,
    126, 129–131, 173–174, 176–178,
    182–183, 196, 205, 220, 233, 234,
    245, 296
Rawls, John 87, 197
Reagan, Ronald 135
reality television 117, 123, 262, 271
Rear Window 127
reconstruction, rational and historical
    220–227
recording 10, 33, 34, 89, 92, 106, 108, 123,
    200, 256, 262, 276
records 27, 33, 67, 101, 104, 110–111, 124,
    162, 267, 295, 303–304, 306–307
reductionism 3, 13–14, 41–42, 174, 197–203
reference list, the 24–39, 40, 43, 45, 61,
    64–65, 69, 73, 87, 91, 97, 137, 147,
    194, 198, 199, 229, 233–234, 237,
    247, 254, 273, 300
reflection 36, 126, 174, 176, 181–182, 189,
    194, 220
regulation *see* privacy, law of; privacy,
    regulation (level 6)
Rehnquist, Chief Justice William 166
Reiman, Jeffrey 184, 286
release-and-forget 251–253
religious contexts 24, 25, 31, 32, 36, 37, 80,
    91, 97, 106, 107, 116, 148, 151, 157,

174, 181, 183–184, 189, 219, 220, 224–226, 245, 264, 271
Rembrandt 108
reserve 30, 37, 142–143, 155, 181
Reservoir Dogs 149
revenge porn *see* pornography
Rhinehart, Luke 137
Richards, Neil 167–168
Richardson, Samuel 295–296
right to be forgotten 275, 277
right to be let alone 8–11, 13–14, 16, 18, 33, 54, 67, 71, 133, 134, 166, 167, 175, 181, 183, 188, 241, 244
right to life 8, 9–10
Ringley, Jennifer 136–140, 213
Robinson Crusoe (Defoe) 96–97
Roe v Wade 29, 163, 164–165, 167, 212
    see also abortion
roles, role occupancy *see* privacy, role-based
Romanticism 183
Rorty, Richard 220
Rössler, Beate 29, 39, 78, 99, 123, 133, 138–140, 153, 178–179, 181, 193–198, 245
Rozanov, Vassily 185
rubber hand illusion 235
Rubenfeld, Jed 70–71
Russell, Bertrand 61

safe cities 289, 290
St Ciarán 91
St James of Cyrrhestica 271
St John the Dwarf 31
Saramago, José 127
Sartre, Jean-Paul 186–187, 242–243
Saudi Arabia 289
Scheler, Max 191
schizophrenia 113, 232
Schmidt, Eric 122, 295
Schoeman, Ferdinand 2, 23, 74, 142, 143, 145, 162, 182, 294
scrutiny 21, 24, 26, 31, 33, 34, 36, 39, 88, 90, 91, 101, 115, 119, 147, 194–195, 196, 201, 213, 222, 248, 271, 278, 288, 308
seamfulness 259
search
    for information 21, 89, 94, 106, 109, 111, 120, 219, 251–252, 253, 277, 296, 303
    physical 58, 97, 114, 154, 163, 274, 287
seclusion 16, 69, 90, 96, 219, 241
secrecy 16, 18, 27–28, 68–69, 74, 88, 92, 110, 117, 121, 130, 137, 172–173, 174, 184, 220, 222, 226, 229, 232, 244–245, 248, 271, 283, 288
security 1, 8, 21, 28, 53, 55, 77, 92, 104, 109–110, 114, 170, 189, 190, 192,

210, 215, 250, 272, 277, 285, 306, 307
self, the 16, 17, 61, 95, 113, 118–119, 137, 176, 181, 184–188, 217, 226, 231–235, 236, 283, 301
self-consciousness 101, 112, 123
sensibility 272
sensitive matters 11, 90, 104, 105, 109, 129, 148, 180, 210, 223, 250, 253, 271, 274, 292, 297
servants 95, 105, 219, 223, 225, 243–244
sex 21, 29, 32, 37, 39, 41, 61, 68, 74, 83, 90, 109, 114, 132, 136, 150, 163, 173, 182, 185, 189–193, 223, 251, 259, 262, 270, 283, 284, 288
Shakespeare, William 100, 113
    King Lear 113
    Othello 230
shame 112, 121, 124, 134, 135, 189, 191, 196, 213, 226, 232, 268, 283, 291, 295
Shils, Edward 195
Silber, Cathy 221–222
Simmel, Arnold 234
Simmel, Georg 30, 142–143, 174, 224
Singapore 289
Sipple, Oliver 258
slander 8, 284
slavery 55–56, 105, 223
smart cities 289–290
smart objects/services 119, 147, 259–260, 303
smartphone 125, 154–155, 256, 257, 265, 277, 289–290, 301, 302–303
Smith, Adam 183, 286, 287, 294
Snowden, Edward 93–94, 307–308
social change 2, 20, 59, 103, 105, 126, 145, 155, 158, 164, 189–190, 193, 205, 212, 214, 215, 219, 270, 300, 304, 307
social credit system (China) 106, 309
social distance 211, 223–224, 241, 304
social justice *see* justice
social machines 246
social media 48, 70, 72, 106, 120, 124, 126, 130, 135, 150, 171, 257–258, 271, 277, 278, 292–293, 301, 303, 308
social networks 31, 48, 72, 79, 124, 126, 127, 131, 146, 185, 189, 195, 210, 246, 258, 265, 292–293
social stability 174, 226, 283, 290
social status 106, 115, 146, 195, 219, 222–224
Socrates 92–93
Solid (platform) 281
solitary confinement 97
solitude 18, 32, 35–36, 37, 48, 68, 91, 96–97, 98, 128, 131–132, 174, 181, 188, 212, 225, 241, 244, 271

Solove, Daniel 1–2, 3, 14–15, 16–17, 18–19, 21, 40–44, 45, 47, 51, 59–75, 85, 86, 87, 114–116, 157, 159–160, 167–168, 171, 175, 176, 207, 209, 228, 230, 236, 280
Somaliland 224
South Korea 213–214, 289, 305
Sparkes, A. W. 49
state, the 1, 39, 57, 70–71, 80, 83, 107, 118, 157, 158–160, 164, 177, 195, 242, 243, 247, 254, 263, 269–270, 272, 274–275, 280, 287, 294, 296, 299, 304
Stevenson, Robert Louis 123
Stirner, Max 31
Stockholm syndrome 117
Strachey, Lytton 95
streakers 155
surveillance 13, 21, 22, 23, 24, 93, 97, 100, 105, 107, 109–110, 114, 116–122, 127, 134, 146, 147, 154, 157, 161, 165, 185, 187–188, 193, 197, 213, 216, 234, 241, 258, 272, 274, 276, 283, 285–286, 288–290, 294, 296, 297–298, 302, 303, 304, 307, 308
surveillance capitalism 120, 126, 172, 278–279

Taiwan 305
tattoos 82, 100, 123
taxation 29, 43–44, 48, 49–50, 59, 74, 77, 91, 175, 288
Taylor, Linnet 167
technological change 2, 21, 55, 59, 152, 155, 167–169, 189–190, 210, 300, 301, 302
technology giants (private sector companies) 1, 70, 107, 120, 134, 164, 169, 258, 260, 275, 279–280, 282, 293
telepathy 94
telephone tapping 26, 92–93, 145–146, 163, 308
terrorism 93–94, 297
Texas Heartbeat Act 165
theology 80, 219
thermal imaging 58, 146
Thomas, William 286
Thomson, Judith Jarvis 12–14, 15, 16, 20, 22, 41–42, 43, 52, 167, 198–202, 209–210
Through the Keyhole 218
Tinder 189
Titchener, Edward 119
Tocqueville, Alexis de 286, 294
toilets 48, 95, 172, 213–214, 215–216, 223, 225, 232, 259, 270, 288

totalitarianism 70, 106, 107, 173, 177, 229, 243, 269–270, 285
track and trace 302–305
tracking (online) 70, 107, 281, 303
trade secrets 8, 28
transparency 34, 113, 127, 189, 198, 248, 259, 264–265, 274, 291–292, 305
trespass 10, 215
trolling 258, 277, 279, 285
Truman Show, The 117–118
Trump, Donald 165
trust 51–52, 92, 116–118, 143, 164, 180, 181, 281–282
trust law 281
Tuareg males 115, 223–224
Twitter 27, 258, 279, 293

Uighurs 51
underwear 33, 106, 184
United Kingdom 95, 114, 170, 218, 283, 297, 301, 302, 304
United States Constitution 160, 162–165, 167, 192, 212, 284
    Fifth Amendment 183
    Fourteenth Amendment 167
    Fourth Amendment 58, 163, 183, 287
United States law 8, 10–12, 13, 29, 40–41, 57–58, 158, 162–166, 183–184, 202, 273–274, 275, 282, 301
United States Supreme Court 29, 41, 58, 68, 160, 162, 163–166, 192, 212
United States v Jones 58
Universal Declaration of Human Rights 14, 270
upskirting 56, 122, 161
USA PATRIOT Act 307
user interface 257, 260
utilitarianism 3, 172, 212, 291–294
utility 124–125, 130

vaccination 1, 306
Veale, Michael 158
veil, veiling 49, 90, 115–116, 143, 155, 215, 219, 223–224
Véliz, Carissa 134
vendetta 230
Venice 286
Victorian England 95, 190
Video Privacy Protection Act 162
voice/virtual assistants 122, 146, 259–260, 278
voluntarism 131–132, 263, 264
voyeurism 56, 61, 67, 122–123, 127, 136, 149
vulnerable persons 21, 70, 114, 120–121, 170–171, 177, 191, 263–264, 283

Wacks, Raymond 1, 4, 16, 116, 158
Warren, Samuel D. 7–11, 12, 13, 15, 16, 20,
  22, 33, 41, 43, 52, 54, 67, 74, 81, 91,
  134, 160, 165–166, 168, 183, 204,
  209, 235, 244
Wasserstrom, Richard 27–28
webcams 99, 136–140, 213–214, 259
  see also cameras; photography,
  photographs
WeChat 293
welfare 110, 120–121, 134, 174, 177, 179,
  250, 263–264
Wesley, John 116
West, Dame Rebecca 35, 268
Westin, Alan 18, 21, 30, 32, 34, 37, 38–39,
  51–52, 71, 93, 132, 134, 149, 163,
  165–166, 245, 262, 297
Whitman, James 165
WikiLeaks 285
Wilde, Oscar 135
Willem-Alexander, King of the
  Netherlands 301
windows 103, 104–105, 108, 143,
  199–201, 225

witches 95
withdrawal 3, 16, 61, 67–69, 89, 108,
  131, 133, 136–139, 140, 141,
  162, 174, 183, 194, 210, 224,
  229, 231, 232, 244, 267,
  270, 288
Wittgenstein, Ludwig 31, 45, 59, 60–65, 66,
  91, 94, 145
Wordsworth, William 183
World Trade Center 307
World Wide Web 70, 82, 93–94, 99, 107–108,
  110, 136, 139, 253, 265, 275, 277,
  281, 293
  see also Internet
Wyndham, John 94

Xinjiang 51

yellow press 8, 92, 219

Zuboff, Shoshana 126
Zuckerberg, Mark 175, 292–293,
  309

EU authorised representative for GPSR:
Easy Access System Europe, Mustamäe tee 50,
10621 Tallinn, Estonia
gpsr.requests@easproject.com

www.ingramcontent.com/pod-product-compliance
Lightning Source LLC
Chambersburg PA
CBHW051949270326
41929CB00015B/2581